Promoting the "Human" in Law, Policy, and Medicine

Global Health, Human Rights and Social Justice

VOLUME 1

The titles published in this series are listed at *brill.com/ghhr*

Bartha Maria Knoppers, Distinguished James McGill Professor Emerita.

Promoting the "Human" in Law, Policy, and Medicine

Essays in Honour of Bartha Maria Knoppers

Edited by

Edward S. Dove
Vasiliki Rahimzadeh
Michael J. S. Beauvais

BRILL | NIJHOFF

LEIDEN | BOSTON

Canadian Institutes of Health Research | Instituts de recherche en santé du Canada

This work was supported by the Canadian Institutes of Health Research – Canada Research Chair in Law and Medicine (950-217983).

Cover image: *Fallingwater*. © Richard Roblin, 1990. Reprinted with kind permission of Eve Roblin.

Library of Congress Cataloging-in-Publication Data

Names: Knoppers, Bartha Maria, honouree. | Dove, E. S. (Edward S.), editor. | Rahimzadeh, Vasiliki, editor. | Beauvais, Michael J. S., editor.
Title: Promoting the "human" in law, policy, and medicine : essays in honour of Bartha Maria Knoppers / edited by Edward S. Dove, Vasiliki Rahimzadeh, Michael J. S. Beauvais.
Description: Leiden ; Boston : Brill/Nijhoff, 2025. | Series: Global health, human rights, and social justice, 2949-8589 ; volume 1 | Includes index. | Identifiers: LCCN 2024046919 (print) | LCCN 2024046920 (ebook) | ISBN 9789004688537 (hardback) | ISBN 9789004688544 (ebook)
Subjects: LCSH: Medical laws and legislation. | Human reproductive technology–Law and legislation. | Stem cells–Research–Law and legislation. | Health insurance–Law and legislation. | Genomics–Data processing. | Bioethics. | Gene editing. | Science and law. | Human rights. | Knoppers, Bartha Maria.
Classification: LCC K3601 .P76 2025 (print) | LCC K3601 (ebook) | DDC 344.04/1–dc23/eng/20241008
LC record available at https://lccn.loc.gov/2024046919
LC ebook record available at https://lccn.loc.gov/2024046920

Typeface for the Latin, Greek, and Cyrillic scripts: "Brill". See and download: brill.com/brill-typeface.

ISSN 2949-8589
ISBN 978-90-04-68853-7 (hardback)
ISBN 978-90-04-68854-4 (e-book)
DOI 10.1163/9789004688544

This book is printed on acid-free paper and produced in a sustainable manner.

Contents

Foreword

> *Everyone has the right to freely participate in the cultural life of the community, to enjoy the arts and to share in scientific advancement and its benefit.*

Article 27 of the Universal Declaration of Human Rights,[1] of which we celebrated in 2023 the 75th anniversary, seems to me a perfect starting point to illustrate an important part of Professor Bartha Maria Knoppers' legacy. Not only because of the discussion I had with her on the scope of this provision—with minor divergences sometimes—but more importantly for what I think was a strong driver in her work and action.

As stated in an Editorial published in Nature in 2023, "Article 27 is particularly remarkable, because it enshrines the enjoyment of science… as a fundamental right to be protected."[2] Throughout her academic career, Bartha has addressed many different issues for which science was always essential. In the biomedical field, from medically assisted reproduction to biobanking, from genetics to Big Data and data protection, from stem cells to genomics, Bartha's research has greatly contributed to the relevant debate and work in the fields concerned.

The international dimension of her professional career is to be underlined, as well as the willingness not to stick to research and teaching, but also to take an active part in the development of standards. The Council of Europe has greatly benefited from Professor Knoppers' expertise and experience to that end. Her important contributions in the development of legal instruments for genetics and medicine is to be acknowledged in this context. Professor Knoppers contributed extensively to building the evidence base around the ethical, social, and legal challenges that emerging genetic technologies raised. Her legal rigour and analytical skills ensured her scholarly contributions provided a very strong basis for the intergovernmental work. Her scholarship informed, for example, the Council of Europe Committee of Ministers of Recommendation (2016)8 on the processing of personal health-related data, including genetic data, for insurance purposes.[3]

---

1 Proclaimed by the United Nations General Assembly in Paris on 10 December 1948.

2 Editorial, "How the 'right to science' can help us overcome the many crises we face today" (2023) 623 Nature 887.

3 Council of Europe, 'Recommendation CM/Rec(2016)8 of the Committee of Ministers to the member States on the processing of personal health-related data for insurance purposes, including data resulting from genetic tests' (adopted by the Committee of Ministers on 26 October 2016 at the 1269th meeting of the Ministers' Deputies), available at: https://search.coe.int/cm/Pages/result_details.aspx?ObjectId=09000016806b2c5f.

Of Dutch origin, having studied in France and in the United Kingdom, and living in Canada, we can say that Professor Knoppers got the "best out of two worlds." In any case, she definitely has a very broad and relevant analysis of the issues at stake. Inviting her to contribute to the strategic discussion initiated on the occasion of the 20th anniversary of the Council of Europe Convention on Human Rights and Biomedicine (Oviedo Convention) in October 2017 was therefore obvious. In her presentation on genetics, genomics, and human rights, she referred to Article 27 of the Declaration of Human Rights, which was made legally binding by Article 15 of the International Covenant on Economic, Social and Cultural Rights. She also referred to the Framework for Responsible Sharing of Genomic and Health-Related Data of the Global Alliance for Genomics and Health, an achievement in which she had a leading role and which several authors in this volume rightfully praise for its groundbreaking policy commitment to the human right to science.

Professor Bartha Maria Knoppers, throughout her career, has certainly contributed to making Article 27 actionable, not only through scientific advancement, but also through her passion to foster the cultural life of communities. I have no doubt that she will continue in her future commitments to be a driving force, with freedom of speech and thought.

Laurence Lwoff, *Head of Human Rights and Biomedicine Division, Council of Europe*

Preface

Bartha Maria Knoppers, PhD, OC, OQ, AdE, FRSC, FCAHS vacated the Canada Research Chair in Law and Medicine in May 2024, having held the position since 2001. In May 2023, she stepped down from her position of Director of the Centre of Genomics and Policy (CGP) at McGill University, a research centre she founded in 2009 when she moved "over the mountain" from the Université de Montréal. She remains deeply connected to McGill , both as Distinguished James McGill Professor Emerita and as Founding Director of the CGP.

This volume is as much about the scholarly and policy contributions of Professor Knoppers as it is a testament to her profound impact on the lives of all those who are featured within its pages. The three of us count ourselves among the luckiest to have learned from, laughed with, and reached newer heights because of Professor Knoppers. We embarked on this journey in part as a token of our infinite well of gratitude for how she has shaped us as scholars and as humans. Her mentorship at nearly every stage in our own careers is the guiding light toward which we gravitate in supporting the next generation of thinkers and change-makers in the fields of law, medicine, and ethics. We believe this collection reflects both the breadth and depth of Professor Knoppers' influence on the field. Readers will also find relatable stories and experiences of their interactions with Professor Knoppers that are told by diverse people of all ages, career stages, professions, and scholarly disciplines. Beyond this collection of essays, we have no doubt that more chapters in future books will be written by those whom Professor Knoppers inspired and whose ideas have her distinct intellectual imprint.

Above all, we curated this collection to remind us that humanity is the tie that binds. The "human" is what gives every data point its significance, and every duty its activator. It is the betterment of humanity through scientific advancement that Professor Knoppers prioritized throughout her career, and from which we lovingly take the torch to continue in our own work.

We owe this volume to our enthusiastic contributors. That 57 busy, accomplished individuals unhesitatingly agreed and submitted texts without delay for this project is a testament to Professor Knoppers' unique role in the lives of many. Or, to use one of Professor Knoppers' favourite Latin maxims—*res ipsa loquitur*.

We have also benefited from the gracious assistance of countless wonderful colleagues, each of whom we are fortunate to have in our own networks because of Professor Knoppers. We thank Yann Joly and Ma'n H. Zawati for their genuine enthusiasm for the project and their generous and wise guidance on various editorial choices. We are thankful for Nadine Thorsen's brilliant support in organizing a retreat for us to meet in the Eastern Townships of Quebec and discuss the book in person, and for coordinating financial support. We thank Rose-Marie Hozyan for her cheerful support in keeping us updated with Professor Knoppers' novel-length CV. We are also grateful to Micheline Nalette for helping us identify the photographer of a portrait of Professor Knoppers—Patricia Brochu. We thank Lauren Danahy at Brill for her enthusiasm for the project from its inception, and Akiko Hakuno at Brill who bravely assisted us in coordinating the endless tasks that publishing a collection like this requires. We are grateful to the Canada Research Chair in Law and Medicine for making this volume available under an open-access licence.

Above all else, we are deeply indebted to Professor Knoppers for her support of this project and for her boundless care as a colleague, mentor, and friend. This book is for her.

Edward S. Dove, Dublin, Ireland
Vasiliki Rahimzadeh, Houston, USA
Michael J. S. Beauvais, New York, USA
September 2024

List of Contributors

Denise Avard
is former Research Director of the Centre of Genomics and Policy at McGill University, Canada.

Michael J. S. Beauvais
is a doctoral candidate at the Faculty of Law, University of Toronto, Canada.

Alexander Bernier
is a lawyer and doctoral candidate at the Faculty of Law, University of Toronto, Canada.

Martin Bobrow
is Emeritus Professor of Medical Genetics at the University of Cambridge, and honorary faculty at the Wellcome Sanger Institute, UK.

Andrea Boggio
is Professor of Legal Studies and Faculty Fellow of the Center for Health and Behavioral Sciences at Bryant University, USA.

Pascal Borry
is Professor of Bioethics at the Centre for Biomedical Ethics and Law (Department of Public Health and Primary Care) at the KU Leuven, Belgium.

Jasper A. Bovenberg
is a lawyer and founder of the Legal Pathways Institute for Health and Bio-Law, Haarlem, the Netherlands.

Maxwell Brodie
is an advanced standing student in the BCL/JD program at the Faculty of Law at McGill University, Canada.

Annelien Bredenoord
is President of Erasmus University Rotterdam, the Netherlands.

Anne Cambon-Thomsen
is Emeritus Research Director of the CNRS (National Centre for Scientific Research) in the Centre for Epidemiology and Research on Population Health

(CERPOP, National Institute of Medical and Health Research, Inserm, and University Toulouse III - Paul Sabatier, France).

Ruth Chadwick
is Professor Emerita at Cardiff University, UK.

Don Chalmers
is Distinguished Emeritus Professor of Law at the University of Tasmania, Australia.

Ellen Wright Clayton
is the Craig-Weaver Chair in Pediatrics, Professor of Law and Professor of Health Policy in the Center for Biomedical Ethics and Society at Vanderbilt Medical Center and University, USA.

Timothy Caulfield
is Professor in the Faculty of Law and the School of Public Health, and Research Director of the Health Law Institute at the University of Alberta, Canada.

R. Alta Charo
is the Warren P. Knowles Professor Emerita of Law and Bioethics at the University of Wisconsin at Madison, USA.

Edward S. Dove
is Professor of Law at the School of Law and Criminology, Maynooth University, Ireland, and Honorary Professor at the School of Law, University of Edinburgh, UK.

Jan M. Friedman
is Professor of Medical Genetics at the University of British Columbia and a Senior Investigator at BC Children's Hospital Research Institute, Vancouver, Canada.

Henry T. Greely
is Professor of Law and Professor by courtesy of Genetics at Stanford School of Medicine and Director of the Center for Law and the Biosciences, Stanford University, USA.

Calvin Wai-Loon Ho
is Associate Professor at the Monash Law School, Monash University, Australia, Research Fellow at the Centre for Medical Ethics and Law of the University of

Hong Kong; and Fellow of PHG Foundation, University of Cambridge, and of the Royal Society for Public Health in the UK.

Rose-Marie Hozyan
is an an Executive Administrative Assistant at the Rosalind and Morris Goodman Cancer Institute at McGill University, Canada.

Judy Illes
is Professor of Neurology, Distinguished University Scholar, and Distinguished Professor in Neuroethics at the University of British Columbia, Canada.

Rosario Isasi
is Associate Professor of Human Genetics, Adjunct Professor of Law and Director, Program in Genome Ethics and Policy at the Dr. John T. Macdonald Foundation Department of Human Genetics at the University of Miami Miller School of Medicine, USA.

Amalia M. Issa
is Founding Director & Professor of Precision Personalized Medicine & Targeted Therapeutics, Springfield, PA, USA, former Chair of Health Policy and Public Health at the University of the Sciences of Philadelphia, and Adjunct Professor of Family Medicine at McGill University, Montreal, Canada.

Yann Joly
is a James McGill Professor at the Faculty of Medicine and Health Sciences, Department of Human Genetics and the current director of the Centre of Genomics and Policy at McGill University, Canada.

Pilar Nicolás Jiménez
is Coordinator of the Chair in Law and the Human Genome Net. Law Faculty at the Universidad del País Vasco / Euskal Herriko Unibertsitatea, Spain.

Jeffrey Kahn
is the Andreas C. Dracopoulos Director of the Berman Institute of Bioethics and Levi Professor of Bioethics and Public Policy, Johns Hopkins University, USA.

Kazuto Kato
is Professor of Biomedical Ethics and Public Policy at the Graduate School of Medicine, Osaka University, Japan.

Jane Kaye
is the Director of the Centre for Law, Health and Emerging Technologies (HeLEX) in the Faculty of Law at the University of Oxford, UK and Professor of Health Law and Policy at Melbourne Law School, University of Melbourne, Australia.

Erika Kleiderman
is a doctoral candidate in bioethics at the École de santé publique, Université de Montréal, Canada.

Patricia Kosseim
is the Information and Privacy Commissioner of Ontario, Canada.

Claude Laberge
is Emeritus Professor of Medicine and Pediatrics at the Faculty of Medicine at Laval University, Canada.

Mark Lathrop
is Scientific Director of the Victor Phillip Dahdaleh Institute of Genomic Medicine and Professor in the Department of Human Genetics at McGill University, Canada.

Graeme Laurie
is a Professorial Fellow at the School of Law, University of Edinburgh, UK.

James V. Lavery
is Professor and Conrad N. Hilton Chair in Global Health Ethics in the Hubert Department of Global Health in the Rollins School of Public Health, and Faculty of the Center for Ethics, Emory University, USA.

Trudo Lemmens
is Professor and Scholl Chair in Health Law and Policy at the University of Toronto, Canada.

Laurence Lwoff
is head of the Human Rights and Biomedicine Division of the Council of Europe.

Patrick A. Molinari
is legal counsel at Lavery and Professor Emeritus at the Faculty of Law, Université de Montréal, Canada.

Fruzsina Molnár-Gábor
is Professor of International Medical and Health Law and Data Protection Law at the Faculty of Law and BioQuant, Heidelberg University, Germany.

Eric M. Meslin
is the former President and CEO of the Council of Canadian Academies, and Adjunct Professor in the Dalla Lana School of Public Health, University of Toronto, Canada.

Dianne Nicol
is a Distinguished Professor Emerita in the Faculty of Law and member of the Centre for Law and Genetics at the University of Tasmania, Australia.

Alycia Noë
is a student at the Faculty of Law, McGill University, Canada.

Alexandra Obadia
is a lawyer and Chief Legal and Data Officer at CATALIS Quebec, Canada.

Ubaka Ogbogu
is Professor and Associate Dean of Research in the Faculty of Law at the University of Alberta, Canada.

Nicole Palmour
is an Academic Associate and Coordinator at the Centre of Genomics Policy, McGill University, Canada.

Dimitri Patrinos
is a lawyer and doctoral student at McGill University's Faculty of Law.

Vasiliki Nataly Rahimzadeh
is Assistant Professor in the Center for Medical Ethics and Health Policy at Baylor College of Medicine, USA.

Vardit Ravitsky
is President and CEO of the Hastings Center, Full Professor at the Bioethics Program, School of Public Health, University of Montreal, Canada, and Senior Lecturer on Global Health and Social Medicine at Harvard Medical School, USA.

Emmanuelle Rial-Sebbag
is a Research Director in health law in the Centre for Epidemiology and Research on Population Health (CERPOP, National Institute of Medical and Health Research, Inserm, and University Toulouse III - Paul Sabatier, France) and Associate Lecturer in Bio-Law and Bioethics at University Toulouse III - Paul Sabatier, France.

Mark A. Rothstein
is Director of Translational Bioethics at the Institute for Clinical and Translational Science, University of California, Irvine, USA.

Jacques Simard
is Vice-Dean of Research and Innovation and Professor in the Department of Molecular Medicine, Faculty of Medicine at the Université Laval, Canada.

Michèle Stanton-Jean
is an historian and bioethicist who has served in senior roles for the governments of Quebec and Canada.

Jennifer Stoddart
is a lawyer and historian, and the sixth Privacy Commissioner of Canada (2003-2013).

Adrian Thorogood
is a lawyer and acts as Legal Advisor and Data Governance Manager for the Terry Fox Research Institute, Canada.

Nadine Thorsen
is a financial administrator for the Centre of Genomics and Policy at McGill University, Canada.

David Townend
is Associate Dean (Research and Enterprise) and a Professor of Law at The City Law School, City St George's, University of London, UK.

Susan E. Wallace
is Honorary Lecturer of Population and Public Health Sciences at the University of Leicester, UK.

Eva Winkler
is an oncologist and Heisenberg Professor for Translational Medical Ethics at the University of Heidelberg, Germany.

Rumiana Yotova
is an Assistant Professor in International Law at the Faculty of Law of the University of Cambridge and a Fellow and Director of Studies in Law in Gonville and Caius College.

Ron Zimmern
is a public health physician and Chairman of the Board of Trustees for the PHG Foundation, University of Cambridge, UK.

Ma'n H. Zawati
is Associate Professor at McGill University's Faculty of Medicine and Health Sciences, Department of Human Genetics and the Research Director of the Centre of Genomics and Policy.

Introduction

Edward S. Dove, Vasiliki Rahimzadeh, and Michael J. S. Beauvais

1 Honouring Professor Bartha Maria Knoppers

This volume honours the academic career of Professor Bartha Maria Knoppers (or more simply, "BMK" to almost everyone who knows her), who retired from the Canada Research Chair in Law and Medicine in April 2024, a post she continuously held for more than 20 years. We are delighted that more than 50 of Professor Knoppers' friends and colleagues have contributed to this academic encomium. Each would, we surmise, remark on the challenge of writing an essay or vignette that adequately captures the stellar accomplishments of this intellectual giant of health law and ethics. Indeed, the chapters in this volume demonstrate that there are few areas in the broad field of health law where Professor Knoppers has not intellectually explored or established her name; from civil liability for doctors to reproductive technology, gene patents to stem cell research, from confidentiality and privacy law to consent to treatment and consent to participate in research, from human genetics to biobanks, and from human rights to the integrity of scientific research and researchers themselves.

Born in the Netherlands and raised in Alberta, Ontario, and Quebec, Professor Knoppers was shaped by the varied landscapes and communities in which she lived. She first pursued her undergraduate degree in French and English literature at McMaster University in Hamilton, Ontario. She continued her passions by obtaining a masters in comparative literature from the University of Alberta in Edmonton before transitioning to law.

Professor Knoppers attended McGill University's Faculty of Law where she earned her degrees in common law (1978) and civil law (1981). From her early years as a law student in the late 1970s one can already see an interest in questions about the obligations of clinicians to their patients, especially in light of new reproductive technologies.[1] She pursued further studies at the Université de Paris I (Panthéon-Sorbonne), obtaining a *diplôme d'études*

1 See e.g. Bartha Maria Knoppers, 'The "legitimization" of artificial insemination: promise or problem?' (1978) 1 Family Law Review 108; Bartha Maria Knoppers, 'Les notions d'autorisation et de consentement dans le contrat médical' (1978) 19 Cahiers de Droit 893.

 | DOI:10.1163/9789004688544_002

approfondies (1981) and doctorate in comparative medical law (1985) under the supervision of Professor André Tunc. During her doctoral years, she also obtained a diploma of legal studies at Trinity College, University of Cambridge (1981). It was at Cambridge that Professor Knoppers made the acquaintance of Dr Patrick Steptoe and Professor Sir Robert Edwards, the pioneers of in-vitro fertilization. This keen interest in the legal and ethical aspects of emerging health technologies—informed by questions such as who benefits? Who owes what to whom?—would be enduring.

Following her doctorate at the Sorbonne, Professor Knoppers became an Assistant Professor in the Faculty of Law at the Université de Montréal. She held this position for five years, focusing on family law and the rights of children, before becoming a Senior Researcher at the Centre de recherche en droit public at the Université de Montréal. She became a Full Professor in 1996 and turned to health law (also known as medical law). It was during this time that Professor Knoppers gained an international reputation for successfully funding a robust research program in health law and ethics, with a specific focus on human genetics/genomics. She has impressively served as principal investigator or co-investigator for more than 180 competitively funded research projects over her career, and through that funding, built teams, or families even, of scholars that often also become friends. This, we hasten to add, was especially pioneering given the stark gender inequalities faced by many women in academia. Some of her successful and substantial grants included from the Fonds pour la formation des chercheurs et l'aide à la recherche on the "Legal, Ethical Issues and Commercialization of Human Genetics" (99-ER-107) in the early 1990s. At the early stages of the famed Human Genome Project, this project was a novel area of investigation. Professor Knoppers was among the earliest investigators to be awarded funding in the early 2000s from the newly formed Genome Quebec and Genome Canada to explore "Genomics in Society: Responsibilities and Rights" (R0009887), and cemented Professor Knoppers' career long interest in the impact of scientific research and emerging genetic technologies on humanity.

In 2009, Professor Knoppers moved "over the mountain", returning "home" one might say, to establish the Centre of Genomics and Policy (CGP) in the Faculty of Medicine at McGill University. It was here that the three of us were lucky enough to cross paths with her. The CGP is now ably led by Professor Yann Joly (Director), Professor Ma'n Zawati (Research Director), and Lindsay Dayton (Executive Director). Thanks to Professor Knoppers' leadership and mentorship of countless research assistants and academic associates, the CGP remains a powerhouse in research grant success and policy formulation across

Quebec, Canada, and the globe in the more than 15 years since its founding. A perusal of its website gives some indication to the numerous research projects underway or completed,[2] and the abundant publications that have resulted from those projects (at the time of writing, these number over 1000).[3]

Among the nearly 150 other leadership roles Professor Knoppers has held, she founded the Public Population Project in Genomics (P^{3}G) and CARTaGENE, Quebec's population biobank, in the early 2000s. She has led the Policy Committee of the Canadian Stem Cell Network and chaired the Ethics Working Party of the International Stem Cell Forum. She has chaired the Ethics and Governance Committee of the International Cancer Genome Consortium, the Ethics Advisory Panel of the World Anti-Doping Agency, and co-chaired the Regulatory and Ethics Work Stream of the Global Alliance for Genomics and Health. She holds five doctorates *honoris causa* and is a Fellow of the American Association for the Advancement of Science, the Hastings Center, the Canadian Academy Health Sciences, and the Royal Society of Canada. She is also an Officer of the Order of Canada and of Quebec, and was awarded the 2019 Henry G. Friesen International Prize in Health Research, the 2020 Till and McCulloch Award for science policy, and was appointed to the International Commission on the Clinical Use of Human Germline Genome Editing. In 2021, Professor Knoppers received the Lifetime Achievement Award from the Canadian Bioethics Society during their 32nd annual conference in recognition of her significant contributions to bioethics in Canada.

2 The Humanity of Professor Knoppers

The three of us first embarked on this project in late May 2023, following the "stepping down but not out" soirée for Professor Knoppers at McGill University. Identifying a unifying theme for the essays in a proposed Festschrift was relatively straightforward. Rather immediately the theme of "humanity" sprang to mind. Across the decades of intellectual outputs—including dozens of

2 Centre of Genomics and Policy, 'Research Projects', available at: https://www.genomicsandpolicy.org/en/funding/index.

3 Centre of Genomics and Policy, 'Publications', available at: https://www.genomicsandpolicy.org/en/publications/index.

books,[4] hundreds of articles, and over 600 talks—and despite their varying topic and scope, we imagined the chapters would likely allude to Professor Knoppers' reflections on what it means to be human in the face of a new technology and in the advance of medical science, be it in relation to the values of dignity, solidarity, equity, fairness, mutual trust and respect, or universality. And indeed, what emerges from all the chapters and vignettes in this volume is the full *humanity* of Professor Knoppers—her talent, charisma, warmth, compassion, and kindness, and her love of world travel. We ourselves have recognized the same attributes in our own relationships with Professor Knoppers. Most evidently, this volume manifests the cherished relationships, conviviality, comradery, and bonhomie forged across decades, disciplines, and continents.

Many individuals in this volume have known Professor Knoppers for decades; we, more humbly, have known her only from her time and ours at the CGP since the second decade of the 2000s. We are most grateful, then, that so many of Professor Knoppers' dearest friends and collaborators have offered thoughts on how her work has promoted deeper understanding of humanity across law, policy, and medicine.

In the immediate sense, what prompted this project was Professor Knoppers' stepping down from the Canada Research Chair in Law and Medicine, and our desire to honour her pioneering leadership and legacy in the broad field of health law and ethics. But in a more abstract sense, we wanted to embark on an intellectual project of its own that would explore in greater detail what the "human" means in law, policy, and medicine. What this volume demonstrates is just how vast Professor Knoppers scholarly networks stretch, well beyond law and well beyond the academy and into think tanks, governments, companies, hospital wards, and laboratories.

As noted by van Beers, Corrias, and Werner, the concept of humanity can be invoked in myriad ways: as a quality (e.g. to describe the human origin of certain biotechnological entities), as a norm or guideline (e.g. when it is stated that technologies should be developed and applied with respect for our humanity), and as a designation of a group (e.g. the human genome being, in a

4 See e.g. Katherine Connell-Thouez and Bartha Maria Knoppers, *Contemporary Trends in Family Law: A National Perspective* (Carswell 1984); Bartha Maria Knoppers, *Professional Liability in Canada. Canadian Institute for the Administration of Justice* (Editions Yvon Blais 1988); Bartha Maria Knoppers (ed), *Canadian Child Health Law: Health Rights and Risks of Children* (Thompson Educational Publishing, Inc. 1992); Bartha Maria Knoppers (ed) *Populations and Genetics: Legal and Socio-Ethical Perspectives* (Martinus Nijhoff 2003); Yann Joly and Bartha Maria Knoppers (eds), *Routledge Handbook of Medical Law and Ethics* (Routledge 2014).

symbolic sense, "the heritage of humanity").[5] Humanity can also comprise our biological and genetic characteristics and can be influenced by our socio-cultural understandings. We editors take the view that to be human is to say something about who we are at the most fundamental level, individually and collectively, and how we work together to define the kind of world we want to live in and leave to future generations.

As the chapters in this volume well demonstrate, Professor Knoppers has prioritized humanity and safeguarding human dignity at every turn in her career. And, the contributions in this volume show how much Professor Knoppers' love of literature (poetry as much as novels) has influenced her academic career in law and defined the ways in which she weaves literary themes in, as Ellen Wright Clayton discusses in her chapter, genetics and the rights and corresponding duties of family members.

Professor Knoppers also applies an outlook of promoting humanity and safeguarding human dignity to her teaching and mentoring of students and early career scholars as well as to patients and prospective research participants in population biobanks, data linkage studies, and clinical trials. She has forged an intellectual path for normative, conceptual, and empirical scholarship that situates the human at the centre of ethico-legal analysis and normative instruments, notably by bringing to the fore the human right to science, genomic and health-related data sharing, genome editing, human reproductive technologies, stem cell research, the rights of children, and population health. Moreover, Professor Knoppers has always kept actual patients and research participants—both current and future—in sharp focus, protecting them against instrumentalization and commodification and promoting their interests as moral agents of intrinsic value.

Promoting humanity is as ambitious and important an undertaking today as it was in the aftermath of World War II and the birth of the bioethics field following the Nuremberg Trials. We live in an evolving world in which biotechnological advances continually raise complex questions about the form and function of the "human" itself, and what role law, policy, and ethics play in helping chart its responsible development. Ensuring that the normative values of individuals and communities align with technological advancement continues to be a common theme for ethicists and policy makers even as the technologies themselves evolve, from sequencing the first human genome to

5 Britta van Beers, Luigi Corrias, and Wouter Werner, 'Introduction: probing the boundaries of humanity' in Britta van Beers, Luigi Corrias, and Wouter Werner (eds), *Humanity across International Law and Biolaw* (Cambridge University Press 2014) 14.

animal cloning, through to our current era of artificial intelligence and germline gene editing. Professor Knoppers has long considered how law, policy, and ethics ought to shape the design and use of new biotechnologies in an environment that accords full respect for the dignity and benefit of human beings.[6] Her work in the Human Genome Organization (as Chair of its International Ethics Committee from 1996-2004) and in the drafting of UNESCO's 1997 Universal Declaration on the Human Genome and Human Rights testify to this. Professor Knoppers was also a founder of the Global Alliance for Genomics and Health and based its groundbreaking Framework for Responsible Sharing of Genomic and Health-Related Data on the human right to science. We now proceed to discuss how this volume's contributors engage with Professor Knoppers' promotion of humanity in law, policy, and medicine.

3 Content and Structure of the Book

Reflective of her international outlook and deportment, we have invited Professor Knoppers' colleagues and academic friends from around the globe to reflect on these ideas. Across 16 chapters and 32 "vignettes," readers will be able to discern the various conceptual frameworks and approaches that authors have invoked to reflect on what it means to be human, and how promoting the human at the present and future crossroads of ethics, law, and policy can ensure the engines of scientific progress turn toward the interests of all humans, communities, and populations. While diverse in content, the chapters suggest several common themes.

3.1 *Theme 1: Protecting and Promoting Humanity through Fairness and Equity*

A first theme we identify is Professor Knoppers' long-standing effort to eliminate genetic discrimination and genetic exceptionalism (e.g. the perception that one's genes ipso facto determine their current and future health), which

6 Among other works, see e.g. Bartha Maria Knoppers, 'Genomics and policymaking: from static models to complex systems?' (2009) 125 Human Genetics 375; Bartha Maria Knoppers, 'Population studies: return of research results and incidental findings Policy Statement' (2013) 21 European Journal of Human Genetics 245; Bartha M Knoppers, 'Does policy grow on trees?' (2014) 15 BMC Medical Ethics 87; Susan E Wallace and Bartha M Knoppers, 'Harmonised consent in international research consortia: an impossible dream? (2011) 7 Genomics, Society and Policy 35; Bartha Maria Knoppers and Michael J S Beauvais, 'Implementing the human right to science in the context of health: introduction to the special issue' (2024) 11 Journal of Law and the Biosciences lsae018.

several authors in this volume trace back at least to 1991, with Professor Knoppers' report to the Law Reform Commission of Canada on genetic discrimination.[7] One of the prospective themes of this report proposed that the human genome at the level of the species be treated as the common heritage of humanity, and addressed the potential for genetic discrimination if genetic exceptionalism or determinism held sway.

In Chapter 1, Maxwell Brodie and Yann Joly engage directly with this first theme of promoting genomic fairness and equity. Brodie and Joly bring readers into the business world of direct-to-consumer (DTC) pharmacogenetic (PGx) testing and shed light on consumer experiences of applying for group health insurance in Canada. PGx testing optimizes drug prescriptions based on deep analysis of multimodal genotypic and phenotypic data. PGx testing can reduce adverse reactions and thereby lower healthcare expenditures, but at what cost to patients and families? Brodie and Joly highlight partnerships between insurance companies and PGx testing providers, discuss the clinical benefits for stakeholders, and also explain some of the significant ethical, legal, and social risks that PGx testing can pose, such as privacy violations, genetic discrimination, and potential misinterpretation of test results, with important consequences for the current and future health of patients. The authors emphasize the need for clear guidelines, regulatory approval, and standardized consent practices to protect consumer privacy and ensure informed consent. They also advocate for public awareness campaigns to educate consumers on Canada's Genetic Non-Discrimination Act, a federal statute that was passed in 2017, and good privacy practices to mitigate risks and enhance the responsible adoption of PGx testing.

We also see this theme in Chapter 9. Erika Kleiderman and Vardit Ravitsky explore the notion of "seriousness" when used to describe genetic conditions. They consider the discursive work, as well as policy relevance, of using seriousness to justify clinical interventions for genetic conditions. They argue that the term "serious" is often ambiguously defined, leading to inconsistent application and decision-making by policy makers and practitioners alike. The authors propose a human rights-based approach, inspired by Professor Knoppers' work, to unveil both objectivist and constructivist perspectives of health and disease. They argue that such a dual approach can add conceptual breadth to understanding seriousness in the context of

7 Bartha Maria Knoppers, *Human Dignity and Genetic Heritage* (Protection of Life Series: A Study Paper prepared for the Law Reform Commission of Canada) (Law Reform Commission of Canada 1991).

genetic disease. The human rights approach also emphasizes, as the authors suggest, the right to the highest attainable standard of health and the right to science, advocating for a balance between biomedical definitions and the lived experiences of patients. By doing so, Kleiderman and Ravitsy aim to ensure equitable access to genomic technologies and enhance the ethical framework guiding their use.

Pascal Borry engages with the human rights of a specific patient group in Chapter 10, namely children and young adults. He connects Professor Knoppers' advocacy for children's issues in medicine, public health, and health research with the best interests of the child principle under the UN Convention on the Rights of the Child. He notes how Professor Knoppers' work prioritized balancing the child's welfare with their burgeoning autonomy. He examines Professor Knoppers' work in newborn screening (also explored by Jan Friedman in Chapter 8), the storage of newborn blood spots, and paediatric data sharing. In each of these areas he notes how Professor Knoppers has focused on the human values underpinning law and policy to ensure that the best interests of individual children and children as a group remain paramount.

Relatedly, Ellen Wright Clayton invites us to consider the inner workings of families in Chapter 14 and how familial relationships help or impede patients from disclosing genetic test results. Drawing upon Professor Knoppers' use of an epithet from Jane Austen's *Pride and Prejudice*, Clayton in turn draws upon Professor Knoppers' work concerning the moral obligations of probands to notify their at-risk relatives about adverse genetic test results. She argues that we should examine what decisions probands themselves take with respect to genetic test results that are relevant for at-risk relatives. Turning to recent empirical work that interrogates proband's disclosure decisions, she encourages us to adopt a more modest position that is about considering disclosure rather than an obligation to disclose.

A final illustration of this theme can be seen in Henry (Hank) Greely's Chapter 13. A friend and colleague of Professor Knoppers since the 1990s, Greely turns to issues of human diversity and equity long-present in Professor Knoppers' work. Looking back to early efforts to ensure broad representation within human genetic databases from the Human Genome Organization and the Human Genome Diversity Project to more recent ones involving the Global Alliance for Genomics and Health and the Human Cell Atlas, Greely traces a "universalist" thread in Professor Knoppers' work. He highlights Professor Knoppers' emphasis on inclusiveness as one dimension of scientific equity. Greely engages in an intellectual debate with Professor Knoppers, explaining differences in their appraisal of the human right to benefit from scientific advancement and how this right ought to impact technology governance. He attributes their disagreement to a difference in outlooks; Professor Knoppers is a "dreamer" — albeit in the best way possible and as an indefatigable, hardworking one—and he a "fox" (per Isaiah Berlin's famous essay), seeing "myriad, intersecting, reinforcing, and conflicting groups that have at least somewhat different values."

3.2 *Theme 2: The Art and Science of Policymaking*

A second theme is Professor Knoppers' long-standing interest not only in international law and human rights, but also in policymaking, especially in population biobanks. Ma'n H. Zawati and Alycia Noë focus on this in Chapter 2. They illustrate how Professor Knoppers' work in biobanking policy helped secure the "human" by, among other things, adapting models of consent and governance that would enable future research. Zawati and Noë discuss the importance of trust-based interactions in biobanking, the role of broad consent, and the complementarity of hard and soft law approaches to sustain biospecimen resources. Professor Knoppers' work in promoting international data sharing frameworks and biobank interoperability is highlighted as crucial for ethical and efficient biobanking moving forward.

Crafting effective policy often entails combining real world evidence with human values. In Chapter 4, Meslin and Lavery highlight the dual nature of policymaking in genomics as both a structured, scientific endeavour and a creative, artistic process. They argue that policymaking often appears "messy" due to the need for negotiation and compromise. Yet, it can also be a methodical and orderly task akin to basic science. Professor Knoppers, Meslin and Lavery argue, is both an artist *and* a scientist of policymaking for emerging technologies. They highlight the humanistic dimensions of policymaking, using historical and contemporary examples to illustrate how effective policy can inspire and reflect societal values. The authors emphasize the trade-offs between protectionist and overly promotional biotechnological advancements, and demonstrate, using historical cases (e.g. recombinant DNA and the Asilomar conferences), the difficulties of striking such a balance.

3.3 *Theme 3: Comparative Law and Bioethics*

Professor Knoppers has maintained long-standing interest in, and made significant contributions to, comparative law and bioethics in equal measure. A lawyer by education and training, Professor Knoppers has instantiated the empirical value of comparing legal frameworks to better harmonize technology policy as well as guide our actions as members of a community and polity.

This commitment to comparative law and policy is the third theme reflected across several chapters in this volume.

In Chapter 3, Ruth Chadwick examines the role of applied ethics in addressing emerging global challenges. Chadwick and Professor Knoppers have collaborated extensively over their careers, co-authoring many highly cited ethics horizon-scanning articles.[8] Chadwick situates applied ethics in her chapter within historical and contemporary contexts, noting its evolution from philosophical inquiries to addressing practical issues in medicine and technology, fields in which Professor Knoppers' scholarship has distinctively shaped. She discusses the complexity of ethical expertise, the integration of ethical considerations into public policy, and the necessity of Professor Knoppers' pluralistic and interdisciplinary approach to research collaboration. Chadwick concludes with advocating for anticipatory and global perspectives in ethical deliberations concerning emerging applications of new technologies where such deliberations can only hint at, but not explicitly define, future ethical controversies and challenges.

Often what is ethical is not legal, and what is legal is not always ethical. Anne Cambon-Thomsen and Emmanuelle Rial-Sebbag elaborate on this paradox in Chapter 5, and discuss the disciplinary boundaries of bioethics and the law in France. While bioethics and the law can be complementary, Cambon-Thomsen and Rial-Sebbag note that the tensions of positivism and principlism, internormativity, interdisciplinarity, and interoperability must be reconciled. In taking a deeper look at the development and evolution of French bioethics laws, they shed light on the interdisciplinary pluralism in Professor Knoppers' own work and note how the trend toward greater public involvement in responding to bioscientific advances is the future direction that bioethics laws should take. Memorably, they introduce a "B.A.R.T.H.A. approach" that captures Professor Knoppers' unique methods and collaborations in bioethics that transcend a single law or individual, squarely focusing on the whole of humanity.

8 Bartha Maria Knoppers and Ruth Chadwick, 'The Human Genome Project: under an international ethical microscope' (1994) 265 Science 2035; Bartha Maria Knoppers and Ruth Chadwick, 'Human genetic research: emerging trends in ethics' (2005) 6 Nature Reviews Genetics 75; Bartha Maria Knoppers and Ruth Chadwick, 'The ethics weathervane' (2015) 16 BMC Medical Ethics 58; Bartha Maria Knoppers, Ruth Chadwick, and Michael JS Beauvais, 'Biomedical Research Policy', in Edward S Dove and Niamh Nic Shuibhne (eds) *Law and Legacy in Medical Jurisprudence: Essays in Honour of Graeme Laurie* (Cambridge University Press 2022).

Andrea Boggio and Rumiana Yotova take a fresh perspective on Professor Knoppers' comparative legal work to bring a humanistic yet pragmatic approach to governing biomedicine through international human rights law. Drawing upon Professor Knoppers' conviction that we must "reach beyond the moral appeals of bioethics," they examine in Chapter 11 how international human rights became progressively integrated into Professor Knoppers' academic and policy work throughout her career. They begin with Professor Knoppers' early work on conceptualizing the human genome as the common heritage of humanity and on global public goods before appraising her use of international human rights law—specifically, the human right to benefit from scientific advancement—in biomedical governance. They then examine how Professor Knoppers has used the rights of future generations under international human rights law in the governance of heritable human genome editing that cannot, as the authors contend, "be solved once and for all by morality or law."

This theme is also well illustrated in Chapter 16. Calvin W. L. Ho reminds us of Professor Knoppers' signature cosmopolitan and comparative law methodology to ground his chapter on the governance of artificial intelligence applications in human health. Focusing on the human right to benefit from scientific advancement, he works with Professor Knoppers' human rights-based approach to evaluating biotechnologies. He calls attention to the "human-centred and public-spirited" aspects of this approach before applying it to the regulation of polygenic risk scoring software. Ho argues that treating science as a cultural phenomenon accentuates its participatory dimensions and that regulating polygenic risk scoring software must meaningfully involve diverse stakeholders to ensure that all can benefit.

3.3 *Theme 4: Responsibly Sharing Data to Protect and Promote the "Human"*

A fourth theme reflected in the chapters in this volume is Professor Knoppers' efforts to craft laws, policies, and ethical frameworks that enable the responsible sharing of data. Adrian Thorogood and Fruzsina Molnár-Gábor underscore Professor Knoppers' significant contributions to international data sharing of genomic and health-related data in Chapter 16. They identify unique threads in Professor Knoppers' oeuvre: the integration of human rights, bioethics, and data governance to ensure a comprehensive assessment of the rights and interests of various stakeholders in collaborative genomics. They argue that Professor Knoppers prioritizes actual and future patients, insisting on the benefits of collaborative data sharing to improve our knowledge of health and, in turn, eventually improve health outcomes. Thorogood and Molnár-Gábor construct an overarching vision from Professor Knoppers' work that enables science to serve humanity and activates humanistic values to inform science policy. This universalist vision should be nurtured in the face of skepticism about the over promises of -omics research and in an increasingly fragmented data protection landscape.

Similarly, in his Chapter 8 on newborn screening, Jan Friedman bridges a topic for which Professor Knoppers has been a renowned expert for over three decades—newborn screening and whole-genome sequencing. Engaging with Professor Knoppers' varied contributions in this area, Friedman argues that whole-genome sequencing in newborns fails to meet standard public health criteria for newborn screening. Connecting clinical validity and clinical utility with the ethical, legal, and social dimensions that underpin newborn screening policies, he warns that we should resist the temptation to implement whole-genome sequencing within a newborn screening program. Doing so would ensure that society maximizes the benefits of screening programs for newborns while minimizing the risks.

A core component of responsible data sharing are the ethical norms and practice of consent, respecting the physical and moral integrity of persons. In Chapter 15, Susan Wallace considers Professor Knoppers' contributions to the development of model consent tools as a way to enable data sharing while also assisting individuals in understanding their options in complex situations. How can such consent tools encourage rather than silo dialogue between research stakeholders, including principal investigators, research ethics committees, and participants? Recalling that no perfect consent form (or process) exists, Wallace underscores the importance of trust in relationships where health and genetic data are implicated.

3.5 *Theme 5: Anticipating the Future Human?*

Technologies advance faster than the policies meant to govern them. We also cannot predict with certainty how technologies will be used. A final theme in this volume therefore relates to anticipatory governance, and how Professor Knoppers' scholarship has helped forge a responsible path for existing governance processes and systems to guard humanity in the face of grave uncertainty and risk—our sense of human dignity, fairness, and mutual respect for each other and our planet.

In Chapter 7, for example, Alta Charo takes both a literal and metaphoric deep dive into what makes us human, versus, say, a woolly mammoth, orange juice, or a synth from *Star Trek*. To what extent can humans be bioengineered before we can no longer claim humanness? These questions matter, Charo argues, as they have consequences for the rights and duties we owe to humans and developing embryos, as some US courts would have it. She discusses how categorization and naming play a crucial role in our understanding of identity and authenticity, especially as science blurs the lines between natural and synthetic life. Using examples like the efforts to resurrect the woolly mammoth and the complexities of defining gender and species, Charo examines how these definitions impact social and moral considerations. She highlights the tension between biological essentialism and the social need to redefine categories for practical purposes, ultimately questioning—and engaging conceptually with—what it means to be genuinely human.

Ron Zimmern likewise considers the connections between individuals and populations in Chapter 12. He brings together Professor Knoppers' work on the human genome as the common heritage of humanity, global public goods, and the human right to benefit from science with a public health focus. He argues that Professor Knoppers' emphasis on the "human" in these issues has led her to focus on the individuals affected by a particular disease or on those who could stand to benefit in the future. He calls for greater attention to this relationship between individuals and populations and for the individual—the human—to be at the centre of healthcare. As Zimmern provocatively queries at the end of his chapter: "Medicine has benefited hugely from science and in particular the genomic revolution, but has it done so at the expense of the 'human'? And what can be done to restore the 'human' to the centre of medical practice?"

4 Concluding Thoughts

We hope this volume not only faithfully honours the rich legacy of Professor Knoppers and provides a suitably abundant and diverse demonstration of her intellectual labour, but that it also provides a window into the humanity of Professor Knoppers herself. Understanding how humanity is "promoted," we think, better elucidates the concept; not by attempting the arduous task of trying to define humanity, but rather showing how it has manifested in the various contexts of Professor Knoppers' personal and professional life. This volume is, then, in some sense, a colourful portrait of Professor Knoppers. Through stories and memories—and yes, also analysis of case law, statutes, guidelines, and policies—we intend that readers come to see how Professor Knoppers, through her work and her humanity, has contributed so much to the development of our understanding of who we are and who we ought to be as diverse individuals and members of the global community, and why every human deserves to share in scientific advancement and its benefits, and enjoy the beauty of life itself.

CHAPTER 1

DTC Pharmacogenetic Testing and Health Insurance: Good for Consumers, Good for Business?

Maxwell Brodie and Yann Joly

Prologue

It is in a 1991 forward-looking study paper for the Law Reform Commission of Canada that Professor Bartha Knoppers first tackled the challenging topic of genetic discrimination. It is interesting to note that she started by introducing discrimination in this context as a double-edged sword: (1) a means of informing one's personal decision or (2) a means of imposing the decisions of others. On that last aspect of discrimination, a domain of potential tension identified by Professor Knoppers was that of personal insurance. Here again, she rightly identified the opposing stakes raised by discrimination: on one hand, private insurers needed access to applicants' health data to successfully operate their businesses; on the other hand, applicants excluded by the process would feel as victims of an injustice.

A few years after the publication of this inspiring landmark report, I would join Professor Knoppers' team at the Université de Montréal. At that time, I was given a unique opportunity to coordinate a Pan-Canadian task force on Genetic and Life Insurance that published a Points-to-Consider policy paper on the topic in the Canadian Medical Association Journal in 2003. Enthused by the policy implications and potential to advocate for a more equitable society, I took over this topic which has brought me from the Council of Europe to the Global Alliance for Genomics and Health, and eventually led me to conceive the International Genetic Discrimination Observatory. This unique international network is now represented in over 28 countries and jurisdictions, with experts working collaboratively to investigate and address genetic discrimination. Yet, genetic discrimination is an elusive target and the description of its dual nature put forward by Professor Knoppers in 1991 remains as accurate now as it was then. Perhaps it is the best explanation as to why attempting to completely prevent genetic discrimination might be a wrong way to approach this pervasive challenge. The chapter that follows this prologue tackles the potential risk of genetic discrimination in the context of pharmacogenomic tests marketed through group health insurance. It

 | DOI:10.1163/9789004688544_003

serves as a wonderful illustration of the complex nature and competing interests raised by discrimination in genetics. I hope Professor Knoppers enjoys the read!

Yann Joly, Montreal, June 2024

1 Introduction

Pharmacogenetic (PGx) testing considers how genetic variations impact a person's response to drugs. PGx seeks to promote personalized medical care by allowing healthcare professionals to examine patients' genetic variations to optimize treatment, prevent adverse drug reactions, and reduce costs to healthcare systems.[1] Increasingly, group health insurance providers have partnered with PGx testing companies to cover, in part or in full, PGx testing for a growing variety of drugs. Should patients be hopeful for prospective health benefits, or apprehensive of the potential privacy, autonomy, economic, psychosocial, and discrimination issues at play? This chapter first provides an overview of PGx testing. Then, the rise of coverage from insurance companies will be explored to assess the potential benefits and harms of this trend.

2 Context

2.1 *PGx Current Outlook*

Drugs are not "one size fits all." The efficacy of many drugs varies drastically from patient to patient, especially for drugs seeking to treat psychiatric disorders. Approximately 50%–60% of patients prescribed an antidepressant do not adequately respond to it.[2] Up to 30% of patients diagnosed with schizophrenia do not respond to prescribed medication during treatment,[3] causing the selection of the appropriate medication to treat schizophrenia to be driven largely by trial-and-error with the patient.[4] A similar situation exists

1 See Adam Jameson and others, 'What are the barriers and enablers to the implementation of pharmacogenetic testing in mental health care settings?' (2021) 12 Frontiers in Genetics 1; Ling Jing Li and others, 'Moving towards the implementation of pharmacogenetic testing in Quebec' (2024) 14:1295963 Frontiers in Genetics 1.

2 Maurizio Fava, 'Diagnosis and definition of treatment-resistant depression' (2003) 53 Biological Psychiatry 649, 655.

3 John Lally and others, 'Treatment-resistant schizophrenia: current insights on the pharmacogenomics of antipsychotics' (2016) 9 Pharmacogenomics and Personalized Medicine 117.

4 Jameson and others (n 1), 2.

in relation to the risk of adverse reactions to these drugs. Approximately 40% of patients on antidepressants experience an adverse side-effect.[5] Thus, using the words of Canadian physician William Osler, there is a "great variability" in patient's response to many drugs.[6]

At the same time, studies estimate that between 91% and 99% of the population have a genotype which is clinically significant in the efficacy of some drugs or in the risk of adverse reactions to drugs.[7] Therefore, PGx testing has the potential to prompt a more personalized approach to psychiatry, which better tailors the chosen drugs and dosages to the individual. A randomized controlled trial has found a 30% decrease in adverse drug reaction when pre-emptive PGx testing is carried out and subsequent medication prescription is guided by those results.[8] With the advancement of PGX research, knowledge of which drugs are impacted by drug-gene interactions is also increasing for medications outside the psychiatric field.[9] All of this has resulted in a significant amount of relabeling of drugs, with over 440 US Food and Drug Administration (FDA) drug labels and 150 Health Canada drug labels being annotated to include PGx information.[10]

This expansion of knowledge about the drugs implicated in drug-gene interactions makes PGx testing of increasing value for patients, but also for the healthcare system and broader society. With the growth of prescriptions for medication treating mental health disorders, the cost borne because of inadequate or adversely reacted-to medication is of rising significance. Studies have suggested that PGx testing can reduce medication costs and hospitalization costs (from drug toxicity) by between $1036 to $3962 USD per patient per year.[11] In a microsimulation model of care for major depressive disorder in British Columbia over a 20-year period, the model found that PGx testing resulted in a 37% decrease in the development of refractory depression. This caused a reduction in the total cost of care by $956 million, or just under $5000 per

5 ibid., 2.

6 Allan D Roses, 'Pharmacogenetics and the practice of medicine' (2000) 405 Nature 857.

7 Li and others (n 1), 1; Danya Kabbani and others, 'Pharmacogenomics in practice: a review and implementation guide' (2023) 14 Frontiers in Pharmacology 1, 2.

8 Jesse J Swen and others, 'A 12-gene pharmacogenetic panel to prevent adverse drug reactions: an open-label, multicentre, controlled, cluster-randomised crossover implementation study' (2023) 401 The Lancet 347, 353

9 Jameson and others (n 1), 2.

10 PharmGKB, 'Drug Label Annotations', available at: https://www.pharmgkb.org/labelAnnotations.

11 Li and others (n 1), 1.

patient, over the 20 years. PGx testing also resulted in an average increase in life expectancy of 0.381 quality-adjusted life years, as well as 1,869 fewer deaths and over 21,000 fewer hospital admissions in the sample size of 194,149 patients.[12]

Despite the great potential of the PGX science, PGx testing has yet to become as widespread as one may expect. This is in large part due to significant challenges that have arisen which pose obstacles to the growth of the field. One of these challenges is cost. In Canada, PGx testing can cost between $199 to $2310,[13] with an average price of $738.[14] The absence of certification and regulatory approval of some direct-to-consumer PGx tests, which may not be as effective as clinical PGx testing, raises further doubts about whether the significant costs of PGx tests (including direct-to-consumer tests) makes investing into PGx testing worthwhile.[15] Moreover, for many, the side-effects that will be prevented can certainly be unpleasant, but they are relatively mild.[16] Among the Canadian direct-to-consumer PGx testing companies, only one provided an initial screening test to help consumers determine whether a PGx test was likely to be cost-effective for them.[17] Secondly, the lack of clear guidelines concerning PGx has stunted its growth. In a survey of French psychiatrists, 94.5% indicated that professional recommendations regarding PGx testing were "rather unclear, or not clear at all."[18] While organizations like the Clinical Pharmacogenetic Implementation Consortium (CPIC) have published guidelines on drug-gene interactions and their therapeutic recommendations,[19]

12 Shahzad Ghanbarian and others, 'Cost-effectiveness of pharmacogenomic-guided treatment for major depression' (2023) 195 Canadian Medical Association Journal 1499, 1503-1504.

13 Li and others (n 1), 1.

14 Ghanbarian and others (n 12), 1503.

15 Chad A Bousmam, 'Encountering pharmacogenetic test results in the psychiatric clinic' (2022) 67 Canadian Journal of Psychiatry 95; Canadian Medical Association,'CMA Policy: Direct-to-Consumer Genetic Testing' (2017), available at: https://www.cma.ca/sites/default/files/2018-11/cma-policy-direct-to-consumer-genetic-testing-pd17-05-e.pdf.

16 Health Quality Ontario, *Multi-gene Pharmacogenomic Testing That Includes Decision-Support Tools to Guide Medication Selection for Major Depression: A Health Technology Assessment*, vol 21 (Ontario Health 2021), 45-46; Ilhem Berrou, Adrusha Ramsunder, and Rachel Palmer, 'Making the case for pharmacogenomics in the management of mental health conditions' (2023) 310 Pharmaceutical Journal 1.

17 GenXys, 'TreatGx: Medication Decision Support', available at: https://www.genxys.com/clinical-decision-support-system/.

18 Benjamin Laplace and others, 'Acceptability of pharmacogenetic testing among French psychiatrists, a national survey' (2021) 11 Journal of Personalized Medicine 446.

19 Clinical Pharmacogenetics Implementation Consortium, 'Publications', available at: https://cpicpgx.org/publications/. See also PharmGKB, 'Publications', available at: https://

communication issues between scientific researchers and healthcare professionals have led to the underdevelopment of *clinical* guidelines on the use of PGx testing in clinical practice.[20]

We query whether emerging partnerships between Canadian PGx testing companies and group insurers will stimulate the clinical translation of PGx or rather create additional ethical, legal, and social issues related to PGx testing that could negatively impact public trust in PGx. A fear of incidental findings or sensitive information falling into the wrong hands, such as insurance companies, may be an impediment to the uptake of PGx testing.[21] Indeed, while a survey by McCarthy and others suggested that fears of genetic discrimination from PGx testing is low, there were "significant differences" between racial groups, with the non-Caucasian group expressing greater concern about discrimination than their Caucasian counterparts.[22]

2.2 *Insurance Companies Collaborating with PGx Testing Providers*

Insurance companies are increasingly partnering with PGx testing providers to cover PGx testing. While Canada's publicly funded healthcare system covers many medical services, some aspects of healthcare are not covered especially for adult patients (e.g. dental services, prescription drugs, ophthalmic exams). Group health insurance offered through an employer or organization can supplement the provinces' healthcare plans and cover many of these additional services.[23] Many insurance companies now offer to cover some PGx tests, although this service varies across insurance providers. The following table (Table 1.1) illustrates the growing numbers of complex partnerships established between Canadian group health insurance providers and PGx testing companies, while Table 1.2 provides key information on PGx testing companies.

www.pharmgkb.org/pgkbPublications; KNMP, 'Farmacogenetica', available at: https://www.knmp.nl/dossiers/farmacogenetica.

20 Li and others (n 1), 3.

21 ibid., 4.

22 Michael J McCarthy and others, 'Attitudes on pharmacogenetic testing in psychiatric patients with treatment-resistant depression' (2020) 37 Depression and Anxiety 826, 846.

23 Canada Life, 'Group benefits', available at: https://www.canadalife.com/insurance/group-benefits.html.

TABLE 1.1 Partnerships between Canadian group health insurance providers and PGx testing companies

Insurer	Partner PGx testing provider	Coverage overview
Beneva	Biron Genetics	Covers PGx testing with Biron Genetics for those on disability leave. Under their group insurance, PGx testing prescribed by a physician carried out in an authorized laboratory is covered
Canada Life	"Pillcheck", by GeneYouIn	Preferential pricing for PGx test offered by this company
Desjardin Insurance	No specified partner provider	To be refunded, a PGx tests must be prescribed by a physician for an established diagnosis under its accident and insurance coverage
Equitable Insurance	Rx-Report, by Personalized Prescribing	Discounted price of $399 CAD + HST (a 20% discount) for PGx testing with this company for Equitable Insurance members with a mental health condition
Green Shield Canada	"Treat Gx", by GenXys	Covers PGx testing from those providers for those with depression or anxiety
Manulife	Rx-Report, by Personalized Prescribing	Covers PGx testing from this company for those with some mental health conditions, including anxiety, depression, chronic pain, ADHD, or a neurological condition
Medavie Blue Cross	"Pillcheck", by GeneYouIn	Preferential pricing for PGx test from this company
RBC Insurance	Rx-Report, by Personalized Prescribing	Test is completely covered for those on disability claim due to mental health condition. 20% off for all plan members
Sunlife	"Treat Gx", by GenXys; Biron Genetics	Group insurance coverage of PGx testing with Treat Gx and Biron Genetics for those with mental health and chronic pain medication

Prices are in Canadian Dollars. HST = harmonized sales tax.

TABLE 1.2 PGx testing companies: key information

	Biron health group	GeneYouIn	GenXys	Personalized prescribing
Year of Incorporation	1952	2012	2014	2013
Country	Canada	Canada	Canada	Canada
Name of PGx Test	Biron Genetics	Pillcheck	TreatGx	Rx-Report
Samples Processed Outside Canada	No	Unclear	Unclear	Unclear
Genes included in the Test	*ABCB1, ABCG2, ADRA2A, ANKK1, BDNF, CACNG2, CES1, CNR1, COMT, CYP1A2, CYP2A6, CYP2B6, CYP2C19, CYP2C9, CYP2D6, CYP3A4, CYP3A5, DRD, DRD3, FAAH, GRIK1, GRIK4, HLA-A*31:01, HLA-B*15:02, HTR2A, HTR2C, HTR7, INSIG2, lncRNA, MC4R, MTHFR, OPRM1, SLC6A2, SLC6A4, SLC6A5, TH, TPH2, UGT1A1, UGT1A4, UGT2B15, UGT2B7*	*ADRB2, ABCG2, CYP1A2, CYP2B6, CYP2C8, CYP2C9, CYP2C19, CYP2D6, CYP3A4, CYP3A5, DYPD, F2, F5, G6PD, NAT2, NUDT15, OPRM1, SLCO1B1, TPMT, UGT1A1, UGT2B15 VKORC1*	*ABCG2, ADD1, ADRB2, ANKK1, COX1(PTGS1), CYP2B6, CYP2C19, CYP2C9, CYP2D6, CYP2A6, CYP3A5, DYPD, F2, F5, FKBP5, GNB3, GRIK4, HLA-A, HLA-B, HTR2A, HTR2C, IFNL3, KCNIP4, MC4R, MT-RNR1, NUDT15, OPRM1, PRKCA, SLCO1B1, TCF7L2, TNF, TPMT, VKORC1, YEATS4*[a]	*ABCB1, ACE, ADGRL3, ADM, ADRA2A, ADRB1, ADRB2, BDNF, CACNA1C, CCK, CHRNB2, COMT, CRHR1, CYP2B6, CYP2C19, CYP2D6, DBH, DRD1, DRD2, DRD3, FAAH, FKBP5, GABAα, GAD1, GNB3, GRIA1, GRIK4, GRIN1, GRIN2B, HTR1A, HTR1B, HTR2A, HTR2C, HTR3A, HTR3B, HTR3B, HTR7, IDO1, IL10, IL1B, IL6, MAO-A, MAO-B, MC4R, MTHFR, NPY, NR3C1, NR3C2, SERPINE1, SLC1A2, SLC6A2, SLC6A3, SLC6A4, SNAP25, TH, TNFα, TPH1, TPH2*

a Abdullah Al Maruf and others, 'Pharmacogenetic testing options relevant to psychiatry in Canada: options de tests pharmacogénétiques pertinents en psychiatrie au Canada' (2020) 65 Canadian Journal of Psychiatry 521. The information on the genes included in the TreatGx test is based on data from 2020.

TABLE 1.2 PGx testing companies: key information (*cont.*)

	Biron health group	GeneYouIn	GenXys	Personalized prescribing
Base Cost (without tax or insurance coverage)	One test type (i.e. mental health or pain): $349; Both tests: $499; Both tests + Nutrigenomic test: $599	$599	$499	$699
Secondary Use of Data	Yes: use of anonymous or aggregate data for research and data analysis, but will generally ask for consent	Yes: use of anonymized aggregated data for unspecified purposes	Yes: research and development. May disclose aggregated anonymized data to third parties for same purpose	Yes: research and other purposes
To Whom Are Results Returned?	The patient and their physician if the patient consents for their data to be shared	The patient and their healthcare provider who prescribed the test (if prescribed)	The patient	The patient and their healthcare provider if coordinates of one is provided by the patient
Destruction of Data	Kept as long as necessary to perform the service requested. Then anonymized or destroyed	Once a test is complete, it is destroyed after 30 days	Kept as long as necessary to perform the service	Kept for 25 years unless the client requests that it be destroyed

3 Assessment of the Benefits to Stakeholders

The growth of insurance coverage for PGx testing prompts investigation into the motivations behind these complex partnerships between insurance providers and PGx testing providers. What is there to gain, and who stands to benefit? The most notable stakeholders to the growth of insurance coverage of PGx testing are: (i) the PGx testing providers, (ii) the insurers, (iii) the insured, and (iv) the healthcare system. The way in which insurance coverage of PGx testing can benefit all these parties has yet to be precisely measured at this early point in time, but several potential advantages from these partnerships seem possible. These will now be explored in more detail, followed by an evaluation of the potential risks.

3.1 *PGx Testing Companies*

Despite its potential health benefits, PGx testing has not been widely adopted by clinicians. In the US, while PGx testing and research is more extensive than many other countries, it has been estimated that only 13% of US care providers reported ordering a PGx test for psychotropic medications in the year preceding a 2018 study.[24] It is expected that Canadian numbers are similar, if not less.[25] Naturally, as many patients may be unaware of the existence or benefits of PGx testing, clinicians are likely going to have a major impact on patients' knowledge and perception of PGx tests. If clinicians do not inform patients, or show ambivalence towards PGx tests, patients may be more cautious or reluctant to trust these new therapeutic options. Thus, if PGx testing providers are to expand the uptake of PGx testing, they must at least in part target clinicians. Maruf and others have summarized psychiatrists' hesitation to incorporate PGx testing into two central headings: (i) a belief that PGx testing is not ready to be incorporated into psychiatry, and (ii) a lack of awareness of what options are available and suitable for their practice.[26] Under both headings of objections, partnering with well-known group insurance companies can positively contribute to the advancement of the interests of PGx testing providers. The main reason for this is that those partnerships facilitate the gathering of a large amount of PGx information by private companies offering the tests. This data may be used for research, to gather evidence as to the effectiveness and utility of PGx testing. If PGx testing providers are to convince clinicians of the suitability of PGx testing, it will be by demonstrating evidence of improved health outcomes for patients on a large segment of the population. As insurance companies continue to cover an increasing number of PGx tests, it is hoped that physicians, patients, and regulators will learn about PGx's benefits and become more willing to embrace these tests.

---

24 Leland E Hull, 'VA primary care and mental health providers' comfort with genetic testing: survey results from the PRIME care study' (2018) 34 Journal of General Internal Medicine 799, 799–800.

25 Abdullah Al Maruf and others, 'Pharmacogenetic testing options relevant to psychiatry in Canada: options de tests pharmacogénétiques pertinents en psychiatrie au Canada' (2020) 65 Canadian Journal of Psychiatry 521, 522.

26 Ibid.

While clinicians play a central role in the advancement of PGx testing, patients themselves are evidently also very important. Many of the PGx tests outlined in the table above are direct-to-consumer tests that do not require a referral from a healthcare professional, which arguably, could be illegal in parts of Canada.[27] A lower price for the consumer could significantly reduce the barriers blocking their access to PGx testing. But also, insurance providers advertising the opportunity for their customers to benefit from PGx testing can better allow PGx testing providers to market their tests. In other words, PGx testing providers, who are relatively unknown to the public, will benefit from the newsletters, press releases, and marketing materials output by the insurance providers to their much wider audience.

PGx testing providers can benefit from other, secondary research carried out on the data collected from the PGx test. Consent forms typically ask for the patient's consent to allow them to carry out research using the anonymized and aggregated data of the patient or to share that anonymized data with others (i.e. broad consent). The secondary research carried out using this data could help advance the knowledge on drug-gene interactions, and the drugs impacted by them. As PGx knowledge progresses, the utility of PGx testing increases, and the testing providers will benefit from the increased demand for PGx testing. Such gradual acceptance of broad consent for secondary research use of protected data in OMICS research is a pro-scientific research realization which owes much to Professor Knoppers' conceptual work and engagement. One of us (YJ) remembers with fondness some of the stimulating early intellectual debates we had on the validity of broad consent in Canadian law and according to international guidelines with other scholars such as Professors Zawati, Caulfield, Dove, and Chadwick (all of whom feature in this book).

3.2 *Insurers*

For the insurance providers, the benefit they derive is from the improvement in health, or reduction in adverse effects and symptoms within their pool of policy holders. Such an outcome would result in financial savings for the insurer given that they bear the burden of compensating the insured in the event of occurrence of any illness covered by the policy. For example, an employee who is off work for chronic pain and covered through a group health insurance plan for missed work could come back to work more rapidly, or avoid adverse effects to their medication, which could result in more productive work and

27 Michael Lang and Ma'n H Zawati, 'The app will see you now: mobile health, diagnosis, and the practice of medicine in Quebec and Ontario' (2018) 5 Journal of Law and the Biosciences 142.

less expensive treatments to cover. This would reduce the financial amount the insurance company would be required to pay out during the employee's absence.

3.3 *Insured Persons*

According to Article 15(1)(b) of the internationally legally binding International Covenant on Economic, Social and Cultural Rights (1966), everyone has the right "to enjoy the benefits of scientific progress and its applications." Professor Knoppers realized the potential of this "dormant" human right to stimulate scientific research in genomics and promote a more collaborative research environment for the benefit of all humanity. Her writings greatly contributed to the recent revival of the "right to science."[28] This work inscribed itself in a natural continuity with previous work on individuals' shared interest in the human genome and related emerging duties of solidarity, reciprocity, and universalism.[29]

The links of the human right to science and promoting PGx testing for insured persons are clear, as are the potential benefits of PGx testing for insured persons. If PGx testing provides actionable information relating to the likely effectiveness and probability of side effects for medication prescribed to the insured person, they would benefit from any positive health outcomes. Given the frequency of adverse effect to drugs in some fields (e.g. psychiatry) and the low efficacy and high toxicity in others (e.g. anti-cancer drugs),[30] there is much to be gained from this. With insurance coverage, the cost of PGx testing decreases for consumers, such that PGx testing, if useful, is more likely to be cost-effective for them. This would have repercussions at the individual level (as per above description) and at the collective level through the gathering of additional evidence of different genotypes and the way they impact drug responses.

---

28 See e.g. Rumiana Yotova and Bartha M Knoppers, 'The right to benefit from science and its implications for genomic data sharing' (2020) 31 The European Journal of International Law 665.

29 See e.g. Bartha M Knoppers and Yann Joly, 'Our social genome?' (2007) 25 Trends in Biotechnology 284; Bartha Maria Knoppers and Ruth Chadwick, 'Human genetic research: emerging trends in ethics' (2005) 6 Nature Reviews Genetics 75.

30 Jameson and others (n 1), 2; Doreen Z Mhandire and Andrew KL Goey, 'The value of pharmacogenetics to reduce drug-related toxicity in cancer patients' (2022) 26 Molecular Diagnosis & Therapy 137.

3.4 *Other Parties*

As discussed earlier, the healthcare system as a whole can benefit from PGx testing. Reducing the prevalence of ineffective prescriptions, adverse reactions causing hospitalizations, and other costly aspects of psychiatry can reduce the financial burden of diseases on the healthcare system. Of course, as mentioned, whether the high costs of some PGx drugs outweigh their potential cost-saving effect on the healthcare system is a complex and controversial question.[31] Regardless, the healthcare system will undoubtedly be impacted by the partnership between PGx testing providers and insurers. Finally, employers may also stand to benefit. A reduced prevalence of adverse reactions to medication and an increase in the effectiveness of psychiatric care for mental health illnesses, for example, can reduce the amount of time employees take off work and can boost employees' morale and productivity at work.[32]

4 Assessment of the Ethical, Legal and Social Risks to Stakeholders

The growth of partnerships between group health insurers and PGx testing companies also gives rise to several risks for consumers. This section explores the privacy, discrimination, and health risks for consumers that are most prominently engaged by these partnerships.

4.1 *Privacy and Consent*

Over time, our understanding of privacy has evolved. Whereas privacy may originally have simply referred to secrecy (i.e. a "right to be left alone"), it now encompasses informational autonomy (i.e. the ability to control how your personal information is processed).[33] As with other types of genetic tests, PGx testing raises privacy risks for consumers. These concerns can occur in the context of inappropriate collection, use, storage, and transfer of personal information. Concerns are heightened in the context of PGx testing because genetic information can provide a detailed picture of a person's health, in addition to their drug responses, including genetic disorders and specific illnesses. The sensitivity of genetic information is further increased given its connection

---

31 Catherine R Virelli and others, 'Barriers to clinical adoption of pharmacogenomic testing in psychiatry: a critical analysis' (2021) 11 Translational Psychiatry 509.

32 Arne Beck and others, 'The effect of depression treatment on work productivity' (2014) 20 American Journal of Managed Care 294.

33 Ellen Wright Clayton and others, 'The law of genetic privacy: applications, implication, and limitations' (2019) 6 Journal of Law and the Biosciences 1, 2.

to other types of sensitive data; for example, genetic information can often allow one's ethnicity to be inferred.[34] Moreover, the information gathered from a genetic test can reveal personal information of family members of the tested person.[35] Despite this, people vary widely in their level of concern for their privacy when undergoing genetic testing,[36] and studies demonstrate that users frequently lack knowledge about the relevant privacy considerations at play in genetic testing.[37]

Given that genetic information is a sensitive type of personal data,[38] PGx testing providers should require users' consent to collect, use, process, or transfer genetic information. This consent cannot merely be implied; PGx testing companies should require explicit and informed consent from their users. Yet, the mere signing of a consent does not obviate privacy concerns. For consent to be *informed*, the PGx testing providers should be transparent and clear on the purposes of collection and the ways personal information will be processed. Special attention should be paid to portraying the relationship between insurers and the PGx companies clearly and concisely. This would prevent cases of insured persons accepting the test because they feel it is required by their insurance provider or state of health. Despite this, there is considerable variance in the level of detail with which the purposes and means of data collection and processing are described in the consent forms of PGx testing companies we reviewed for this chapter. This aligns with the results of a US study that included 35 PGx testing providers; it highlighted an elevated level of variability in consent practices, as well as that many testing providers that did not publicly share their consent practices. Moreover, there was a lack of consensus on the content of the informed consent.[39]

---

34 Mark D Shriver and others, 'Ethnic-affiliation estimation by use of population-specific DNA markers' (1997) 60 American Journal of Human Genetics 957.

35 Johanna Rahnasto, 'Genetic data are not always personal—disaggregating the identifiability and sensitivity of genetic data' (2023) 10 Journal of Law and Biosciences 1, 9, 13.

36 ibid., 4; Ellen Wright Clayton and others, 'A systematic literature review of individuals' perspectives on privacy and genetic information in the United States' (2018) 13 PLOS ONE 1, 5–9.

37 Kirpal S Panacer, 'Ethical issues associated with direct-to-consumer genetic testing' (2023) 15 Cureus e39918.

38 Office of the Privacy Commissioner of Canada, 'Interpretation Bulletin: Sensitive Information' (2022), available at: https://www.priv.gc.ca/en/privacy-topics/privacy-laws-in-canada/the-personal-information-protection-and-electronic-documents-act-pipeda/pipeda-compliance-help/pipeda-interpretation-bulletins/interpretations_10_sensible/.

39 Susanne B Haga and Rachel Mills, 'A review of consent practices and perspectives for pharmacogenetic testing' (2016) 17 Pharmacogenomics 1595, 1597–1598.

It is now worth exploring important privacy considerations which users ought to be aware of prior to consenting to PGx testing.

In the consent forms and privacy policies analyzed from Canadian PGx testing providers, one commonality was the practice of allowing anonymized and aggregated data to be used for secondary research.[40] Yet, in the context of PGx testing, there are questions about the extent to which genetic information can ever truly be anonymized. Only a small amount of genetic information is required to re-identify a person by matching this information with other genetic data and associated metadata that is publicly available.[41] Moreover, what may nowadays be considered unidentifiable, and therefore anonymous, may in the near future be considered identifiable because of advancing technologies and the growing number of public genomic databases which allow ever smaller amounts of OMICS data to be linked back to an individual's identity.[42]

For consent to be truly informed, there must be transparent disclosure from the PGx testing provider as to the purposes and means of processing data. In many instances in this study, this information appeared to be lacking. Consent forms and privacy policies were frequently unclear as to where the data would be processed and whether the data would ever be processed outside of Canada. Information regarding the security systems relating to the storage of the data was rarely mentioned. When they were, PGx testing companies typically merely stated that adequate security measures would be implemented to protect the security of the information.[43] One point of considerable variance between PGx testing companies were policies concerning the destruction of PGx information. While PGx testing companies similarly contained clauses allowing individuals to withdraw their consent for PGx testing companies to conduct further analysis on their samples, there was considerable variance on the maximum time period the data could be stored by a company when individuals had not withdrawn their consent. This time period ranged from

40 See e.g. Pillcheck, available at: https://www.pillcheck.ca/; Biron Health Group, 'Privacy Policy', available at: https://www.biron.com/en/privacypolicy/.

41 Charles Dupras and Eline M Bunnik, 'Toward a framework for assessing privacy risks in multi-omic research and databases' (2021) 21 The American Journal of Bioethics 46.

42 Global Alliance for Genomics and Health, 'GDPR Brief: can genomic data be anonymised?' (10 October 2018), available at: https://www.ga4gh.org/news_item/can-genomic-data-be-anonymised/; Rahnasto (n 35), 20-21.

43 See e.g. Biron Health Group (n 40); For an exception, see Personalized Prescribing, 'Privacy Policy', available at: https://personalizedprescribing.com/privacy-policy/.

30 days[44] to 25 years depending on the company.[45] On the positive side, many consent forms expressly stated that personal information would not be shared with insurers or employers.[46]

Importantly, based on a review of their website and online documents, PGx testing providers did not appear to provide any information on whether their tests have been approved or recommended by any regulatory body, such as Health Canada. This is problematic and puts into question the clinical relevance of the test. Compared to the US, Health Canada has moved much more slowly and with great restraint to regulate PGx.[47] While genetic testing marketed as test kits are subject to federal regulation under the Medical Device Regulations,[48] genetic tests offered as laboratory services (where DNA samples are sent to a laboratory) fall under provincial regulation and do not require approval by Health Canada.[49] The PGx testing providers analyzed in the context of our study seem to all send their DNA samples to a laboratory, implying that they are not subject to the federal regulation. There is also very little information provided on the laboratories used by the PGx testing providers. Overall, the lack of transparency in the existence of regulatory approval undermines the ability of the consumer to evaluate the utility and trustworthiness of the PGx test.

As remarked by Haga and Mills, "the variability in laboratory consent practices may reflect the ambiguous status and shifting perception about PGx testing."[50] For some, PGx testing does not engage the same privacy considerations as disease-based genetic testing, as the results are less sensitive in nature.[51] This statement is disputable given the pleiotropic nature of PGx data, with some PGx markers also providing information about disease predispositions.[52] Furthermore, the lack of transparency and occasional wide discrepancy

44 Pillcheck (n 40).

45 Personalized Prescribing (n 43).

46 Pillcheck (n 40).

47 Medication Management, 'Pharmacogenetic testing in Canada – what plan sponsors need to know' (2021), available at: https://www.benefitscanada.com/wp-content/uploads/sites/7/2021/11/MedManagement_Inagene_2021_ENG-nov-2021.pdf.

48 Medical Device Regulations, SOR/98-282 (Canada).

49 See Yann Joly and Emma Ramos-Paque, 'Approval of new pharmacogenetic tests: is the Canadian regulatory process adequate?' (2010) 8 Canadian Journal of Law and Technology 215, 224-225.

50 Haga and Mills (n 39), 1602.

51 Nuffield Council on Bioethics, *Pharmacogenetics: ethical issues* (Nuffield Council on Bioethics 2003), 62.

52 Mariamena Arbitrio and others 'Pharmacogenomics biomarker discovery and validation for translation in clinical practice' (2021) 14 Clinical and Translational Science 113.

between PGx testing providers poses challenges to uninformed consumers and may damage the public perception of the PGx testing industry. This is problematic, particularly when individuals seeking PGx testing are unlikely to read the consent forms. It would thus be desirable to have more homogenous consent practices which ensure a minimum standard of privacy that is consistent with what consumers would expect when undergoing PGx testing. Haga and Mills highlight that researchers and clinicians share this desire for greater standardization.[53] At the same time, exceptions should be expected, especially for tests targeting a different audience. For example, consent forms for preemptive PGx testing (prior to any medication being needed) may wish to provide more information on the long-term uses and consequences of PGx testing, while PGx testing at the point of care (when medication is needed now) may focus more on the utility of PGx testing in treatment selection and dosing.[54]

4.2 *Discrimination*

Genetic discrimination involves an individual or a group being negatively treated, unfairly profiled, or harmed, relative to the rest of the population, based on actual or presumed genetic characteristics.[55] It remains a relatively uncommon phenomenon, but one of increasing significance given the fast rise of genetic testing. Genetic discrimination is most relevant in the insurance context, where people with particular genetic diseases or predispositions to disease known by insurers may face greater challenges obtaining coverage or be deemed uninsurable.[56]

In response to genetic discrimination complaints and the worry that the public would be unwilling to undergo genetic testing out of concern of being discriminated against, many lawmakers worldwide have passed legislation seeking to prohibit genetic discrimination particularly in the context of insurance and employment.[57] In Canada, the insurance industry chose not to act on recommendations made by the Canadian Genetics and Life Insurance Task Force, which included Professors Joly and Knoppers along with representative of the life insurance industry and other stakeholders,[58] the situation continued

53 Haga and Mills (n 39), 1598.

54 ibid., 1601.

55 Beatrice Kaiser and others, 'A proposal for an inclusive working definition of genetic discrimination to promote a more coherent debate' (2024) 56 Nature Genetics 1339.

56 Amy Fernando and others, 'Still using genetic data? A comparative review of Canadian life insurance application forms before and after the GNDA' (2024) 9 Facets 1.

57 ibid.

58 Bartha M Knoppers and Yann Joly, 'Physicians, genetics and life insurance' (2004) 170 Canadian Medical Association Journal 1421.

to escalate between them and some patient organizations such as Huntington Society of Canada and the Canadian Breast Cancer Association. Eventually these groups and other organizations regrouped as the Canadian Coalition for Genetic Fairness to promote the adoption of the Genetic Non-Discrimination Act (GNDA).[59] The GNDA makes it a criminal offence for a provider of goods or services to require a person to undergo a genetic test, or to disclose the results of a genetic test, in the context of an agreement or contract to receive said good or service.[60] Given the broad wording used in the law, the prohibition would apply to the context of a private personal or group insurance contract.

Insurance companies could also be interested in having access to PGx testing results for underwriting. PGx information would be relevant to insurers in two settings: (i) in the process of determining the premiums for people applying for insurance coverage, and (ii) in resolving claims and deciding whether to cover an injury suffered by a policyholder.[61] If insurers could access PGx information, it could lead to adverse outcomes for those who underwent PGx testing. For example, should a PGx test reveal that existing drugs for a particular illness they have are more likely to cause adverse reactions, insurers may wish to charge that individual higher premiums to reflect the heightened health risk this represents for the health of that person. Alternatively, if an insured person makes a claim based on an illness for which they have not followed the prescription-related advice from a PGx test (e.g. taking a medication which was contraindicated by a PGx test), the insurer may be inclined to deny the claim. However, in addition to the legal protection afforded by the GNDA, the risk of genetic discrimination in this field is greatly reduced by three factors: (1) the health risk presented by an insurance candidate can only be assessed once at the beginning of an insurance contract; (2) many PGx tests are insufficiently validated to be used by personal insurers for underwriting; and (3) according to the GNDA and Canadian data privacy legislation, the use of PGx results collected in the context of group health insurance should not be communicated (to an insurer) without obtaining an explicit, informed, written consent from the person.

This could explain why only a minority of PGx patients surveyed by McCarthy and others expressed concerns about genetic discrimination arising from PGx testing.[62] The Nuffield Council on Bioethics has also stressed that the likelihood of genetic discrimination arising out of PGx testing is considerably

59 Genetic Non-Discrimination Act, SC 2017, c 3 [GNDA] (Canada).

60 ibid., s 7; Reference Re Genetic Non-Discrimination Act, 2020 SCC 17 (Canada).

61 Nuffield Council on Bioethics (n 51), 69.

62 McCarthy and others (n 22), 845-846.

lower than for genetic tests for single-gene disorders.[63] There are many other non-genetic health-related questions related to a person's lifestyle (e.g. whether they smoke, drink, exercise, eat a healthy diet) which will have a greater impact on the risk assessment carried out by the insurer. For this reason, the Nuffield Council on Bioethics stated that it was unlikely that PGx testing information would be widely used for underwriting purposes.[64]

While one may believe that the prohibition on genetic discrimination under GNDA fully protects individuals from PGx discrimination, it is important to stress the limited scope of the law. As it is formulated, the GNDA prohibits the imposition of a genetic test or the disclosure of the results of a genetic test, in the context of contracts or agreements to provide goods or services. Importantly the law defines a genetic test as a test that analyzes DNA, RNA, or chromosomes for purposes such as the prediction of disease or vertical transmission risks, or monitoring, diagnosis, or prognosis. Given this formulation and the inclusion of the open expression "such as" in the law, it appears likely but not completely certain that, if there were to be a court case, the scope of the Act would be considered to encompass PGx test results. Importantly, only the imposition of a genetic test, or required disclosure of test results, are prohibited by the GNDA. If an individual had to pay a higher premium for their personal insurance given that they are not taking the medication usually recommended for their condition (as a result of a PGx test), it is uncertain that the GNDA would apply. This is because in this last example, the insurer had not required genetic test results or based their decision on the results of such tests; instead, the decision is based on a refusal of a person to take medication as prescribed by their physician. Interestingly, the application of the GNDA to this case is unclear regardless of whether test results suggested that the individual should take the same drug as the majority group of the population, or rather use an alternative medicine better suited to their PGx profile.

Therefore, while the risk of PGx discrimination is low, it is not completely theoretical. In response, efforts should concentrate on raising public awareness of good privacy practices and the potential for genetic discrimination and the legal protections in place by the GNDA. Doing so would render PGx test users' consent more informed and would promote their privacy interests. Moreover, public awareness of GNDA would reduce the likelihood of insurance applicants unnecessarily disclosing their protected PGx testing results and avoid any discriminatory use from an uninformed or ill-intended insurer. However, we should not forget that other health information beyond genomics

63 ibid.

64 Nuffield Council on Bioethics (n 51), 70.

can also be used in a discriminatory or stigmatizing manner for an insurer. This is in fact quite relevant to the case of PGx testing by private companies for psychiatric disorders. The knowledge by such companies that a person submitting a DNA sample is afflicted by a psychiatric disorder, and perhaps the specific type or category of disorder, is highly sensitive personal information. The communication of this information to friends, co-workers, or other insurance companies could result in a clear violation of a person's dignity, privacy, psychological integrity, and autonomy, and be a source of intense psychological distress and more for that person. As such, both employers and the PGx companies involved in these collaborations should have robust, legally and ethically-attuned policies to manage their interaction and respect the employees' privacy. The employer, or the health insurer, should not receive any identifying information about employees that are availing themselves of the opportunity to get tested. The PGx testing companies should have clear, legally and ethically-attuned consent and data privacy information available for consumers. They should require only the minimal amount of personal information that is necessary for them to conduct the test and to return the results to the individual, or their physician. Future research use is only acceptable if clearly indicated on the consent material and if all reasonable measures to prevent data breach and re-identifcation have been taken.

4.3 *Health*

Psychosocial and medical risks may also materialize due to an increase in PGx testing, in the context of partnerships between PGx testing companies and group insurers, especially if medical or pharmaceutical specialists are not involved. The first risk would be that a PGx test that is not clinical grade provides erroneous results to a person. The person could then potentially incur harm by following the results of the PGx test to adjust their dosage or take a different drug.

As with other direct-to-consumer tests, there is also a risk that the consumer will misinterpret otherwise relevant test results. Should the consumer misinterpret a PGx test, and for example cease to take their prescribed medication, this could have harmful health effects. For this reason, PGx testing companies should provide information about the clinical validity of their test and explicitly state that consumers should not act upon the PGx test results without first consulting their healthcare provider.[65]

65 See e.g. Personalized Prescribing, 'Informed Consent and Choices', available at: https://personalizedprescribing.com/pages/informed-consent-and-choices/.

In addition, if public attention is increasingly drawn to the way genetics impact a person's response to medical care, there is a risk of a deterministic attitude being taken towards treatment. In other words, patients may increasingly come to believe that their prospect for recovery from an illness is solely based on their genetics. To prevent this, it is important to increase public awareness through the media about the role, benefits, and limitations of PGx in medicine, including the problems of genetic determinism.

5 Conclusion

This chapter's review of the ethical, social, and legal implications of growing collaborations between health insurers and PGx testing companies is particularly interesting in the context of this Festschrift. It is a welcome occasion to remind ourselves of the far reaching impact that our mentor Professor Knoppers has had on the field of genomics law and policy. Indeed, while she did not write on the specific topic of PGx, her work on key policy questions (e.g. consent, privacy, discrimination, communication of results) has transcended the narrowly defined genetic discipline and is considered a major source of legal and policy writing for all OMICS research and care fields. Moreover, her visionary and innovative contribution has influenced developments in other medical disciplines, including the neurosciences, end-of-life care, paediatrics, and oncology.

PGx testing has the potential to personalize many aspects of care, especially for mental illnesses and chronic pain. Several impediments, such as high costs and a lack of clinical guidance, have stunted the growth of PGx testing. The rapid rise of insurance coverage of PGx testing raises the potential for broader uptake of PGx tests by the public. At the same time, this partnership between PGx testing providers and insurers gives rise to privacy, discrimination, and psychosocial risks for consumers. These risks need to be carefully addressed to avoid incidents that could seriously undermine public trust in PGx.

This chapter has underlined the rapidly growing interrelations between PGx testing companies and group health insurers in Canada, and the considerable variability in consent and privacy practices used in this context. Currently, patients are unlikely to be alert to relevant ethical, legal, and social risks when undergoing PGx testing. While some PGx testing providers offer relatively clear and understandable consent forms, a broader effort should be concentrated on creating a minimum standard of privacy and transparency across PGx testing companies which is commensurate with what consumers should expect and is required by Canadian law and good privacy practices. Notably, PGx testing companies vary considerably in their policies vis-à-vis the conservation and destruction of PGx data. Consent forms of PGx providers are also frequently lacking in their description of where data is processed, what secondary uses will be made of PGx data, and what security systems are in place to protect consumers' data.

While PGx testing is less likely to lead to genetic discrimination compared to other types of genetic testing, consumers should remain vigilant. The development of public information campaigns promoting greater awareness of the GNDA and its limited scope of application, as well as of good privacy practices applicable to genetic data, would bolster the efficacy of existing protections and prevent careless behaviours from consumers. While PGx testing providers, employers, insurance companies, and consumers all stand to benefit greatly from partnerships between PGx testing companies and group insurers, greater attention must be placed on clarifying the terms of these partnerships and the legal and ethical implications for consumers to avoid costly setbacks.

VIGNETTE

25 Years of Enriching Collaboration with Bartha M. Knoppers

Jacques Simard

For over 25 years, I've had the great privilege to work closely with Professor Bartha Maria Knoppers on numerous research projects of international scope, particularly in the context of the interdisciplinary and international INHERIT BRCAS team from 2001 to 2013. During that time, I had the opportunity to exchange with her on numerous salient topics, such as the emergence of ethical duties to disclose genetic research results, the potential for inequitable access to healthcare related to personalized medicine, the legal liability and uncertain nature of risk prediction, the challenges for intrafamilial communication of cancer genetic risk, as well as the debate on genetic discrimination in the context of life insurance related to stratified medicine.

These studies have paved the way for our future collaborative endeavours. From 2013 to 2018, Bartha and I were the co-leads of the large-scale applied project titled "Personalized Risk Stratification for the Prevention and Early Detection of Breast Cancer" (PERSPECTIVE). This project was followed by the related project "PERSPECTIVE: Integration and Implementation" from 2018 to 2024, for which Bartha was the co-lead of one of the major implementation components. The overarching goal of these projects was to develop risk stratification tools that would improve personalized breast cancer risk assessment thereby allowing more cost-effective prevention to those most likely to benefit, and to determine actionable cost-effective strategies based on real world experience for the implementation of a risk-stratified screening approach within its socio-legal environment, and healthcare organization structures.

Her unique expertise has been invaluable not only in the funding of all these cutting-edge interdisciplinary projects, but more importantly in our capability to achieve our deliverables in a timely manner. It goes without saying that she has been an indispensable pillar within our interdisciplinary team. There is no doubt that her dedicated involvement gave me the audacity and the courage to undertake these translational studies in cancer genomics. It is worth mentioning that, despite her extreme workload and global travel, she was always reachable and available. It is still unclear to me which time zone her internal body clock is set to!

DOI:10.1163/9789004688544_004

Bartha is a true trailblazer, exceptionally talented, and a most prolific and highly influential researcher who consistently establishes successful collaborations worldwide. She has always conducted her research activities in accordance with the highest possible ethical standards, rigour and integrity. Such a broad expertise, coupled with a great sense of humanism, has ensured a thorough health technology assessment, knowledge mobilization, and the establishment of the most appropriate socio-ethical and legal framework needed to accelerate the translation of results into healthcare improvements, both at the individual and the population level for the common goods.

Throughout her exemplary career, she has demonstrated a ground-breaking leadership, innovation, creativity, and dedication to developing world-class research across the disciplines of ethics, law, and health sciences. She has furthermore provided a highly stimulating training environment while being an indispensable mentor to a new generation of interdisciplinary researchers in law and medicine. Indeed, I had the chance to witness her full wholehearted dedication to education, and she has been recognized as an inspiring role model for her students who highly praise her exceptional qualities as a motivating, competent, and most respectful teacher.

As a testimony to her exceptional career, her peers have celebrated her with numerous most prestigious accolades that demonstrate the great magnitude of the esteem they have for her, the impact of her visionary work, and her wonderful legacy. I feel privileged to have her personal contact details and I am sure that I will keep seeking her incomparable wisdom for many years.

VIGNETTE

A Lifetime of Collaboration

Denise Avard

I have known Bartha as a colleague, mentor, and, most importantly, as a friend for more than thirty years. We both were highly involved in promoting the health and wellbeing of children. When we first met, I was working as Director of the Canadian Institute of Child Health (CICH) in Ottawa, while Bartha was on the Board.

One of the our earliest collaborations was when Bartha produced a book entitled *Canadian Child Health Law*,[1] a cornerstone piece regarding the well-being of children in Canada. In this book she addresses the implications for Canada to honour what was then the new United Nations Convention on the Rights of the Child (1990) into domestic law and help promote the inclusion of children in research. It was very timely because this book provided a fact-based portrait of the health and rights of children just as Canada became a signatory to the Convention.

Several years later I moved to Montreal and Bartha invited me into her team to integrate my child health background with her work in pediatric genetics at the CRDP (Centre de recherche en droit public) at the Université de Montréal. Concerns over DNA testing, screening, and data banks with children's information further enhanced our bond to promote children's health and rights.

I helped her move from Université de Montréal to McGill University (the two solitudes!), with all the stress of moving a team the size of a whole village, and with all the excitement of a new start. At McGill, Bartha created the Centre of Genomics and Policy, which became a world-class research centre committed to providing policy advice to international, national, and regional organizations and governments.

One of the many qualities of Bartha, and one of her biggest assets, is her ability to motivate, inspire, and promote multidisciplinary collaborations. This has been her modus operandi throughout her career. Her early interest in the ethical and judicial impact of genetic and genomics facilitated this approach by combining science, ethics, sociology, psychology, medicine, and law.

1 Bartha Maria Knoppers, *Canadian Child Health Law: Health Rights and Risks of Children* (Thompson Educational Publishing 1992).

The collaborative approach paved the way to the creation of the HumGen website, a clearing house of public policies on socio-ethical issues related to human genetics, which facilitated the access and validation of various genomics policies globally.[2] Remember, this was the late 1990s, still the early days of the internet, and yet already Bartha was interested in this new communication technology! I shall say no more and leave to her colleagues the discussion of many successful collaborative projects frequently summarized using a creative ACRONYM, "A Coded Resume Of Names Yielding Messages."

Bartha has always been an exceptional orator. During a scientific presentation, she commands a crowd's attention and skillfully makes complex bioethical concepts understandable. Laughter can do a lot to captivate an audience and generate instant comprehension of the issues.

Bartha has also always been an ideal travel companion. I vividly remember our awkward coffee shop moment in Amsterdam, when we unintentionally walked into a "coffee shop" (in other words, a marijuana café), dressed in full business attire, as we were heading to meet a potential funder. Also, our stay in a hotel in Kijkduin, an oasis of tranquility located near sandy beaches and dunes on the North Sea, was a great source of inspiration and relaxation.

Bartha, despite your "retirement," your passionate commitment to high standards and your collaborative spirit will keep making the world a better place.

---

2 See e.g. Denise Avard and Bartha Maria Knoppers, 'Genetics and Society Project' (2000) 3 Community Genetics 102.

CHAPTER 2

If We Build It, They Will Come: Population Biobanks and the Enduring Legacy of Bartha Maria Knoppers

Ma'n H. Zawati and Alycia Noë

1 Introduction

Back in 2009, *Time* magazine named biobanks as one of the ten ideas changing the world.[1] Little did I[2] know that in that same year, I would be ushered into this vastly expanding field of study. I had just recently been licensed as a lawyer and was eyeing a master's degree under the supervision of Professor Knoppers. Here I was, a young researcher, a newly minted member of the Quebec Bar, looking to build a niche in the ethical, legal, and policy issues associated with genomics. Despite being new to the field, Professor Knoppers chose to not only involve me in research projects on this topic, but to also connect me with all the major actors in this field. "This is Ma'n, a future world expert in the field of biobanking," she would say at networking events. While she did her best to inflate the hype around me as a researcher, the hype around biobanks, however, was growing stronger. In fact, the Office for the Privacy Commissioner of Canada stated in 2011 that: "Biobanking stands to fundamentally change the way we prevent, diagnose, and treat disease."[3] With that, biobanking also promised to challenge traditional approaches to the ethical, legal, and social regulation of medical research.[4] Legal and ethical challenges associated with biobanks include, but are not limited to, informed consent, data sharing with

1 Alice Park, '10 Ideas Changing the World Right Now' *Time* (12 March 2009), available at: https://content.time.com/time/specials/packages/article/0,28804,1884779_1884782_1884766,00.html.

2 The use of "I" in this text refers to the co-author Ma'n H Zawati (MHZ). MHZ would like to acknowledge the funding provided by the FRQS J1 Research Career Award.

3 Office for the Privacy Commissioner of Canada, 'Banking for the Future: "Informing" Consent in the Context of Biobanks' (IV International Seminar on the UNESCO Universal Declaration on Bioethics and Human Rights, Barcelona, 2011).

4 ibid.

researchers, international collaborations, data security, privacy and confidentiality, commercialization and return of results.[5]

Professor Knoppers' unique contribution to this field of study cannot be understated. More importantly, her efforts have not only included the creation of Quebec's first populational cohort study, CARTaGENE, but also laid the groundwork for policy development and international interoperability of biobanking standards. Are the traditional ethical and legal principles equipped to address the issues arising from the use of such novel technologies and research initiatives? The answer was no. After all, "ethics does not consist of a static set of theories or principles that can unproblematically be 'applied' to new situations."[6] Rooted in the "Human," Professor Knoppers' legacy in the world of biobanking contributed to a better understanding of the relationships underpinning population biobanks, where, for the first time, the values of reciprocity, solidarity, and universalism were introduced and adapted into this novel context.[7]

It is important to state that Professor Knoppers' contribution to this field has not been limited to policy development or publications (which is astounding: as of the time of writing, when searching "Bartha Knoppers" and "biobank" in Google Scholar, an impressive 331 search results come up); it has also included founding vital organizations and sitting on key committees aimed at moving this conversation forward, fostering innovation and achieving international consensuses. Indeed, she was the Founder and Chair of the Public Population Project in Genomics and Society (P^3G) Consortium and of CARTaGENE.[8] She served as Co-Chair of the Sampling/ELSI Committee of the 1000 Genomes Project and as a member of the Scientific Steering Committee of the International Cancer Genome Consortium (ICGC).[9] She was Chair of the International Ethics Committee of the Human Genome Organization (HUGO), Co-Chair of the Governance Ethics Working Group for the Human Cell Atlas (HCA),[10] and a

5 Heather Widdows and Sean Cordell, 'The ethics of biobanking: key issues and controversies' (2011) 19 Health Care Analysis 207.

6 Bartha Maria Knoppers and Ruth Chadwick, 'Human genetic research: emerging trends in ethics' (2005) 6 Nature Review Genetics 75.

7 ibid.

8 Public Population Project in Genomics and Society, available at: https://www.p3gobservatory.org/; CARTaGENE: a new era of research, available at: https://cartagene.qc.ca/en/.

9 The International Genome Sample Resource, available at: https://www.internationalgenome.org/; The International Cancer Genome Consortium, 'International network of cancer genome projects' (2010) 464 Nature 993.

10 Human Genome Organization, available at: https://www.hugo-international.org/; Human Cell Atlas, available at: https://www.humancellatlas.org/.

member of UNESCOs International Bioethics Committee (IBC).[11] She was also co-founder and on the Board of Directors of the Global Alliance for Genomics and Health (GA4GH),[12] where she was instrumental in putting in place its international Regulatory and Ethics Work Stream.[13]

Synthesizing Professor Knoppers' legacy on biobanks in one chapter is an impossible feat. That said, we hope to highlight important milestones over her illustrious career and show that for biobanks to prosper, a solid normative ecosystem, namely policies and legislation, need to be put in place. Accordingly, this chapter will concentrate on population biobanks, a category that was the focus of much of Professor Knoppers' scholarly work on biobanks over the past three decades. We will begin with an overview of their characteristics and purpose. This is a necessary starting point for the chapter, as any ethical or legal study of population biobanks must keep their purposes at the forefront. The chapter then uses CARTaGENE as a case model to showcase the web of complex, multidirectional human relationships underlying population biobanking initiatives. We then delve into Professor Knoppers' legacy both in legislative and policy approaches to the regulation of biobanks. The Estonian Human Genes Research Act, which Professor Knoppers helped to draft, will be presented as a case in point. Next, the chapter explores policies that have proved important for biobanking initiatives. Through the exploration of Professor Knoppers' crucial contributions in international organizations such as HUGO and UNESCO, the chapter highlights how prospective policymaking is key for international cooperation in biobanking, and how it offers flexibility and malleability that legislation might not always provide. As will be seen in this chapter, in the phrase "if we build it, they will come," the "it" here does not refer to the population biobank initiative per se, but rather to the set of policies, both internal and external, that one needs to put in place to allow population biobanks to fulfill their purpose in an efficient, ethical, and equitable manner.

11 Aleksandra Draper, 'Bartha Knoppers – Complex ethical and legal question on data use are increasingly pertinent' (*eTRIKS*, 18 October 2016), available at: https://www.etriks.org/2016/10/18/bartha-knoppers-complex-ethical-and-legal-questions-on-data-use-are-increasingly-pertinent/.

12 Global Alliance for Genomics and Health, available at: https://www.ga4gh.org/.

13 Global Alliance for Genomics and Health, 'Regulatory and Ethics Work Stream (REWS)', available at: https://www.ga4gh.org/work_stream/regulatory-ethics/.

2 Population Biobanks

2.1 *Biobank Typology*

Research biobanks are an organized and searchable collection of biological samples and associated health data (e.g. genomic data, health records, questionnaire responses to lifestyle questions) held for the purpose of future biomedical research.[14] There are numerous types of biobanking initiatives.[15]

While there is no fully recognized and formalized classification system for biobanks, many researchers have nonetheless attempted to classify biobanks in the literature.[16] When classified by research goals, there are three types of biobanks: population-based biobanks, disease-specific biobanks, and public health biobanks.[17]

In general, disease-specific biobanks are the most selective with their recruitment of participants as they recruit for a particular disease.[18] These biobanks, due to their focus on a given illness, aim to identify biomarkers to improve diagnosis and to identify novel therapeutic strategies.[19] Examples include biobanks centered on infectious diseases, such as the University of San Francisco AIDS Specimen Biobank and CanCOGeN HostSeq,[20] and those with a concentration on cancer prevention, such as the International Cancer Genome Consortium and Ontario Tumour Bank.[21] On the other hand, public health biobanks survey a cross-section of the population to monitor the health

---

14 Laura Annaratone and others, 'Basic principles of biobanking: from biological samples to precision medicine for patients' (2021) 479 Virchows Archiv 233, 233.

15 Edward S Dove, 'Biobanks, data sharing, and the drive for a global privacy governance framework' (2015) 43 Journal of Law, Medicine & Ethics 675, 676-77.

16 Annaratone (n 14), 234.

17 Karine Sargsygan, Berthold Huppertz, and Svetlana Gramatiuk (eds), *Biobanks in Low- and Middle-Income Countries: Relevance, Setup and Management* (Springer 2022), 19; Peter Dabrock, Jochen Taupitz, and Jens Ried (eds), *Trust in Biobanking: Dealing with Ethical, Legal and Social Issues in an Emerging Field of Biotechnology* (Springer 2012), 7-11.

18 ibid.

19 Luigi Coppola and others, 'Biobanking in healthcare: evolution and future directions' (2019) 17 Journal of Translational Medicine 1, 5.

20 Lisa Loeb Stanga and others, 'The California HIV/AIDS Research Program: History, Impact, and HIV Cure Initiative' (2017) 33 AIDS Research and Human Retroviruses S-1; HostSeq, available at: https://genomecanada.ca/challenge-areas/cancogen/hostseq/.

21 Junjun Zhang and others, 'International Cancer Genome Consortium Data Portal – a one-stop shop for cancer genomics data' (2011) 2011 Database 1; Ontario Tumour Bank, available at: https://ontariotumourbank.ca/.

and well-being of the population as well as changes in the nature of diseases passing through the monitored population (e.g. Statistics Canada Biobank).[22]

The significance of both disease-oriented and public health biobanks became clearer with the emergence of the COVID-19 pandemic. COVID-19 swept through the world within months of its appearance, threatening human health and leaving devastation in its wake. In order to further our understanding of the virus and its associated disease and to develop a vaccine, researchers needed biological samples from COVID-19 patients. For example, samples from the Banque québécoise de la COVID-19 (BQC19) spurred research that identified genetic isoforms that are protective against COVID-19 severity and COVID-19-specific immune modifications found in severely ill patients, to name a few research advancements directly resulting out of a COVID-19-specific biobanks.[23] As such biobanks, such as UK Biobank, BQC19, and CanPath (including CARTaGENE), have a key role to play in epidemic/pandemic preparedness and prompt response. Some even say that biobanks are foundational as they are "mediators between clinical practice and research."[24]

Finally, there are population-based biobanks that recruit participants by random selection among a particular population (e.g. Quebec residents). [25] As we have chosen to centre the chapter on Professor Knoppers' contributions to the sustainability of population biobanks, the goals of population biobanks will be explored in greater detail in the next section of this chapter.

2.2 *Population Biobanks*

The Council of Europe's definition of population biobanks is a common starting point for discussions concerning the regulation of biobanks. Population biobanks are:

> [Collections of biological materials having the following characteristics]: i. the collection has a population basis; ii. it is established, or has been

22 Government of Canada, 'Statistics Canada Biobank', available at: https://www.statcan.gc.ca/en/microdata/biobank; Angela M Brand and Nicole M Probst-Hensch, 'Biobanking for epidemiological research and public health' (2007) 74 Pathobiology 227, 231.

23 Sirui Zhou and others, 'A Neanderthal OAS1 isoform protects individuals of European ancestry against COVID-19 susceptibility and severity' (2021) 27 Nature Medicine 659; Rose-Marie Rébillard and others, 'Identification of SARS-CoV-2-specific immune alterations in acutely ill patients' (2021) 15 The Journal of Clinical Investigation 1.

24 Dovile Juozapaite and others, 'The COVID-19 pandemic reveals the wide-ranging role of biobanks' (2023) 11 Frontiers in Public Health 01, 01.

25 Philip Awadalla and others, 'Cohort profile of the CARTaGENE study: Quebec's population-based biobank for public health and personalized genomics' (2013) 42 International Journal of Epidemiology 1285.

> converted, to supply biological materials or data derived therefrom for multiple future research projects; iii. it contains biological materials and associated personal data, which may include or be linked to genealogical, medical and lifestyle data and which may be regularly updated; iv. it receives and supplies materials in an organised manner.[26]

Population-based biobanks are appealing because they diminish the need to correct any bias upon selection of participants.[27] Examples of population-based biobanks include the Estonian Genome Project,[28] CARTaGENE (Quebec),[29] the UK Biobank,[30] and All of Us (USA).[31] These projects collect health data for future, unspecified research. Just like disease-specific biobanks, their aims are future-oriented, whether that be new therapies or increased diagnostic capabilities. They provide "ready and waiting" data samples from a heterogeneous population for research projects that are yet to be known.[32] Ultimately, population biobanks seek to understand the genomic variation, lifestyle choices, and environmental factors that are correlated with and may contribute to disease risk and other aspects of human health.[33] By doing so, population biobanks have a key role to play in disease prevention and diagnosis.[34]

2.3 *From Individuals to Populations Back to Individuals: the Birth of CARTaGENE*

All population biobanks are built and used for future generations. While there may be inadvertent gains for individuals contributing samples and associated data to biobanks today, the goal truly is future benefits to society, thanks,

26 Council of Europe, 'Recommendation Rec(2006)4 of the Committee of Ministers to member states on research on biological materials of human origin' (15 March 2006), available at: https://search.coe.int/cm/Pages/result_details.aspx?ObjectID=09000016805d84f0.

27 Awadalla and others (n 25).

28 Quirin Schiermeier, 'How Estonia blazed a trail in science' (Nature, 22 January 2019), available at: https://www.nature.com/articles/d41586-019-00209-7.

29 CARTaGENE (n 8).

30 Rory Collins, 'What makes UK Biobank special?' (2012) 379 The Lancet 1173.

31 National Institutes of Health, 'All of Us Biobank', available at: https://allofus.nih.gov/funding-and-program-partners/biobank.

32 Bartha Maria Knoppers and others, 'Modeling consent in the time of COVID-19' (2020) 7 Journal of Law and the Biosciences 1, 5.

33 Muin J Khoury and others, 'The emergence of epidemiology in the genomics age' (2004) 33 International Journal of Epidemiology 936, 940.

34 Ozren Polasek, 'Future of biobanks – bigger, longer, and more dimensional' (2013) 54 Croatian Medical Journal 496, 498.

in part, to future medical research.[35] Furthermore, unlike clinical trials, this future research cannot be specified in the same detail as it is unknown at the time of participant consent.[36] The potential downstream applications of research using biobanking data and samples are vast in scope, including, but not limited to, early diagnosis of disease, new treatments, and improved public health initiatives.

As such, population biobanks are less directly fixated on individuals than conventional research and challenge the traditional, individualist conception of autonomy.[37] Traditionally, provision of healthcare has been based on autonomy—an individual patient being entitled to make an informed decision for themselves, empowered by all relevant information and without interference.[38] In a research setting, as the therapeutic benefit is much lower than in day-to-day healthcare, the physician-researcher was said to have a higher expectation when informing participants.[39] The same can be said for cosmetic surgery and organ donation.[40] However, population-based biobanking is focused on the collective or common good.[41] This necessarily means that a participant is not entering into a relationship simply with the biobank. In reality, when a participant agrees to donate genetic material and health information to a biobank, they are also entering into relationships with the general public and researchers seeking to use their samples and data, forming an intricate multi-lateral web of trust.[42] For these relationships to function well, they must be based in reciprocity. This means that the relationships of a biobank are sustainable due to mutuality for the parties.[43] For example, individuals contribute samples for

35 Bartha Maria Knoppers and Michael JS Beauvais, 'Three decades of genetic privacy: a metaphoric journey' (2021) 30 Human Molecular Genetics R156, R157.

36 Bartha Maria Knoppers and Ma'n H Abdul-Rahman (Zawati), 'Biobanks in the Literature' in Bernice Elger and others (eds), *Ethical Issues in Governing Biobanks: Global Perspectives* (Routledge 2016), 14.

37 Ma'n H Zawati, *Reciprocity in Population Biobanks: Relational Autonomy and the Duty to Inform in the Genomic Era* (Elsevier Academic Press 2021), 95.

38 Ma'n H Zawati, 'Liability and the legal duty to inform in research' in Yann Joly and Bartha Maria Knoppers (eds), *Routledge Handbook of Medical Law and Ethics* (Routledge 2014), 199

39 Suzanne Philips-Nooten and Robert P Kouri, *Éléments de responsabilité civile médicale* (Éditions Yvon Blais 2021), 227–236.

40 Zawati (n 38), 200.

41 Ma'n H Zawati, Bartha Knoppers, and Adrian Thorogood, 'Population biobanking and international collaboration' (2014) 81 Pathobiology 276.

42 Ma'n H Zawati and Bartha Knoppers, 'Population Biobanks and the Principle of Reciprocity' in Pierre Hainaut and others (eds), *Biobanking of Human Biospecimens: Principles and Practice* (Springer 2017), 105.

43 Zawati (n 37), 82.

the common good, but have their data and samples protected and are subject to ongoing engagement from the biobank.

CARTaGENE is a population-based biobank founded by Professor Knoppers and Professor Claude Laberge.[44] It was the first of its kind in Quebec and is currently made up of data and biological samples on 43,000 Quebecers, aged 40 to 69 at the time of recruitment.[45] The data collected for this biobanking initiative was extensive and included health information, socio-demographic information, physiological measures, and biological samples (blood, serum, and urine).[46] This amounted to an impressive 11,452 data points on a given participant.[47] The extensiveness and depth of the biobank was part of the strategy to encourage future research on chronic disorders as the targeted population was most at risk for developing these disorders in the next decades.[48]

Overall, the founding of CARTaGENE shows just how much Professor Knoppers was ahead of her time. CARTaGENE may have been the first population-based biobank in Quebec, but it is also much more and has influenced biobanking nationwide and internationally. At the national level, for example, CARTaGENE paved the way for the development of the Canadian Partnership for Tomorrow's Health (CPTP, now called CanPath),[49] which harmonized the biobanking data of seven Canadian regions.[50] With CanPath, there is now a comprehensive and uniform biobank holding the genomic, clinical, behavioural, and environmental data on 330,000 Canadians for prospective research.[51] Professor Knoppers' work at CARTaGENE echoed her vision for Canadian biobanks. She believed in consensus building and national consolidation aimed at facilitating streamlined access to data and samples. Indeed, CARTaGENE helped to usher in an era where relational autonomy and broad consent gained prominence along with pan-Canadian collaboration in biobanking.

CARTaGENE showed just how much a novel conception of autonomy was necessary for the functioning and long-term benefits of biobanks to be

44 Meghan Mast and Katelyn Verstraten, 'Would You Deposit Your DNA in a 'BioBank'?' (*The Tyee*, 11 March 2014), available at: https://thetyee.ca/News/2014/03/11/DNA-BioBank/.

45 CARTaGENE (n 8).

46 Awadalla and others (n 25).

47 CARTaGENE, 'Data catalogs', available at: https://cartagene.qc.ca/en/researchers/data-catalogs.html.

48 Awadalla and others (n 25).

49 CanPath, 'CPTP Transition Complete' (9 April 2019), available at: https://canpath.ca/2019/04/cptp-transition-complete/.

50 Trevor JB Dummer and others, 'The Canadian Partnership for Tomorrow Project: a pan-Canadian platform for research on chronic disease prevention' (2018) 190 Canadian Medical Association Journal E710; CanPath, 'Regional cohorts', available at: https://canpath.ca/cohorts/.

51 CanPath, 'About the Study', available at: https://canpath.ca/about/.

realized. The individualist conception of autonomy, with its unidirectional attention on participants, fails to make sense of the multilateral relationships that are necessarily implicated in population biobanks.[52] For example, an individualistic conception of autonomy, as it considers the participant-researcher relationship to be unidirectional, would require that population biobanks obtain the consent of participants every time a researcher accesses samples and data. Re-consenting every participant in a biobank when a new research project arises risks delays and creates unnecessary barriers to research projects. CARTaGENE instead favoured a relational conception of autonomy that one can argue was based in reciprocity. This model of autonomy highlights that no actor works in isolation from the environment in which they live.[53] Unlike individualist autonomy, relational autonomy acknowledges that a person's autonomy is affected by their interpersonal relationships.[54] In the case of a biobank, the expectation of reciprocity in these interpersonal relationships sustains the biobank. Reciprocity is premised on the ideal that "individuals will 'help benefit others at least in part because [they] have received, will receive, or stand to receive beneficial assistance from them'."[55] Participants decide to give samples to the biobank due to the promise of future benefit for society.[56] Researchers use this data to help contribute to knowledge generation that is key for public interests to be realized.[57] And, finally, the public has a vested interest in the biobanking initiative as most are funded by public money and the biobanks have promised contributions to general knowledge and common good.[58] In this model, the individual participant remains important, but the interests of the public and of researchers must also be taken into account when designing the inner workings of a biobank through internal policies.[59]

CARTaGENE took these complex, ongoing, multi-faceted human relationships into account in a few ways. Firstly, spearheaded by Professor Knoppers,

52 Zawati (n 37), 95.

53 Jennifer K Walter and Lainie Friedman Ross, 'Relational autonomy: moving beyond the limits of isolated individualism' (2014) 133 Pediatrics S16, S19.

54 Natalie Stoljar and Kristin Voigt, *Autonomy and Equality: Relational Approaches* (Routledge 2021), 1.

55 Zawati (n 37), 82. Tom L Beauchamp and James F Childress, *Principles of Biomedical Ethics* (7th edn, Oxford University Press 2013), 174.

56 Louise Locock and Anne-Marie R Boylan, 'Biosamples as gifts? How participants in biobanking projects talk about donation' (2016) 19 Health Expectations 805, 807.

57 Deepshikha Batheja and others, 'Understanding the value of biobank attributes to researchers using a conjoint experiment' (2023) 13 Scientific Reports 1.

58 Vladimir Balaz, Tomas Jeck, and Miroslav Balog, 'Economics of biobanking: business or public good? literature review, structural and thematic analysis' (2022) 11 Social Sciences 1, 14.

59 Zawati (n 37), 121.

CARTaGENE adopted a broad consent approach to consenting. Broad consent is consent for future, unspecified research coupled with good governance practices and ongoing participant engagement. For example, the CARTaGENE consent materials contain a broad description of how data and samples will be used: "data and samples collected from them [participants] will be used for health and genomic studies in the future."[60] Significantly, this is not the same as open or blanket consent. It does not constitute a "carte blanche."[61] Broad consent is said to be sufficient "as long as [...] broad consent is thorough and includes a discussion of the goals and relevant process."[62] In other words, broad consent adds obligations onto the biobank. These obligations ensure that the reciprocity in biobanking relationships is maintained.

This is why CARTaGENE's consent document includes obligations such as coding of data and samples to protect confidentiality,[63] research ethics committees review to ensure the scientific and ethical validity of proposed studies involving the biobank,[64] access committee review of applications for access to data and samples, and newsletters to inform participants of the current developments of the biobanks.[65] Coding and research ethics review committees are obligations to protect the confidentiality and good use of biobanking samples. These are obligations that provide safety to the participants who donate. Newsletters to inform participants, as discussed above, reinforce the hope and desire of beneficial results from donating to a biobank. Newsletters are not the only form of public engagement, of course, especially as they imply one-way communication to the public. Bi-directional engagement through public consultations, including citizen forums, are also a useful approach. This is important as "reciprocity recognizes the public as a distinct party whose opinions and thoughts [...help to] shape policies and the overall direction of a research project."[66] The initial public consultation for the CARTaGENE

60 CARTaGENE, 'Information Brochure for Participants', available at: https://cartagene.qc.ca/files/documents/consent/brochure_en_0505.pdf, 2.

61 Bartha Maria Knoppers and others, 'Framing genomics, public health research and policy: points to consider' (2010) 13 Public Health Genomics 224, 331.

62 Timothy Caulfield and Bartha Maria Knoppers, 'Consent, privacy and research biobanks' (2010) Policy Brief no. 1 Genomics, Public Policy, and Society 1 at 5, citing Ants Nõmper, *Open Consent: A New Form of Informed Consent for Population Genetic Databases* (Tartu ülikooli kirjastus 2005).

63 ibid.

64 Mark A Rothstein and others, 'Broad consent for future research: international perspectives' (2018) 40 IRB: Ethics & Human Research 7, 9.

65 CARTaGENE, 'The CARTaGENE voice: Happy Holidays and Happy New Year 2024', available at: https://cartagene.qc.ca/files/documents/newsletter/Infolettre_participants_Decembre2023_V1_EN.pdf.

66 Zawati and Knoppers (n 42), 107.

project was undertaken to hear the thoughts of the Quebec population on the project but also to encourage future participation in the project.[67] This public consultation was key for evaluating the possible efficacy of broad consent for the CARTaGENE project. For example, Quebec residents were asked about the major challenges of project participation and their perceptions and attitudes towards the project.[68] Gaining a better understanding of the public's perception of the CARTaGENE project allowed the project to be welcoming and accommodating for participants.

While broad consent was contentious at the time of its adoption by CARTaGENE, it is well established today, thanks to its introduction by this initiative. It structures the "web of trust" so that the multiple relationships that flow through a biobank, namely between the participants, the community of researchers, the public, and the biobank, are sustainable and in good working condition to facilitate the goals of the biobank initiative. By ensuring proper disclosure of all available information at the time of consent and clarity as to decision-making and governance of the biobank, broad consent is key for trust in these relationships. Individuals agree to be participants for the greater good of the public, rather than purely for themselves.[69] This decision is made easier when they have clarity as to how their data and samples will be used. Broad consent also builds in transparency for the future as either online registries of research projects or newsletters in lay terms inform participants as to the latest research with their contributions to the biobank. Furthermore, broad consent forms underscore the limits on the possible research that can be performed, while simultaneously removing barriers to research that would exist if participants had to reconsent to each research project that utilized their samples. Finally, during the process of broad consent, the rights and obligations of each party involved in the biobanks are explicitly stated. For example, the biobank must detail how they will safeguard data and samples, the process of withdrawal of consent must be stated clearly, and return of results is written in as an obligation to participants and the public.

The impact of the use of broad consent in CARTaGENE cannot be overstated. After years of debate,[70] broad consent is now incorporated into the

67 Béatrice Godard, Jennifer Marshall, and Claude Laberge, 'Community engagement in genetic research: results of the first public consultation for the Quebec CARTaGENE project' (2007) 10 Community Genetics 147.

68 ibid, 148.

69 Zawati and Knoppers (n 42), 106.

70 See e.g. Susan Wallace, Stephanie Lazor, and Bartha Maria Knoppers, 'Consent and population genomics: the creation of generic tools' (2009) 31 IRB: Ethics & Human Research

Canadian Tri-Council Policy Statement (TCPS2-2022).[71] In Canada, it is now the standardized approach to consent for the "storage of data and human biological materials for future unspecified research" (i.e. biobanking). This framework outlines the appropriate information that must be provided by researchers to prospective applicants for valid broad consent. This includes, but is not limited to, the type, identifiability, and amount of data collected and stored, the voluntariness of consent, a general description of the nature and types of future research, the risks and potential benefits of storage of data and biological materials, governance of the biobanking initiative, and more.[72]

The following section discusses Professor Knoppers' role in developing legislative guidance and policies that helped to further shape an amenable environment for collective scientific endeavours like population biobanks.

3 Professor Knoppers' Legacy in Biobanking Legislation and Policy Development

While internal governance structures are significant for the proper functionality of biobanks, biobanks are also situated within a broader ecosystem. This ecosystem, composed of legal and policy guidelines, must be supportive of these endeavours to ensure their sustainability. Professor Knoppers realized this early in her work and has held several key positions and led countless initiatives to contribute to the development of strong biobanking projects.

3.1 *Towards Prospective Legislation: The Example of Estonia's Human Genes Research Act*

Very few countries have laws that directly address biobanking. Estonia's Human Genes Research Act of 2000 (HGRA) stands out for its prospective nature. Professor Knoppers played a direct role in the drafting of this legislation, which is

15; Kristin Solum Steinsbekk, Bjorn Kare Myskja, and Berge Solberg, 'Broad consent versus dynamic consent in biobank research: is passive participation an ethical problem' (2013) 21 European Journal of Human Genetics 897.

71 Canadian Institutes of Health Research, Natural Sciences and Engineering Research Council of Canada and Social Sciences and Humanities Research Council of Canada, 'Tri-Council Policy Statement: Ethical Conduct for Research Involving Humans – TCPS 2 (2022)' (Government of Canada 2022), Chapter 3, Section E.

72 ibid, Art 3.13 and its application.

commonly considered to be the benchmark against which other biobanking legislation is measured.[73]

The Estonian Genome Project was one of the first population biobanks in Europe.[74] The goals of the biobank were to promote genetic research, to collect information on the Estonian population, and to use genetic research results to improve public health.[75] Today, the cohort size of the Estonian Biobank is more than 200,000 individuals, representing approximately 20% of the Estonian adult population.[76] Researchers at the University of Tartu, where the biobank is housed, have published over 830 peer-reviewed papers using data from the project.

Prior to the launch of the Estonian Genome Project, the founders of the project felt it necessary to create a legal framework to regulate the biobank and associated activities.[77] This demonstrated both a strong sense of responsibility that the researchers had towards the Estonian public, but also their belief in the advantages of legal regulation of biobanking activities. The HGRA was drafted by an interprofessional committee including geneticists, lawyers, physicians, data protection specialists, and Estonian politicians.[78] Professor Knoppers was asked to make comments on the draft version of the HGRA as a foreign expert.[79]

As required by the HGRA, all participants in the Estonian Biobank must sign an informed consent form. Since the passing of the Act, the broad consent approach has been legally recognized as the approach to consenting for biobanks. The mandate for broad consent was revolutionary in 2000, the year that the HGRA was passed by the Estonian Parliament. While broad consent was controversial at the time of the founding of CARTaGENE, it was all the more radical when the HGRA was drafted. Some critics argued that broad consent is not properly informed consent as the participant is agreeing to future, unspecified research.[80] However, Professor Knoppers' work showed that broad consent-related documents can still provide key information to the participant,

73 Jüri Raidla and Ants Nõmper, 'The Estonian Genome Project and the Human Gene Research Act' (2002) 2 Baltic Yearbook of International Law 51, 53.

74 Liis Leitsalu and others, 'Linking a population biobank with national health registries – the Estonian experience' (2015) 5 Journal of Personalized Medicine 96.

75 Raidla and Nõmper (n 73), 52.

76 Estonian Biobank, available at: https://genomics.ut.ee/en/content/estonian-biobank.

77 Raidla and Nõmper (n 73), 53.

78 ibid.

79 ibid.

80 Gert Helgesson, 'In defense of broad consent' (2012) 21 Cambridge Quarterly of Healthcare Ethics 40, 43; Bjørn Hofmann, 'Broadening consent: and diluting ethics?' (2009) 35 Journal of Medical Ethics 125.

rendering them capable of making an informed decision. Although the specific title of a research project cannot be provided, these documents can describe the epidemiological objectives of research originating from the biobank, the longitudinal nature of biobanking, the manner in which their samples will be preserved, the security safeguards surrounding their data, and more.[81] In other words, it crystallizes not only voluntary, informed consent, but the continuous nature of such a process thanks to long-term engagement with the participants. From this information, a competent individual can decide if the outlined conditions and protections are sufficient for them to consent to future studies. Just like in Canada, this view has now gained international approval in the international bioethics community over the years, as seen, for example, in 2016, when the World Medical Association and the Council for International Organizations of Medical Sciences/World Health Organization (CIOMS/WHO) recognized that broad consent for future unspecified research was "an acceptable alternative" to specific consent for biobanks.[82]

3.2 *Policies Do Not Grow on Trees*

Professor Knoppers' contribution was not limited to helping draft legislation; she also focused on preparing the groundwork for the development of anticipatory, international, and interoperable policies and ethics frameworks in the field of biobanking. Policy can provide flexibility that law cannot. While it is vital to know where the certainty and guaranteed enforcement of the law is needed in biobank regulation (e.g. privacy law and data protection laws), it is equally important to identify where policy could be a better approach. Professor Knoppers was one of the first to call for the expanded use of policies.

It is important to realize that policymaking does not happen overnight. It is not simply an ethicist thinking up a solution and writing it down; it is a delicate art and science that is grounded in precedent, just like scientific research in a lab is grounded in past publications and preceding experiments and a court judgment in a common law system is guided by jurisprudence.[83] It is an endeavour that requires an extraordinary amount of effort, consensus, and trust.[84] Furthermore, policymaking is complicated by the fact that it must

81 Zawati and Knoppers (n 42), 100.

82 Rothstein and others (n 64), 7.

83 Bartha M Knoppers, 'Does policy grow on trees?' (2014) 15 BMC Medical Ethics 1.

84 Friends of CIHR, 'Prof. Bartha Knoppers – 2019 Friesen Lecture at U Ottawa' (YouTube, 18 September 2019), available at: https://www.youtube.com/watch?v=TnA6f4Jr2FI.

evolve with the times as "[e]thical thinking [...] inevitably [...] evolve[s] as the science does."[85]

In the context of biobanks, ethical policymaking has a unique set of requirements. These were outlined in Professor Knoppers' seminal paper "Does policy grow on trees?". She argued that the numerous and sometimes contradictory requirements of policymaking for biobanks makes it a unique task requiring expertise, experience, goodwill, consensus, egos being set aside, openness to criticism, and frank discussions. Policies must:

- be in plain language;
- address numerous issues simultaneously;
- be context-specific;
- integrate multiple disciplines into the decision-making;
- consider many different cultures and backgrounds;
- facilitate harmonization (ideally internationally), compliance, and oversight;
- include all relevant stakeholders;
- be aspirational in nature;
- be practical; and
- be principled.[86]

These reflections concerning what constitutes good policies arose from Professor Knoppers' involvement in policy drafting initiatives concerning the good governance of biobanks and databases. Significantly, she played a role in drafting the UNESCO Universal Declaration on the Human Genome and Human Rights (1997) and the HUGO statements, both of which crystallized the idea of a web of trust.

3.2.1 UNESCO Declaration

Professor Knoppers has been concerned with the ethics of genetic research and biobanking since the early days of the Human Genome Project. Her work with Ruth Chadwick laid out what they considered to be the ethical and legal norms that inspired that project.[87] They included autonomy, privacy, justice, equity, equality, and respect for human dignity.[88] They believed that these internationally agreed upon concepts, if written into an international instrument, could serve to harmonize regulations of genetic research and biobanking internationally by serving as a framework to model domestic regulations

85 Knoppers and Chadwick (n 6), 78.

86 Knoppers (n 83), 1.

87 Bartha Maria Knoppers and Ruth Chadwick, 'The Human-Genome Project: Under an international ethical microscope' (1994) 265 Science 2035.

88 ibid.

off of.[89] Professor Knoppers considered this an urgent step to fully realize the value of research on the human genome and biobanks.[90] As a result, she was a member of UNESCO's International Bioethics Committee and its Legal Sub-Committee and helped to draft UNESCO's Universal Declaration on the Human Genome and Human Rights.[91] This Declaration evolved from concerns over the ever-changing nature of medicine and genetic research. Just as Professor Knoppers felt that international guidance was necessary, the UNESCO community agreed that an international instrument would be useful to provide guidance as to how to best approach preservation of human rights in the tricky arena of human genetics.[92]

This Declaration is significant in that it hinted that current approaches to ethics and regulation that centered on individuals would be insufficient. As discussed above, the field of ethics would need to adapt with science. The Declaration clearly calls attention to the need to administer biobanks and further research involving the human genome for the common good, but also square this collective interest with human dignity and rights.[93] It laid the groundwork for an approach to biobanking that promotes the human, but in a different way. Rather than focusing on individual autonomy, biobanking requires relational autonomy to succeed. The individual is still protected due to obligations from both the biobank and researchers, but the biobank also has goals of being beneficial for society, which require a different approach than individual protections. The Declaration suggested, for the first time in an international instrument, that research involving the human genome and research on a grander scale pose new, complex, ever-evolving ethical problems that will require innovative approaches.

89 ibid.

90 Bartha Maria Knoppers and Ruth Chadwick, 'The ethics weathervane' (2015) 16 BMC Medical Ethics 1.

91 Sean Foley, 'Shouldn't there be a law against that?: Facing our fear of genetic innovation' (*CBC* Radio, 24 July 2020), available at: https://www.cbc.ca/radio/ideas/shouldn-t-there-be-a-law-against-that-facing-our-fear-of-genetic-innovation-1.5340925; Friends of CIHR, 'Prof. Bartha Knoppers – The 1997 Universal Declaration on the Human Genome and Human Rights' (YouTube, 16 July 2021), available at: https://www.youtube.com/watch?v=SGrQz_04pSI.

92 Shawn HE Harmon, 'The significance of UNESCO's Universal Declaration on the Human Genome and Human Rights' (2005) 2 SCRIPTed 18, 20.

93 The Universal Declaration on the Human Genome and Human Rights (adopted 11 November 1997 UNGA Res 53/152) Art 1.

3.2.2 HUGO Statements

The Human Genome Organization, like UNESCO, is an international organization. The organization came to being in 1988 at the first ever meeting on Genome Mapping and Sequencing that took place in Cold Spring Harbor, New York.[94] From its initial size of 42 scientists, it has grown exponentially and currently has over 2,000 researchers from over 92 countries as members.[95] The goals were lofty. The HUGO Organization aimed to become a "U.N. [United Nations] for the human genome."[96] With such a goal, it was only logical that Professor Knoppers ended up becoming a member of the HUGO Ethics Committee. The organization's goals and her goals for the international interoperability and cooperation of genetic research, specifically through biobanks, were very much aligned.

As such, in the early 2000s, this Committee adopted six statements that built on the UNESCO Declaration and further outlined the fact that the genome is a "shared public good."[97] The most significant HUGO statement for biobanks is the 2002 "HUGO Statement on human genomic databases."[98] The first two recommendations make it clear that "human genomic databases [biobanks] are global public goods" and that all individuals, groups, and institutions involved in biobanking initiatives should aim to "foster the public good."[99] This wording strongly emphasizes the diversity of stakeholders in biobanking initiatives. Just like the UNESCO Declaration laid the groundwork for an alternative approach to the "human" in biobanking, the HUGO Statements took it a step further. By highlighting that biobanks are "public goods," the HUGO Statements underscore why it is so important to remember individual participants, the individuals in society who could be helped by the biobanking initiative, the individual researchers, and more. While the individual participant is important, so are the public and researchers. These multilateral relationships must all be fostered to ensure the success of biobanking initiatives and to safeguard individual participants, many of whom participate simply out of a desire to help or contribute

94 Human Genome Organization, 'About HUGO: Introduction', available at: https://www.hugo-international.org/about-us/#:~:text=History,a%20period%20of%20two%20decades.

95 Dorothy C Wertz and Bartha Maria Knoppers, 'The HUGO Ethics Committee: Six innovative statements' (2003) 1 New Review of Bioethics 27.

96 Human Genome Organization, 'About Us: History', available at: https://www.hugo-international.org/history/.

97 ibid.

98 HUGO, 'Statement on human genomic databases. December 2002' (2003) 14 Journal International de Bioéthique 207.

99 ibid, Recommendations 1 and 2.

to science. This emphasis on the multilateral relationships in biobanking was significant as it went on to influence policies of biobanking, such as those that came out of P³G.

3.3 *"These Walls Were Not Meant to Shout Out Problems, You Have to Face Them"*[100]*: P³G*

Given the nature of biobanks and human genetic research more generally, a policy shift espousing the concepts of "reciprocity, mutuality, solidarity, citizenry and universality"[101] was necessary. Such a shift symbolized a move away from individualistic autonomy as the pivotal concern in the interaction between the participant and the biobank to an appreciation for the need for a communal, collective approach, an approach that valued the numerous relationships that occur in biobanking.[102]

This rejigging of policy concerning biobanking required an organization that could lay down consistent biobanking policies worldwide. One such organization is P³G. P³G was founded in 2004, after several years of planning by Professor Knoppers and her team.[103] It was an international, non-profit consortium with a goal of harmonizing biobanking internationally through collaboration and sharing.[104] At its start, P³G served four different population-based biobanking projects: CARTaGENE (Quebec), GenomEUtwin (a biobanking project involving eight EU countries), the Estonian Genome Project, and the UK Biobank.[105] Over time, many more biobanks were added to the consortium: the Western Australia Genome Health Project, the Singapore Tissue Network, and the NuGene Project, to name a few.[106] During the decade of its existence, P³G played a pivotal role in harmonizing international approaches to biobanking, with a focus on the type of data available in biobanks, the approach to consenting, and templates to ensure the data could be shared with ease.[107]

100 *The Sound of Music*, 1965.
101 Knoppers and Chadwick (n 6), 75.
102 Knoppers and Chadwick (n 90), 1; Knoppers and Chadwick (n 6), 75.
103 Sylvie Ouellette and Anne Marie Tassé, 'P3G – 10 years of toolbuilding: From the population biobank to the clinic' (2014) 3 Applied & Translational Genomics 36.
104 Bartha M Knoppers and others, 'Population Genomics: The Public Population Project in Genomics (P3G): a proof of concept?' (2008) 16 European Journal of Human Genetics 664.
105 Ouellette and Tassé (n 103).
106 Susan Wallace, Stephanie Lazor, and Bartha Maria Knoppers, 'Consent and population genomics: the creation of generic tools' (2009) 31 IRB: Ethics & Human Research 15.
107 Ouellette and Tassé (n 103), 36.

3.3.1 Data Sharing

P³G was founded on a principle of promotion of the common good.[108] Population research using samples from biobanks requires a large number of samples. As such, the best use of biobanks would occur if data for each biobank could be pooled. Chapter 6 in this volume is dedicated to international data sharing, but we will briefly touch on it here as P³G laid the groundwork for consistency of data sharing between biobanks.

Before the P³G project, it was rather difficult to share data across biobanks as the data was often collected and recorded in numerous ways.[109] For example, there was little to no harmonization of what variables were recorded and how these data items were stored. This made it difficult for data stored in biobanks around the world to be used in combination, even if the biobanks purported to focus on the same disease or have the same goals. To address this problem, P³G collaborated with biobanks to create a tool, via a subproject entitled DataSHaPER (Data Schema and Harmonization Platform for Epidemiological Research), that enabled biobanks to harmonize methods of collection and data storage.[110] The DataSHaPER tool was not meant to be a prescriptive list of the data that biobanks were obliged to collect, but rather was designed to be a flexible tool to ensure that the data that biobanks chose to collect could be done in an internationally consistent manner allowing for pooling of the data later on.[111] Additionally, DataSHaPER took into consideration that many of these biobanking projects were well underway and offered feedback on both retrospective and prospective harmonization.[112] This innovative solution laid down the groundwork for what we now term "federated systems" in large biobanks and databases, where access to the data could be performed without needing to transfer data between different jurisdictions. In fact, DataSHaPER paved the way for a harmonization rate of 62% of the variables that they prescribed to be collected.[113] This led to the aggregation of the

---

108 Bartha M Knoppers and Yann Joly, 'Our social genome?' (2007) 25 Trends in Biotechnology 284, 286.

109 Susan Wallace and Bartha Maria Knoppers, 'The Role of P3G in Encouraging Public Trust in Biobanks' in Peter Dabrock, Jochen Taupitz, and Jens Ried (eds), *Trust in Biobanking: Dealing with Ethical, Legal and Social Issues in an Emerging Field of Biotechnology* (Springer-Verlag Berlin Heidelberg 2012).

110 Public Population Project in Genomics and Society, 'DATASHAPER', available at: https://www.p3gobservatory.org/datashaper/presentation.htm; Isabel Fortier and others, 'Quality, quantity and harmony: the DataSHaPer approach to integrating data across bioclinical studies' (2010) 39 International Journal of Epidemiology 1383.

111 Fortier and others (n 110), 1385.

112 ibid, 1388.

113 Ouellette and Tassé (n 103), 37.

data of 6.9 million individuals as of 2011.[114] Furthermore, newer versions of the tool have been created, inspired by DataSHaPER.[115] Much of the newer work has been concentrated on mitigating the worries of data harmonization on carrying forward errors in original datasets. In other words, the newer research has worked to address management errors that may have been missed by original data harmonization approaches, with the goal of deepening the meaning of data stored in biobanks.[116]

Furthermore, P^{3}G, alongside collaborators, developed a Code of Conduct for responsible data sharing in a biobank context.[117] The Code begins by underscoring the necessity of data sharing to support and promote genomic research, both nationally and internationally. It aimed to fill a void in international policy guidance concerning the topic and without guidance, there is little hope of international collaboration and uniformity.[118] The "International Data Sharing Code of Conduct" elucidated seven principles and procedures to promote "greater access to and use of data."[119] These principles are quality, accessibility, responsibility, security, transparency, accountability, and integrity.[120] These principles are not ranked. Each of them is equally significant for responsible data sharing. Furthermore, it stressed that these principles are key to ensuring equitable, ethical, and efficient data sharing.[121]

As this Code of Conduct has served as the backbone for numerous projects to build on, it is important to understand what each principle demands of those sharing data. First, quality states that scientists involved in data sharing endeavours must be "*bona fide* researchers" who have proof of their academic or peer reviewed standing.[122] Next, accessibility necessitates that "curators of databases [...] promote sharing [of data] to generate maximum value" for the public.[123] One way to foster accessibility, as was seen in the CARTaGENE project's inclusion in CanPath, is by standardizing data collection and storage processes. Third, data must be shared in a responsible manner. Responsibility

114 ibid.

115 University of Michigan, 'Cross-Cultural Survey Guidelines' (2016), available at: https://ccsg.isr.umich.edu/chapters/data-harmonization/.

116 Cindy Cheng and others, 'A general primer for data harmonization' (2024) 11 Scientific Data 1, 9.

117 Bartha Maria Knoppers and others, 'Towards a data sharing Code of Conduct for international genomic research' (2011) 3 Genome Medicine 1.

118 ibid.

119 ibid, 2.

120 ibid.

121 ibid.

122 ibid.

123 ibid.

calls for governance structures that are shared with "funders, generators, and users of data," mechanisms of appropriate management, capacity building and more.[124] To ensure security, data management and security mechanisms must have oversight and mechanisms for "identifying and tracking data generators should be international."[125] Transparency ensures that the public is aware of the ongoing data sharing through public accessibility of publications, intellectual property, and industry involvement.[126] Websites can help to facilitate this access to information. As a related principle, accountability requires "efficient monitoring and good governance" alongside "ongoing public engagement that is tailored to the nature of the database and local cultures."[127] Finally, integrity requires mutual respect between all relevant stakeholders, prevention of harms, reporting practices for irresponsible research, and sanctions for breach of the Code.[128]

3.3.2 *Generic Consent Clauses and Other Documents*

In 2007, the P³G Board of Directors adopted a "Charter of Principles." These principles are promotion of the common good, responsibility, mutual respect, accountability, and proportionality.[129] These principles served as guidance for any projects undertaken by P³G, such as the development of generic information pamphlets, consent forms as well as access agreement clauses.[130] After years of experimenting with different models, it became clear that proposing a finalized consent form or an access agreement may be useful for some jurisdictions, but that it risks not being adaptable to all. Given that the goal of P³G is to facilitate international collaboration, the use of generic clauses was deemed most appropriate. In order to properly underscore the "human" in biobanking, any policy guidance on consent need to highlight the non-negotiable aspects of the consenting process in the unique context of biobanks, but also needed to be adaptable to the specific geographic location and cultural norms of each biobank—keeping in mind the potential benefits this will reap to the different stakeholders (including the participant). Indeed, rather than draft a full consent form for a particular project, the idea was to draft generic clauses that would be included under specific themes in every document developed. This allowed researchers to benefit from the proposed language, provided them

124 ibid.
125 ibid.
126 ibid.
127 ibid.
128 ibid.
129 Ouellette and Tassé (n 103), 36.
130 ibid, 38.

with flexibility on adding more information or jurisdictional specifications and had the value of formulating core elements that needed to be found in any such document.

That last part is crucial. Core elements for consent forms allowed P³G to underscore key issues that must be considered and addressed when informing participants, such as broad consent to future research projects.[131] The purpose is twofold. It ensures that participants are empowered with all information available to make an informed decision, including information about the unusual issues that arise from biobanks. It also ensures that administrators of the biobanks are aware of how to discuss issues with participants and are, to a certain extent, educated on the ethical quandaries of biobanking.

The same approach was taken with access agreements, where generic clauses were created as well to provide legal departments with useful language to incorporate into their institutional agreements. This approach allowed access agreements to be drafted with clear language to ensure that researchers using data and samples from biobanks are aware of their obligations. The access agreements also form a boundary between what are acceptable uses of the biobanking data and what are unacceptable uses as there are outlined sanctions for inappropriate behaviour.[132] To make this more practical on a global scale, P³G frequently engaged in international comparative review of policies and legislation to draft language that would be compatible with as many norms as possible.

4 Conclusion: An Enduring Legacy and a Pathway to the Future

It is without a doubt that the regulatory landscape of biobanks would not be what it is today without the contributions of Professor Knoppers. Biobanks require a strong "web of trust" to function at their fullest capacity. Legislative and policy guidelines that support broad consent, international collaboration, and data sharing are a part of the framework that enables and supports biobanks. With her founding of CARTaGENE and assistance in drafting the Estonia law on biobanking, HGRA, Professor Knoppers has helped to usher in a global acceptance of broad consent. She helped to show how broad consent does not diminish the importance of the individual, but rather reframes it in the biobanking context where the individual is engaged in multilateral relationships

131 Wallace and Knoppers (n 109), 193.

132 Bartha Maria Knoppers and others, 'A P3G generic access agreement for population genomic studies' (2013) 31 Nature Biotechnology 384.

with several actors. Her conception of broad consent includes biobanks outlining commitments they make to the participants regarding their data and samples. This reinforces the participant's trust in the future-based initiative. Furthermore, policymaking has been central to the building of strong biobanks. With the UNESCO Declaration, the HUGO statements, and the building of P³G, Professor Knoppers has had a role to play in the drafting of countless policies that support the "web of trust" within biobanks. The UNESCO Declaration and HUGO statements state explicitly that all stakeholders must be considered in the drafting of internal policies for biobanks and the P³G project provides ample resources to biobanks to aid them in the development of internal policies that are consistent with international partners. This work has provided a pathway to the future, with initiatives such as GA4GH and its Regulatory and Ethics Work Stream becoming increasingly visible as standard-setting organizations developing policies, frameworks, and tools that facilitate the sharing of genomic and health-related data at an international level.

Professor Knoppers' work with CARTaGENE, UNESCO, HUGO, P³G, and others has provided the initial building blocks for yet another level of tool building. A prime example of this is the development of the Framework for Responsible Sharing of Genomic and Health-Related Data by the GA4GH, developed by its Regulatory and Ethics Work Stream and partners, including P³G.[133] The Framework has since been translated into 15 languages and gone on to guide all tools developed by GA4GH,[134] and continues to guide researchers, clinicians, clinical laboratories, data generators, data custodians, data access committees, ethics review boards, and others in their future biobanking and data sharing endeavours.[135]

In the years since Professor Knoppers' first contributions to the policy and governance of biobanks, biobanking initiatives have expanded greatly and have shown themselves to be vital tools for public health interventions, development of new treatments, precision medicine, and more. Trust is central to the sustainability of biobanking initiatives as it supports the multiple relationships found in biobanks—namely the relationships between the research community, the participants, the public and the biobank. Professor Knoppers' contributions have not only shed a light on these interactions, but have built an ethical, equitable, and efficient policy ecosystem that sustains them over time.

133 Bartha Maria Knoppers, 'Framework for responsible sharing of genomic and health-related data' (2014) 8 The HUGO Journal 1.

134 Global Alliance for Genomics and Health, 'Our products: Framework for responsible sharing of genomic and health-related data', available at: https://www.ga4gh.org/product/framework-for-responsible-sharing-of-genomic-and-health-related-data/.

135 ibid.

VIGNETTE

A Cameo on BMK

Claude Laberge

Very soon after agreeing to provide a cameo of 500 words for this Festschrift, I came down with the dreaded case of writer's block[1]—but not from the classical etiologies. By itself, the list of BMK's contributions, publications, and representations in the continuously evolving fields of genetics-genomics-epigenomics and their ELSI implications would instantly fill a whole chapter in this book.

So where to begin? Well, perhaps at the beginning:

I first met Bartha Maria Knoppers (a.k.a. BMK) 40 years ago when she came to my lab in Quebec City. My colleague Charles R. Scriver (CRS) of McGill University sent BMK to get acquainted with and learn about newborn screening, to represent him at a coming meeting in Chicago organized by Lori B. Andrews.

On her visit she met my colleague and friend Jean H. Dussault (JHD) who also had been invited to the same symposium. For ten years in the RMGQ (Réseau de médecine génétique du Québec [Quebec Network of Genetic Medicine]), Jean developed and validated newborn screening for congenital hypothyroidism.[2]

The subjects of BMK's research at the time were consent in medical law and the social impact of new biotechnologies such as IVF. Serendipitously, on that same visit, she met my colleague Jacques E. Rioux, the "father" of the first IVF baby in Quebec. Metaphorically, a loop was closed.

Both eventually attended the symposium on newborn screening.

Back in Quebec City, Jean told me that he had found the person we needed to consolidate the emerging international network of neonatal hypothyroidism screening (1:4-5000 births).[3] She accepted without hesitation given her expertise in international human rights law.

Thereon, I became a colleague of BMK, a scientific advisor, and a friend.

---

1 Dennis Upper, 'The unsuccessful self-treatment of a case of "writer's block"' (1974) 7 Journal of Applied Behavior Analysis 497.

2 Jean H Dussault and Claude Laberge, '[Thyroxine (T4) determination by radioimmunological method in dried blood eluate: new diagnostic method of neonatal hypothyroidism?]' (1973) 102 L'union Medicale Du Canada 2062.

3 Jean H Dussault and others, 'Preliminary report on a mass screening program for neonatal hypothyroidism' (1975) 86 The Journal of Pediatrics 670.

Our first joint paper, published in 1989,[4] was on informed consent in DNA sampling. Informed consent has been BMK's guiding principle, and a cornerstone of her advocacy for distributing the benefits of science and knowledge for humanity. It also metamorphosed the traditional research "subjects" into "participants," and thus helping to materialize what were otherwise mythical benefits.

The rest is history as can be ascertained through the careers of the members of her Montreal School of Thought and Curiosity. In medieval times, she would have been an abbess of high renown.

In that School, genetics and derived biological sciences are viewed as belonging in the social space, based on scientific data, where they should be debated and challenged, but also consensually integrated in the regulatory policies available at the time, even innovating if necessary. Thus, she became a *magistera* at networking, dedicated to interdisciplinary contributions, futuristic considerations and ethical, legal, and social issues in genetics/genomics.

Sometimes, foundational philosophy is hidden in forgotten scripts of less-read volumes: such as, defining genomics as a social and humanities science, morphing biology into our humanity.[5]

As a footnote to explain how she met and meets with the top international players in genomic policy and production, remember that she was recruited as a colleague by two members of Canada's Medical Hall of Fame: CRS and JHD.

Over her illustrious career, BMK has many times over surpassed the policy research covered in that initial newborn screening symposium. Indeed, she has created space for intellectual communities to flourish around nearly all emerging genetic technologies since.

4 Bartha M Knoppers and Claude Laberge, 'DNA sampling and informed consent' (1989) 140 Canadian Medical Association Journal 1023.

5 Bartha M Knoppers and Claude Laberge, 'The Social Geography of Human Genome Mapping' in Zbigniew Bankowski and Alexander Capron (eds) *Genetics, Ethics and Human Values: Human Genome Mapping, Genetic Screening and Therapy* (CIOMS 1991); Claude M Laberge and Bartha Maria Knoppers, 'Rationale for an integrated approach to genetic epidemiology' (1992) 6 Bioethics 317.

VIGNETTE

Nice and Smart

Jennifer Stoddart

People who are gifted, innovative, or highly creative are rarely also unfailingly pleasant, kind, and aware of others around them. These super-bright constellations usually burn in their own trajectory, often leaving husks of various kinds, if not social chaos, in their wake.

So, when in the autumn of 1977 a law school acquaintance, in a different academic stream than mine, invited me to a group dinner to meet the editor of the McGill Law Journal, I was slightly nervous at the prospect of having to converse with such an important person in the academic legal world. But I met a warm, fun-loving young woman, un-judgemental of others and obviously very quick-witted.

Fortunately, Bartha Knoppers included me in her group of friends, all law students of the time, who were somewhat out of the ordinary in different ways.

She and her husband Daniel left Montreal for Cambridge and Paris, bringing back small children and the reputational basis for their stellar academic careers. Life in an august apartment building on Sherbrooke Street, inhabited by a group of young rising lawyers, was busy. Small children ran the hallways but there was always laughter and a warm welcome.

Bartha became a professor at the Université de Montréal and her interest in the legal status of different persons soon led her naturally to the rapidly developing field of genomics.

In implementing the increasingly important research grants she obtained, she drew on a widening group of research assistants, some undergraduate, some graduate, and some even retired! All could be useful, she thought, in an approach which deviated from traditional academic work patterns propped up by a rigid hierarchy.

Her various assistants showed their appreciation of her confidence in them by impressive productivity, personal loyalty, and an ongoing contribution as a group to policy developments around the use of genomic knowledge.

As always, Bartha inspired others. Her self-discipline is legendary. Rising very early to write, or later, Zoom to different time zones, she could put in a full working day, often followed by social events. Dinners and concerts were favourite activities, including spending time with friends, research associates, and students.

DOI:10.1163/9789004688544_008

Travel to international forums became more and more frequent as time passed and her reputation grew, not only for academic excellence but also for being reliable and pleasant, never taking her now larger-than-life aura too seriously.

Others in this collection of tributes have narrated her intellectual accomplishments and her well-deserved multiple honours from various governments and learned societies. But it is her humanity, her many friendships, her care for others, and her nurturing of future talent that deserve recognition as well, as they show how the qualities of empathy and humility importantly enhance the search for scientific knowledge.

CHAPTER 3

Anticipatory International Ethics

Ruth Chadwick

1 Introduction

Ethics is sometimes criticized for addressing issues too late, and sometimes for discussing hypothetical problems that may never materialize. There is of course a place for thought experiments about unlikely-seeming developments, as they may help identify the principles on which our responses are based, but ethics may also be anticipatory in other ways, preparing possible real-world solutions to scenarios that can be foreseen. In thinking about the possibility and nature of appropriate anticipatory international ethics, I will attempt to situate a discussion of Professor Bartha Knoppers' contribution in relation to ongoing theoretical debates about ethics. These debates include what might be expected of ethics in so far as it is applied to contemporary issues. They engage questions concerning the nature of ethical expertise (if any) and about the possibility of global ethics. Second, it will be relevant to look at the particular role of ethics in policy, the relationship between different disciplines, what exactly is "applied," and how ethics is subject to change. I will argue that Professor Knoppers' work demonstrates attention to the ways in which ethical issues are framed, with an eye to changes both actual and anticipated, while keeping a focus on human good and human rights.

2 Applied Ethics: What Can It Do?

What is now known as applied ethics came to prominence as a field of study in the last quarter of the twentieth century. Its emergence followed a period in which the primary focus, among philosophers in the Anglo-American tradition, was the analysis of moral language rather than addressing practical problems.[1] Indeed, ethics was often regarded as emotive.[2] In an effort to contribute to progressive clarity in moral discussions, philosophy devoted itself to metaethics.

1 See e.g. Richard B Brandt, *The Problems of Normative and Critical Ethics* (Prentice-Hall 1959).

2 See e.g. Charles L Stevenson, *Facts and Values: Studies in Ethical Analysis* (Yale University Press 1963).

The importance of applied ethics arguably first came to the forefront in a medical context, where expanding commitments to human rights and developments in technology gave rise to challenging ethical issues related, for example, to the allocation of scarce resources such as kidney dialysis machines, the use of heart-lung devices, and organ transplantation protocols. Questions such as the extent to which healthcare professionals should intervene to extend life, along with the definitions of life and death themselves, became extensively debated in the field of bioethics (emerging in the 1970s[3]), which studies, in an interdisciplinary way, the ethical, legal, social, and philosophical issues arising from medicine, the life sciences, and emerging technologies.

On the other hand, while applied ethics may appear to be a relatively recent development, some philosophy scholars have always envisioned its application. Since the time of Plato, philosophers have been concerned with problems of living in the real world. Plato's *Republic*, for instance, concerned as it was with the nature of justice, discussed inescapable questions relevant to how one should live. Plato also had things to say about control of reproduction in a selective way, an issue still very controversial today in the context of technologies such as gene editing.[4]

David Armstrong has written critically about attempts to give applied ethics a long history, saying that "It is only by *inventing* (my emphasis) a history going back to Hippocrates that bioethics can demonstrate its universal and timeless truths."[5] This claim, I would suggest, conflates two different things—the longevity of certain issues and the diversity of approaches used to analyze these issues. Approaches do change, not only with time but also with place, and this should not be a matter of surprise or regret. As we shall see below, applied ethics need not be regarded as the application of universal principles to particular problems. What exactly is "applied" is precisely a matter for debate.

Applied ethics is, of course, by no means confined to bioethics. Applied ethical issues arise in any area of life where the interests of individuals or groups conflict, including not just national groups but even the interests of different species. Thus, to highlight areas especially relevant to science and technology, in which Professor Knoppers' work is situated, environmental ethics has

3 Van Rensselaar Potter's book, *Bioethics: Bridge to the Future* (Prentice-Hall 1971) was published in 1971, although he was using the term as a bridge between humankind and nature, and was disappointed by its subsequent individual and medical focus.

4 See Julia Annas, 'Plato's *Republic* and feminism' (1976) 51 Philosophy 307.

5 David Armstrong, 'Embodiment and ethics: constructing medicine's two bodies' (2006) 28 Sociology of Health and Illness 866.

acquired increasing importance as the world grapples with issues of climate change, for example. Ethics in relation to artificial intelligence (AI) raises the issue of the disruptive power of technology. The collection, storage, and use of Big Data has given rise to ongoing discussions about privacy, surveillance, and human rights. As issues continue to emerge, debate is ongoing about how to respond and what ethical resources are available to do so.

3 Ethical Expertise

It is by now an expectation that ethics will feed into public policy through, for example, membership of ethicists on committees and specialized ethics committees (in research, for example). Academic researchers, in this as in other fields, are routinely required to demonstrate the impact of their work. There are, however, different scenarios. In some cases a public policy committee includes a single ethicist. The disciplinary background of the occupant of this seat may vary. In other cases there are committees described as ethics committees but which involve other disciplines. What is the involvement of ethicists meant to achieve? If it is thought that it is the role of ethics to apply ethical thinking to social issues and come up with authoritative advice for policy, the question arises as to what kind of expertise professional ethicists have. What might be meant by expertise in this context is problematic. There is understandable skepticism regarding whether any one group of people has privileged access to the truth about what ought to be done.

Arguably this is not the sense of expertise that is involved in feeding ethics into policy. Are there alternative notions of expertise that might be available?[6] One possibility is that expertise in ethics involves familiarity with a range of views, skills in reasoning and argumentation, and an ability to facilitate debate. In so far as this is the case, what is purported to be applied ethics expertise, in the policy arena, could involve a commitment to a kind of ethical pluralism.

This also requires thinking about the role of different disciplines that might be involved. For philosophy, reasoning skill is prioritized rather than a deep understanding of one tradition. In applying ethics to particular issues, discussions from more than one perspective are to be preferred to discussions from only one. There are both theoretical and practical reasons why universalism may be unlikely to work, but for some, this liberal approach constitutes a kind

6 Jenneth Parker, 'Moral Philosophy – Another 'Disabling Profession?' in Ruth Chadwick (ed), *Ethics and the Professions* (Avebury 1994).

of relativism, which may be regarded as undesirable if it implies that nothing can be ruled out. The role of law here is particularly helpful, in particular international law which has evolved greatly with Professor Knoppers' contributions, and which highlights both the similarities and divergences between approaches in different parts of the world that influence policy.

Social science approaches to ethics have also become increasingly important. They highlight the ways in which the notion of expertise can be contested, especially in biomedical ethics, where there might be differences of opinion between healthcare professionals and patient groups. In the debates about human genomics, for example, this has been a prominent feature feeding into debates about the concept of disability and what counts as a "serious" condition (as Kleiderman and Ravitsky elaborate in this volume).

A more radical challenge to the notion of expertise comes from those who see applied ethics, and in particular bioethics, as an assertion of power on the part of a certain group. Bioethicists themselves, from this perspective, might be regarded as a professional group who have been very successful in attracting large amounts of funding for their research and who have acquired seats at the policy table. Bioethics can then be seen, not merely as a field of study—even as a field of study that has input into policy—but as a site of struggle where ethicists claim to have a special role.

In addition to these challenges to applied ethics in general, however, there are particular issues about the relationship between ethics, on the one hand, and developments in science and technology, on the other. While there are of course questions to be asked about who has expertise to apply to issues and what form that takes, there are also questions concerning the *identification* of the ethical problems about which philosophical and legal reasoning is required: about whether this is a matter for particular professional groups or whether they can be identified from outside by so-called ethical experts. This will be examined further below.

4 Can Ethics Be Global?

In thinking about anticipatory *international* ethics, we have to consider what is meant by the term "international." Strictly speaking, "international" refers to things that involve two or more countries, whereas "global" refers to the whole world. Although there are certainly ethical issues that pertain to situations involving a smaller number of countries, I will focus here on the discussions about global ethics. The possibility of global ethics has produced a large literature, along with debates about its nature. For present purposes, I will confine myself to making two key distinctions. The first distinction is between global *issues* and global *approaches*. Some issues that require ethical (and policy) attention are global in nature, such as climate change. Research in human genomics also has global dimensions, in so far as this research has implications for all, and the human genome has been described as the "common heritage of humanity."[7]

The second distinction concerns what counts as a global approach to ethical issues. One possibility is that ethical theories that have been developed in one part of the world *expand* to meet challenges that are global in scope. This might be seen as a form of ethical colonialism, however—the export of Western traditions to other parts of the world.[8] Nigel Dower drew a distinction between an ethics that is global in scope and an ethics that is global in acceptance.[9] What is needed for successful international application is clearly more than an ethic that is global in scope. It may be that what is desirable is not just applying theories or principles in a new way, but reconfiguration of the conceptual scheme in ways that can command wide if not universal agreement. Harmonization in this area will be a process, not an endpoint.[10] So, in thinking about the possibility of international applied ethics, it is necessary to think about what, if anything, is "applied," which I now turn to discuss.

5 What Is "Applied"?

In the theoretical debates within the field there are different models concerning what is involved in applied ethics. It is tempting to think that in order for ethics to be applied, there must be *something* such as a theory to apply, which is indeed one possible model of applied ethics. The "fruits of theory" approach depends on the view that in applied ethics *some* theory is applied, but admits a variety of possible theories. Brown characterizes the fruits of theory approach

7 See e.g. Faith Kabata and Donrich Thaldar, 'The human genome as the common heritage of humanity' (2023) 14 Frontiers in Genetics 1282515.

8 See e.g. Ademola Kazeem Fayemi and OC Macaulay-Adeyelure, 'Decolonizing bioethics in Africa' (2016) 3 BEOnline 3 68.

9 Nigel Dower, 'Global Ethics, Approaches' in Ruth Chadwick (ed), *Encyclopedia of Applied Ethics* (Vol 2) (2nd edn, Elsevier 2012).

10 Ruth Chadwick and Heather Strange, 'Harmonisation and Standardisation in Ethics and Governance: Conceptual and Practical Challenges' in Heather Widdows and Caroline Mullen (eds), *The Governance of Genetic Information: Who Decides?* (Cambridge University Press 2009).

as the thesis that "Applied ethics is application of ethical theory."[11] This is to be distinguished from the "engineering" approach, which holds that there is one particular theory which can be drawn upon to apply to practical problems as and when they occur[12] and which will produce answers as a result of this application. As agreement is lacking on any *one* theory, the engineering approach has relatively few adherents, but the fruits of theory approach—that applied ethics must involve application of *some* ethical theory—remains one popular conception of applied ethics.

Contemporary applied ethics, in so far as it *is* an application of theory, relies to a large extent on ethical theories which take their starting point in the eighteenth and nineteenth centuries: deontology and utilitarianism. Deontological ethics draws on the thought of Immanuel Kant in a tradition that stresses respect for persons and notions of human rights and dignity, without necessarily being a strict application of Kant's own philosophy. Similarly, utilitarian ethics, or some form of consequentialism as it is employed today, rarely attempts to reproduce the thought of Jeremy Bentham or John Stuart Mill as such. While the former has arguably influenced present day conceptions of human dignity to which appeal is sometimes made in discussions of human genomics, the latter faces a potential problem in the international context. Where utilitarianism tells us to seek the greatest happiness of the greatest number, the number of people to take into account across the world is so large that it has led to consequentialism being described as the "ethics of fantasy."[13]

An alternative to applying high-level theory is the deployment of mid-level principles as found in Beauchamp and Childress' influential text, *Principles of Biomedical Ethics.*[14] Mid-level principles are said both to be in accordance with the "common morality" and to be reconcilable with different underlying theories. This in part explains their appeal. The notion of the common morality on which the approach depends has nevertheless been questioned: common to whom? The "four principles" in Beauchamp and Childress comprise autonomy, beneficence, non-maleficence, and justice. Thus autonomy, for example, can be supported both from a Kantian and a utilitarian point of view, although the interpretation of autonomy will be different in each case. Utilitarian ethics

11 James M Brown, 'On applying ethics' (1987) 22 Royal Institute of Philosophy Lecture Series 81.

12 See e.g. Arthur L Caplan, 'Can applied ethics be effective in health care and should it try to be?' (1983) 93 Ethics 311.

13 See John Leslie Mackie, *Inventing Right and Wrong* (Penguin 1977).

14 Tom L Beauchamp and James F Childress, *Principles of Biomedical Ethics* (Oxford University Press 1979). This book is now in its eighth edition and marked its 40th anniversary in 2019.

portrays the agent as choosing to maximize their utility, while the Kantian moral agent's exercise of autonomy is in accordance with what is right, rather than a pursuit of the good.

The four principles have been regarded by some of their advocates as forming the basis of a global bioethics in that they represent values that can be supported by anyone, although they may be so for different reasons. The extent to which ethics can be harmonized has moved centre stage in an era of globalization, at least as far as pragmatic guidelines are concerned for the conduct of research. People from very different cultures might support autonomy and justice, although they might mean different things in different contexts. The transferability of the four principles to different cultural contexts has however been subject to challenge, as has the priority commonly accorded to the principle of autonomy (although Beauchamp and Childress themselves push against this interpretation of autonomy).[15] It is important to note that the application of the four principles does not represent the application of a theory as such: they represent a useful framework for highlighting the moral dimensions of a situation, but a great deal of work is required in thinking about prioritizing, balancing, and specifying them.

Even within the fruits of theory model, including Kantianism, utilitarianism and principlism, there is criticism of the degree of abstraction which they exhibit. Other models thus attempt to take a more contextual and relational approach[16] leading to criticism also of the universalism as found in documents such as the Universal Declaration of Bioethics and Human Rights.[17] Feminist ethics, for example, critically examines issues of power, and assesses issues from the perspective of marginalized parties. In discussions of reproductive technology, for example, feminist ethics will not in an abstract way discuss the status of the embryo or fetus, or the right to life. Nor does feminist ethics accept the notion of the sole (which might be regarded as prominent in several other approaches) autonomous individual; rather, it will look at the position of the woman who has to carry the fetus or who has to undergo assisted reproductive techniques, and the ways in which power relations in society have an impact on options and decision-making. It is thus not only the individual case that is at stake—the distribution of power in the wider social context is also important.

15 Søren Holm, 'Autonomy' in Ruth Chadwick (ed), *Encyclopedia of Applied Ethics* (Academic Press 1998).

16 Priscilla Alderson, 'Abstract ethics ignores human emotions' (1991) 68 Bulletin of Medical Ethics 13.

17 Mary C Rawlinson and Anne Donchin, 'The quest for universality: reflections on the Universal Draft Declaration on Bioethics and Human Rights' (2005) 5 Developing World Bioethics 258.

In the light of considerations such as this, and also disagreements between different theories, anti-theorists explore the desirability of doing applied ethics without theory. One way in which this finds expression is in judgement about particular cases. Particularism objects to the search for universally applicable principles on the grounds that what counts as a reason in one case may not be so in another.[18] The approach of casuistry starts from cases and principles (analogous to case law) emerge from these, rather than being developed in the abstract and applied from above.[19] Specific developments and particular cases may affect the development of appropriate theory, and some argue that there is room for a bottom-up rather than a top-down approach.

One may thus distinguish a number of general models for doing applied ethics: theory application, mid-level principle application, feminist contextualism, and case-based casuistry. The first two apply some form of theory and may be described as top-down models; the middle two apply traditions of reflection that emphasize context; the last is a very bottom-up model that applies one case to another. In regard to issues related to science and technology, top-down models are perhaps more common, with much of the literature in biomedical or scientific ethics tending to illustrate this model. Context models exercise a stronger role in discussions of the responsibilities of professionals. Casuistry is no doubt the least common approach to doing ethics in science and technology, in part because many of the ethical problems associated with science and technology are so unprecedented that argument by case analogy is a stretch. In the kind of global ethics exemplified by Professor Knoppers' work, mid-level principles have largely been applied, informed by comparative international law and ethical consensus or harmonization in so far as it can be established.

6 So What Is Applied Ethics Applied *To*?

On the fruits of theory model, one concern is that principles developed in one field of expertise, such as philosophy, are (mistakenly) applied to another area of activity, such as the healthcare professions.[20] There are questions here about whether it is possible or desirable for principles to be developed externally rather than internally to the profession in question.

---

18 Jonathan Dancy, *Ethics Without Principles* (Oxford University Press 2004).

19 Albert R Jonsen and Stephen Toulmin, *The Abuse of Casuistry: A History of Moral Reasoning* (University of California Press 1988).

20 Alasdair MacIntyre, 'Does applied ethics rest on a mistake?' (1984) 67 Monist 537.

Arguably a prior task of applied ethics is, indeed, to elucidate what the ethical issues actually *are* and there is a concern, especially in ethics as applied to the professions, that those working in the field will uncritically accept problems defined in a particular way.[21] Put simply, what does applied ethics apply *to?* Contemporary debates about ethical aspects of developments in science and technology frequently focus on issues such as informed consent, safety and risk, privacy and security, conflict of interest, and professional responsibility. It is important to ask if significant matters of ethical concern are overlooked, such as the factors that influence the choice of areas of research, including societal and economic factors.

Relevant ethical questions include, not only external governance of science, but also ethics of scientists (and engineers) "internal" to the professions. Issues here arise concerning the responsibilities of scientists with regard to setting the research agenda, the conduct of research, the use of the results, and communication with different sections of the public and with potential users. The move from programs of promoting public understanding towards public engagement in science and technology has led to debates about how upstream in the research and development process such engagement should be. Is there a role for public involvement in deciding what research is carried out, or should the role of the public be limited to discussing the impact of research on society? The increasing commercialization of science and the changing social context in which scientists operate, overlap with business ethics, including questions about the "publish or perish" syndrome; the pressures of commercialization on the setting of research priorities; sharing of the benefits of the outcomes of research; and the question as to whether there are some things (e.g. living organisms) that should not be commercialized, and which should therefore be outside the patenting system. Seen in this light, questions about the social value of science become particularly urgent.

It may be the case that this is not a situation in which an either/or approach (ethics or science) towards identifying relevant issues to be addressed is desirable, but that it should be a collaborative venture. Thus, policymaking on science needs to include the perspectives of both science and ethics so that greater insight can be achieved through dialogue. This has been a key feature of the work of bodies such as the Human Genome Organization's Ethics Committee, which Professor Knoppers chaired. Under her leadership, influential statements were produced on topics such as the principled conduct of genetic

21 Onora O'Neill, 'The power of example' (1986) 61 Philosophy 5.

research and on benefit-sharing.[22] These were anticipatory in so far as they identified emerging issues and embodied a human-centred ethic, acknowledging human rights, human dignity, and freedom. On the one hand, it is essential that ethics in this area is scientifically informed; on the other hand, it is also the task of ethics to question assumptions about aspects of science that may raise issues of ethical importance but which may have been overlooked.

7 Science, Emerging Technologies, and Ethical Evolution

The assessment of science and technologies is made more problematic by the ways in which they extend the reach of human power across ever wider spatial and temporal scales.[23] The revolutionary power of AI, for example, has already been mentioned. Arguably, issues of scientific and technological ethics once seemed marginal in relation to ethical reflection on politics and economics, but contemporary world politics and economics have themselves been transformed by science and technology—and science and technology challenge ethics itself. These considerations lend weight to the view that over and above the assessment of individual technologies, there is a need for attention to technology's overall impact on the human condition. This is more apparent in continental philosophy than in Anglo-American applied ethics.[24]

Even within the Anglo-American tradition, however, there are special challenges: first, there is rapid development not only in science and technology themselves but also in the opportunities and potential for use (and the potential for dual use). The speed of change requires a similarly swift response on the part of society in terms of ethics, policy, and legislation. As stated at the beginning of this chapter, it is frequently argued that ethical deliberation comes too late, although in the case of the Human Genome Project the fact that ethical research was funded alongside the science and genomics has undoubtedly had a marked influence on ethics. This is especially so in the ways in which the challenges posed by the speed of change are further complicated by the fact that the development of technologies arguably pose questions for ethical frameworks themselves. In other words, we can no longer continue to think in

22 Human Genome Organization (HUGO) (1996) *Statement on the Principled Conduct of Genetics Research*. Human Genome Organization (HUGO) (2000) *Statement on Benefit-Sharing*. All the Statements are available on the HUGO website hugo-internatinal.org.

23 Hans Jonas, 'Technology as a subject for ethics' (1982) 49 Social Research 891.

24 Carl Mitcham and Helen Nissenbaum, 'Technology and Ethics' in Edward Craig (ed) *Routledge Encyclopedia of Philosophy* (Routledge 1998).

ways that were once comfortable. This is not just a point about how attitudes *do* change: certain ways of thinking turn out to be no longer *thinkable*. This is because new technologies push ethical frameworks to the limits so that their application is at best uncertain. So even for those who subscribe to a "fruits of theory" approach, it is therefore not simply a matter of "applying" ready-made theories to the possible implementation of technological advance—developments in the life sciences and other technologies can lead us to rethink theories and even concepts. Ethical theories emerge in particular social and historical contexts, so why should we assume that they can automatically apply in other contexts? Thus in the early days of the Human Genome Project, there was much discussion about genetic exceptionalism and the extent to which genetics requires rethinking of ethical doctrines such as the importance of confidentiality, since blood relatives have an interest in genetic information about those to whom they are related. The thesis of genetic exceptionalism was, however, hotly contested by arguments that genetic information is not different in kind, only in degree, from other kinds of medical information.[25]

Whatever model of applied ethics is preferred, there are questions that inevitably arise. Developments in science and technology give rise to different categories of questions. The first concerns what should be done about the new possibilities with which we are presented, such as whether or not it is desirable to try to extend the normal human lifespan by, say, fifty years. There is a question here about where the burden of proof should lie: some argue, in relation to such possibilities of human "enhancement," that the onus is on those who want to prevent such developments from occurring. Either way, these possibilities need to be considered in the light of the social and political context. For example, in so far as new technologies have the potential to offer benefits, what are the issues of equity of access and concerning the sharing of the benefits between different population groups? This is the second type of question. Analogous questions apply to consideration of the distribution of any attendant burdens or disadvantages.

Third, there is the question of what is new and what is the same. When new developments occur, they not uncommonly give rise to anxieties about possible consequences, and these anxieties find expression in some commonly used arguments that are not always easily identifiable with any particular theory. In part, this may arise from previous experience of things going badly wrong. However, anxiety may arise precisely because there is no prior experience on which to draw. In other words, what is feared is the unknown.

---

25 Thomas H Murray, 'Is genetic exceptionalism past its sell-by date? On genomic diaries, context, and content' (2019) 19 American Journal of Bioethics 13.

Even then, however, there may be an appeal to experience of things going seriously wrong in other fields when human beings "go too far." The response to certain developments, conceptualized as the crossing of limits or boundaries that should not be crossed, may be at least in part an expression of such a view. The playing God objection to new developments is frequently voiced in arguments about science and technology. It is not always clear what the objection amounts to or how seriously it should be taken: it may rely on a sense of the "natural" or "fitting." In so far as it points to undesirable consequences of the exercise of new powers, however, it may suggest caution. Advocates of caution sometimes deploy the precautionary principle, which has been used by a number of policymaking bodies. Slippery slope arguments are also frequently used in arguments about taking new steps—and typically envisage something unpleasant at the bottom of the slope (for example, scenarios of mass reproductive cloning).[26]

Finally, and at a deeper level, new developments lead to challenges concerning our interpretation of the very concepts at stake. New technologies can lead to a new understanding of concepts such as life, death, health, and disease. In the post-genome era, one of the purported outcomes is that there will be different disease classifications as we are able to rely less on symptoms and more on explanations of underlying mechanisms. The way we think about our identities as individuals and as members of groups may also be affected, as information continues to be forthcoming about ways in which we are related, genetically speaking, to each other and to other species.

What is particularly challenging for applied ethics, however, is the way new technologies may lead to reconsideration of our *ethical* concepts. Autonomy, for example, and as already noted above, is a concept that is the focus of considerable discussion. There are different aspects to the debate, including the issue of cultural specificity, the criticism of individualism, and the attempt to produce a relational interpretation, as in some feminist work in bioethics. Privacy has been challenged from a variety of directions: surveillance technologies, social media interoperability of databases and data mining, and whole-genome sequencing.

Applied ethics in this context requires not just application of principles, but reflection on how principles ought to be interpreted and how they evolve alongside science and technology. These have been key features of Professor Knoppers' work in applied ethics in a series of articles (see below). Her work involves both a comparative assessment of what principles are being invoked; to what

26 See e.g. Wibren van der Burg, 'The slippery-slope argument' (1992) 3 Journal of Clinical Ethics 256.

extent they command agreement across cultures; how they are being and should be interpreted; and how they are applicable, if they are, to particular issues.

Over the past thirty years, Professor Knoppers and I have worked together to map the ways in which ethical framings have changed in the light of scientific developments and emerging technologies. In 1994 in our article on the Human Genome Project (HGP), we identified an emerging consensus around principles of autonomy, privacy, equity, justice, and quality of science.[27] Later, as genetic research moved increasingly from Mendelian genetics to studying natural human variation at the level of the genome, we identified a shift in emphasis towards principles of reciprocity, mutuality, solidarity, citizenry, and universality.[28] The principles we identified in the 1994 article were not replaced: they continued to be invoked, but with new twists and interpretations. For example, conceptions of autonomy arguably became more nuanced, to include ideas about self-definition, for example, in relation to genomics as well as self-determination. Approximately another decade later, we looked again at trends in appeals to ethical concepts and principles in international research (not specific to genomics alone) and identified another six: governance, security, empowerment, transparency, the right not to know, and globalization.[29] We also noted that these ethical trends motivated a more politically actionable human rights approach, along with emerging calls for interoperability and harmonization of data—argued to be necessary in order to promote data sharing and maximization of potential medical benefits from the data and samples being collected in various jurisdictions.

Then, in our chapter in the 2022 book, *Law and Legacy in Medical Jurisprudence*,[30] we began by looking to the past to examine the development of three species of human rights: the rights of children and decisionally vulnerable adults, the right to benefit from scientific advancement, and the rights of future generations. We then turned to the future, looking at the possible ethical impact of developments in epigenomics and microbiomics, genome editing, and COVID-19. We noted the continuing pressing need for solidarity

---

27 Bartha Maria Knoppers and Ruth Chadwick, 'The Human Genome Project: under an international ethical microscope' (1994) 265 Science 2035.

28 Bartha Maria Knoppers and Ruth Chadwick, 'Human genetic research: emerging trends in ethics' (2005) 6 Nature Reviews Genetics 75.

29 Bartha Maria Knoppers and Ruth Chadwick, 'The ethics weathervane' (2015) 16 BMC Medical Ethics 58.

30 Bartha Maria Knoppers, Ruth Chadwick, and Michael JS Beauvais, 'Biomedical Research Policy: Back to the Future?', in Edward S Dove and Niamh Nic Shuibhne (eds) *Law and Legacy in Medical Jurisprudence: Essays in Honour of Graeme Laurie* (Cambridge University Press 2022).

and justice at a time when there are not only urgent questions about science serving the interests of humanity as a whole (rather than the few), but also when the future of the species is challenged, for example by enhancement technologies and by climate change.

Writing this present chapter only a few years later, the prospects seem increasingly dramatic in their possible impact and we have to ask whether what we have to contemplate is not simply a *co-evolution* of ethics and science, but rather a *revolution* in the light of the potentially disruptive power of technologies. While translational genomics (broadly understood as the take up and use of genomic knowledge[31]), both in the clinic and public health, may involve co-evolution along the lines we have identified in our previous writing, arguably developments in AI will be radically disruptive, not only socially and economically, but also ethically. Attention to social context is necessary in evaluating the implications for ethics, including social media, divisiveness in society, and post-truth.

8 Conclusions

Although the debates about the relative merits of theory and anti-theory continue, along with arguments about the nature of expertise, if such exists, what cannot be doubted is that there are pertinent questions to be addressed. It is necessary to continue to discuss the proper relationship between science, law, social science, and ethical theory: just as there are questions about the relationship between science and technology and ethical theory, there are also questions about as the ways in which the so-called "common morality," on which principlism, for example, draws, is to be described. Applied ethics requires collaboration, not only between lawyers, philosophers, and professionals, but also between different academic disciplines. *How* they are to collaborate is an ongoing question.[32]

The repertoire of philosophical theoretical approaches is very diverse, and yet applied ethics may sometimes be regarded as privileging certain ways of framing the issues. What has to be borne in mind is that these issues constitute lively debates *within the field*. As the following quotation, from the bioethics

31 Sheri D Schully and Muin J Khoury, 'What is translational genomics? An expanded agenda for improving individual and population health' (2014) 3 Applied Translational Genomics 82.

32 Vilhjálmur Arnason, 'Sensible discussion in bioethics: reflections on interdisciplinary research' (2005) 3 Cambridge Quarterly of Healthcare Ethics 329.

literature, shows, there are voices in bioethics who are pointing to two challenges that need to be addressed:

> [...] how to shift to locus of bioethical dialogue to bring to the foreground implicit assumptions that frame central issues and determine whose voices are to be heard and how to sharpen the vision of a global bioethics to include the perspectives of the marginalized as well as the privileged.[33]

The point about "framing" in the above quotation is important. Any theoretical approach "frames" the issues in a particular way, drawing attention to what the "framer" considers to be the salient points of a situation. Such approaches, however, can be blind to other concerns—for example, those anxieties that members of different publics may have, whether or not they are key stakeholders in some specific issue, for example by virtue of being a member of a patient organization.

Any purported resolution of an ethical issue depends on some theoretical presuppositions. The above analysis suggests that it is important to have regard to what frame is being imposed. The work of Professor Knoppers has exemplified attention to this framing and how it changes. Philosophers, lawyers, scientists, and social scientists have complementary roles to play. Comparative and empirical research can map changes in concepts, and expose the limitations of certain forms of argument in particular contexts. There needs to be ongoing negotiation about the nature of the problems being addressed and identification of areas of possible conflict of interest, in ways that are not just reactive but also anticipatory as well as global.

33 Anne Donchin and Debora Diniz, 'Guest editors' note' (2001) 15 Bioethics 111.

VIGNETTE

Vivid Memories with Bartha Knoppers

Annelien Bredenoord

The first time I met Bartha was at the International Stem Cell Forum Ethics Working Group in Uppsala, Sweden in October 2011. Having just started as an assistant professor in bioethics, I was deeply impressed by her work and leadership in the field. It seems that everyone in bioethics and health law has read her work with Ruth Chadwick, "Human genetic research: emerging trends in ethics,"[1] which was published in Nature Reviews Genetics in 2005, right when I had embarked on my PhD project in the field of the ethics of reproductive genetics.

From the moment we first crossed paths on various international committees and conferences, I have been consistently inspired by her unwavering dedication, boundless intellect, and compassionate approach to addressing the most pressing ethical dilemmas of human bioscience. The committee meetings and conferences were always inspiring and fun, taking us to adventurous locations, and we always wrapped up the day with drinks. Bartha was sure to have her signature drink in hand: whisky on the rocks! I can remember meetings we had in Uppsala, Banff, Boston, Montreal (several times), not to mention several locations in the Netherlands.

Bartha's guidance and mentorship have been invaluable to me throughout my career, shaping not only my professional trajectory but also my perspective on the intricate intersection of law and bioethics, and on combining academic leadership with a friendly atmosphere. I am ever so grateful also to the letters of reference that Bartha was always willing to write for me when applying for full professorship in Utrecht. (She also always had inspiring stories about her Dutch lineage and her sister living in Utrecht!)

In the last few years, I have moved to Erasmus University Rotterdam to become a full-time executive as Rector Magnificus, and more recently as President of the University. With this busy role, we have not had the opportunity to see each other for quite some time. As Bartha prepares to embark on the next chapter of her journey, I hope she appreciates and remembers fondly the profound impact she has had on the fields of law and bioethics internationally, and also as an inspiration for academics like me!

1 Bartha Maria Knoppers and Ruth Chadwick, 'Human genetic research: emerging trends in ethics' (2005) 61 Nature Reviews Genetics 75.

 | DOI:10.1163/9789004688544_010

VIGNETTE

A Tribute to Bartha Maria Knoppers: Dear Friend and Collaborator

Mark A. Rothstein

Bartha and I met at a genetics conference in the late 1980s, but we both attended so many conferences in those days that I'm not exactly sure where or when our initial meeting occurred. In retrospect, it was inevitable that we would meet and later work together on numerous projects for over three decades. In the 1980s there were very few legal academics studying, publishing, and attempting to shape public policy on genetics. Today, there are hundreds of people around the world working on these important issues, and many of them were mentored by or at least influenced by Bartha, her work, and that of her protégés.

On a personal level Bartha and I have many parallels. Our birthdays are only three days apart (although I am two years older). We both are married to law professors, have two grown children, and are dog lovers. We have also had many similar professional activities. For example, we both served as chair of the Social Issues Committee of the American Society of Human Genetics and were advisers to the US National Institutes of Health and Genome Canada. We also faced many years of challenges in directing interdisciplinary bioethics research institutes.

Our collaborations increased in the 1990s. In 1995, when I was Director of the Health Law and Policy Institute at the University of Houston, Bartha taught a two-week intersession course on International and Comparative Health Law, which stressed the importance and challenges of global efforts in health law. In 1996, we published the first of many co-authored articles, this one on comparative genetics laws for the European Journal of Health Law.[1]

Working on international and comparative ethics, law, and policy often requires foreign travel. I made several trips, but Bartha has been the ultimate frequent flyer. Some of our joint travels, including to Lausanne, Stockholm, and

1 Mark A Rothstein and Bartha Maria Knoppers, 'Legal aspects of genetics, work and insurance in North America and Europe' (1996) 3 European Journal of Health Law 143. The most recent co-authored article was published just this past year. See Mark A Rothstein and others, 'International scope of biomedical research ethics review' (2024) 385 Science 145.

DOI:10.1163/9789004688544_011

Valencia, were especially memorable, as were trips with her McGill colleagues to Mexico City, Turin, and other places.

In 2016, Bartha and I organized a session on international biobanking for a conference in Vienna. One day, we decided to have a mid-afternoon snack of Viennese pastries at a famous hotel. When the bill came for €35, I paid it by credit card on a mobile card reader and mistakenly added a €700 tip! After I noticed the mistake, I spoke to the restaurant manager, and he said to come back in the evening. When I returned, he kindly gave me a copy of the voided credit card charge and a new one for €35. I asked him how I could leave a tip on the new charge, and he replied: "Sir, you've already done enough for one day."

My interest in international and comparative health law and bioethics is due to Bartha's influence. The daunting logistical, linguistic, cultural, and legal challenges of this research were made manageable by Bartha's insights and experience, as well as her personal relationships with experts in many countries. In the last decade we published the results of five major studies exploring the common elements of international research ethics. Bartha and I viewed this and other scholarship as a means to the end of facilitating important health research while also promoting such values as autonomy, dignity, transparency, privacy, cultural sensitivity, and justice.

Over the years, I have had the privilege of working with many of Bartha's graduate students, post-docs, and colleagues. At first, I thought she was extraordinarily fortunate to be surrounded by such diverse and talented individuals. I soon learned it wasn't luck. Bartha attracted the best and brightest from Canada, the United States, and other countries because she is a fantastic leader, role model, and mentor. She demonstrates the importance of hard work, detailed preparation, meticulous research, independent analysis, and lucid writing, all achieved with collegiality, integrity, and a keen sense of public service. Some of her junior colleagues have remained with her for years in positions of increasing responsibility. Others have accepted leadership roles in academia, government, nonprofit organizations, or commercial entities around the globe. Evidence of her successful guidance of emerging scholars is found in the authoritative contributions to this volume by some of her many proteges, along with contributions from some of her long-time friends and colleagues.

I've learned so many things from my association with Bartha that it is difficult to single out a particular item, but one thing is clear. The next time we go out for pastries, I'm going to let her leave the tip.

CHAPTER 4

Policymaking as a Humanistic Endeavour: On the Art and Science of Genomics Policy Development

Eric M. Meslin and James V. Lavery

1 Introduction

Policymaking is sometimes referred to as "messy," an adjective meant to suggest the many complex factors—personal, emotional, political—that inform and inspire the process.[1] It recalls the description famously (but incorrectly) attributed to Otto von Bismarck: "Laws are like sausages. It is best not to see them being made."[2] The reference to the messy bits and pieces that are pleasantly packaged for more polite company's consumption has become a meme of sorts for the policy community. It is meant to convey the role of negotiating, compromise, and trade-offs, but also where anecdotes stand in for data, ends matter more than means, and personalities rather than good arguments play an outsized role.

This generalization is not altogether fair since much of policymaking is the antithesis of messy: it is tidy, ordered, and (in the view of many) boring; where the main business is keeping the wheels of government and society turning, and the bureaucracy functioning. It is writing bills to fund roads and the post office, drafting regulations for clean water, and issuing licenses for restaurants.

1 Janice Gross Stein, 'Policy is messy because the world is messy. Get used to it' (2001) Policy Options 73, available at: https://policyoptions.irpp.org/magazines/2001-odyssee-espace/policy-is-messy-because-the-world-is-messy-get-used-to-it/.

2 We say "attributed to" since there is little evidence that von Bismarck said these words, or even words to this effect. A review of this quote reveals a much more interesting origin, however:

> Quotation researchers Fred Shapiro, Garson O'Toole ... have traced it to the American poet, John Godfrey Saxe (1816-1887). Saxe, a popular poet in the mid-19th century, is mostly remembered today for setting the ancient parable from India about the blind men and the elephant to verse and making the story popular in the United States ... The law and sausages idea was attributed to Saxe as early as 1869, and that's the first appearance of that phrase. What he said was, "laws, like sausages, cease to inspire respect in proportion as we know how they are made." [University Chronicle. University of Michigan (27 March 1869) books.google.de. Daily Cleveland Herald (29 March 1869), McKean Miner (22 April 1869)], available at: https://professorbuzzkill.com/2018/05/01/bismarck-laws-and-sausages/.

Even when the topics are controversial, the processes still follow accepted practices and requirements. In this way policymaking resembles basic science—using tested methods to answer or define a question in pursuit of a broader societal goal. It has a routine, an approach, a type of bureaucracy.

But one person's messiness is another person's art: "politics is the art of the possible, the attainable—the art of the next best."[3] In this sense, policy as "messy" is not pejorative but speaks instead to the creative actions and strategies undertaken in the policy arena. As art, policy can then be judged subjectively. Although we expect that few would immediately identify policymaking or its outcomes in artistic terms, it takes little effort to identify policies, or policy-inspiring actions, with artistic character, such as those in Abraham Lincoln's *Gettysburg Address*, which laid out "the great task" for the nation to "have a new birth of freedom." Or JFK's inspirational call to go to the Moon ("We do these things not because they are easy, but because they are hard") which inspired, instigated, and shaped US federal policy. There are policy documents with actual physical beauty, such as the Magna Carta, virtually every illuminated vellum emerging from the Vatican, or the Rosetta Stone. Collectively, these examples reveal the humanistic dimensions of the policy enterprise and even its potential for inspirational elegance.

In this chapter, drawing on our own experience, we present two different but complementary perspectives on policymaking. The first perspective is policymaking as a structured process more akin to a *scientific pursuit*. The second perspective is policymaking as a creative act, or *artistic endeavour*. Recalling Voltaire's dictum "le mieux est l'ennemi du bien" (the perfect is the enemy of the good), we will argue that elements of both perspectives are often what animates policymaking and policy debates of today. No policy is ever perfect[4] and not every policy will have scientific and artistic attributes. Unsurprisingly, this is because policymakers themselves do not have all these skills. Some are gifted in content expertise, others in procedural knowledge, others in soft skills. A small number, and we believe Professor Bartha Maria Knoppers is one of them, function effectively in policymaking because they have many of these skills and attributes.[5]

---

3 von Bismarck was quoted in *St. Petersburgische Zeitung*, 11 August 1867, available at: https://www.shmoop.com/quotes/politics-art-of-impossible.html.

4 Eric M Meslin, 'If perfect isn't possible, Is the good "good enough? Placebo, Post-trial provisions and the Politics of Helsinki' (2013) 5 World Medical Journal 185.

5 We are not surprised by this: Bartha's career trajectory included graduate training in French poetry, before switching over to law and then health law with a particular focus on biosciences and biotechnologies (especially genetic and reproductive). For most of her career, she has had an abiding commitment to the most vulnerable in society—especially children—

These ideas—policymaking as scientific and artistic, boring and exciting, messy and tidy—animate our approach in this chapter. By using illustrative case examples, we hope to make progress towards a description of humanistic policymaking of the kind that reflects the enormous contributions of the honoree of this volume. By doing so, we also aim to suggest that humanistic policymaking—however difficult to define—provides a meaningful defence against the inadvertent or wilful disregard of fundamental human rights and interests in the design and implementation of social policy. Like art, humanism in policymaking can be understood as a form of confrontation. Certain ideas and considerations are important enough to the human condition, and to fairness and decency in society, to warrant robust representation. As is the case for art, humanistic representation in policymaking often requires courage, ingenuity, and creativity.

2 Two Perspectives on Policymaking

An advanced search in the *Oxford English Dictionary* of the term "policy" results in 65 entries, 82 meanings, and 322 quotations, occurring in various parts of speech: nouns (652), adjectives (94), verbs (56), adverbs (7), prepositions (2), plus one instance each of a prefix and suffix.[6] We adopt a similarly inclusive approach to using the term here, referring to policy in some instances as a *document or written statement* (e.g. the policy for responsible research in a university); as one of many types of governance *tools* (e.g. "there are many policy approaches we can take to this problem, ranging from legislation to guidelines"); and as a *way of behaving* and thinking that follows from a set of ideas or beliefs (e.g. "it is my policy that I always treat people equally"; "it is the policy of this government to support multiculturalism").

But we also refer to the related term "*policymaking*" for which the OED lists only twelve definitions and one meaning: "(a) n. The devising of policies, esp. by a government or political party; (b) adj. that makes or is associated with the making of policy."[7] It is policymaking in this inclusive sense—that is, the different aspects of developing, writing, editing, contributing to, advising on,

---

and has used her many platforms in the academy and on advisory committees in the public and private sectors to speak on behalf of human rights, from the right to benefit from science to the right to be treated with respect.

6 Oxford English Dictionary, 'Policy', available at: https://www.oed.com/search/advanced/Meanings?textTermText0=Policy&textTermOpt0=Definition&tl=true.

7 Oxford English Dictionary, 'Policy-making', available at: https://www.oed.com/search/dictionary/?scope=Entries&q=policy-making.

agreeing to, negotiating about, reviewing, and evaluating—that is the central focus of this chapter.

We suggest two perspectives to consider when discussing policymaking. The first is policymaking as a structured endeavour that follows accepted rules. This is policymaking as a *scientific pursuit*. The second perspective sees policymaking as a type of creative expression, seeking sometimes novel solutions to problems or proposing imaginative approaches that had not been envisioned previously. This is policymaking as an *artistic endeavour*. If our intuitions about humanistic representation as a core feature of art are correct, we believe that both perspectives are necessary for "good" policy.

2.1 *Policymaking as a "Scientific" Pursuit*

There is a certain appeal to referring to policymaking as a scientific pursuit. Good science is objective, based on accepted values, approaches, and methods. It is rarely messy. Messy science is bad science—sloppy design begets sloppy research which begets sloppy data which begets useless findings and conclusions. Perhaps that is why there is no Bismarckian sausage-making equivalent to doing science. The worst one can say about doing science may have been described by science journalist Stephen Battersby:

> Science is not a whirlwind dance of excitement, illuminated by the brilliant strobe light of insight. It is a long, plodding journey through a dim maze of dead ends. It is painstaking data collection followed by repetitious calculation. It is revision, confusion, frustration, bureaucracy and bad coffee. In a word, science can be boring.[8]

Of course, there are the occasions when science transcends boredom. This happens when one experiences that (rare) moment of joy or pleasure when nature reveals a truth no one in the world has known before.[9] Some of these truths may even be described as beautiful or elegant.[10] In his 2015 *New Yorker* piece, "What is elegance in science?", Patrick House revisits familiar examples, such as the laws of planetary motion by Kepler and Newton, or the simplicity of Einstein's formula $E = MC^2$ or the structure of DNA arising from the work of

8 Stephen Battersby, 'Let's face it, science is boring' (16 December 2009) New Scientist, available at: https://www.newscientist.com/article/mg20427392-300-lets-face-it-science-is-boring/.

9 The physicist Richard Feynman wrote about this type of joy in Richard P Feynman, *The Pleasure of Finding Things Out: The Best Short Works of Richard P. Feynman* (Basic Books 1999).

10 Ian Glynn, *Elegance in Science: The Beauty of Simplicity* (Oxford University Press 2010).

Watson, Crick, and Franklin.[11] House recounts the story of Crick's 1957 paper "Codes Without Commas," in which he claimed that individual amino acids only occur in a specific order of three bases: an idea Crick wrote about in his memoir that "seemed so pretty, almost elegant." This "elegant" idea turned out to be wrong, recalling HL Mencken's caution: "Explanations exist; they have existed for all time; there is always a well-known solution to every human problem—neat, plausible, and wrong."

Like some aspects of science, some aspects of policymaking can be boring: endless committee meetings, hearings, data gathering, followed by parliamentary/legislative rules that require specific steps for the discussion, introduction, and final approval of a piece of legislation before it becomes law. While they may not be exciting, these procedures are necessary for converting an idea into action within the norms of procedural and deliberative fairness in liberal democracies. Framing policymaking as a scientific pursuit means that the process adheres to specific rules of behaviour, different procedures that must be followed depending on the policy problem that is being solved.

But there are also moments of excitement, even joy, when the collective power of policy*makers* is brought to bear on a wicked problem[12] or supporting a meaningful initiative: enacting anti-discrimination legislation, establishing Canada's Charter of Rights and Freedoms, or authorizing funding of the Human Genome Project. Moreover, there are occasions where policy has a transcendent moment—where the right approach is found to overcome a seemingly unbridgeable divide between competing interests. An example from the life sciences was the passage of the 1974 US National Research Act (NRA).[13] Signed into law by President Richard Nixon, the NRA established the first US bioethics commission, which wrote the historic Belmont Report,[14] leading to the establishment of the regulations for the protection of human subjects that

11 Patrick House, 'What is elegance in science?' (17 April 2015), available at: https://www.newyorker.com/tech/annals-of-technology/what-is-elegance-in-science.

12 The original description of "wicked problems" was advanced in Horst WJ Rittel and Melvin M Webber, 'Dilemmas in a general theory of planning' (1973) 4 Policy Sciences 155. But others have picked up this term and approach including, for example, Australian Public Service Commission (2007) *Tackling Wicked Problems: A Policy Perspective* (2007), available at: https://www.enablingchange.com.au/wickedproblems.pdf. See also Brian W Head, *Wicked Problems in Public Policy: Understanding and Responding to Complex Challenges* (Palgrave Macmillan Cham 2022), available at: https://link.springer.com/book/10.1007/978-3-030-94580-0.

13 National Research Act (Public law 93-348-July 12, 1974), available at: https://www.govinfo.gov/content/pkg/STATUTE-88/pdf/STATUTE-88-Pg342.pdf.

14 US National Commission for the Protection of Human Subjects of Biomedical and Behavioral Research, *The Belmont Report: Ethical Principles and Guidelines for the Protection of*

(with changes over time) remain in effect today in the US and have been used as a model by other countries.[15]

Some might say that the products of the NRA, especially The Belmont Report and the system of institutional review, were transcendent in the field of research ethics,[16] but what was particularly inspiring about the NRA, in our view, was the process that led to its passage in the first place. Led by the indomitable Senator Ted Kennedy, Democratic and Republican legislators who disagreed on fundamental issues of human rights, the use of children or fetuses in research, and the authority of the state to regulate science nevertheless *agreed* to support a law that would create a system for the protection of human participants. But they agreed for different reasons: some were convinced of the necessity of advancing research while protecting individuals against discrimination; others provided support because they believed that using regulation was preferable to legislation; others recognized the symbolic importance of the new system, having been made aware of the infamous Tuskegee studies on untreated syphilis during Kennedy Senate hearings.

Whether boring or exciting, messy or elegant, just as science has specific tools, approaches, instruments, and methods for undertaking research, policymaking has its own "box of tools." Figure 4.1 provides an illustration of the many tools available to policymakers.

Among the most formidable of these many tools, policymaking also purports to share with science a commitment to use evidence when making decisions. Shortly after he was elected in 2015, Canadian Prime Minister Justin Trudeau said: "We are a government that believes in science—and that good scientific knowledge should inform decision-making." His remarks mirrored those of US President Barack Obama who, six years earlier in his 2009 Inaugural Address said: "We'll restore science to its rightful place and wield technology's wonders to raise health care's quality and lower its cost." These twin statements stood as an affirmation of the argument that policymaking should be informed by

---

Human Subjects of Biomedical and Behavioral Research (1979), available at: https://www.hhs.gov/ohrp/regulations-and-policy/belmont-report/index.html.

15 The regulation in the US, now known informally as the Common Rule, is described in federal regulations as 45 CFR 46. A review of the International Compilation of Human Research Standards lists more than 1000 guidelines from more than 130 countries. See Office for Human Research Protections, 'International Compilation of Human Research Standards', available at: https://www.hhs.gov/ohrp/international/compilation-human-research-standards/index.html.

16 See e.g. the chapters in James F Childress, Eric M Meslin, and Harold T Shapiro (eds), *Belmont Revisited: Ethical Principles for Research with Human Subjects* (Georgetown University Press 2005).

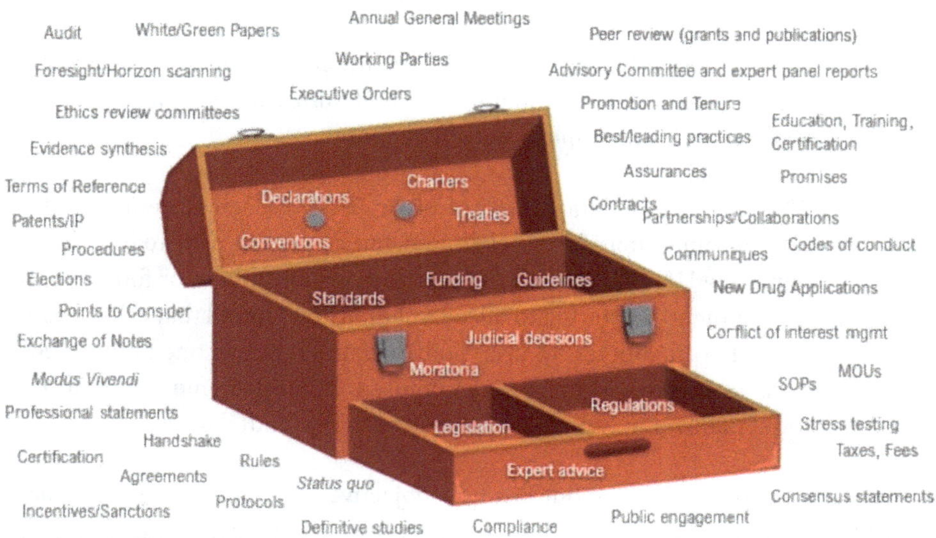

FIGURE 4.1 Policy tools[17]

evidence and data.[18] The use of the term evidence-informed (an improvement over "evidence-based") suggests an objectivity usually reserved for science.[19] Yet we also know that the rhetoric conceals more difficult truths, as the celebrated economist John Maynard Keynes captured best when he said wryly: "There is nothing a government hates more than to be well informed; for it makes the process of arriving at decisions much more complicated and difficult."[20] Many have pointed to former UK Secretary of State for Levelling Up, Housing and Communities, Michael Gove's oft-parodied 2017 quote, as further evidence (pun intended) that the effort to link policymaking with science and the expertise that underlies good science is not universally supported, when he said in a SkyNews interview: "I think people in his country, have had enough

17 One of us (EMM) created this graphic, and used it for the first time when giving the Bartha Maria Knoppers Inaugural Lecture: "Policy as an International Language in Bioethics: What We Can Learn from Genomics" (16 October 2023, McGill University). It is reproduced here with permission.

18 See for example, JA Muir Gray, 'Evidence based policy making' (2004) 329 BMJ 988; Tjede Funk and others, 'Translating health information into policy-making: a pragmatic framework' (2022) 126 Health Policy 16.

19 Ross EG Upshur, 'If not evidence, then what? Or does medicine really need a base?' (2002) 8 Journal of Evaluation in Clinical Practice 113.

20 Cited in Robert Skidelsky, *John Maynard Keynes: A Biography. Vol. 2: The Economist as Saviour, 1920-1937* (Macmillan 1992).

of experts from organizations with acronyms that have got things so wrong in the past."

In a more thoughtful way, Ian Boyd, the former Chief Scientific Advisor of the UK Department of Environment, Food and Rural Affairs, expressed a similar concern about how people think about *data*:

> When I think of data I think of binary or hexadecimal numbers. This betrays something of my background, but it was a surprise to me when in Defra, the UK Department of State with responsibility for food and the environment, we started to talk about data and I found that other people saw data very differently. Everybody had different preconceptions about data. Some seemed to be very confused. It had become trendy to talk about data, but few people appeared to think about data.[21]

To this list of concerns about just how objective and science-like policymaking can be, one can add the rise of misinformation and disinformation,[22] the decreasing trust in scientists, and the political selectivity of cherry-picking data.[23] These factors collectively have been shown to undermine the confidence that the public places in policymakers generally, leading to respected groups such as the International Science Council to recommend a pivot away from the product to the producers:

> The traditional linear model of disseminating scientific knowledge to policy-makers and the public is outdated. It ... assumes that trust in science is solely a matter of educating the public and addressing misinformation. Trustworthiness [in the messenger] is more important than trust in [the] messages.[24]

---

21 Ian L Boyd, 'The stuff and nonsense of open data in government' (2017) 4 Scientific Data 170131. Boyd's observation is reminiscent of Mary Poovey's *A History of the Modern Fact: Problems of Knowledge in the Sciences of Wealth and Society* (University of Chicago Press 1998), in which she argues that even this basic unit of knowledge—the fact—is not as "objective" as one might first think.

22 Council of Canadian Academies, *Fault Lines: The Expert Panel on the Socioeconomic Impacts of Science and Health Misinformation* (Council of Canadian Academies 2023).

23 Alexander Furnas, Timothy LaPira, and Dashun Wang, 'Partisan disparities in the use of science in policy' (Northwestern University, Institute for Policy Research Working Paper WP-24-05, 2024), available at: https://www.ipr.northwestern.edu/our-work/working-papers/2024/wp-24-05.html.

24 International Science Council, 'The Contextualization Deficit: Reframing Trust in Science for Multilateral Policy' (The Centre for Science Futures 2023), available at: https://council.science/publications/reframing-trust-in-science/.

In contrast with the depiction above of policymaking as a legalistic, quasi-scientific endeavour, we propose a complementary narrative: policymaking as an artistic endeavour. At first blush, this is not so fanciful an idea, since "the art of" is a common phrase meant to convey mastery, skill, and expertise covering everything from tennis games to war games.[25] From this it is a short step to the art of policymaking.[26]

2.2 *Policymaking as an Artistic Endeavour*

From Plato to the present day, philosophers, theologians, and crafts-persons have sought to define and explain the meaning of art for themselves and for others, and how to distinguish mere art from great art. As with most debates involving subjectivity, these cannot be settled definitively. To say that policymaking is a *type of art,* therefore, will invite this same debate. It is not conventional to think of policy and governance strategies for new technologies as works of art, or those engaged in policymaking as artists. We tend to think of them in more technocratic and administrative terms, perhaps with some attention to their design, but not as human creations that communicate and represent unique expressions of personal and social meaning—i.e. as works of art. Many (including us) share the view that human values play a significant role in policymaking, and that there is no such thing as value-free policy.[27] We accept that just as Verdi, Puccini, Van Gogh, Picasso, Tolstoy, and Walcott were great artists in the performing, visual, and literary arts, so too has art been used as an effective tool in policy development.[28] Certainly the rhetorical

25 We asked ChatGPT what "the art of" means (using tennis and war as examples) and it returned the following:

> Saying "the art of" typically refers to the skill, technique, or craftsmanship involved in a particular activity or discipline. It suggests a level of mastery or expertise in the subject matter, whether it be cooking, writing, negotiation, or any other endeavour. It involves not only hitting the ball effectively, but also anticipating your opponent's moves and adapting your game accordingly. Like any art form it requires practice, dedication, and continuous refinement to achieve proficiency." The "Art of War" is a classic treatise on military strategy written by the ancient Chinese military strategist Sun Tzu. It explores principles of warfare, including tactics, maneuvering, deception, and the importance of understanding oneself and the enemy.

26 See e.g. Harold Varmus, *The Art and Politics of Science* (W.W. Norton 2009); George Shambaugh and Paul J Weinstein, *The Art of Policymaking: Tools, Techniques, and Processes in the Executive Branch* (2nd edn, Sage Publications 2016).

27 Heather E Douglas, *Science, Policy, and the Value-Free Ideal* (University of Pittsburgh Press 2009).

28 Our colleague Timothy Caulfield, a student of Bartha Knoppers, and his brother Sean, a distinguished international artist, convened successful meetings where artists and scientists were brought together. The resulting products were both published and displayed.

flourishes of Winston Churchill, Mahatma Gandhi, and Alexander Hamilton qualify as artistic acts; but so, too, have been the creative actions of invisible administrators and civil servants tasked with crafting regulation and guidelines to meet the moment. What might we gain by imagining policymaking in this way?

One advantage of the analogy might be that it can help us grasp a deeper appreciation of the instigators and creators of policy—the artists—who imagine these processes, and who craft and nurture them into being. In the world of art, critical attention is divided between the works of art themselves and the artists who create them. Their stories, their histories and their aspirations figure prominently in how we view the works that they create and the weight these works carry as cultural artifacts. When significant policy achievements, such as "Obamacare," or FDR's "The New Deal," or Tommy Douglas's historic contributions to the creation of Canada's universal healthcare system[29] are so closely associated with individuals, it is rarely because the policies are exemplary in purely technical terms. More often, it is because the policies reflect something important about the creator's humanity, an expression of their compassion or solidarity and even defiance of political opposition. This description would be as fitting for Verdi's *La Traviata,* Picasso's *Guernica,* or Tolstoy's *The Kingdom of God is Within You* as it would be for President Obama's Affordable Care Act.

To extend the analogy, the tools in Figure 4.1 might be thought of as the policymaking equivalent of the painter's oils and brushes, the writer's notebooks and pens (or laptops), or the composers' instruments and scoresheets. Each tool is used for a specific purpose and requires special skills and mastery. The art of policymaking suggests that there are some crafts persons who are simply better at their work than others: some are better at imagining paths forward on complex and contentious issues; some are better at converting messy ideas into soaring prose; others have mastered the craft of gaining support, and still others have perfected their skills in negotiation and consensus building. Some are better at strategic thinking, others at implementation. Some are better with words, others with deeds. As the saying goes, some are playing chess while others are only playing checkers. Whether these skills are innate or acquired, we suspect that like all who aspire to the highest levels of excellence in their field,

See Sean Caulfield, Curtis Gillespie, and Timothy Caulfield (eds), *Perceptions of Promise: Biotechnology, Society and Art* (University of Alberta Press 2011); Sean Caulfield and Timothy Caulfield (eds), *Imagining Science: Art, Science and Social Change* (University of Alberta Press 2009).

29 Vincent Lam, *Extraordinary Canadians: Tommy Douglas* (Penguin Books Canada 2013).

the policymaker learns the tools by some combination of practice and mentoring, spending many hours doing so.[30]

Key to the artistic perspective we are advancing is a humanistic commitment to solving a problem that affects human beings. Artists have the ability to see other human beings as worthy of their attention, care, and concern. In essence, artistic expression—whatever its form—is an act of reaching beyond oneself and the service of one's own interests to recognize and illuminate an important feature of the human condition. Artists must have an understanding and appreciation of the inherent beauty of the human experience, as well as the implications for fellow human beings of its inevitable trials and tribulations. And the necessary vulnerability, compassion, intelligence, and perseverance to achieve representations that honour its significance and complexity.

Admittedly, this perspective may not be what comes immediately to mind when we think of policymakers. Indeed, if recent polling about the dramatic decline in the public's trust and confidence in governments is any indication,[31] the prospect of other-regarding behaviour and "appreciation of the vulnerability of the human experience" must sound like a fantasy world. That said, there are examples of policymakers who share precisely these same traits—who are committed to subduing the many forces in the complex process of policymaking that discourage the kinds of vulnerability, compassion, and other-regarding orientation that we are so quick to celebrate in great artists.

We now turn to the art of policymaking in genomics, using cases familiar to our honoree, Professor Bartha Maria Knoppers, and for some of which she played a key "artistic" role. Our objective in selecting these is to highlight how

30 The idea of needing 10,000 hours to master a skill, popularized by Malcolm Gladwell in *Outliers: The Story of Success* (Little, Brown and Company 2008), is probably a significant under-count for those working in policy, especially those who complete undergraduate and/or graduate training, internships, and a variety of staff positions before taking on elected or appointed positions. For example, William Lyon MacKenize King was Canada's longest serving Prime Minister for 21 years and 154 days, the equivalent of 187,656 hours.

31 See e.g. the 2022 OECD report which found that "just over 4 in 10 respondents had a high or moderately high trust in their government.": OECD, *Building Trust to Reinforce Democracy: Summary brief presenting the main findings from the OECD Trust Survey* (2022), available at: https://www.oecd.org/governance/trust-in-government/oecd-trust-survey-main-findings-en.pdf; see also the Pew Research Center study that tracked public trust in the US federal government from 1958–2023 and concluded: "public trust in government, which has been low for decades ... returned to near record lows," and that "less than 2-in-10 Americans say they trust the government in Washington to do what is right 'always' or "most of the time"", available at: https://www.pewresearch.org/politics/2023/09/19/public-trust-in-government-1958-2023/.

different policy tools were used to advance some of the humanistic interests we describe above.

3 Policymaking in Genetics and Genomics

The life sciences have continuously presented daunting technical and ethical challenges for those in the business of charting appropriate public policy. Genomics and biotechnology have a unique history of both exciting and frightening the public imagination, and of stimulating the legislatures' impulse to act (usually by prohibiting worrisome technology). From early examples of *in vitro fertilization* to more recent developments in gene editing, the full meaning and implications of the emergence of genetic and genomic technologies—both beneficial and harmful—is often unclear, making their regulation more difficult. The policymaking process is often unable (or incapable) of keeping pace with the science it is trying to regulate, and where the ethical, legal, and social issues are complicated. Thomas Friedman captured this conundrum in *Thank You for Being Late*:

> If it is true that it now takes ten to fifteen years to understand a new technology, and then build out new laws and regulations to safeguard society, how do we regulate when the technology has come and gone in five to seven years? This is a problem.[32]

And because the benefits and harms can have very different meanings and implications for different stakeholders, one of the challenges for policymaking has been to thread the needle between prohibiting, permitting, and encouraging research, development, and innovation. This is the "palette" that policymakers must work with: to create strategies that not only solve a problem (e.g. how best to regulate a technology), but also to represent the various interests held by diverse stakeholders, in a way that also preserves some meaningful expression of compassion and social solidarity.

These complementary issues are intended to bring policymakers and stakeholders into dialogue with one another in an effort to make the interests explicit, to deliberate about constructive ways to support and constrain the technologies, and to moderate any potentially corrupting advantages of power and privilege over those technologies that some stakeholders enjoy. Generating

32 Thomas L Friedman, *Thank You For Being Late: An Optimist's Guide to Thriving in the Age of Accelerations* (Farrar, Straus and Giroux 2016).

the kinds of evidence about stakeholder and public engagement strategies that would help policymakers realize these goals reliably has proven to be a difficult challenge.[33] But the key point for our purposes here is that stakeholder, community, and public engagement are other-regarding activities that require many of the same attitudes among those seeking the perspectives of affected communities that artists bring to their work. Engagement strategies are vehicles for acknowledging that emerging technologies can affect the interests of different stakeholders differently—creating value for some while setting back the interests (creating harm) for others. And for learning about how policy might be crafted intelligently and compassionately to optimize the impact of these implications.

Given the context above, here are three case examples of policymaking in genomics that reflect the humanistic perspective we are endorsing.

3.1 *Recombinant DNA Research, Cloning, and Gene Editing: The Art of the Moratorium*

In the early 1970s, molecular biology was having a moment. Coming two decades after the structure of DNA had first been fully described, new technologies to cut, paste, and splice pieces of DNA were the subject of intense scientific investigation. Among the more notable of these studies were a particular group of studies the prime example of which was a proposal by Nobel laureate Paul Berg and his graduate student Janet Mertz in 1971 to splice a monkey virus, SV40, into an *E. coli* cell. Following a Gordon Conference in June 1973, letters calling for temporary halts in the research to allow time for risks to be adequately assessed were submitted to *Science*,[34] an action previously unheard of.

Many of the letter writers, including Singer and Berg, then organized a historic meeting at the Asilomar Conference Center north of San Francisco in 1975 to discuss these studies in more detail, to seek a consensus on the types of studies that should proceed (or not), and to propose guidelines for future use. They were joined by other scientists, journalists, government officials, and members of the public (a first in science policymaking for genetics). The resulting recommendations[35] were adopted by the National Institutes of Health (NIH) and remain substantially intact to the present day.[36] While there has been a great

33 James V Lavery, 'Building an evidence base for stakeholder engagement' (2018) 361 Science 554.

34 Maxine Singer and Dieter Soll, 'Guidelines for DNA hybrid molecules' (1973) 181 Science 1114.

35 Paul Berg and others, 'Asilomar conference on recombinant DNA molecules' (1975) 188 Science 991.

36 NIH Guidelines for Research Involving Recombinant or synthetic nucleic acid molecules, available at: https://www.osp.od.nih.gov/wp-content/uploads/NIH_Guidelines.pdf.

deal written about these discussions, much of it by the participants themselves,[37] we draw the reader's attention to the creative acts of policymaking that the rDNA case instigated. In his pitch-perfect analysis of moratoria for the National Bioethics Advisory Commission (NBAC) more than three decades later, Cook-Deegan assessed the use of a moratorium (or in his words, "a ban I don't want to call a ban") and the broader policy paradigm it helped to generate:

> The voluntary moratorium, largely conceived and imposed by the molecular biology community on itself, thus was supplanted by a federally sanctioned set of guidelines and a prospective group review process. No violations of the voluntary phase of the recombinant DNA moratorium are known to have occurred.[38]

When seen in the broader context of the letters written by scientists, the Asilomar meeting, and the subsequent NIH guidelines, the moratorium can be seen as a nimble, creative, and even defiant example of policymaking—in artistic terms, perhaps an influential new "school of thought."

The moratorium approach also inspired policy strategy following the announcement of Dolly the cloned sheep in 1997. Among President Clinton's first actions on learning this news was to announce a ban on the use of federal funding for cloning research, and then to ask NBAC to "undertake a thorough review of the legal and ethical issues," which it produced in 90 days, recommending among other things that "it is morally unacceptable for anyone in the public or private sector, whether in research or in the clinical setting, to attempt to create a child using somatic cell nuclear transfer cloning." Further recommendations included: continuing the ban on the use of federal funding; requesting the private sector to voluntarily comply with the moratorium; suggesting that professional and scientific societies make clear that this would be an irresponsible and unprofessional act; and a call for federal legislation to prohibit cloning to create a child.

In the case of the Asilomar recombinant DNA moratorium, its main purpose can be described as a way for the scientific community to register its legitimate concern that they were not confident enough in the safety of the science to proceed apace, and that they wished to defer research until those concerns were addressed. A less charitable explanation may have been that they preferred

37 Paul Berg and Maxine F Singer, 'The recombinant DNA controversy' (1995) 92 Proceedings of the National Academy of Sciences USA 9011.

38 Robert Cook-Deegan, 'Do Research Moratoria Work?' in National Bioethics Advisory Commission, *Cloning Human Beings: Volume II Commissioned Papers* (1997), available at: https://bioethicsarchive.georgetown.edu/nbac/pubs/cloning2/cc8.pdf.

self-regulation over government regulation. We suspect both were true. In the case of human cloning, the referral to NBAC served a different policymaking end: by announcing that the topic would be first addressed by a federal advisory committee, the President effectively controlled the pace and positioning of the policy debate. Until NBAC reported, any congressional action would be seen as premature and uninformed. This had a type of neutralizing effect on the debate: cloning was "on the table" but pushed slightly to one side pending the report of the commission. This allowed other policy business to proceed. While the 90-day deadline was lightning-fast for advice for the commission to work, three months in Washington, DC was a lifetime.

Moratoria are not ancient artifacts of long-ago genetics debates. More recently, a proposed moratorium on heritable gene editing shared some similarities with past efforts in that there was a call for a pause in research. But unlike the US-centered examples above, this call recognized the scientific and moral issues as global in impact from the outset. They called for, among other things: a "global moratorium on all clinical uses of human germline editing," a "fixed period" which would "provide time to establish an international framework," and the recognition that once a framework was established that "nations may choose to follow separate paths."[39]

3.2 *Embryonic Stem Cell Research*

In 1998, two science reports shocked the world: Jamie Thomson and John Gearhart had identified and derived human embryonic stem cells and embryonic germ cells respectively,[40] 35 years after Canadians Till and McCulloch had shown that hematopoietic stem cells existed.[41] Two days after the announcements, the *New York Times* reported that Advanced Cell Technology (ACT), a Worcester, Massachusetts biotech company issued a press release announcing it developed a human-cow hybrid cell by removing the nucleus of the cow egg, and replacing it with the nucleus of a human cell.[42] The three events

39 Eric S Lander and others, 'Adopt a moratorium on heritable genome editing' (2019) 567 Nature 165.

40 James A Thomson and others, 'Embryonic stem cell lines derived from human blastocysts' (1998) 282 Science 1145; Michael J Shamblott and others, 'Derivation of pluripotent stem cells from cultured human primordial germ cells' (1998) 95 Proceedings of the National Academies of Sciences USA 13726.

41 Andrew J Becker, Ernest A McCulloch, and James E Till, 'Cytological demonstration of the clonal nature of spleen colonies derived from transplanted mouse marrow cells' (1963) 197 Nature 452. It is a testament to Till and McCulloch's integrity that first authorship was given to their graduate student, Andrew Becker.

42 Nicholas Wade, 'Researchers claim embryonic mix of human and cow' (12 November 1998) New York Times, available at: https://www.nytimes.com/1998/11/12/us/researchers-claim-embryonic-cell-mix-of-human-and-cow.html.

catapulted this boutique branch of science to the front pages of print media and therefore to the front benches of legislatures around the world. Nowhere was this more evident than in the United States.

Important though the science was, the stem cell research story initially unfolded within the unusual US policy ecosystem, where research is regulated differently depending on whether it is funded by the federal government or the private sector. Of particular importance was that research involving the human embryo or fetus was the subject of especially strict regulations, consistent with American public policy on the beginning and end of life, abortion, and the moral status of the fetus. There existed at this time federal legislation giving authority to the NIH to fund human embryo research,[43] but placed limits on that research by way of an amendment attached to the legislation funding the research. In other words, research on embryos was permitted except where it was prohibited.[44]

It was against this background that the Thomson and Gearhardt reports, supercharged by the ACT press release, gave Clinton and his White House a policy challenge, which they faced in several creative ways. The first response came in correspondence President Clinton sent to NBAC on 14 November 1998 (see Figure 4.2), which said in part:

> This week's report [in the *New York Times*] of the creation of an embryonic stem cell that is part human and part cow raises the most serious ethical, medical, and legal concerns. I am deeply troubled by this news of the experiments involving the mingling of human and non-human species. I am therefore requesting that the National Bioethics Advisory Commission consider the implications of such research at your meeting next week, and to report back to me as soon as possible.

Using a federal advisory committee to review and study an issue was not uncommon in the US, but few other countries had access to such an expert and well-financed resource.[45] In 1998, all eyes were on NBAC as it deliberated

43 National Institutes of Health Revitalization Act. Public Law 104-43 (1993), available at: https://www.congress.gov/bill/103rd-congress/senate-bill/1.

44 The ban was called the Dickey-Wicker Amendment (DWA), named after its two Republican co-sponsors Jay Dickey and Roger Wicker. The DWA was added to every bill funding the NIH from 1995 until the present day.

45 Eric M Meslin and Summer Johnson, 'National Bioethics Commissions and Research Ethics' in Ezekiel J Emanuel and others (eds), *The Oxford Textbook of Clinical Research Ethics* (Oxford University Press 2008).

THE WHITE HOUSE
WASHINGTON

November 14, 1998

Dr. Harold Shapiro
Chair
National Bioethics Advisory Commission
Suite 3C01
6100 Executive Boulevard
Bethesda, Maryland 20892-7508

Dear Dr. Shapiro:

This week's report of the creation of an embryonic stem cell that is part human and part cow raises the most serious of ethical, medical, and legal concerns. I am deeply troubled by this news of experiments involving the mingling of human and non-human species. I am therefore requesting that the National Bioethics Advisory Commission consider the implications of such research at your meeting next week, and to report back to me as soon as possible.

I recognize, however, that other kinds of stem cell research raise different ethical issues, while promising significant medical benefits. Four years ago, I issued a ban on the use of federal funds to create human embryos solely for research purposes; the ban was later broadened by Congress to prohibit any embryo research in the public sector. At that time, the benefits of human stem cell research were hypothetical, while the ethical concerns were immediate. Although the ethical issues have not diminished, it now appears that this research may have real potential for treating such devastating illnesses as cancer, heart disease, diabetes, and Parkinson's disease. With this in mind, I am also requesting that the Commission undertake a thorough review of the issues associated with such human stem cell research, balancing all ethical and medical considerations.

I look forward to receiving your reports on these important issues.

Sincerely,

Bill Clinton

FIGURE 4.2 President Clinton letter to NBAC, 14 November 1998

in public. As described in more detail elsewhere,[46] NBAC met three days after receiving Clinton's letter in Miami, Florida from 17–18 November 1998 where, following a late-night drafting session and further discussion in open session the next day, they replied to the President's request with a letter of their own, effectively calling out the ethical issues, cautioning against research until the risk were known. This "exchange of letters" had the effect of pausing any

46 Eric M Meslin and Harold T Shapiro, 'Bioethics inside the Beltway: some initial reflections on NBAC' (2002) 12 Kennedy Institute of Ethics Journal 95.

policymaking.[47] NBAC then went about its business over the next 8 months, preparing to submit its final report in September 1999,[48] which was widely expected to recommend supporting federal funding for stem cell research. However, the President preempted NBAC's final report through a press statement on 14 July 1999 (see Figure 4.3), the relevant parts of which were that a ban already existed to use federal funds to creating of human embryos in research, and since stem cells might be available in the private sector (and therefore out of the reach of federal regulation), no additional legal response

THE WHITE HOUSE

Office of the Press Secretary

For Immediate Release **Contact 202/456-6047**
July 14, 1999

Statement by the President

Back in November, when I asked my National Bioethics Advisory Commission (NBAC) to look at the ethical and medical issues surrounding human stem cell research, I recognized the enormous medical potential of such research. The scientific results that have come out in just the past few months already strengthen my basis for hope that one day, stem cells will be used to replace cardiac muscle cells for people with heart disease, nerve cells for hundreds of thousands of Parkinson's patients, or insulin-producing cells for children who suffer from diabetes.

But I also understand that stem cell research raises ethical concerns that need to be addressed, and the national dialogue has highlighted a range of opinions that must be respected.

First, I want to reaffirm the ban I issued in 1994 prohibiting the use of Federal funds for the creation of human embryos for research purposes. No other legal actions are necessary at this time, because it appears that human embryonic stem cells will be available from the private sector. Publicly funded research using these cells is permissible under the current Congressional ban on human embryo research.

Second, I will continue to insist that any Federally supported human stem cell research be held to the highest ethical standards. The NIH guidelines, with input from NBAC, will be the principal mechanism to ensure this outcome, while helping scientists turn the promise of stem cell technology into reality.

Finally, I would like to thank Dr. Harold Shapiro, Chairman of the National Bioethics Advisory Commission, and other Commission members for their hard work and thoughtful consideration of a very complex and sensitive set of issues.

FIGURE 4.3 White House Statement, 14 July 1999

---

47 It should go without saying that while email and the internet existed, formal correspondence at that time often relied on use of letters and fax machines.

48 The chronology of the NBAC deliberations and process can be found in its report, *Ethical Issues in Human Stem Cell Research* (US Government Printing Office 1999).

was required, allowing for NIH Guidelines ("with input from NBAC") to be the main policy tool for permitting stem cell research to take place in the US.

President George W Bush inherited the stem cell issue from the Clinton administration and his policymaking repertoire was similar. His first policy statement on stem cell research was announced on television to a national audience on 9 August 2001. Pressured by his supporters and opponents, Bush consulted with ethicists and lawyers before giving his primetime remarks. The President's nationally televised speech included a key policy statement that was buried five paragraphs in:

> As a result of private research, more than 60 genetically diverse stem cell lines already exist. They were created from embryos that have already been destroyed, and they have the ability to regenerate themselves indefinitely, creating ongoing opportunities for research. I have concluded that we should allow federal funds to be used for research on these existing stem cell lines, where the life and death decision has already been made.[49]

Just as Clinton and Bush sought to appease different stakeholders, Barack Obama also weighed in on the debate when he moved into the White House in 2009, using an Executive Order, with a self-explanatory title—"Removing Barriers to Responsible Scientific Research Involving Human Stem Cells"[50]—to communicate his policy decision to re-authorize federal funding of ES cell research.

The stem cell and rDNA debates were not existential moments in the history of genetic policymaking. But they did illustrate the value of deftly using different policymaking tools to open up space for debate and allow different opinions (especially strongly held ones) to be heard while providing a structure for meeting the diverse interests.

3.3 *The United Nations International Declaration on the Human Genome and Human Rights*

Stimulated by the growing international attention arising from the Human Genome Project and the announcement of the cloned sheep Dolly in the

49 George W Bush, 'Address to the nation on stem cell research' (9 August 2001) in *Public Papers of the Presidents of the United States: George W. Bush* (Book II, GPO 2001), available at: https://www.govinfo.gov/content/pkg/PPP-2001-book2/pdf/PPP-2001-book2-doc-pg953-2.pdf.

50 Executive Order 13505 (9 March 2009), available at: https://obamawhitehouse.archives.gov/the-press-office/removing-barriers-responsible-scientific-research-involving-human-stem-cells.

United Kingdom, UNESCO undertook to develop an international declaration that would take account of these emerging issues in the context of bioethics and human rights. If there ever was a nominee for best artistic policymaking style, the adoption of declarations by multilateral organizations like UNESCO would surely qualify as among the prime candidates. From the use of international diplomacy with its formal protocols and procedures, to the reverential preambular statements providing a historical context and provenance to situate debate, this policy environment resembles a theatre performance, a symphony, or epic poem—with different actors and characters playing specific roles.

In the policymaking toolbox illustrated in Figure 4.1, declarations function in a specific way: as aspirational documents with quasi-legal status.[51] Unlike treaties or conventions which create legal obligations for countries, declarations carry no such equivalent weight other than that which is attributed to them by governments, judicial bodies, and other groups. In the history of bioethics, declarations have figured prominently in policymaking. Among the most well known is the World Medical Association's Declaration of Helsinki, first adopted in June 1964 by the World Medical Assembly and amended 10 times thereafter (and counting).[52] But many organizations use this tool precisely because of its status as a type of political speech, designed to reflect broad consensus views on difficult topics, calling for action by others, and otherwise serving notice of the topic's importance.

The 1997 UNESCO Declaration, now formally the United Nations Universal Declaration on the Human Genome and Human Rights, shared all these features. And given its context as the first *universal* declaration the UN adopted focusing on a bioethics topic, it occupies a special place in that history. We recognize it here for an additional reason: Professor Knoppers was among a small group of experts directly responsible for developing the Declaration's draft language. Indeed, as we note below, she played a key role in providing the rationale and language for a key piece of the Declaration's text.

The development of the declaration occurred by way of two connected processes: first, convening experts in law, ethics, science, and policy to draft the language; second, convening government representatives who would receive

51 As non-lawyers, we make no claim to promoting or defending a strict legal interpretation of declarations, other than to note that they carry a different legal status than other instruments.

52 World Medical Association, Declaration of Helsinki – Ethical Principles for Medical Research Involving Human Subjects, available at: https://www.wma.net/policies-post/wma-declaration-of-helsinki-ethical-principles-for-medical-research-involving-human-subjects/.

the experts' document and negotiate the final language.[53] This division of labour made sense: content experts in genomics, international health and human rights, ethics, and science would jointly agree to text that satisfied the requirements that UNESCO adopted; the group of government experts would ensure that the final language would be acceptable to their governments and in so doing increase the likelihood that the recommendations proposed would be adopted and implemented.

What was not anticipated in this process was the sensitivity to certain issues and terms arising from the Declaration's creation, which only emerged during the Meeting of Government Experts to Finalize the Draft Declaration on the Human Genome and Human Rights in Paris in July 1997. As has been widely published, a draft text had been prepared by the committee of experts in 1996, which among other things proposed the language of Article 1. In its original form it read:

> The human genome underlies the fundamental unity of all members of the human family, as well as the recognition of their inherent dignity and diversity. It is the common heritage of humanity.

The reference in the second sentence to "the common heritage of humanity" was placed there intentionally and with specific reference to a long-standing tradition in law and international relations that includes other terms such as "common heritage of mankind," "common heritage of humankind," and the "common heritage principle."[54] This legal principle has been applied in many domains, from the sea to outer space, and from heritage to biodiversity.[55] Importantly, however, the application of this historical legal concept to genetics

---

53 Professor Knoppers was one of the academic experts who drafted the original text. One of us (EMM) was one of the government experts, appointed by the United States in its Observer capacity. Neither was aware of the others' role in the development of this document until a fortuitous conversation in 2023. There were many dates leading up to its adoption by the UNESCO General Conference on 11 November 1997 and then endorsement by the UN General Assembly on 9 December 1998. Our focus here is limited to the former. See United Nations, Universal Declaration on the Human Genome and Human Rights, available at: https://www.ohchr.org/en/instruments-mechanisms/instruments/universal-declaration-human-genome-and-human-rights.

54 See e.g. Prue Taylor and Lucy Stroud, *Common Heritage of Mankind: A Bibliography of Legal Writing* (Fondation de Malte 2013); Kemal Baslar, *The Concept of the Common Heritage of Mankind in International Law* (Martinus Nijhoff Publishers 1997).

55 See e.g. Graham Nicholson, 'The common heritage of mankind and mining: an analysis of the law as to the high seas, outer space, the Antarctic, and world heritage' (2002) 6 New Zealand Journal of Environmental Law 177.

and genomics was proposed more than a decade earlier by Bartha herself, in a commissioned study undertaken for the Law Reform Commission of Canada.[56]

Applying the language of "common heritage of humanity" to the human genome thus made good conceptual and legal sense. Although the Human Genome Project was only a decade into its effort to map and sequence the entire human genome, it was well accepted that there was very little genetic variation between individuals—perhaps no more than 1 percent. And yet, following several days of negotiations and discussions, the Meeting of Government Experts concluded on 11 July 1997 with an agreement to amend Article 1 as follows:

> The human genome underlies the fundamental unity of all members of the human family, as well as the recognition of their inherent dignity and diversity. *In a symbolic sense, it is the heritage of humanity.* [Italics added].

Gone was the word "common." Added was the modifier "in a symbolic sense." The final text, with the modified Article 1, was adopted unanimously by 77 nations present at the UNESCO General Conference on 11 November 1997.[57]

The case of the Universal Declaration may be seen in two ways. First, when seen as an example of a policymaking process that follows the rules and procedures of multilateral organizational governance, the amendments to the original text substantively changed the intended meaning of the expert group proposal, and in so doing effectively undermined the legal meaning and history of the term. It was as if the phrase "common heritage of humanity" was considered a suggestion, open for improvement rather than as an accepted principle of comparative international law.[58]

---

56 Bartha M Knoppers, 'Human Dignity and Genetic Heritage' in *Protection of Life Series: A Study Paper for the Law Reform Commission of Canada* (Department of Justice, Canada 1991), available at: https://www.lareau-legal.ca/Human.pdf (which has been applied in many domains from the sea to outer space, and from heritage to biodiversity).

57 There were several other phrases, terms, and proposals that were changed or adopted in the final document. This chapter is not the place to review those. We wish only to draw attention, by use of this single example (Article 1), of the complex way in which the art of policymaking manifested in the agreement reached on this specific instrument. As a point of information, the US was an Observer to the proceedings, as it was not a Member of UNESCO at this time. Therefore, it did not (nor did Meslin) vote on the final text of the Declaration, on any of the revisions.

58 It is noted that the expert group that drafted the original declaration was not invited to the meeting of government experts in July 1997. Had they done so it is possible that the case for maintaining the original text may have been made more forcefully. That said, the

Another way of understanding this case example is that the role played by the drafting committee of experts was substantively different from the role played by the government representatives, but without a way of engaging both together, neither benefited directly from the expertise of the other. It is the nature of these roles, and the special expertise each brought to the table, that is instructive for understanding the art of policymaking. Both were necessary, but as we show below, each group had different responsibilities, obligations, and functions. In simple terms, the role of the expert committee was to work towards a document that was of the highest scientific, legal, and ethical quality. The role of the government, in contrast, was to work towards a different type of outcome: a document that stood the best chance of achieving consensus support from the assembled representatives themselves, the support of the UNESCO General Conference, and ultimately the UN General Assembly. Importantly, both groups fulfilled their responsibilities. Each group used both "scientific" and "artistic" approaches.

It is ironic that what might have made the original text an example of policymaking at its "artistic" best was lost through the messy process of consensus-seeking around a final policy product. Even though the word "symbolic" was added as a qualifier, it did little to replace the damage done by undermining an accepted legal concept. As with many challenging issues through the ages, it may be, more simply, that the artists presented a vision that ran too far ahead of the fears and narrow political interests that so often have the final say in matters of policy.

4 Beyond the "Art and Science of Policy"

The Wikipedia definition of "art" provides a useful caution against viewing art, and its products, too narrowly:

> Art is a diverse range of human activity and its resulting product[s] … involve creative or imaginative talent generally expressive of technical proficiency, beauty, emotional power, or conceptual ideas.[59]

Although the definition includes the need for "imaginative talent," it stops short of acknowledging that the production of art (especially great art) often

committee of government representatives included many who were experts in law, ethics, science, and genomics.

59 Wikipedia, 'Art', available at: https://en.wikipedia.org/wiki/Art.

requires artists to run counter to popular opinion and to challenge convention and established norms and practices, all while demonstrating unusual technical prowess. The "artistic temperament," which is invoked so often to celebrate the character and personality of famous artists, invariably involves moral courage, moral clarity, impatience, sometimes debilitating compassion, a susceptibility to beauty, a deep understanding of the social and political contexts they are operating within, and an indefatigable commitment and perseverance in the face of personal and societal challenges. The phrase "the art and science of policy" is likely understood by most scientists and policymakers to be referring to art in purely figurative terms. But perhaps such a reading requires its own caution. We ignore the critical importance of something akin to the artistic temperament in "the art" of policymaking at our peril. The relevance of the hallmarks of artistic temperament for complex policymaking seems profoundly obvious. But there are mysterious forces at play that perpetuate an unnecessary suspicion of ideas like compassion, love, and solidarity in the pursuit of effective policy, and an ignorance of how this temperament humanizes and enriches the process and outcomes of policymaking.

The ideas we have shared in this chapter have been inspired by our abiding admiration of Professor Knoppers. We have had the extraordinarily good fortune to have worked closely with her as co-authors, fellow advisory committee members, and research collaborators. In each of these domains, we have been privileged to watch her apply her unique talents to some of the world's most difficult policy issues, especially those emerging from biotechnology and genomics. There is no doubt that Professor Knoppers' extraordinary success has been due, in part, to the authentic artistic temperament that she brings to all of her work. Our modest hope in the production of this chapter is that we have opened a small window onto an underappreciated feature of policymaking, but one that is familiar to Professor Knoppers and those who know and admire her. In doing this, we wish to ensure that the unique contributions of Professor Knoppers, the artist, are not obscured by the enormous contributions of Professor Knoppers, the international legal scholar and policy icon.

VIGNETTE

Bartha Maria Knoppers: Accolades from the Antipodes

Dianne Nicol and Don Chalmers

"I am an optimist, romantic, idealist, you name it—but I'm a realist."[1]

These words were used by our esteemed colleague, Bartha Maria Knoppers, specifically to describe her position on the European Union's current data protection law, the General Data Protection Regulation (GDPR). But in our view, they sum up her approach to tackling the big ethical, legal, and social implications (ELSI) of human genomics more broadly. This is a topic that she has engaged in with great passion for the past 40 years. We would both like to think that we, too, might be remembered for sharing this passion, this optimism, romanticism, and idealism—but also this realism.

It all began for us in 1992, lagging several years behind the start of Bartha's ELSI scholarship. At that time, one of us was teaching and the other was learning about contract law. In conversations with a visiting torts lecturer, the renowned US health lawyer Professor Rob Schwartz, we discussed developments in the new field of genomics, and particularly the emergence of the curious ELSI acronym. For those of us who were to become ELSI scholars, this new field of study was the most significant turning point of our careers. The fact that 3–5% of funding allocated to the Human Genome Project (HGP) was promised to ELSI research illustrated that we were not alone in recognizing the vital need for this research. The genomics science and policy communities also showed deep commitment to ELSI research, a commitment that continues to this day.

The establishment of the HGP ELSI program provided us with the impetus to form our own collaborative team with colleagues from our university and the University of Melbourne (Drs Margaret Otlowski and Loane Skene, as they then were) to research the ELSI of genomics in Australia. Our Centre for Law and Genetics at the University of Tasmania was established some two years later. Although our mission was to examine these ELSI from a

1 Global Alliance for Genomics and Heath (GA4GH), 'Ethics of genomic data sharing: an interview with Bartha Maria Knoppers' (13 April 2018), available at: https://www.ga4gh.org/news_item/ethics-of-genomic-data-sharing-an-interview-with-bartha-maria-knoppers/.

uniquely Australian perspective, we always recognized that this research had to be undertaken against the background of the developing international ELSI research landscape. Although Australian funding agencies did not have an explicit commitment to fund ELSI at that time (unlike Genome Canada, for example), we have been fortunate to receive generous support from the Australian Research Council.

Already by the start of the 1990s Bartha was shaping what would be the great international ELSI debates—debates that continue to this day. She was already writing about privacy, confidentiality and discrimination, patenting and trading in human genetic material, human dignity, and informed consent. In the mid-1990s she was largely responsible for triggering debate about the ELSI of banking human tissue for genomics ("biobanking" as it later became known). The particular ELSI of return of research results and incidental findings, secondary uses of data, data sharing, and Big Data soon became the focus of her presentations and academic writings. We and many others faithfully followed.

From the outset, Bartha was also shaping much of the international ELSI policy environment, including pivotal early roles on the Human Genome Organization Ethics Committee and in drafting the UNESCO Universal Declaration on the Human Genome and Human Rights, to which we had input through the eminent Australian judge, the Honourable Justice Michael Kirby. This linkage between human genomics and human rights (particularly the right to science) has shaped much of Bartha's subsequent work, particularly through her integral role in the formation and development of the Global Alliance for Genomics and Health (GA4GH). We are honoured to have been given the opportunity to participate in many of these international discussions, and particularly in the Regulatory and Ethics Work Stream of GA4GH.

It is timely now to reflect on where the science of genomics has come in the past 40 years. It was a science that had a patchy past, at times both glorious and dubious, with profound social consequences. Its promises had to be fulfilled and its threats contained. That containment had to be addressed within the regulatory spectrum from professional ethics to legislation. It could not be left to professional self-regulation. It had to involve the broader community and it had to be international in scope. The science of genomics and the ethical regulation of genomics have come a long way since that time. It is fortunate that, because the international ELSI debates started early, this progress has largely been hand-in-glove.

Genuine international voices and fortunately, shared common themes, emerged early on in the debates about how this science should proceed, and how genomic research should be translated into clinical practice, both safely and ethically. The choir of voices were many but there were, we are sure we all agree, some gifted, golden, and gracious voices who also took on additional conductors' tasks. As Founding Director of the Centre of Genomics and Policy, within the Department of Human Genetics at McGill University, Bartha has held an internationally influential and magisterial position in the development of genomics policies and regulation of these international genomics issues.

Bartha's contributions have gone beyond her own scholarly works to gathering and leading these voices around the world and finding the common themes. Bartha, we would all agree, has been one of our most influential voices. She has been one of the leading international authorities in shaping the regulation of our imagined genomic futures. Her publications and thinking have been at the international vanguard and have permeated and influenced genomics international ELSI scholarship and practice, and will continue to do so long into the future.

We acknowledge her internationalism, intellectual integrity, and her commitment to the ethical imperative of community and individual benefit.

VIGNETTE

Overheard BMK

Timothy Caulfield

Top 10 Bartha Maria Knoppers' Quotes Overhead at Conference Coffee Breaks (I may be paraphrasing…)

10) "Seriously, I don't need a computer. I'll just write this grant on an Air Canada barf bag." (She got the grant.)
9) "Look, 'interdisciplinary' means *interdisciplinary*. It doesn't mean disciplining your trainees two different ways."
8) "What do you mean wine isn't a claimable expense? It is essential to the creative process!"
7) "Is it true that at the Cold Spring Harbor Laboratory they make you *share* a bathroom? Barbaric!" (Ok, that one might have been me.)
6) "In Montreal we serve real croissants, not stale hockey pucks."
5) "Ethics, law, and science policy are not simply 'add ons.'" (Note: This position changed scholarship and research funding in Canada.)
4) "Where's the espresso?"
3) "Being a great mentor can change a person's life." (So true. And she changed mine.)
2) "We are gonna make this happen!" (And she made it happen, every time.)
1) "Friends, conversations, laughter, literature, art, good food, and energizing creativity. What more do you need?" (What more, indeed?)

CHAPTER 5

Bioethics "Laws": Paradox or Way of the Future?

Emmanuelle Rial-Sebbag and Anne Cambon-Thomsen

> When you work you are a flute through whose heart the whispering
> of the hours turns to music. ...
> And I say that life is indeed darkness save when there is urge,
> And all urge is blind save when there is knowledge,
> And all knowledge is vain save when there is work,
> And all work is empty save when there is love; ...
> And what is it to work with love? ...
> It is to charge all things you fashion with a breath of your own spirit, ...
> Work is love made visible
>
> KHALIL GIBRAN, *The Prophet* (Knopf 1923).

1 Introduction

Professor Bartha Maria Knoppers' work has been characterized by interdisciplinary approaches. Her career has largely dealt with exploring the interplay between law and bioethics, a particularly complex challenge. So, centering on the theme of how both bioethics and the law treat the human seems most appropriate to pay tribute to her. Human activities and aspirations can be specified by five Ts: Time, Tools, Technology, Treatments, and Treasures. These dimensions are intrinsic to the bioethics laws in France, which undergo regular revisions. The revisions take into account the current implementation of the law, new issues brought up by advances in science and technology and the evolution of societal attitudes regarding bioethical questions. As an introduction we wish to underline these dimensions and the relevant contributions of Professor Knoppers.

Time frames all human activities. Time can be perceived as both a strength or as a constraint. Time for the formulation and implementation of bioethics laws is an essential feature as we will see below.

DOI:10.1163/9789004688544_015

Tools and Technology go hand-in-hand as bioethics laws attempt to address both their existing and future capacities. Law is a tool to regulate and a binding instrument. Bioethics also has its own analytical tools.

The law addresses various aspects of biomedical advancements, involving numerous tools, techniques, and technologies. Evaluating the law's effects and consulting stakeholders through various means are crucial steps in revising laws as the tools and technologies evolve. The process of revising the law is in itself also a tool.

Treatment. The core focus of bioethics laws lies in advancing treatments in biomedicine and ensuring regulations are in place to facilitate these advancements responsibly. These laws are integral in upholding fundamental rights and values within our society. Laws protect fundamental rights and values of individuals and communities.

Treasures. Health and its progress, in addition to being desirable, are considered a kind of treasure in our society, and this gives a specific dimension to the bioethics laws. Both knowledge and health are being seen not only as a right but as treasures to be protected and made accessible and the bioethics laws make explicit what we consider licit to do regarding these treasures.

Professor Knoppers has consistently shown deep interest in the bioethics laws in France and always followed their developments closely. As a renowned international bioethics expert[1] and as a specialist of comparative health law,[2] she embodies two other "T" dimensions in her work: *Talent* and *Trust*. In the chapter that follows, we explore some normative challenges of combining bioethics and law approaches, and how the French bioethics laws have managed to reconcile them. This allows us to examine how Professor Knoppers' interdisciplinary scholarship has managed these differences and has contributed to the advancement of human health, policy, and bioethics debates throughout her illustrious career.

2 Is Bioethics Law an Oxymoron?

Lawyers, social scientists, and humanities scholars have long debated when and how the law should intervene on addressing bioethical issues in practice. These questions were at the heart of Professor Knoppers' research, positioning

1 See e.g. Centre of Genomics and Policy, available at: https://www.genomicsandpolicy.org/en/research/international_partnerships.

2 See e.g. Bartha Maria Knoppers, 'Foreword' in Andrea Boggio, Cesare PR Romano, and Jessica Almqvist (eds), *Human Germline Genome Modification and the Right to Science: A Comparative Study of National Laws and Policies* (Cambridge University Press 2020).

her work as that of a lawyer looking at the interplay between law and other types of norms, such as ethics or policy. The relationship between bioethics and law raises two main questions for us: (1) *are bioethics and laws fundamentally different?* and (2) *when and for what purposes should bioethics and the law be brought together?*

2.1 *Bioethics: A Conceptual and Methodological Approach*

In order to see how bioethics and the law might interact, we must first define each of these terms and those that might be understood as similar. Bioethics and law are distinct in nature, even if they overlap. Bioethics is rooted in moral theory and ethics that circumscribe a set of values and principles that should guide human activity towards the good. Bioethics applies moral theories to health and the use of new health technologies. Beauchamp and Childress propose four foundational bioethics principles,[3] comprising autonomy (appropriate information and consent), non-maleficence (do no harm), beneficence (act for the good), and justice (non-discrimination, equal access). In medicine or research, professionals must balance these principles in given situations to ensure that their actions can be considered moral. These principles aim to resolve dilemmas that may arise in the medical or research decision-making process, and should provide, in a deliberative manner, an acceptable strategy for the benefit of patients/research participants. Although these principles can be considered universal, the way they are implemented in different countries may differ,[4] and take into account cultural, social, and legal traditions.

The law consists of binding rules adopted by democratic institutions and enforced by a controlling one. Laws are usually adopted when the institutions (parliaments, governments) consider that an issue falls within the scope of the law, as defined in their constitution or constitutional framework. In France, the adoption of bioethics laws[5] was decided at the end of the 1980s, following several reports[6] calling for binding rules that respect the individual and

---

3 Tom L Beauchamp and James F Childress, *Principles of Biomedical Ethics* (8th edn, Oxford University Press 2019).

4 Daniel Callahan, 'Universalism & particularism: fighting to a draw' (2000) 30 The Hastings Center Report 37.

5 Loi n° 94-653 du 29 juillet 1994 relative au respect du corps humain; loi n°1994-954 du 29 Juillet 1994 relative au don et à l'utilisation des éléments et produits du corps humain, à l'assistance médicale à la procréation et au diagnostic prénatal; Loi n° 94-548 du 1 juillet 1994 relative au traitement de données nominatives ayant pour fin la recherche dans le domaine de la santé et modifiant la loi n° 78-17 du 6 janvier 1978 relative à l'informatique, aux fichiers et aux libertés.

6 Conseil d'État, Sciences de la vie, De l'éthique au droit, La documentation française, Notes et Etudes documentaires, 1988; «Avis sur les sciences de la vie et les droits de l'homme», CNCDH 21/12/1989.

their dignity.[7] The codification of bioethics in law is based on the position that patients and research subjects are entitled to special protections. The CNCDH (Commission nationale consultative des droits de l'Homme) has therefore justified the need for a law on life sciences by stating that "the state of current biomedical practices and the dangers that some of them may pose to the rights of individuals make it necessary for the legislator to take a stand."[8] At the time of the debate on the first bioethics laws, there was a need to adapt previous outdated legislation in France (such as that on organ donation) and to adopt new rules that took account of certain medical advances (e.g. assisted reproduction), but with the same objective of ensuring that individuals have a say in their medical situation.

Policies[9] differ from laws in that they are procedures and measures that institutions adopt and impose different duties on various actors. The main objectives of policies are to establish harmonized standards for the conduct of biomedical activities and common rules for a certain degree of harmonisation of practice. They are usually guidelines that are not binding, except in certain cases where compliance is required.

From a practical point of view, when laws are enacted in the field of health, they are intended to protect and secure the rights of individuals. This means that health professionals, such as doctors or researchers, are expected to provide healthcare or carry out research in accordance with the requirements set out in legislation. Therefore, these professionals are legally responsible and can be held liable for non-compliance. Most healthcare and human research regulations require that patients and research participants are adequately informed about how the medical or research procedures will be carried out and that they give appropriate consent. The modalities of informed consent may differ depending on the medical procedure (e.g. medical follow-up, organ donation, assisted reproduction, research,) and on the person involved (e.g. minors, persons incapable of giving consent) and sometimes need to be in writing (e.g. genetic testing). As an example, the practice of obtaining informed consent from a bioethics perspective is motivated not necessarily by legal obligation, but rather to cope with the principle of autonomy and respect for persons. In her scholarship, Professor Knoppers has consistently promoted both the legal

7 This vision commenced in 1988 with the adoption of the law on research, known as the Huriet-Serusclat law, Loi n° 88-1138 du 20 décembre 1988 relative à la protection des personnes qui se prêtent à des recherches biomédicales.

8 CNCDH (n 6).

9 Marion Danis and Rahul Nayak, 'Health Policy' in Henk ten Have (ed), *Encyclopedia of Global Bioethics* (Springer 2016).

and normative bioethics significance for patients and research participants, ensuring a humanistic application of emerging technologies as well as in how societies govern these technologies.[10] Taken together, policies activate ethical norms through rules and also translate the rule of law into practice.

2.2 *Bioethics and Laws: Effective Boundaries?*

Students often point out the differences between law and bioethics.[11] First, law and bioethics differ in the way they are adopted and, second, how they are implemented in our legal systems. Laws are enacted through a parliamentary process intended to represent the will of the people. Law-making therefore manifests a democratic process, even if the people are not invited to participate directly, but through their representatives. Making laws then means making rules binding on concerned parties.[12]

Bioethics, in contrast, is aspirational and deliberative. Even if bioethics laws are considered as standards, the process by which rules are created stem from deliberations between many stakeholders.

Professor Knoppers shifted away from the strict requirement for lawyers to confine their analysis solely within legal boundaries. Instead, she advocated for a broader approach, acknowledging that in areas where the law lacks clear guidance—such as in ethical dilemmas, policy considerations, or emerging scientific fields—it is essential to incorporate various perspectives and integrate bioethical norms and values. Integrating such broader perspectives is crucial for understanding the impact of new technologies on healthcare and ensuring policies respond to the needs of individuals and communities.

Law and bioethics, while distinct fields, intersect in many ways. They share common concerns and influence one another. Therefore, they should not be treated as separate entities, according to Professor Knoppers, but rather viewed as interconnected elements that must be brought together to address complex health innovations. Bioethics' flexibility is particularly useful for lawmakers, administrators, and judges, as it enables them to interpret legal principles and apply them to specific cases.

---

10 Rosario M Isasi and Bartha M Knoppers, 'Governing stem cell banks and registries: emerging issues' (2009) 3 Stem Cell Research 96; Edward S Dove, Yann Joly Y, and Bartha M Knoppers, 'Power to the people: a wiki-governance model for biobanks; (2012) 13 Genome Biology 158.

11 Alexander M Capron and Vicki Michel, 'Law and bioethics' (1993) 27 Loyola of Los Angeles Law Review 25.

12 Bartha Maria Knoppers, *Conception artificielle et responsabilité médicale. Une* étude *de droit comparé* (Éditions Yvon Blais 1986).

But for this normative interplay between bioethics and law to be effective, the following tensions must be resolved.

2.3 *Positivism and Principlism*

Professor Knoppers was trained as a lawyer in both France and Canada, and has always drawn on her skill sets in comparative law.[13] As such, she rejects analytical approaches that only rely on positivist interpretations of the law and that do not also account for moral norms.[14] Since her earliest writings, she has insisted on the need not to limit the questions raised by new health technologies only to legal texts, but to expand analyses to ethics and policy questions.[15] Her more integrated legal analysis follows the law as it evolves from development, to negotiation, implementation, and evaluation.

2.4 *Internormativity*

To effectively address the challenges presented by an integrated positivist and principlist approach to bioethics policy making for innovative health technologies, an adaptive methodological approach is crucial. Professor Knoppers exemplifies this inclusive approach in her work, recognizing the importance of expanding competencies beyond just legal expertise on research teams. Professor Knoppers has furthermore found that this interconnected approach can be a suitable way to tackle intractable ethical challenges in emerging health technologies and becomes especially necessary when legal norms fail to address emerging situations that require regulation.

Bioethics and the law operate on different timelines, which allows bioethics policies to respond more rapidly than the law to new ethical issues raised by emerging technology. Indeed, Professor Knoppers has been vocal that not every new technology compels the creation or modification of laws. She has always underscored the importance of evaluating whether existing laws could adequately address the technological novelty or if alternative normative sources can regulate it effectively. The decision to amend or introduce new laws should only be made if fundamental rights are at risk.

---

13 ibid.

14 'Legal positivism', Oxford reference, available at: https://www.oxfordreference.com/display/10.1093/oi/authority.20110803100058162.

15 See e.g. Bartha Maria Knoppers and Ruth Chadwick, 'The Human Genome Project: under an international ethical microscope' (1994) 265 Science 2035.

2.5 *Interdisciplinarity*

Interdisciplinarity calls for collaborations between disciplines. It can be deployed either at an individual level, for a researcher to acquire skills in various disciplines or, at a more collective level in making stakeholders collaborating together.

Internal interdisciplinarity. As researchers in the humanities and social sciences, we have specialized expertise in disciplines such as ethics, philosophy, sociology, and anthropology. The international community has pushed for bioethics to be a recognized field of empirical research that is not limited to a single discipline, but rather requires that researchers acquire skills across several disciplines. For this reason, some lawyers, notably Professor Knoppers,[16] have developed competencies in ethics, philosophy, and genetics, which enable them to more fully grasp the technical and policy relevant implications for law or policy making purposes and which in turn strengthens their policy-making ability. However, many countries do not recognize bioethics as a main discipline, as is the case in France.[17] This reality has probably influenced the adoption of bioethics laws in this country.

External interdisciplinarity. In order to address challenges that affect several scientific communities, there is a need to discuss complex issues in an interdisciplinary way, as Professor Knoppers' research clearly demonstrates.[18] Bioethics is inherently interdisciplinary. As a result, rigorous bioethics research in emerging technology captures views of multiple stakeholders to inform whether and why such technology is ethically acceptable.

Transdisciplinarity. In recent years, it has been argued that interdisciplinarity should be more open to end users, patients, research participants, and the general public, in order to better contribute to the development of ethical or legal standards in a participatory way. The transdisciplinary[19] approach aims to involve more community members as experts in formative policy discussions to ensure that the questions raised by health innovations are formulated and prioritized according to community need, and also to enhance community

16 See e.g. Michael JS Beauvais and others, 'Frontline Ethico-Legal Issues in Childhood Cancer Genetics Research' in David Malkin (ed), *The Hereditary Basis of Childhood Cancer* (Springer 2021).

17 Henri-Corto Stoeklé, Christian Hervé, and Guillaume Vogt, 'Bioethics as a science: an epistemological and methodological reflection' (2020) 13 Ethics, Medicine and Public Health 100473.

18 Bartha Maria Knoppers and Ruth Chadwick, 'Human genetic research: emerging trends in ethics' (2005) 6 Nature Reviews Genetics 75.

19 Gunther Tress, Bärbel Tress, and Gary Fry, 'Clarifying integrative research concepts in landscape ecology' (2005) 20 Landscape Ecology 479.

buy-in of proposed solutions. This method is fully in line with the current expectations of both patients and policymakers, and has also been a key part of the recent work of Professor Knoppers.[20]

2.6 *Interoperability*

Finally, science is a global endeavour. However, laws are jurisdictional and can differ from the local, regional, national, European, and international levels. This mismatch can create ethical and legal tensions that make regulations of emerging technology not interoperable. This problem, also known as the fragmentation/defragmentation challenge, is well known in international law.[21] At least two fundamental questions therefore emerge: (1) *What is the optimal scope of regulation?* and (2) *How, if at all, can regulations be harmonized to facilitate application across jurisdictions*?[22] In bioethics, interoperability is a challenge because jurisdictions tend to adopt rules and regulations that are in line with their own societal norms but may differ in other jurisdictions, leading to fragmentation. Such tensions are ripe for scholarship in comparative law, for which Professor Knoppers is an international authority.

Laws restrict what can and cannot be done, including in medicine and biomedical research. Although it may be technically feasible to develop an innovative technology, the law may deem it socially unacceptable, as seen with genome editing in embryos. In France, "Bioéthique à la française"[23] incorporates the moral and cultural vision needed to respond effectively to emerging technology. We now turn to explore this more in depth.

---

20 Yann Joly and others, 'The GA4GH Regulatory and Ethics Work Stream (REWS) at 10: An Interdisciplinary, Participative Approach to International Policy Development in Genomics' in Marcelo Corrales Compagnucci and others (eds), *The Law and Ethics of Data Sharing in Health Sciences* (Springer 2023).

21 Pierre-Marie Dupuy, 'A doctrinal debate in the globalisation era: on the "fragmentation" of international law' (2007) 1 European Journal of Legal Studies 25.

22 For example, regarding "health," in the EU competencies are shared between domestic Member State laws and EU laws (supporting competency according Article 168 of the EU Treaty on the Functioning of the European Union), but the EU grasps new areas as most of the new rules are adopted through EU Regulations, which should lead to better harmonization.

23 Kristina Orfali, 'French Bioethics: The Rhetoric of Universality and the Ethics of Medical Responsibility' in Catherine Myser (ed), *Bioethics Around the Globe* (Oxford University Press 2011).

3 The Bioethics Laws in France: A Way to Reconcile?

Few jurisdictions have decided to expressly incorporate bioethical principles into legislation. France has been a pioneer in integrating bioethical principles into its legal framework since the 1980s. The creation of the Comité Consultatif National d'Ethique pour les sciences de la vie et de la santé (CCNE) via presidential decree in 1983 marked the beginning of this journey.[24] It is striking that the installation of a national body with an independent advisory and reflection function regarding bioethics issues precedes the implementation in law of bioethics principles. The CCNE's continued existence shows the complementarity of the two paths. This demonstrates an attempt to capture both law and bioethics complexity, not to choose between law or bioethics complexity. The CCNE's missions have been strengthened by law itself, showing that the paradoxical situation of bioethics and law described above is smoothed through this coexistence.

3.1 *The Path of Bioethics into Laws*

Protecting individuals participating in health-related research was the aim of the first French law regulating biomedical research in 1988.[25] This legislation incorporated international bioethical principles and rules from documents such as the World Medical Association's Declaration of Helsinki into national law. It is remarkable that this approach placed the "human aspect" at the heart of the legislation. The law is not presented as a way to regulate research, but rather as a means to protect research participants. And it is not without consequence that the committees examining research protocols, the composition of which is described in this law, are designated as "committees for the protection of persons" and not as usually in most countries as "research ethics committees." The law's general applicability is also worthy of consideration.

The law's obligations and protections apply to all actors in research, whatever their institutional situation. This is in contrast to the wide use of ethics committees that are responsible for an institution, whose independence may not be guaranteed. The law has evolved over time,[26] but the core humanistic characteristics of the legislative text remain.

---

24 Décret n°83-132 du 23 février 1983 portant création d'un Comité consultatif national d'éthique pour les sciences de la vie et de la santé.

25 Loi n° 88-1138 du 20 décembre 1988 relative à la protection des personnes qui se prêtent à des recherches biomédicales.

26 LOI n° 2012-300 du 5 mars 2012 relative aux recherches impliquant la personne humaine.

We believe that the bioethics law is the best example of this complex interplay between ethics and law. Before discussing its content and how revisions are conducted, it is worthwhile recalling that the French bioethics law does not comprehensively cover all areas of human activity where bioethical principles are at stake. For example, biomedical research is in a different law, which we have just discussed, and issues pertaining to medical aid in dying are currently being debated in a separate legislative process at the time of writing.

The first bioethics law in 1994 required that it be revised after five years of application. An obligation to periodically revise the law is found in all successive versions of the bioethics law. Three revisions have occurred over the 30 years since the law's enactment: one in 2004, one in 2011, and one in 2021.[27] The present indicated period for revision is seven years, unless circumstances require earlier revision. This never occurred but the fact that there are provisions to face a possible new unexpected situation requiring urgent action is to be underlined. This obligation to revise takes into account both the evolution of the scientific and technological landscape and the evolution of societal positions on bioethics issues. It is also a characteristic of the profoundly human aspect of such laws: the domain is not frozen and must evolve to continue to frame the field in a human-centric manner. This very much echoes what Professors Knoppers and Chadwick were writing in 2005: "Ethics does not consist of a static set of theories or principles that can unproblematically be 'applied' to new situations."[28] And this is reflected also in the legislator's creation of the obligation to revise the bioethics law from the law's inception.

3.2 *The Evolution of the Content of Successive Bioethics Laws*

In brief, the domains addressed in the present bioethics law are as follows.

1. Assisted Human Reproduction: This includes regulations on who can receive assistance, the conditions under which it is provided, and the rights of children born as a result of such assistance. These issues are addressed under the general umbrella of reaffirming bioethical principles while promoting access to new technologies.
2. Organ and Tissue Donation: The law addresses the donation—for either therapeutic or research purposes—of blood, cells, organs, and even whole bodies after death, balancing the principles of solidarity and autonomy. Balancing solidarity and autonomy likewise informs access to genetic information potentially medically useful to family members.

27 LOI n° 2021-1017 du 2 août 2021 relative à la bioéthique.

28 Knoppers and Chadwick (n 18).

3. Big Data: Regulations are provided for the use of genetic testing in healthcare, the application of algorithmic tools that use large data sets, and imaging for clinical care or research.
4. Support of Responsible and Free Health Research: The law outlines conditions for conducting research on embryos, embryonic cells, and induced pluripotent cells, as well as the use of genetic information in research. It also introduces the concept of a program of research, a broader concept than a research project.
5. Quality and Safety in Healthcare: Recommendations are made for practices in various medical fields, including prenatal and neonatal screening, medical termination of pregnancy, and fertility preservation. This part also deals with issues such as troubles in sexual development and measures of healthcare organization, e.g. in prescribing and managing the various genetic tests or for the use of faeces for treatment purposes (microbiota), and the therapeutic use of autologous cells.
6. Governance and Public Debate: The law details the roles of various authorities and committees, including an expanded role for the CCNE in public debates on bioethics. The CCNE's expanded mandate includes societal questions that are beyond biological approaches (for example, a new technology coming from digital or physics domains and has health applications). It furthermore creates the Agence de la biomédecine (Biomedical Agency), which is responsible for the application and enforcement of the bioethics law.

The final part sets the seven-year revision period. It is remarkable that many of the law's subjects are those that have been at the heart of Professor Knoppers' research for 40 years. We also note that her wise counsel has been sought for a number of these revisions.

Our purpose is not to go into detail on these different domains and their regulation, but rather to show that the law's vocation is to reconcile conflicting values and principles across areas of application. We believe that the law is the translation of the duality of bioethics and law described in the first part of this chapter. There is a contrast between the overarching framework, an architecture that appears notably in the titles of the articles of the law, referring to principles, which is very close to analytical bioethics texts or ethics committee recommendations, and the detailed technical and organizational elements addressed in the text.

3.3 *Examples of the Evolution of Content*

The revisions of bioethics laws over time provide a fascinating insight into how legal frameworks adapt to ethical and scientific advancements. A notable area of focus has been the regulation of research on human embryos and the use of derived cell lines, a domain of particular interest for Professor Knoppers.[29] Initially, such research was prohibited, but over time, the laws evolved to allow exceptions, then conditional authorizations, and most recently, a shift to declarations instead of authorizations for certain types of research. Whereas with an authorization, one has to wait until they get an approval, with a declaration one simply informs the authority of the research that is conducted. A similar trend has emerged regarding the conditions for research on human embryos, once it was considered possible. Initially, the research that could be performed was strictly limited to therapeutic purposes such as for the improvement of in-vitro fertilization techniques, or the development of a cure for a defined condition. Over time, the regulations broadened to encompass a wider range of research, removing the strict requirement for a therapeutic objective, but keeping a medically-oriented research purpose. Most recently, permitted categories of research encompass biological knowledge in a more general sense.

In the realm of genetic testing, the evolution of laws concerning the sharing of genetic information with family members, while safeguarding medical confidentiality, personal autonomy, and the right to informed choice, has been a significant area of focus. (See also Chapter 14 in this volume.) This has been an enduring interest of Professor Knoppers.[30] Initially, the responsibility for sharing actionable genetic information was recognized as a moral duty. Over time, this responsibility has been formalized into a legal obligation, with various approaches to its implementation.[31]

The most recent legal amendments have introduced a legal responsibility for patients to share critical genetic information if withholding such information could lead to severe consequences for family members. For example, sharing information about a pathogenic variant could have facilitated genetic counselling for reproductive choices, thus preventing the birth of a child with a severe condition. Or if an early detection of a genetic variant could have been medically actionable, allowing an appropriate prevention or early treatment, whereas an advanced disease became untreatable due to a failure to communicate the information. Initially, a complex mechanism was proposed, involving a national agency tasked with notifying family members anonymously if the individual directly affected chose not to disclose the information themselves.

---

29 Bartha Maria Knoppers, Sylvie Bordet, and Rosario Isasi, 'The Human Embryo: Ethical and Legal Aspects' in Cathy Vaillancourt and Julie Lafond (eds) *Human Embryogenesis: Methods in Molecular Biology* (Humana Press 2009).

30 Bartha Maria Knoppers, 'Genetic information and the family: are we our brother's keeper?' (2002) 20 Trends in Biotechnology 85.

31 Marine Gaboriau, 'L'information génétique familiale: secret, autonomie et responsabilité' (2014) 1 Cancer(s) et psy(s)122.

However, this system proved to be ineffective due to operational complexities. Subsequent revisions simplified the process, allowing the disclosure of information to be performed by the medical doctor who ordered the genetic test. If the notified individuals seek further details or wish to undergo genetic testing, they can obtain more comprehensive information from a medical genetics specialist.

The bioethics law has also evolved to address the challenges associated with incidental findings in large-scale genomic testing, an area where Professor Knoppers has been particularly active and which has sparked significant global discussion.[32] Initially, the law restricted the return of test results to those directly related to the initial scope of the prescription for testing. However, the most recent amendments have introduced a requirement to inform patients about the potential for incidental findings and to ascertain their preferences regarding the disclosure of such findings through informed consent. This change in regulation, marking a significant shift in the approach to genetics in the 2021 bioethics law, extends to the sharing of critical genetic information with family members and applies even when incidental findings emerge during research.

Another notable shift in the law's focus is its expansion from strictly medical or research-related matters to broader societal issues for which biotechnologies offer a possible answer. A prime illustration of this evolution is the adaptation of medical assistance for procreation policies. Initially designed as a medical response to infertility, the application of medical assistance for procreation has been broadened to include all women, encompassing female couples.[33] This particular change to the bioethics law garnered significant media attention, underscoring a broader trend towards integrating societal considerations into bioethics legislation. This media focus created an imbalance in the public perception of the purpose of the law, while in fact the law itself is covering many other important areas.

One can wonder whether such examples reflect a slippery slope that would constitute the model of evolution of the bioethics laws whereby society just needs a certain time to "swallow" innovations. We believe that this slippery slope view is a superficial analysis and a deeper look is required.

3.4 *Relations between the Content and the Process*

This evolution, while adhering to the same underlying principles, has various facets and different bases.

---

32 Bartha Maria Knoppers, Ma'n H Zawati, and Karine Sénécal, 'Return of genetic testing results in the era of whole-genome sequencing' (2015) 16 Nature Reviews Genetics 553.

33 René Frydman, 'Quatrième loi de bioéthique 2021: un passage progressif du médical au sociétal pour la procréation' (2021) 37 Médecine/Sciences (Paris) 1087.

Firstly, there is a focus on observing actual conditions: the types of research being conducted, how existing laws are applied, emerging scientific developments, techniques, and knowledge, as well as the suitability of current regulatory measures. This approach shifts from cautious experimentation in uncertain conditions to a comprehensive evaluation of real-world practices, ultimately guiding the development of evidence-based policy. This is a way to face the "evidentiary time lag," which occurs between the moment when a technology is considered ready and in principle applicable and the moment when data on issues actually encountered through its application are available. This is a time period with considerable uncertainty on how to optimally apply the technology; revising the law allows us to take this into account.

Secondly, there is a comparative analysis of how other countries approach similar issues, which is particularly relevant to highlight in connection with Professor Knoppers' expertise in comparative law. Rather than focusing solely on French regulations and practices, this approach emphasizes the overarching human consequences and the need to protect vulnerable populations. For instance, the approach considers the importance of preventing disparities in access to healthcare; certain validated medical advancements may be available in other countries but not in France, making them accessible only to those with greater financial means. This situation may prompt the promotion of such treatments or the research leading to their development, even if they were previously unauthorized, based on the principles of equity and equality, provided that there is societal acceptance or desire for them, taking a more comprehensive view of the field.

Finally, there is improvement in the way public debates and consultations are conducted for each subject. As already noted, the public consultation has radically changed since the preparatory phase of the first bioethics law. As expressed at the time of the first revision of the law by Jennifer Merchant:

> Hence, with the CCNE settling more comfortably into its role as a purely consultative organism, and the growth and emergence of the civil society, especially grass-roots and interest groups, France has now firmly placed both feet into the modernity of biomedical practices and their consequences. Chances are that this new-found role of France's civil society in bioethical issues will soon play an even more important part in the shaping of future law revisions; what was once a process bringing experts to legislation might soon become one of bringing public debate to legislation, something we can certainly hope for.[34]

34 Jennifer Merchant, 'From legislation to debate: the regulation of assisted reproduction, human cloning, and embryonic stem cell (ESC) research in France' (undated), available at: https://web.stanford.edu/dept/france-stanford/Conferences/Bioethics/Merchant.pdf.

The evolution of the various ways of involving the public in bioethics debates prior to the revision of laws is paradigmatic of how civil society is increasingly considered in its various modes of expression. The fact that the CCNE is now open to societal questions and in charge of related public debates, as well as its enlarged mandate to consider the consequences for health of scientific progress in any domain, not only biological sciences, are a sign of the different appraisals of bioethics today.

Behind the content of the law, the process and the debates represent the most "human" aspect, the "humanful" within the "lawful." Analyzing the evolution of the process involving both experts and the public is valuable. The most comprehensive approach in 2018 was the "États généraux de la bioéthique," which combined a variety of complementary methods under the responsibility of the CCNE.[35] This included an online consultation, a series of coordinated debates on the main areas of the law held throughout France and led by regional bioethics structures that reported to the CCNE for the final synthesis. Additionally, a panel of citizens was consulted in a structured manner, and they provided recommendations. These efforts were in addition to meetings of experts organised by the CCNE itself and to reports from various ethics bodies. The "États généraux de la bioéthique" supplemented reports from agencies and institutions such as the Biomedical Agency (l'Agence de la biomédecine), the CCNE in its advisory role, the State Council (le Conseil d'État), the Parliamentary Office for Evaluating Scientific and Technological Choices (OPEST – l'Office parlementaire d'évaluation des choix scientifiques et technologiques), and a parliamentary commission. Comparing the convergence, divergence, and impact of all these elements within the revision process is a research topic for the humanities and social sciences, viewed through the lens of health democracy, that describes how democratic processes are gradually shaping health governance systems.[36] This interdisciplinary dimension, encompassing law, bioethical issues, and diverse scientific communities, is paradigmatic of Professor Knoppers' approach and likely represents the future direction of bioethics laws.

35 Rapport de synthèse des États généraux de la bioéthique. Comité consultatif national d'éthique (Juin 2018), available at: https://www.ccne-ethique.fr/fr/publications/rapport-de-synthese-des-etats-generaux-de-la-bioethique.

36 Jean-François Delfraissy and Pierre-Henri Duée, 'Chapitre 2. La loi de bioéthique: un enjeu de démocratie sanitaire' (2023) 34 Journal International de Bioéthique et d'Éthique des Sciences 33.

4 Conclusion: Bioethics Laws beyond Individuals: B.A.R.T.H.A.'s Approach

Looking back at the history of bioethics, the main stance of scholars who have worked in this field has been to identify and construct a framework (which has evolved into different types of norms) with the aim of protecting the individual in two regards: firstly, as the less powerful party in the medical or research relationship, and secondly, to ensure that their rights are fully protected in relation to the emergence of new technologies. However, while there is an ongoing need to support this approach, Professor Knoppers has expanded the scope of bioethics to look beyond a single law and beyond the individual (whether researcher, patient, or research participant). To achieve this, she has developed methods and collaborations through what we can call the B.A.R.T.H.A. approach.

Bartha's "children." Throughout her career, Professor Knoppers has sought to pass on her knowledge and to involve young researchers in her vision of bioethics and medical law. Several scholars have collaborated with her in various social and humanistic disciplines (law, philosophy, sociology, political science) as well as in the life sciences (medicine, genetics, biology). These scholars are spread all over the world and carry on Professor Knoppers' bioethical tradition. She has strongly supported young researchers by sharing her experience and wisdom in many areas of contemporary biomedicine and by enabling them to network broadly across countries.

Anticipation. Professor Knoppers' research and expertise illustrate the ambition to go beyond the law, which is not always the ideal type of norm for anticipating biomedical progress.[37] Her inter-normative approach has demonstrated the effectiveness of engaging with multiple normative systems to anticipate the necessary frameworks when biomedical innovations emerge. This anticipatory approach has successfully supported technological advancements while safeguarding human rights.[38] It not only allows for balancing scientific progress and the potential risks to individuals but also fosters a convergence between the two, bringing together various disciplines around a shared vision of bioethics.

---

37 Bartha Maria Knoppers and Vural Özdemir, 'The Concept of Humanity and Biogenetics' in Britta van Beers, Luigi Corrias, and Wouter G Werner (eds), *Humanity Across International Law and Biolaw* (Cambridge University Press 2014).

38 As an example, we can refer to the work done during the Human Genome Project (HGP), where Professor Knoppers led the Ethics Committee of the Human Genome Organization (which at the time helped coordinate and enhance efforts in the HGP). See Bartha Maria Knoppers and Lori Luther, 'The Human Genome Organization (HUGO)' (1997) 16 Politics and the Life Sciences 127.

Regulations. Professor Knoppers is a lawyer and she has never denied being one. She has employed the term "regulation" in an expansive sense, not confining it solely to the legal realm. In this context, she undertakes a meticulous legal analysis of the law, not merely to criticize it but also to elucidate and make accessible the rights and obligations that the law bestows. Nevertheless, to account for the intricacies of health innovations and the necessity to refer to norms beyond mere regulations, she has embraced the Ethical, Legal, and Social Implications (ELSI) approach to provide a comprehensive framework, offering a fresh perspective on contemporary bioethics research activities.[39] As a jurist, she applies this normative and conceptual approach in various fields (e.g. genomics, cancer, neurology, data protection), always with the aim of promoting medical progress and protecting the most vulnerable.[40] It is worthwhile noting that "R" could as well be discussed as rights, reflection, and of course research!

Tour de table. Collaboration is at the heart of the research that Professor Knoppers spearheads.[41] She has initiated many of ELSI's contributions to renewed consortia (e.g. in 2013, she became Chair of the Regulatory and Ethics Working Group of Global Alliance for Genomics and Health and a member of its Steering Committee). The same year, she contributed to the recommendations of the European Society of Human Genetics on whole-genome sequencing for clinical care.[42] In 2007, she led key initiatives and programs such as P^{3}G (Public Population Project in Genomics & Society) and CARTaGENE, Quebec's longitudinal cohort and biobank. Moreover, she has served on seemingly innumerable boards and committees. All of these talented contributions are rooted in her legal background and have certainly influenced the way legislators and policymakers have drafted new bioethics regulations and laws.

Human/ity. As we have already mentioned, Professor Knoppers has used bioethics and bioethical laws to reconcile biomedical innovation with the promotion of fundamental personal rights. She has recalled several times the importance of prior information and consent as bioethical pillars, but she went beyond the sacralization of these principles, recalling that they have limits and

39 Lisa S Parker and others, 'Normative and conceptual ELSI research: what it is, and why it's important' (2019) 21 Genetics in Medicine 505.

40 See e.g. Dimitri Patrinos and others, 'Whither health research: the missed opportunities of the child's right to health' (2023) 31 The International Journal of Children's Rights 865.

41 See e.g. Mark A Rothstein and others, 'Concordance of international regulation of pediatric health research' (2023) 260 The Journal of Pediatrics 113524.

42 Carla G van El and others, 'Whole-genome sequencing in health care' (2013) 21 European Journal of Human Genetics 580.

therefore that governance must also play a role in contemporary bioethics.[43] Moreover, the originality of Professor Knoppers' approach has been to explore other "subjects" of rights. Like other bioethics scholars and bioethics laws/ policies, she expanded the perspective beyond just patients and research participants to examine the issues surrounding biomedicine and family members, especially in the field of genetics. This includes their access to information that is protected by professional secrecy but could be relevant to the health of relatives.[44] Additionally, she has investigated the impact of medical advancements on the respect for humanity, particularly in relation to UNESCO's Universal Declaration on the Human Genome and Human Rights, where she was a key promoter of the idea that the human genome is the heritage of humanity.[45] Professor Knoppers has also placed the human rights approach at the core of data sharing in genomics.[46] Moreover, she has made significant contributions to the legal qualification and legal regimes of what can be considered human and what can be considered "things."[47] This question has been and continues to be crucial, given the challenges posed by the development of biobanks and the use and re-use of human biological samples.[48]

Airplanes. Finally, even if we are all committed to reducing our air travel in order to better preserve our planet, we must thank the airplanes for giving Professor Knoppers and all of us the opportunity to meet in person, to exchange views, and to try to move bioethics forward for the benefit of all stakeholders involved in biomedicine and innovation. Let us hope that we still have the chance to go beyond our borders and make bioethics international, while respecting our diversity and cultures, which is probably a proposition with which Professor Knoppers would agree. But we would like to conclude this contribution with another word, a French one, that Professor Knoppers was especially talented at cultivating: "Amitié"—friendship.

---

43 See e.g. Bartha Maria Knoppers and others, 'Modeling consent in the time of COVID-19' (2020) 7 Journal of Law and the Biosciences lsaa020; Kieran C O'Doherty and others, 'Toward better governance of human genomic data' (2021) 53 Nature Genetics 2.

44 Knoppers (n 30).

45 UNESCO, Universal Declaration on the Human Genome and Human Rights (1997).

46 Bartha Maria Knoppers, 'Framework for responsible sharing of genomic and health-related data' (2014) 8 The HUGO Journal 3; Bartha M Knoppers and others, 'A human rights approach to an international code of conduct for genomic and clinical data sharing' (2014) 133 Human Genetics 895.

47 Bartha Maria Knoppers and Henry T Greely, 'Biotechnologies nibbling at the legal "human"' (2019) 366 Science 1455.

48 Anne Cambon-Thomsen, Emmanuelle Rial-Sebbag, and Bartha M Knoppers, 'Trends in ethical and legal frameworks for the use of human biobanks' (2007) 30 European Respiratory Journal 373; Bartha Maria Knoppers, 'Biobanking: international norms' (2005) 33 Journal of Law, Medicine & Ethics 7.

VIGNETTE

Bartha, Biobanking, and Success

Jane Kaye

Where do you start, when you are asked to comment about Bartha Knoppers' contributions to the field? Bartha has had a stellar career and has been involved in establishing so many international initiatives, large-scale interdisciplinary projects, and writing cutting-edge publications that there are too many to recount. Her work has had an incredible impact on the field of international bioethics, especially in genomics. Her publications and activities have been prolific, attesting to a great sense of purpose, vision, and energy, guided by the values instilled through her upbringing.

My first interactions with Bartha were in the field of biobanking and the Public Population Project in Genomics (P³G).[1] This organization was formally established in 2004 under the leadership of Bartha Knoppers and Thomas Hudson, and was funded in 2007 by Genome Quebec and Genome Canada, as well as other funding agencies. In Bartha's words, the aim of P³G was to

> create, harmonize and share methods, tools and information so as to enhance the design of emerging biobanks and to promote compatibility–between studies–of data (e.g. socioeconomic and clinical), samples and supporting infrastructure (eg sample- and data-management systems). The potential for data pooling to optimize statistical power is, thereby, increased and pivotal findings can more rapidly and effectively be replicated or validated.[2]

This was at a time when many countries were establishing national biobanks, designed to be longitudinal resources for many research projects.[3] As former P³G members Sylvie Ouellette and Anne-Marie Tassé noted, "Originally, P³G served four different but complementary population genomics research

1 P3G aimed to facilitate collaboration between many national biobanks in a not-for-profit initiative, providing a public and accessible knowledge database for the international population genomics community.

2 Bartha M Knoppers and others, 'Population Genomics: The Public Population Project in Genomics (P3G): a proof of concept?' (2008) 16 European Journal of Human Genetics 664.

3 Jocelyn Kaiser, 'Biobanks: population databases boom, from Iceland to the US' (2002) 298 Science 1158.

© JANE KAYE, 2025 | DOI:10.1163/9789004688544_016

projects: CARTaGENE (Quebec); GenomEUtwin (FP5 (EC) project involving 8 countries); Estonia's genome project (Estonia); and the UK Biobank (UK). Dedicated to the development and management of multi-disciplinary research infrastructures, it sought to facilitate translational research via tools for prospective harmonization."[4] It soon expanded beyond this in response to the innovations in data science.

It is now hard to believe that before 1999, there was a lack of an agreed definition for biobanks and that they were variously labelled genetic databases, population collections, genome databases, genebank, biolibraries, and human research genetic databases.[5] Bartha was pivotal in Canada and the world stage in starting to formalize and co-ordinate these disparate but similar activities through organizations such as P³G. Although trained as a lawyer, Bartha could understand the science and the need for well-classified and organized population biobanks to further the understanding of the impact of genomics on disease. What is astounding is that she worked with Professor Claude Laberge to establish the CARTaGENE biobank for Quebec. In doing so, Bartha demonstrated her profound intelligence, skills, and capabilities, not just as a lawyer but also as a scientist. I remember reflecting with Bartha on how far biobanking had come in such a short period of time, at the launch of BBMRI-ERIC, the European biobanking research infrastructure. It was just ten years from the launch of P³G in 2003 that BBMRI-ERIC, a bespoke organization, a juridical person, and a corporation under European Union law, was established.[6] Bartha had been an instrumental player in making that happen. Bartha provided leadership in the field of biobanking that was integral to its success. Her intellectual contributions, strategic thinking, and interpersonal skills were—and are—exceptional, and resulted in—and continue to result in—a better world.

4 Sylvie Ouellette and Anne Marie Tassé, 'P3G — 10 years of toolbuilding: from the population biobank to the clinic' (2014) 3 Applied & Translational Genomics 36.

5 Don Chalmers and Dianne Nicol, 'Human genetic research databases and biobanks: towards uniform terminology and Australian best practice' (2008) 15 Journal of Law and Medicine 538.

6 2013/701/EU: Commission Implementing Decision of 22 November 2013 on setting up the Biobanks and Biomolecular Resources Research Infrastructure Consortium (BBMRI-ERIC) as a European Research Infrastructure Consortium OJ L 320, 30.11.2013, p. 63–80.

VIGNETTE

Thirty Years of Learning from Bartha

Pilar Nicolás

It is my honour to write this tribute to Professor Bartha Knoppers, who has been an admirable figure in my academic career, both personally and professionally.

In Spain, Bartha's work has been well-known since the early 1990s. In 1993 she was invited to an important conference held in Bilbao, "El Derecho ante el Proyecto Genoma Humano" (Law and the Human Genome Project). More than 100 speakers from all over the world participated. The publication of the contributions, in four volumes, in English and Spanish, had a great impact and contributed to the creation of a critical mass in "biolaw" in general and ethical and legal aspects of genetics in particular, especially in Spain and Latin America. It was also an opportunity to connect different people who then constructed entirely new lines of research. Bartha wrote a chapter entitled, "Towards Genetic Privacy," contributing ideas that are still maintained and quoted, such as the interpretation of the "triptych-diptych" nature of genetic intimacy.[1]

The Banco Bilbao Vizcaya Foundation as well as the Provincial Government of Bizkaia Chair in Law and the Human Genome at the University of Deusto were created at this conference, and later joined by the University of the Basque Country. In 2024, Bartha gave the inaugural lecture at a conference celebrating our 30th anniversary.

Bartha's contribution goes well beyond her publications and her academic footprint. I had the opportunity to work with her as a member of the Ethics and Policy Committee of the International Cancer Genome Consortium (ICGC), of which she was the Chair. Her work was exceptional. I confess that I was surprised, given her senior level and status, by her inclusive disposition, her ability and desire to listen to others in the room, and her generosity of effort. Her ability to coordinate and her efficiency in achieving objectives and solving problems were decisive in this pioneering worldwide initiative of collaboration in the sharing of genetic data for cancer research. The experiences within this project have been inspiring for many others. I learned a lot at that stage, in

1 Bartha Maria Knoppers, 'Towards genetic privacy' in Fundación BBV (ed), *The Human Genome Project: Legal Aspects* (Fundación BBV Documenta 1995).

many ways, and I owe it to Bartha. I also remember very fondly our face-to-face ICGC meetings in different countries such as Japan or Italy.

The impact of her work has both international breadth and intellectual depth—I think more than she herself realizes. I can say that her influence has been felt, through the contribution of the Chair in Law and the Human Genome, in the regulation of biomedical research in Spain, specifically concerning genetic analysis and the use of biological samples. The benefits of having a Spanish legal framework that guarantees the rights and interests of all those involved in research (of course those of patients and families but also those of researchers) owes much to Professor Knoppers. Thank you, Bartha!

CHAPTER 6

Bartha Maria Knoppers: A Standard-Bearer for Responsible Genomic and Health Data Sharing

Adrian Thorogood and Fruzsina Molnár-Gábor

1 Introduction

Professor Bartha Maria Knoppers has been a tireless promoter of genomic research, collaboration, and data sharing. She is a believer that collaborative genomics not only holds vast promise to advance scientific knowledge and human health, but that such advancement is an ethical imperative. She has had and continues to have a major impact on the field through her contributions in the areas of international policymaking, leadership in international projects, and comparative law and policy research.

Two key areas where Professor Knoppers has tremendously influenced data sharing in biomedicine—both intellectually and practically—are data governance and data protection. In terms of data governance, she has made a significant impact on international policy and practice across the entire data lifecycle, comprising collection, storage, sharing, use, and preservation. From the outset, Professor Knoppers has comprehensively identified and transparently promoted the adaptation of human rights, bioethics principles, and data governance measures to the specifics of information interventions in patient datasets and has advocated for the recognition and mitigation of risks associated with the application of new technologies, while also exploring the potential of science and technology to improve human health.[1] Professor Knoppers has been a long-time champion of the concept of broad consent, particularly in the context of population biobanks and community data resources. This is consent to sharing biosamples or data for wide areas of scientific research, subject to ongoing oversight and transparency. In large part due to her efforts, broad consent has now been widely adopted in practice as well as incorporated in policies and regulations. She has helped to define the ethics of Big Data through the development of data governance strategies and tools to support ethical integration of data from diverse sources into large-scale international

1 Bartha M Knoppers and Claude Laberge, 'DNA sampling and informed consent' (1989) 140 CMAJ: Canadian Medical Association Journal 1023.

 | DOI:10.1163/9789004688544_018

resources. She has pioneered the conceptualization and implementation of data access models that effectively, ethically, and efficiently balance the dual aims of making data available to the broad scientific community while protecting the privacy and autonomy of the research participants and patients whose data are being shared. She has also promoted coordinated ethical oversight of data-intensive health research across sites and jurisdictions through ethics review mutual recognition models.

Beyond scholarship, Professor Knoppers has been a leader in the international scientific community, helping scientists to navigate evolving data protection laws around the world, and reconcile data sharing practices with these laws. Data protection rules take different conceptual approaches to enabling data processing than research ethics. In order to foster international data-intensive scientific research, a harmonization between different approaches must be made possible, between a general permission for data processing and a prohibition with a reservation of permission. The balance between conflicting legal positions and interests is what becomes apparent in both cases in the legal provisions and in their implementation through the organization of data sharing practices. Professor Knoppers has demonstrated this in a leading role, from guiding the ethical and legal work stream of the International Cancer Genome Consortium[2] to shaping Canada's COVID data portal.[3] With her strong contribution to enabling data sharing across borders, she has succeeded in demonstrating that the risks of data processing, which are often perceived as less contoured, are just as important for those affected as the risks posed by the obstacles to data-based research. Furthermore, she has succeeded in addressing these risks in both directions—with nuanced, precise work, creating standardized documents for data processing, without losing the claim that these templates should be used by the scientific community across borders to facilitate their data protection compliance.

As many of this volume's chapters have demonstrated, the "human" is central to Professor Knoppers' work in multifaceted ways. To begin, her domain of interest is human genomics research and medicine—an exploration into the fundamental biological aspects of what it means to be both an individual, a family member, and a member of humankind. She has also focused on the intersection of human values with this very human science. Her contributions on ethical, legal, and social issues (ELSI) have also brought focus to respect for the rights and interests of the humans whose data are analyzed and shared.

2 ICGC Data Portal, available at: https://dcc.icgc.org/.

3 COVID-19 Host Genetics Initiative, available at: https://www.covid19hg.org/.

Humans are not simply Professor Knoppers' intellectual subject matter. Her outsized impact is due not only to her analytic acumen, but also to her tireless attention to human relationships. Professor Knoppers has fostered career-long collaborations and friendships with visionary scientists around the world who lead collaborative initiatives. She has helped to forge an international community of ELSI experts, bringing together diverse perspectives while also fostering a common vision within that community to drive policy harmonization. Finally, Professor Knoppers has delighted in mentoring and collaborating with ELSI scholars both at McGill University's Centre of Genomics and Policy, as well as around the world, to advance our understanding of how to foster human-centred scientific and medical progress. Both of us are extremely honoured to have had Professor Knoppers as a mentor and collaborator. We have been endlessly inspired by her intellectual curiosity, tireless work ethic, wisdom, and wit. Without a doubt she has had a defining influence on both our research interests and career trajectories.

In the following, we will focus on a selection of Professor Knoppers' key contributions in the field of data sharing, in particular to (1) international policy making, (2) data governance approaches to foster responsible data sharing, and (3) accompanying comparative law efforts to harmonise legislation and application practices. We end by highlighting why we believe Professor Knoppers' work is as relevant as ever.

2 Contributions to International Policymaking

Professor Knoppers has long promoted the ethos of data sharing in genomics that was core to the success of the Human Genome Project (HGP), captured by the Bermuda Principles.[4] Indeed, she played an important role in developing the Toronto Statement on community resource projects, which balanced responsibilities of funders, data producers, and data users.[5] Professor Knoppers also led work in international policy-making as Chair of the Human Genome Organization (HUGO) Ethics Committee, which produced a number of Statements supporting data sharing: the Principled Conduct of Genetic Research (1996), DNA Sampling: Control and Access (1998), Benefit Sharing

4 Robert Cook-Deegan, Rachel A Ankeny, and Kathryn Maxson Jones, 'Sharing data to build a medical information commons: from Bermuda to the Global Alliance' (2017) 18 Annual Review of Genomics and Human Genetics 389.

5 Toronto International Data Release Workshop Authors, 'Prepublication data sharing' (2009) 461 Nature 168.

(2000), and Human Genomic Databases (2002).[6] Work to promote genomic data sharing quickly extended to other research-relevant data types, over an extended period of time before and after significant research steps with the data, such as the publication of research results.

Reflecting Professor Knoppers' love for innovative and inspiring legal concepts, the latter statement drew on the concept of human genomic databases as "global public goods," defined as "those whose scope extends worldwide, are enjoyable by all with no groups excluded, and, when consumed by one individual are not depleted for others."[7] The Statement also highlights Professor Knoppers' acknowledgement that the scientific and societal progress (for all) promised by genomics cannot be taken for granted; it must be supported by a commitment to sustainability, excellence, and inclusion.[8]

Professor Knoppers is also well known for her founding role in the Global Alliance for Genomics and Health (GA4GH), an international, public-private collaboration with a mission to promote the responsible international sharing of genomic and related-health data to advance human health, through the development of technical standards and policy frameworks. Under Professor Knoppers' inspirational and innovative leadership, the GA4GH developed and adopted the Framework for Responsible Sharing of Genomic and Health-Related Data.[9] This framework adopted a novel "human rights" approach, aiming to activate the human right of everyone to benefit from scientific progress and its applications, a legally binding right under the United Nations' International Covenant on Economic, Social and Cultural Rights.[10] As a co-lead of the Regulatory and Ethics Working Group/Work Stream, Professor Knoppers brought together hundreds of experts to expand on the Framework through a comprehensive set of principled and pragmatic policies that now comprise the GA4GH Regulatory and Ethics Toolkit. These include a Consent Policy and

---

6 HUGO Ethics Committee, 'Statement on human genomic databases' (2003) 13 Eubios Journal of Asian and International Bioethics 99.

7 ('Knowledge useful to human health belongs to humanity.'; 'Human genomic databases are a public resource.'; 'The free flow of data and the fair and equitable distribution of benefits from research using databases should be encouraged.')

8 'b. Repositories should be established and funded to ensure the continuation of publicly available databases. c. Compatibility should be fostered through the use of common nomenclature, and, where possible, the pooling of databases should be encouraged. d. There is a scientific responsibility to ensure the professional competence of researchers working with data, as well as the quality and accuracy of the data.'

9 GA4GH, 'Framework for Responsible Sharing of Genomic and Health-Related Data' (2014), available at: https://genomicsandhealth.org/about-the-global-alliance/key-documents/framework-responsible-sharing-genomic-and-health-related-data.

10 Adopted 16 December 1966 (signed by 172 parties to date).

a variety of consent toolkits to support ethical and consistent consenting for genomic research and data sharing, addressing a range of contexts, populations, and issues (see Figure 6.1). The Privacy and Security Policy promotes a risk-based approach to promote data accessibility and utility, while mitigating risks of unauthorized access and misuse through proportionate safeguards. The toolkit also provides guidance for consistent, and ideally coordinated, oversight by data access committees and research ethics committees.[11]

Professor Knoppers has also contributed to numerous other national and international health data governance policymaking initiatives, including the OECD Recommendation on Health Data Governance (2016), which recognizes both that access to and re-use of personal health data "can serve health-related public interests and bring significant benefits to individuals and society" and that such data are sensitive and require robust protection.[12] This shows how

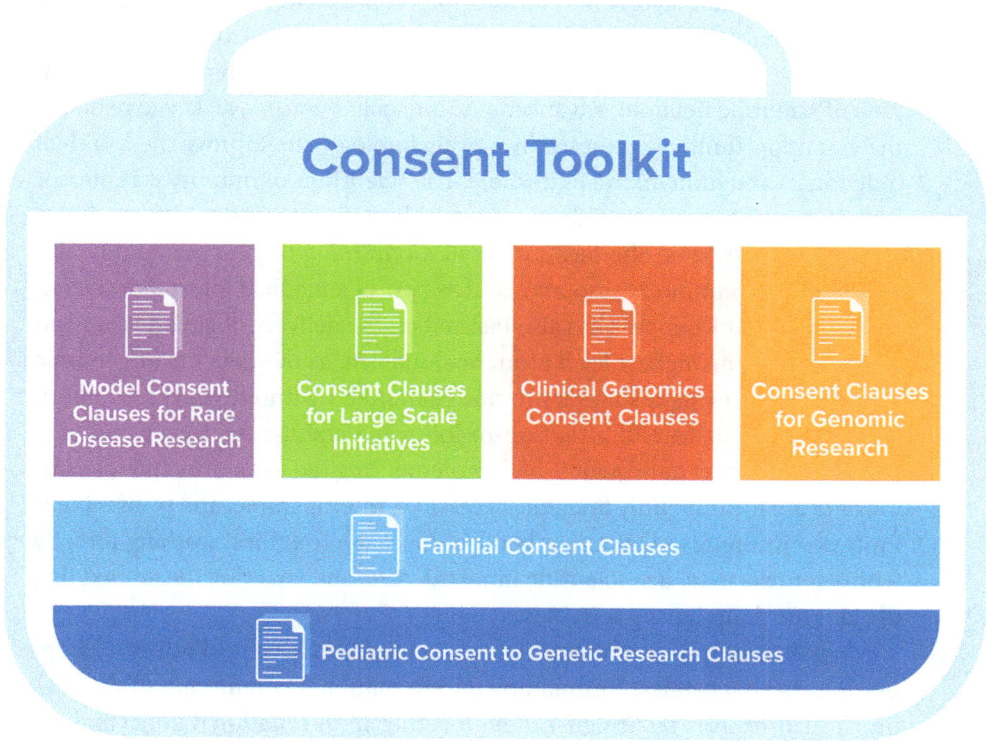

FIGURE 6.1 GA4GH Consent Toolkit[11]

11 GA4GH Consent Toolkit, available at: https://www.ga4gh.org/product/consent-toolkit/. Reprinted with permission from GA4GH.

12 OECD, 'Recommendation of the Council on Health Data Governance' (2016), OECD/LEGAL/0433, available at: https://legalinstruments.oecd.org/en/instruments/OECD-LEGAL-0433.

her approach and successes in promoting stewardship of genomic data are increasingly sought after in broader contexts.

Professor Knoppers is thoughtful about the aims of policy and what it can expect to achieve. In her own words:

> The aims of ethics policymaking in the biomedical research sector are many: avoid being legalistic; be context-specific; speak plainly; address the diversity of issues, disciplines and cultures involved; facilitate harmonization, compliance and oversight; include all relevant stakeholders; be aspirational; be practical and yet, at the same time, be principled. ... It seeks to reconcile universals and particulars, the possible and the hoped-for, as well as acquire legitimacy through use and usefulness over time.[13]

Professor Knoppers tirelessly promotes a characteristic set of human values. Respect for human dignity is at the core of her policy work, including respecting individual autonomy, and protection and inclusion of the vulnerable in science and society. At the same time, Professor Knoppers has been a champion of scientific freedom, advancement, and collaboration, all key to realizing the vast opportunities presented by new technologies to improve the health of individuals and humankind as a whole. The scientific community is Professor Knoppers' tribe, with its faith in progress through knowledge, and its international-mindedness. She has promoted a reframing of genomic and health databases as community resources and as part of a medical information commons. Professor Knoppers has also insisted on the delivery of genetic care and research with the highest level of professionalism, as the benefits of genomic care, research, or data sharing are not guaranteed without concerted effort. Progress requires careful attention to following standards of care and best practices, ensuring data quality, and implementing the FAIR principles, ensuring data are meaningfully findable, accessible, interoperable, and re-useable.[14] Professor Knoppers takes an embedded approach to ethics, working directly with scientists to realize scientific infrastructure, and ensuring the embedding of values in data sharing activities.

More than simply an advocate for a particular human value, Professor Knoppers has been a catalyst for building an international community of international ELSI experts by bringing them together in international policymaking forums. Her intellectual approach has always been centred in comparative law

13 Bartha M Knoppers, 'Does policy grow on trees?' (2014) 15 BMC Medical Ethics 87.

14 Mark D Wilkinson and others, 'The FAIR guiding principles for scientific data management and stewardship' (2016) 3 Scientific Data 160018.

and policy, which requires collaboration across borders. Policy does not grow on trees, but it is made by humans working together. Again in her own words:

> The most essential ingredient for what was (and is, with all policymaking) inevitably a long and arduous process of discussion, drafting and re-drafting is the involvement of people working closely together. Even more important than the expertise and experience of individuals is their goodwill and capacity for consensus. ... Moreover, validation of the content of any policy developed through broad exposure and input strengthens eventual buy-in and use by the scientific community. [15]

3 Responsible Data Governance

As an advocate for both scientific progress and the protection of individuals, Professor Knoppers has championed the robust data governance approaches to promote data sharing and open science in a manner that aligns with data protection and research ethics principles. In particular, she has been a leader in developing the concept and driving the implementation of "data governance frameworks" to support responsible data collection, integration, and data sharing as part of international research collaborations. These data governance frameworks included policies, procedures, and agreements with a dual purpose of protecting individual privacy and respect for legal requirements and research ethics principles, while at the same time facilitating data sharing and open science. But as we note below, Professor Knoppers' work goes beyond best practices for data repositories, and really extends to promoting coordination and harmonization enabling a Big Data approach that integrates data into global resources in an ethical way.

3.1 *Broad Consent*

One of Professor Knoppers' signal achievements has been the conceptualization and promotion of broad consent approaches in genomics research.[16] This is consent to the use of samples and/or data for not-fully specified studies in a broad scientific area, subject to ongoing governance, including oversight, providing regular updates to participants and uses and results, and the ability

15 Knoppers (n 13).

16 Bartha Maria Knoppers, 'Consent revisited: points to consider' (2004) 13 Health Law Review 33.

to withdraw.[17] This concept reflects Professor Knoppers' efforts to marry the principles of infrastructure science and bioethics. The scientific and societal value of large-scale data resources, as well as the public expense of building them, forces us to re-consider them as resources for the research community, rather than individual projects or fiefdoms. This can place tensions on traditional research ethics notions of informed consent, as the details of the studies being conducted or the identities of the researchers conducting the studies cannot be fully specified at the time of recruitment. Professor Knoppers regularly marshals a range of arguments for this approach: data sharing is essential to advance science and improve human health; specific consent approaches place an impractical burden on scientific resources as well as on participants; participants expect that the maximum value be made of their contributions to science; consent to an area of scientific research can still be informed and specific alongside oversight that ensures an integrity of purpose, monitoring, and transparency; and with appropriate privacy and security safeguards the risks of data sharing can be effectively mitigated.[18] Some of Professor Knoppers' strongest advocacy for data sharing and broad consent models has been for vulnerable groups, including children, rare disease patients and persons with dementia.[19] Here she has carefully balanced consideration for the necessity and interest of these communities in scientific advancement, with protection, as well as careful attention to the nuances of reduced autonomy, representation, and inclusion.

Professor Knoppers has continued to defend this principled and practical approach through a protracted debate between broad and dynamic consent. Dynamic consent emphasizes how information and communication technologies can enable ongoing communication between participants and biobanks and data repositories, and can thus enable biobanks to efficiently provide individuals with more continuous and granular control over the sharing and use of

17 Mark A Rothstein and others, 'Broad consent for future research: international perspectives' (2018) 40 IRB: Ethics & Human Research 7; Deborah Mascalzoni and others, 'International charter of principles for sharing bio-specimens and data' (2015) 23 European Journal of Human Genetics 721.

18 Bartha Maria Knoppers and Adrian Mark Thorogood, 'Ethics and big data in health' (2017) 4 Current Opinion in Systems Biology 53.

19 Minh Thu Nguyen and others, 'Model consent clauses for rare disease research' (2019) 20 BMC Medical Ethics 55; Adrian Thorogood and others, 'Consent recommendations for research and international data sharing involving persons with dementia' (2018) 14 Alzheimer's & Dementia: The Journal of the Alzheimer's Association 1334.

their data.[20] The debate reflected different positions on the status of individual autonomy in the context of infrastructure projects, and about the practicality of deploying the necessary infrastructure and ongoing relationships. In reality, the approaches are more complementary than they may appear in the literature debates. Broad consent can be strengthened by a greater commitment to ongoing communication efforts and tools, as well as investment in ongoing participant engagement. Broad consent is also not incompatible with individuals exercising ongoing control (with certain limitations), and this control depends on higher levels of transparency that can be reinforced by mediating technology. Moreover, the appropriate infrastructure, relationship, and type of consent is highly context-dependent, depending on the aims, resources, and population under study. But Professor Knoppers' continued advocacy has been important to remind us that broad consent is simple, ethically robust, and will often be the most practical and appropriate model for respecting autonomy while enabling science in a wide range of data sharing contexts. These questions are increasingly confronting healthcare institutions and systems the world over, as they seek to promote digitization and innovation in privacy-preserving ways.

Never content to limit her impact to the ivory tower, Professor Knoppers has been tirelessly involved working with scientific resources and collaborations to promote the implementation of broad consent and the harmonization of consent language across projects, contexts, and countries. Anyone who has worked closely with Professor Knoppers is likely to have been roped into developing a set of consent clauses to facilitate international data sharing (see e.g. Figure 6.1). The (sometimes seemingly endless) process of collecting, reviewing, integrating, and tinkering with consent language reflects pressures on ethics and governance to adapt alongside science. It also reflects a need for iterative and consultative approaches to arrive at consensus over what information about aims, benefits, risks, safeguards, and unknowns are meaningful and material to individual decision-making.

3.2 *Ethical Data Integration*

Professor Knoppers has long been attuned to the need for robust but flexible ethical approaches for an era of Big Data.[21] The rise of international data sharing initiatives reflects the reality that the value of individual datasets

20 Jane Kaye and others, 'Dynamic consent: a patient interface for twenty-first century research networks' (2015) 23 European Journal of Human Genetics 141.

21 Knoppers and Thorogood (n 18).

lies in our ability to compare and combine them at scale and within networks, especially in the areas of rare diseases and rare genetic mutations. One of Professor Knoppers' signature tools in these areas is the consent filter, developed for initiatives like ICGC-Argo[22] and the Human Cell Atlas.[23] These filters are premised on promoting a set of core consent elements for data sharing, often across different countries and research contexts. Potential data contributors can ensure these elements are incorporated in information and consent documents for prospective research. For legacy data, they can evaluate existing consents against the core elements. The approach is flexible in terms of proposing potential avenues for rectification if core elements are not (clearly) addressed, such as seeking a consent waiver from an ethics body. It emphasizes the important procedural side of ethics, which is not just about trying to interpret strict limits to what can and cannot be shared or pooled, but rather demonstrating that a process is in place to ensure that data integration has both meaningful scientific value, does not increase privacy and security risks, and remains aligned with the reasonable expectations of participants.

3.3 *Data Access*

Professor Knoppers was a key part of innovating on the dimension of data access. For community resources and databases, data access governance primarily aims to establish a balance between ensuring the timely availability of data to the scientific community and protecting the rights and interests of participants. The genomics field has pioneered open science approaches where data are made publicly or broadly available to the community.[24] The field has also been early to recognize the limits to de-identifying genomic and related health data (while maintaining scientific utility), resulting in residual risks to the privacy of participants and their blood relatives. The solution to achieve the most desirable balance between these competing imperatives was controlled access. Controlled access requires scientists interested in accessing genomic data to make a request to a data access committee, who reviews the requests against a transparent but limited set of scientific and ethical criteria. Approved users are provided with access to data subject to contractual, and sometimes also technical, safeguards. Data access agreements include

22 Susan E Wallace, Emily Kirby, and Bartha Maria Knoppers, 'How can we not waste legacy genomic research data?' (2020) 11 Frontiers in Genetics 446.

23 Bartha Maria Knoppers and others, 'Open data in the era of the GDPR: lessons from the Human Cell Atlas' (2023) 24 Annual Review of Genomics and Human Genetics 369.

24 Cook-Deegan, Ankeny, and Jones (n 4).

provisions on data confidentiality, security, and privacy (e.g. "do not attempt to re-identify individuals"). Controlled access also highlights principles of procedural fairness towards the research community, establishing transparent criteria and procedures, as well as timely and reasoned decisions. Controlled access approaches have become widespread for large-scale population research resources, major genomic data archives, and international data sharing initiatives.

The era of Big Data continues to bring new challenges for calibrating data access governance. First, the balance between openness and privacy is dependent on context—the population involved and their preferences; the types of data involved and the level of sensitivity, the types of safeguards employed, etc. Professor Knoppers has supported the realization of diverse approaches to openness, including controlled (but otherwise non-discriminatory) access to global cancer datasets,[25] as well as truly open (i.e. public) data sharing for cell biology[26] and neuroscience.[27] Second, not all data is equally sensitive, leading to the emergence of tiered access approaches, with data types and fields presenting a minimal residual risk of re-identification being released publicly, while other fields and types remaining controlled access. This has been popular in cancer genomics for instance, where tumour mutation and expression data, as well as some limited demographic and clinical data, is often shared publicly, but raw sequence data are only available controlled access. And sometimes, two tiers are not nuanced enough. Professor Knoppers also promoted the development of an intermediate registered-access tier, a form of role-based access where an authenticated individual is granted more granular access to data based on a reliable level of trust and accountability, without the need for a specific request.[28] Professor Knoppers has also seen the value from a security and accountability perspective of providing access to data in the cloud, and the need to adapt access oversight and tiers to the realm of remote access.[29]

---

25 Yann Joly and others, 'Data sharing in the post-genomic world: the experience of the International Cancer Genome Consortium (ICGC) Data Access Compliance Office (DACO)' (2012) 8 PLoS Computational Biology e1002549.

26 Knoppers and others (n 23).

27 Alexander Bernier and others, 'Open data governance at the Canadian Open Neuroscience Platform (CONP): from the walled garden to the arboretum' (2024) 13 *GigaScience* giad114.

28 Stephanie OM Dyke and others, 'Registered access: authorizing data access' (2018) 26 European Journal of Human Genetics 1721.

29 Lincoln D Stein and others, 'Data analysis: create a cloud commons' (2015) 523 Nature 149.

Another current challenge for data access governance is the need to coordinate across resources. It is not simply enough for each data resource to strike a careful balance between openness and protection. Almost as soon as a resource and governance framework is established, an unexpected opportunity arises to combine across resources. This can quickly lead to duplicative oversight processes that slow or halt scientific advancement, without improving protection. Professor Knoppers has led efforts to establish common and coordinated data access governance mechanisms across resources, which often requires thoughtfully navigating trade-offs between delegation, streamlining and efficiency on one hand, and local authority and accountability on the other hand.

3.4 *Ethical Provenance*

These ideas have evolved and been combined into Professor Knoppers' latest concept of ethical provenance, which aims to ensure an ethical supply chain across the data lifecycle from consent to integration to access to use.[30] This would be supported by compatible documents (information sheets and consent forms, data submission agreements, data access review, and data use agreements), and highlights the value of IT tools to more effectively ensure the capture, communication, and enforcement of permissions, conditions, and restrictions across the data lifecycle. Beyond legal harmonization, this endeavour has a decisive impact on standardization. Ethics as a cultural practice in research and medicine guides behaviour in those fields of activity that are not consolidated by legal regulations. However, as an influence on behaviour, it can help to interpret legal regulations and contribute to their further development in the long term. Professor Knoppers' work has provided groundbreaking insights into the norm-interpreting and norm-initiating role of ethics in the practice of data sharing.

4 Comparative Law and Data Protection

Professor Knoppers has also played a leadership role in finding mutual understanding and accommodation between data protection law and international data sharing (as well as alignment with bioethical frameworks).

30 Alexander Bernier and others, 'Recording the ethical provenance of data and automating data stewardship' (2023) 10 Big Data & Society (1-11).

4.1 *Comparative Approaches*

Professor Knoppers has had considerable impact as a comparative legal expert. She has acted as an advisor for global data sharing initiatives, assisting them with legal interpretation and compliance across multiple jurisdictions. One of Professor Knoppers' preferred techniques for providing this practical support is to frame the provision of information on legal requirements as a collaborative, comparative law research project. One of us (AT) had the opportunity to participate in two memorable, ambitious examples of these projects led by Professor Knoppers and her long-time partner in comparative law crime, Mark Rothstein. The first involved a review of privacy frameworks for biobanking spanning 20 jurisdictions.[31] This highlighted a high level of similarities in the principles of regulation, though the formal nature of regulatory instruments often differed. At the time, there was a lack of explicit recognition of broad consent, though it has long been common practice. While some jurisdictions have explicit controls on international transfers, the main barrier to international collaboration was a lack of harmonization of rules. Another exciting project involved a review of frameworks or restrictions related to international, direct-to-participant genomics research. This research involved direct app-based recruitment of individuals from many different countries into a research study, without establishing partnerships with local research institutions. The results of the study reveal a number of unexpected grey areas around applicable legislation and ethics oversight.[32] The project also laid the groundwork for such recruitment approaches, taking advantage of reduced overhead and oversight, while compensating for a lack of local ethics oversight with a robust global ethics review informed by global engagement and incorporating local ethical considerations. As a talented comparative legal scholar, Professor Knoppers' projects have also produced valuable resources not only for referencing legal information, but also for supporting harmonization and cross-fertilization between regulatory frameworks.

Professor Knoppers has a particular passion for clarifying and simplifying the often overlapping and jurisdiction-specific use of terminology surrounding data identifiability and de-identification.[33] Many of Professor Knoppers'

---

31 Mark A Rothstein, Bartha Maria Knoppers, and Heather L Harrell, 'Comparative approaches to biobanks and privacy' (2016) 44 Journal of Law, Medicine & Ethics 161.

32 Mark A Rothstein and others, 'Legal and ethical challenges of international direct-to-participant genomic research: conclusions and recommendations' (2019) 47 Journal of Law, Medicine & Ethics 705.

33 Mark Phillips and Bartha M Knoppers, 'The discombobulation of de-identification' (2016) 34 Nature Biotechnology 1102.

colleagues, including the authors, have participated in one or another of her efforts to establish an international glossary or lexicon for data protection as it relates to scientific data sharing. While such exercises can at first seem pedantic and potentially futile, Professor Knoppers has always used them to promote practical alignment, to bring together communities of ELSI scholars committed to a common purpose of supporting international collaboration, and a legal comparatist's humility of difference.

4.2 *Challenging Problematic Legislation or Legal Interpretation*

Professor Knoppers is not afraid to challenge overly strict legislation or legalistic interpretations of data protection law where it hampers international research collaboration. Professor Knoppers has been critical of conservative interpretations of the identifiability of health research data. She is always the first to point out that legal standards are typically phrased with a regard to reasonable likelihood of re-identification, considering the means. She has also been critical of conservative interpretations that conclude all individual-level genetic data are inherently identifiable. Professor Knoppers has been critical of the absolutist interpretation that pseudonymized health research data, even if effectively anonymized, remains personal data even when processed by a third party without access to the re-identification mechanism.[34]

Her approaches to anonymization and pseudonymization highlight the importance of the context of data processing, a situational approach to data protection and the technical and organizational measures needed to implement it. Her work has intrinsically shown that the context of data processing also includes the context of the application of regulations, with legal and socio-cultural elements influencing the interpretation and application of regional and international standards in different cultural and regulatory environments.

As a long-standing proponent of a bioethical broad consent model for biobanking and data sharing, Professor Knoppers has also been critical of narrow interpretation of the requirement that consent to data processing be "specific" for health research, and has promoted the importance of acknowledging Recital 33 of the European Union's General Data Protection Regulation (GDPR),[35] which permits valid consent to areas of scientific research,

34 Jasper Bovenberg and others, 'How to fix the GDPR's frustration of global biomedical research' (2020) 370 Science 40.

35 Regulation (EU) 2016/679 of the European Parliament and of the Council of 27 April 2016 on the protection of natural persons with regard to the processing of personal data

especially considering that a "stated objective of the GDPR is that processing of personal data should serve humankind."[36] This issue is also closely related to diverging interpretations across Member States about the appropriate lawful basis for health research involving the processing of personal data, with some countries viewing consent as the preferred basis, and other countries preferring a public interest (or legitimate interest) basis. The former view is usually premised on a more flexible vision of the GDPR consent standard, whereas the latter vision is usually premised on a stricter consent standard that cannot be meaningfully achieved for health data repositories. The former view also tends to be linked to a bioethical concept of consent to research participation, whereas the latter tends to reflect a view that GDPR consent for data processing and ethical consent for research participation are separate but overlapping concepts. As both a bioethicist and jurist, Professor Knoppers has been able to nimbly navigate these conceptual distinctions, and simultaneously advocate for harmonized interpretations as well as interim practical solutions.

Above all, Professor Knoppers has raised concerns that "GDPR limitations on data transfers will hamper science globally in general and biomedical science in particular," as a result of a lack of fit-for-purpose transfer mechanisms surviving judicial invalidation and conservative regulatory opinions.[37] In the interest of a high level of data protection, jurisdictions often define their protection rules in a way that they apply to data wherever it is transferred. For this reason, the statutory mechanisms for international data transfers often function as applicable laws: they define the rules that must be complied with, even if the data leaves the respective jurisdiction.[38] At the same time, we lack cross-border rules to avoid conflicts of law in this field, so that researchers collaborating across borders may be subject to different rules regarding their data processing. Even though there are mechanisms that have been developed to recognize the essential equivalence of the level of data protection, such as the concept of "adequacy" in EU law, we have all experienced how difficult it is to assess laws in a third country in such a way that they remain watertight in

---

and on the free movement of such data, and repealing Directive 95/46/EC (General Data Protection Regulation), OJ 2016 L 119/1.

36 Bovenberg and others (n 34).

37 ibid.

38 Fruzsina Molnár-Gábor and others, 'Bridging the European data sharing divide in genomic science' (2022) 24 Journal of Medical Internet Research 37236.

a judicial review.[39] Such regulations ultimately present researchers and their organizations, as well as supervisory authorities, with the enormous task of assessing the level of protection in a third country. Examining the similarities and differences in protection in the various countries and how it is presented in terms of the operationalization of data protection principles, the legal bases, risk assessment, the balancing of researcher and participant interests, and the translation of the result of this balancing into the specification of concrete technical and organizational measures can be informative for collaborative projects and contribute to the promotion of international standardization and harmonization. One of us (FMG) had the opportunity to contribute to the joint efforts in setting such standards, which included a thorough legal comparison between several countries, including European and Canadian regulations, in support of EUCANCan, an international cancer network.[40]

4.3 *Innovative Legal Approaches: Self-Regulatory and Sector-Specific Codes of Conduct*

Professor Knoppers has been a staunch promoter of anticipatory ethics and self-regulatory approaches by the international genomics community, as evidenced by the many international policy frameworks that bear her imprimatur. The participation of researchers in self-regulatory approaches is key: they have the best insight into the details of their activities; co-development supports acceptance, and researchers have a responsibility to contribute to the sector-specific concretization of data protection rules and principles. At the same time, this approach emphasizes the special nature of health data science and its importance for individual health and the common good.

Professor Knoppers has also sought to leverage legislative flexibility in the context of self-regulation, in innovative ways, such as by promoting efforts to develop a GDPR code of conduct for health research.[41] The GDPR provides the opportunity to develop a sector-specific code of conduct outlining technical details to provide greater legal certainty, as well as oversight by a sectoral

39 *Maximillian Schrems* v *Data Protection Commissioner*, ECLI:EU:C:2015:650 (Grand Chamber); *Data Protection Commissioner* v *Facebook Ireland Limited and Maximillian Schrems*, ECLI:EU:C:2020:559 (Grand Chamber).

40 EUCANCan, available at: https://eucancan.com/.

41 Mark Phillips and others, 'Genomics: data sharing needs an international code of conduct' (2020) 578 Nature 31; Fruzsina Molnár-Gábor and Jan O Korbel, 'Genomic data sharing in Europe is stumbling—could a code of conduct prevent its fall?' (2020) 12 EMBO Molecular Medicine e11421.

monitoring body to provide greater accountability.[42] Legal certainty is strengthened as a code of conduct consolidates the relevant data protection rules and creates new specific rules for concrete research areas. It ensures a better balance between the effective implementation of data protection provisions and the guarantee of framework conditions for research. This makes it easier for data subjects to exercise their rights and strengthens the freedom of research. A higher degree of legal certainty is also achieved with regard to monitoring by the supervisory authority. The improved control creates a greater sense of security for those affected, provides proof of compliance with data protection more easily, and exercises privileges for their research. Costs can also be saved. Professor Knoppers has highlighted how such codes could include a combination of detailed rules providing clarity and harmonized interpretations around matters like legal basis, identifiability, and international transfers, as well as higher level interpretative principles such as a commitment to advancing open science and the medical information commons.[43] A code of conduct plays a key role in science communication and acts as a mediator in transparent data processing. The result is a dynamic and discursive set of rules that enables individual and social perspectives to be taken into account in setting standards for health research.

5 Conclusion

Professor Knoppers' contributions to scholarship, science, and regulation are myriad. She has also been a major personal influence for both of us. AT had the opportunity to support Professor Knoppers' work to develop policy frameworks through GA4GH. This experience directly informed AT's research and career interests in developing data governance frameworks for (federated) data sharing initiatives,[44] and has founded AT's passion for working on the interdisciplinary challenges that bring together bioinformatics, IT, and ELSI experts. FMG has had the opportunity to co-lead research projects with Professor Knoppers addressing international data sharing and access across borders.

42 European Data Protection Board, 'Guidelines 1/2019 on Codes of Conduct and Monitoring Bodies under Regulation 2016/679' (2019), available at: https://www.edpb.europa.eu/our-work-tools/our-documents/guidelines/guidelines-12019-codes-conduct-and-monitoring-bodies-0_en.

43 Mark Phillips and Bartha M Knoppers, 'Whose commons? Data protection as a legal limit of open science' (2019) 47 Journal of Law, Medicine & Ethics 106.

44 Adrian Thorogood and others, 'International federation of genomic medicine databases using GA4GH standards' (2021) 1 Cell 100032.

This has set her into an excitement of international standardization, interpretation, and approximation of laws that she has ever since never thought about leaving.

Current trends all reinforce an urgent need to continue to champion Professor Knoppers' ideas and vision. Genomics is going through an unprecedented translation into precision medicine and public health. As a result, the stakes in genomic data are ever higher in terms of made (or missed) opportunities for targeted prevention, diagnosis, and treatment. Data privacy laws are multiplying around the world in addition to other layers of regulation, bringing rigidity that may threaten principled innovation. Hype around artificial intelligence is feeding enthusiasm for ever more health data sharing and re-use, as well as exacerbating concerns about both ineffective, biased, and potentially harmful deployments as well as missed opportunities to improve health. Despite growing disease burdens, pandemics, and environmental threats that cross borders, interest in global collaboration only seems to be ebbing.

Professor Knoppers has shown us how legal research can contribute to a practical enabling of data sharing and scientific progress. For the processing of systematic connections in the data protection arena, dedication is needed to find answers to fundamental questions that are not piecemeal and that also recur in different subject areas. The long-term development, safeguarding, and visualization of such fundamental questions in the interplay of ethical, legal, and social approaches is reflected in the completeness of Professor Knoppers' work. With her work and personality, Professor Knoppers stands for bringing together different legal ideas from different cultures and bringing them into dialogue. It is also never enough for her to find the lowest common denominator between them; she always pushes to bring them together. This provides an innovative boost in two directions: towards harmonization as a reaction to the original systems, and in the development of an international legal culture to promote individual health and health as a public good. Both the convergence to higher-ranking standards and their reflection in national law must take place within the established system of human rights and the rule of law.

What we have always appreciated about Professor Knoppers' approach is that it is always both principled and practical, reflecting her earnest commitment to supporting science as well as her efforts to always be embedded within scientific leadership and practice. What is ethical and what is practical are not necessarily in conflict; they can be one and the same. In Professor Knoppers' view, the pragmatic approach of proportionality, of balancing competing rights and interests, is part and parcel with an ethical worldview.

VIGNETTE

The Great BMK Effect

Patricia Kosseim

As with many young students in university, I struggled to figure out what I wanted to "do with my life." Until I heard of Bartha Maria Knoppers. Then, all became clearer, more focused in my mind. I wanted to do "what Bartha did." Her groundbreaking work in health law and bioethics inspired me to pursue my studies in that direction. Issues of consent and confidentiality fascinated me to no end. Bartha was literally my "aha" moment.

Throughout my career, there have been many touchpoints with Bartha—too many to recount. But a few stand out worthy of mention.

As a student and young lawyer, it was Bartha who asked me to develop and publish the first compendium of federal, provincial, and territorial laws governing secondary use of personal health information. It was that comparative exercise which first sparked my interest in privacy law and eventually set the trajectory of my career. As co-publishers on a few articles, I was filled with enormous pride to have my name associated with "Knoppers, BM" and only wished we could write more together. During my time working as Director of the Ethics Office, at the Canadian Institutes of Health Research, and as Chief Officer, Science and Society, at Genome Canada, Bartha served on external advisory committees to both organizations. She provided me with thoughtful, strategic, and visionary advice that encouraged me and helped stimulate and guide my work over the years. As co-presenters at privacy conferences, I would listen in awe to what Bartha was saying, and though we didn't always agree on all points, I admired her deep knowledge, courage, and ingenuity as she injected new concepts into the conversation, like the principle of solidarity, that would eventually start to sway my thinking. But my greatest privilege was watching Bartha "in action" at international meetings. As a gifted convener of people and ideas, Bartha would actively work the room, bridging laws and cultures across jurisdictions, in the tireless aim of harmonizing international standards to support the development and interoperability of biobanks, and ultimately, improve global health.

Bartha Maria Knoppers is a true pioneer, a pillar of strength, a tour de force, whose professional leadership in the field of health law and bioethics will have changed the arc of research for years to come. But the personal impacts she has had on the lives and careers of others is perhaps her greatest accomplishment.

 | DOI:10.1163/9789004688544_019

Her dedication, mentorship, and generosity have inspired her many students and researchers to become leaders and experts in their own right. They have gone on, far and wide, to mark significant achievements, building on her extraordinary contributions to the field and amplifying the great BMK effect.

Then there's Bartha, the friend. When all is said and done, it's Bartha's human dimension that stand out as most memorable. Her immense kindness, contagious smile, and funny stories from a lifetime of travels around the world are what bring this monument of a person down to earth, approachable and accessible to all those who are lucky to know her.

VIGNETTE

Bartha Knoppers—Colleague and Friend

Martin Bobrow

I think I worked alongside Bartha for over a decade (circa 2005–2017). If I'm wrong, she will politely correct me; she never seems to forget anything, however trivial.

I come from medical genetics. Bartha came from the very different perspective of law and policy, but she has an intuitive understanding of how science works. I came to trust and admire her as much as anyone I have known. A small army of us hold that view. Indeed, I watched her develop rigorous policy and ethical frameworks for complex projects such as the International Cancer Genome Consortium (ICGC), the Global Alliance for Genomics and Health (GA4GH), and several population genomic studies. Genomic studies on large populations were not lacking in ethical pitfalls, and that these generally proceeded smoothly and with strong public support owes much to the excellent guidance provided by Bartha and colleagues.

Perhaps my outstanding memories are not of Bartha gripping the attention of a large audience (which she did with ease), but of checking into a hotel and getting a message nominating a pleasant, reasonable, and accessible restaurant. There I would find Bartha with friends, colleagues, and trainees. They were there to renew acquaintanceships, gather news, and think about the coming meeting (and to eat and drink). These convivial meetings were characterised by an egalitarian informality, high intellectual standard, and a group cohesion based on the loyalty that Bartha created, apparently effortlessly.

What makes Bartha so special? It's an impossible question, but she has a few outstanding characteristics that contribute:

She has (of course) an encyclopaedic knowledge and recall, and a network of resources and people that she can rapidly call on to plug any information gap. She has a prodigious capacity for work, keeping going at apparently full throttle when the rest of the company have degenerated into somnolence. There is a touch of the perfectionist, who goes on improving documents long after lesser mortals thought they were good enough. She is a consummate talent spotter, recruiting excellent people and looking after them carefully and compassionately so that they become not just trainees, but colleagues and friends, keeping in touch with her and ready to help her out for years after their training was

DOI:10.1163/9789004688544_020

completed. She has, to put it another way, founded a substantial tribe to carry on her intellectual traditions.

Most importantly, though, Bartha always approached new ventures in a positive way. Those who work on ethical, policy, or regulatory aspects of biomedical science often find themselves defining problems in proposed lines of research. It can be a somewhat negative experience. Bartha preferred to always seek workable solutions, to help enable appropriate science to proceed for the common good. Bartha was always the optimistic and pragmatist, looking for sensible and decent ways of doing what was worth doing. It was her remarkable ability to pick out the big (and genuine) issues and find ways of melding sound social and ethical practice with workable scientific protocols that led her to successful outcomes, and in turn, that led broader society to reap the benefits from socially valuable scientific discoveries.

Her standards are always high and her judgement rigorous. She has earned equal respect from patient groups, colleagues in her own core disciplines, national and international science administrators, and biomedical scientists. She has left an indelible mark on the practice of human population genomics. It is a privilege to call her both a colleague and friend.

CHAPTER 7

The Sweet Smell of the Rose—Names, Categories, and the Authentic Meaning of Being Human

R. Alta Charo

[H]umans are not their germline.[1]

1 A Human by Any Other Name?

In the first season of the series "Star Trek: Picard,"[2] the oh-so-human (and humane) retired Admiral Picard says to a "synth"—a sophisticated android who is having an emotional crisis after learning her memories were implanted, her character programed, and her body constructed in a laboratory—"Have you ever considered that you are something lovingly and deliberately created?" The synth replies, "You're telling me that I'm not real."

But what would have made the synth real? Or is that impossible? With the increasing power of science not only to analyze, construct, and destroy, but also to create and grow, has come a crisis of our own—a crisis of identity and authenticity as we struggle to reconcile our instincts and our spiritual faiths with the increasingly indistinguishable forms of life we make in our laboratories. And we often play out this struggle in the form of debates over names.

There is a thread that runs through our instinct to place things in categories, to reify those categories by assigning each a name that could apply to every member, and then to define membership by whether the name makes sense. Only those entities with key characteristics are entitled to the name and, therefore, to membership. But over and over, we find that different groupings and different categorical concepts are needed for different purposes, whether it is constructing a sporting event, selling a food item or, most profoundly,

1 Andrea Boggio and others, 'The human right to science and the regulation of human germline engineering' (2019) 2 The CRISPR Journal 134.

2 Wikipedia, 'Star Trek: Picard', available at: https://en.wikipedia.org/wiki/Star_Trek:_Picard.

DOI:10.1163/9789004688544_021

recognizing human rights and responsibilities. There is a tension between tailoring our concepts and rules to our social needs versus the opposite instinct, which is to tether our categories to a biological reality, and so limit the mischief we might make by defining some humans as property and, thereby, appropriate for slavery. Of course, biology is neither so clear-cut nor so appropriate in all situations as to make it the perfect proxy for common sense or social necessities.

2 Essentialism and Relational Properties

The biotechnology company Colossal[3] is best known for its announcement that it plans to bring back the woolly mammoth.[4] Co-founded by Harvard scientist George Church and entrepreneur Ben Lamm, the company has been working to develop technologies to identify the key characteristics of an extinct animal, edit its nearest living relative (the Asian elephant) to recapitulate those characteristics, and gestate the resulting creature. Critics have complained that whatever the resulting creature might be, it will not be a woolly mammoth.[5] On the company website, which highlights headlines from press coverage, the creature is referred to by multiple terms, including "woolly mammoth," "cold-resistant elephant," "hybrid elephant," and "almost elephant."

At what point would it actually be a mammoth? How does one define such an animal, such that it deserves this name? Surely, if it is a member of the same species as the extinct mammoths, that would earn the moniker, yes? But the very definition of species is subject to considerable confusion and debate.[6] It is, of course, a fundamental unit of biological classification. For essentialists, a deity created species and there is an eternal essence for each species, which is static, not evolving.[7] On the other hand, evolutionarily speaking, species are the result of speciation, a process involving change over time, with no qualitative feature—morphological, genetic, or behavioural—considered essential

3 'Home - Colossal' (Colossal), available at: https://colossal.com.

4 Disclosure: I am a paid consultant to Colossal.

5 See e.g. Patrice Kohl, 'Using de-extinction to create extinct species proxies; natural history not included' (2017) 20 Ethics, Policy & Environment 15; Douglas Ian Campbell and Patrick Michael Whittle, *Resurrecting Extinct Species: Ethics and Authenticity* (Palgrave Macmillan 2017); Christian Diehm, 'De-extinction and deep questions about species conservation' (2017) 20 Ethics, Policy & Environment 25.

6 Marc Ereshefsky, 'Species' in Edward Zalta (ed), *The Stanford Encyclopedia of Philosophy* (2022), available at: https://plato.stanford.edu/archives/sum2022/entries/species/.

7 Makmiller Pedroso, 'Origin essentialism in biology' (2014) 64 The Philosophical Quarterly 60.

for membership in a species.[8] And yet many still have an instinctual loyalty to a notion of species essence, that all and only the members of a kind have a common essence—but this is hard to find.

Relational properties, such as interbreeding, genealogy, and occupying a specific niche are also ways to define species. But citing the relations among the organisms of a species does not explain why a particular organism is a member of a certain species. Saying that, because an organism can interbreed with a member of *Homo sapiens*, it must also be a member of *Homo sapiens*, leaves unanswered why those other organisms are already considered *Homo sapiens*. It's an unanswered regress: why are any of them *Homo sapiens*?[9] And yet, by naming an organism, and placing it or not in one category (*Homo sapiens*) can have profound effects on whether it is considered a member of our moral community and has the same rights that we enjoy—to life, to freedom from abuse, whatever.

3 Legal and Philosophical Boundaries of the Human

As Professor Bartha Maria Knoppers and her colleague Professor Henry (Hank) Greely wrote:

> Bioscientific advances are nibbling away at classical legal boundaries that form the bedrock of the normative structures on which societies are based [and] blur legal distinctions between human beings and other living organisms, between living human beings and dead ones, and between human tissues and cells and nonhuman ones. Determining whether some "thing" is now some "one" carries with it profound implications for the rights and obligations the law recognizes for "humans."[10]

There is, of course, a circularity in this discussion. The reason for defining something as inside or outside categorical boundaries, such as "human," is to organize these rights and obligations. But to determine the nature of those

8 Alan R Templeton, 'The Meaning of Species and Speciation: A Genetic Perspective' in Daniel Otte and John A Endler (eds), *Speciation and its Consequences* (Sinauer Associates 1989); Joel D Velasco, 'Species, genes, and the tree of life' (2010) 61 The British Journal for the Philosophy of Science 599.

9 Richard A Richards, *The Species Problem: A Philosophical Analysis* (Cambridge University Press 2010).

10 Bartha Maria Knoppers and Henry T Greely, 'Biotechnologies nibbling at the legal "human"' (2019) 366 Science 1455.

rights and obligations, one must inquire as to the attributes of the entity and whether they make sense for such an assignment.[11] Does it make sense to say an entity that has a genome that is consistent with genomes found in *Homo sapiens* is therefore entitled to "human" rights if that entity has no sentience and no ability to perceive, enjoy, or exercise those rights?[12] Does it matter if that entity is a single cell, a multi-cellular embryo, or a fully differentiated body? Answering this question requires a decision about the purpose of human rights, which in turn influences whether the entity belongs in this category.

This need—to construct definitions and assign names—arises in far less fraught settings. Something as mundane as our breakfast table features foods such as cereals, which (in the United States, at least) are carefully defined and named pursuant to regulations for a food's "standard of identity."[13] These regulations define what a food must contain (and in what proportions) to guard against economic adulteration, so consumers get what they are paying for. And food names must reflect consumer expectations, so they know what they are buying. To some extent, then, the name of an entity must coincide with our common expectation for that entity, regardless of minor technical variations. And those expectations may be at odds with the substantive risks and benefits or other attributes of the food.

The disconnect between public expectation (or, as some might call it, right to know), the chemical constitution of a food, and the key attributes of a food (such as taste, mouthfeel, shelf stability, etc.) has been prominent in debates over the proper naming and labelling of so-called "genetically modified organisms" (GMOs). Despite numerous studies and reports finding that genetic modification and modern bioengineering do not intrinsically make foods any more dangerous or less healthful than conventionally grown versions,[14] a large portion of the public continues to view GMO foods with suspicion, if not outright hostility,[15] often labelling them as "unnatural" with the term referring both

11 Rowan Cruft, 'Rights: beyond interest theory and will theory?' (2004) 23 Law and Philosophy 347.

12 HLA Hart, *The Concept of Law* (Oxford University Press 1961); Hart HLA, *Essays on Bentham* (Oxford University Press 1982); Jeremy Bentham, 'Anarchical Fallacies' in Jeremy Waldron (ed), *Nonsense Upon Stilts: Bentham, Burke and Marx on the Rights of Man* (Methuen 1987).

13 US Food and Drug Administration, 'Standards of Identity for Food', available at: https://www.fda.gov/food/food-labeling-nutrition/standards-identity-food.

14 National Academies of Sciences, Engineering, and Medicine, *Genetically Engineered Crops* (National Academies Press 2016).

15 Brian Kennedy and Cary Lynne Thigpen, 'Many publics around world doubt safety of genetically modified foods' (Pew Research Center, 11 November 2020), available at: https://

to potential danger and to something deeper and more inchoate or spiritual. "It's not exactly a religious view, because it's not something they would have learned in church," Paul Thompson, Professor of Applied Philosophy, has said:

> It's quasi-religious, because it's a particular way of thinking about nature. ... Part of the anxiety about genetically engineered foods is that our view of how the world works is eroding away from underneath our feet ... It's a shame that this anxiety has been attached so strongly to genetically engineered foods, because the feeling really exists in many areas of life.[16]

4 Bioengineering Entities

In the US, the National Bioengineered Food Disclosure Standard defines bioengineered foods as those that contain detectable genetic material that has been modified through certain lab techniques and cannot be created through conventional breeding or found in nature. The Standard establishes requirements for labelling foods that humans eat that are or may be bioengineered, including text on the package that must say "bioengineered food," has the bioengineered food symbol, or has directions to a site to find the disclosure.[17] This labelling does not change the *name* of the food. The corn or soy remains corn or soy in name, even if labelled "bioengineered." But in many ways, the addition of the word "bioengineered" to the label does, in fact, change the name, just as much as calling an entity a "synthetic human" changes its name, and its category, regardless of how the word "human" remains in the name. And with this change, a sort of signalling, one changes how the entity (here, the food) will be regarded by customers or even whether it can or will be sold for consumption.

The use of a modifier can, at times, make a name that might otherwise be misleading into one that can capture a public instinct. For years, for example, dairy farmers and others who sell milk from mammals had argued that plant-based alternatives had no right to call themselves "milk." Following years of debate the US Food & Drug Administration concluded that consumers

---

www.pewresearch.org/short-reads/2020/11/11/many-publics-around-world-doubt-safety-of-genetically-modified-foods/.

16 Steve Talley, 'Are genetically engineered foods natural? A bioethicist responds', available at: https://www.purdue.edu/uns/html4ever/0009.Thompson.natural.html.

17 US Food and Drug Administration, 'How GMOs Are Regulated', available at: https://www.fda.gov/food/agricultural-biotechnology/how-gmos-are-regulated-united-states.

understand that when named with modifiers such as "oat milk" or "soy milk" or "almond milk," consumers understand simultaneously that the product has key similarities to milk (particularly regarding look, mouthfeel, texture, and taste) while still not actually being what they would think of as "milk." As noted in the 2023 guidance, milk is

> [...] strongly rooted in consumers' vocabulary when describing and talking about plant-based milk alternatives. The focus groups indicated that most participants were not confused about plant-based milk alternatives containing milk ... Other research also appears to show that consumers understand that plant-based milk alternatives are distinct products and choose to purchase plant-based milk alternatives because they are not milk.[18]

The absence of confusion, that is, the fact that the public did not misunderstand plant-based alternatives as being the same as milk derived from cows and goats and such, led to the decision to allow the use of the word "milk" even though the plant-based alternatives were manifestly different.

5 Naming, Perception, and Their Consequences for Identity

Such a connection, between the name of an entity, how it is perceived and even how it is regulated has been the subject of other debates related to food. A product that is derived from cells of a cow, for example, would seem to be meat. But federal law in the US defines meat as a product derived from the carcass of an animal. For "cell-based,"[19] "lab-grown,"[20] and "cultivated"[21] meat (just a

18 US Department of Health and Human Services, Food and Drug Administration, 'Labeling of Plant-Based Milk Alternatives and Voluntary Nutrient Statements: Guidance for Industry' (2023), available at: https://www.fda.gov/media/165420/download.

19 Nicole Axworthy, 'USDA And FDA to host joint meeting on cell-based meat regulation' (VegNews.com, 13 September 2018, available at: https://vegnews.com/2018/9/usda-and-fda-to-host-joint-meeting-on-cell-based-meat-regulation.

20 Henry Fountain, 'A lab-grown burger gets a taste test (Published 2013)' (The New York Times, 5 August 2013), available at: https://www.nytimes.com/2013/08/06/science/a-lab-grown-burger-gets-a-taste-test.html.

21 Elaine Watson, '"Cultivated" meat could be the most-consumer-friendly term for cell-cultured meat, suggests Mattson/GFI research' (FoodNavigator-USA, 12 September 2019), available at: https://www.foodnavigator-usa.com/Article/2019/09/12/Cultivated-meat-could-be-the-most-consumer-friendly-term-for-cell-cultured-meat-suggests-Mattson-GFI-research.

few of the names that have been used), there is no carcass. If this means it falls outside the definition of "meat," not only does it change how it is named and labelled for consumer sale, but it also actually changes whether it is regulated by the US Department of Agriculture (which routinely inspects and grades all meat products) or the Food and Drug Administration (which regulates many novel foods).[22]

There is, as noted above, an emotional or even spiritual quality to the public sensibilities surrounding food and its identity. This is nothing, however, to the emotional and spiritual underpinnings of the debates surrounding the names used for elements of human sexuality and reproduction, and the substantive meanings attached to those names.

The naming debate has been going on for generations when it comes to defining male and female, man and woman. Apparently there has been sex testing and separation of men and women in the context of sports since the seventh- or eighth-century BCE origins of Olympic games.[23] The testing has come and gone over the years, as well as changed from requiring women to be paraded naked to have their genitals examined to, in the presumably more dignified recent era, requiring women to provide cells for chromosomal analysis.[24] As with other definitions, these are created to serve a purpose. In this case, it is to ensure a separation of sexes that presumably reflects both a belief in the intrinsic weakness of all women and something intrinsic to fairness in the games, such that they test skill and training rather than physical advantage.[25]

The problem arises, however, both when individual women prove stronger, faster, or more skilled than one of the men in the competition, thus belying the first proposition, and with someone whose chromosomal body is at odds with outward phenotypic expression. The latter can occur, for example, in those who have a Y chromosome that is not expressed, and who develop bodies of typical female form,[26] as has happened to some athletes.[27] One solution,

---

22 "The term "meat food product" means any product capable of use as human food which is made wholly or in part from any meat or other portion of the carcass of any cattle, sheep, swine, or goats, ..." (21 USC §601).

23 John Mouratidis, 'Heracles at Olympia and the exclusion of women from the ancient Olympic games' (1984) 11 Journal of Sport History 41.

24 Laura A Wackwitz, 'Verifying the myth: Olympic sex testing and the category "woman"' (2003) 26 Women's Studies International Forum 553.

25 Graham Dunbar, 'Sex eligibility rules for female athletes are complex and legally difficult. Here's how they work' (AP News, 7 August 2024), available at: https://apnews.com/article/sex-eligibility-tests-female-athletes-07572d23d409126a8e069cb0bced1706.

26 Marianne Legato, *Principles of Gender-Specific Medicine* (Academic Press 2017).

27 Alison Carlson, 'When is a woman not a woman? For 24 years Maria Patino thought she was female. Then she failed the sex test' (1991) Women's Sports and Fitness 24.

therefore, would be to group athletes according to where they fall on a spectrum of physical capabilities, with biological sex (however defined) and social gender rendered irrelevant.

Indeed, mixed attitudes about whether sporting events are about celebrating excellence in outcome versus excellence in effort is evident in the multiple weight classes for boxing (which allows lighter competitors to be appreciated for their skill and training) versus the single class structure of basketball (which has never fronted a short- persons' league) and most other sports. Without clarity about the purpose of the sports spectacle, the credibility of humiliating and often erroneous sex testing will be undone, as little purpose seems to be served by resorting to such a problematic practice.

The problem for sports, therefore, may lie not with what we call people or how we define their sex, but rather by how we choose to use those definitions and names as imperfect proxies for our true concerns about fair competition and reward. Nonetheless, the recent spate of social and legislative penalties aimed at those who are transgender[28] confirms that there is tremendous resistance to abandoning categories that have long been viewed as essential, immutable, and even divinely ordained,[29] the biological reality of persons born intersex or social reality of gender dysphoria notwithstanding.[30]

6 Reproducing the "Human"

Perhaps nowhere has the debate over names and definitions been as intractable as in the context of human reproduction. For example, Professor Knoppers and her colleagues had to begin their own discussion of ethical issues related to embryos by first laying down their philosophy on naming:

> At the outset, it should be noted that there is little agreement concerning appropriate terminology to designate the human embryo. The use of different words for different stages of development is often used to mark a perceived difference in the ethical significance of particular stages. For the sake of simplicity, this paper eschews the use of terms such as

28 American Civil Liberties Union, 'Mapping Attacks on LGBTQ Rights in U.S. State Legislatures In 2024', available at: https://www.aclu.org/legislative-attacks-on-lgbtq-rights-2024.

29 Teresa J Hornsby and Deryn Guest, *Transgender, Intersex, and Biblical Interpretation* (SBL Press 2016).

30 Ryan T Anderson, 'Transgender ideology is riddled with contradictions. Here are the big ones' (The Heritage Foundation, 9 February 2018), available at: https://www.heritage.org/gender/commentary/transgender-ideology-riddled-contradictions-here-are-the-big-ones.

> "zygote," "pre-embryo," "fertilized egg," and others used to describe very early stages of development of the human organism.[31]

These authors were quite correct to note the ethical significance of the names. Use of classic biological terminology to describe stages from fertilization to zygote to morula to blastula to gastrula to organogenesis emphasize the distinctive physical characteristics and the slow emergence of traits associated with a developing foetus or baby.[32] It can help to reinforce the sense that this developing entity has not yet achieved a moral status akin to that of an embryo, let alone a foetus or baby. Indeed, in the 1980s there were many in the field of *in vitro* fertilization who used the phrase "pre-embryo" to help emphasize this distinction,[33] at least while an entity was still developing in a laboratory dish, a time when it might be discarded if the progenitors no longer wanted it for reproductive purposes.

The debate over whether to include such entities within the human community dictates everything from the legality of IVF itself to the role of the state in determining the disposition of such entities when one or the other progenitor no longer wishes to bring it to term. Indeed, the debate has flared up anew in the United States since a startling decision by the Alabama Supreme Court in 2024, holding that *ex vivo* frozen embryos are "minor children" for the purposes of a wrongful death statute that grants tort damages for negligent killing.[34] Many of those opposed to abortion rights celebrated the decision, as a step toward the goal of recognizing personhood in all settings as existing from the moment of fertilization onward.[35] Others recognized the dilemma

---

31 Bartha Maria Knoppers, Sylvie Bordet, and Rosario Isasi, 'The human embryo: ethical and legal aspects' (2009) 550 Methods in Molecular Biology 281.

32 BD Editors, 'Embryo - Definition, Development, Stages and Quiz | Biology Dictionary' (Biology Dictionary, 6 July 2017), available at: https://biologydictionary.net/embryo/.

33 Richard A McCormick, 'Who or what is the preembryo?' (1991) 1 Kennedy Institute of Ethics Journal 1.

34 *Le Page* v *Center for Reproductive Medicine* (SC-2022-0579) (Alabama Supreme Court, 16 February 2024); R Alta Charo, 'Back to the future in Alabama' (2024) 390 New England Journal of Medicine 1253; Rebecca S Feinberg, Michael S Sinha, and I Glenn Cohen, 'The Alabama embryo decision—the politics and reality of recognizing "extrauterine children"' (2024) 331 JAMA 1083; Michelle J Bayefsky, Arthur L Caplan, and Gwendolyn P Quinn, 'The real impact of the Alabama Supreme Court decision in *LePage v Center for Reproductive Medicine*' (2024) 331 JAMA 1085.

35 Nathaniel Weixel, 'How Alabama's frozen embryo decision is shaking the nation: what you need to know' (The Hill, 21 February 2024), available at: https://thehill.com/policy/healthcare/4481856-how-alabamas-frozen-embryo-decision-is-shaking-the-nation-what-you-need-to-know/.

this poses, given the loss of embryos typical of IVF, causing a scramble by many who co-sponsored a bill to create federal law that grants legal personhood at fertilization to nonetheless claim support for IVF as a technology that is pro-natalist and supportive of family formation.[36]

But things only get murkier when the entity is not even created using fertilization of a human egg by human sperm. This may be when it is made instead through somatic cell nuclear transfer (also known as cloning)[37] or, as being developed now, is made by fertilization of gametes that themselves have been made by de-differentiating and re-differentiating somatic cells, a process known as gametogenesis.[38] Already, international professional societies have worked on guidelines for whether and when research on these entities should be governed by the norms that apply to embryo research or some other set of rules.[39] Further, in such situations, debates may occur over whether the resulting entity, or even a live born person conceived in this manner, fits within our human community. Indeed, just such debates took place in the 1990s at the advent of cloning.[40]

This question of what constitutes an "authentic" human (or human embryo) revolves not only on the method by which a cell becomes diploid and developmentally capable, but also by looking at the characteristics of the entity and its potentiality. Nowhere was this more forcefully brought into discussion than by the 2017 paper that introduced the concept of 'synthetic' embryos.[41] This paper, which introduced the term "SHEEFS" to refer to *Synthetic Human Entities with Embryo-like Features*, set out to describe a new way to develop an entity that could recapitulate many of the stages of embryo development, thus serving as a model for the kind of research usually done on IVF embryos, but that would lack one or more key characteristics that typically are cited as the

36 Kelsey Ables, 'Senate Republican blocks bill to protect IVF after Alabama ruling' (The Washington Post, 29 February 2024), available at: https://www.washingtonpost.com/nation/2024/02/29/ivf-bill-senate-republicans-alabama/.

37 National Academy of Sciences (US), National Academy of Engineering (US), Institute of Medicine (US) and National Research Council (US) Committee on Science, Engineering, and Public Policy, *Scientific and Medical Aspects of Human Reproductive Cloning* (National Academies Press 2002).

38 'Conception – Turning Stem Cells into Human Eggs', available at: https://conception.bio. Disclosure: I am a paid consultant to Conception.

39 International Society for Stem Cell Research, 'Guidelines—International Society for Stem Cell Research' (2022), available at: https://www.isscr.org/guidelines.

40 Katheryn D Katz, 'The clonal child: procreative liberty and asexual reproduction' (1997) 8 Albany Law Journal of Science & Technology 1.

41 John Aach and others, 'Addressing the ethical issues raised by synthetic human entities with embryo-like features' (2017) 6 eLife e20674.

basis for according an elevated moral status to human embryos, as compared to other human tissue.[42]

If these entities do lack some key characteristic, then presumably research could be done on SHEEFs that could not be done (by law or professional ethical norms) on IVF embryos, including the widely imposed prohibition on research beyond the appearance of the primitive streak or beyond 14 days of *ex vivo* embryonic development, which dates back to advisory committee recommendations from the 1980s and 1990s in the UK[43] and the US.[44] As the originators of the term note:

> SHEEFs … are different enough from non-synthetic embryos to justify their exemption from research limits on such embryos. But to achieve this will require deep consideration of the conditions under which SHEEFs might develop features that are morally concerning, and a framework that allows research limits to be specified for them.[45]

With the circularity that is typical in these debates around proper naming and categorization, the question then becomes—again—which characteristics in an embryo or embryo-like entity become morally concerning. In considering this question, and what it is that makes something human for the purpose of eligibility for a range of human rights and responsibilities, Professors Knoppers and Greely wrote:

> We care about living organisms that are human in their characteristics, but they do not always need to have exactly human characteristics. "Human beings" typically have two arms and two legs, but we recognize as human those without all those limbs, through amputation or congenital condition, as well as people with artificial limbs.[46]

42 R Alta Charo, 'The hunting of the snark: the moral status of embryos, right-to-lifers, and Third World women' (1995) 6 Stanford Law & Policy Review 11.

43 Mary Warnock, *Report of the Committee into Human Fertilisation and Embryology* (Cmnd.: 9314) (Her Majesty's Stationery Office 1984).

44 Human Embryo Research Panel, National Institutes of Health, *Report of the Human Embryo Research Panel, Volume 1* (1994), available at: https://repository.library.georgetown.edu/handle/10822/559352.

45 Aach and others (n 41).

46 Knoppers and Greely (n 10).

They continue by noting, as have others, that possession of a human genome is certainly not sufficient, lest every cell in our body be given elevated status.[47]

But if the key to moral significance lies in the characteristics, and not the genome, and if the most commonly cited characteristics involve recapitulation of developmental stages coupled with at least hypothetical capacity for development to birth, then in what possible way can the mode of fertilization or other aspect of conception possibly matter? As with the discussions around somatic cell nuclear transfer (cloning), if and when such developments occur, should the entity no longer be deemed a "synthetic" embryo and simply be called an embryo?

Add to these the recent work on human-nonhuman embryo combinations, known as chimaeras, and the resulting entities, according to Professors Knoppers and Greely "challenge the animal-human species divide [thus blurring the boundary of] living, natural persons with legally recognized rights and obligations. … A new classification has the potential to affect and bind all future parties while unsettling the past."[48]

Both scholars also noted in their 2019 piece the *hominum causa omne jus constitutum est* ("all law is created for the sake of men"), a maxim from Roman law. In other words, law *should* create categories that make law function as it is needed to for the proper management of our lives and environment. It must create categories of sufficient clarity that people can understand the rules that might apply. The categories must be sufficiently aligned to be perceived as objective and must accord with emotional reactions sufficiently for people to find them rational, perhaps even instinctual. They must, at the same time, not be rigidly bound to categories as defined by biologists as to undermine sensible social policy, given that biological categories (e.g. male and female; sibling and stranger; dead and alive) may make sense for purposes of research, but not make sense for purposes of constructing fair sports contests, allocating family law rights and responsibilities, or deciding when medical interventions are no longer required as a matter of right:

> There are many examples in which the public has become comfortable with rules based on treating people or things as if they really met the criteria for an underlying biological reality. … A fine example is treating adoptive parents in all respects as if they were their child's biological

47 R Alta Charo, 'Every Cell is Sacred: Logical Consequences of the Argument from Potential in the Age of Cloning' in Paul Lauritzen (ed), *Cloning and the Future of Human Embryo Research* (Oxford University Press 2001).

48 Knoppers and Greely (n 10).

parents. What may determine public acceptance of such fictions is the degree to which they protect the current interests of parties affected by the problem at hand.[49]

7 Concluding Thoughts: What Constitutes the *Authentic* Human?

So, what can one conclude about authenticity, and whether and when an entity is an authentic human? Professors Knoppers and Greely would argue that:

> [L]ike the body, the genome needs only to be "substantially" human. Unusual or rare variations are not disqualifying in themselves but form part of the decision. The same is true of humans with some tissue from nonhuman organisms or some mechanical implants. ... Similarly, some version of "substantially" could be applied to definitions of brain death, not to require some kind of "higher brain death" rule but to avoid complexity when small bits of living brain, either in vivo or in vitro, are used to assert that the legal natural person still lives.[50]

This would, as they note, allow for a fair degree of discretion when judges, juries, legislators, regulators, and the public interpret that word "substantially," as well as allow for cross-border culturally determined variations. But perhaps that is indeed better than a fruitless effort to rigidly define authenticity by tying social categories to definitions constructed for different purposes, such as biological research. Instead, one can ask the same question posed by Juliet, when speaking to a lover who bore the name of a family sworn to enmity with her own: "Tis but thy name that is mine enemy: What's Montague? It is not hand nor foot, Nor arm, nor face, nor any other part. What's in a name? That which we call a rose, By any other name would smell as sweet."[51]

It is in the purpose of names that one may determine the authenticity of those named. And if the purpose is to determine rights and responsibilities as between and among those named, then Professors Knoppers and Greely have the right of it when they argue that this is "necessarily situated in the context of relationships. ... From an appreciation of these relationships emerge ethical

49 R Alta Charo, 'Biological truths and legal fictions' (1998) 1 Journal of Health Care Law and Policy 701.

50 Knoppers and Greely (n 10).

51 William Shakespeare, *Romeo and Juliet* (1597), 'Scene II. Capulet's Orchard', available at: http://shakespeare.mit.edu/romeo_juliet/romeo_juliet.2.2.html.

principles that reflect the complexity of both the human person and new technologies."[52] It is this same complexity that directs us to shy away from reliance on simplistic uses of biological categories, and to take on the more challenging task of deciding for ourselves with whom and for whom we must honour human rights and responsibilities. Today that task may focus on embryos and organoids. Tomorrow, it may be for synths.

52 Bartha Maria Knoppers, 'Of biotechnology and man' (2004) 7 Public Health Genomics 176.

VIGNETTE

Trademark Bartha

Jeffrey Kahn

It is my honour to offer a few words about my opportunities to collaborate with Bartha over the years, as our careers have overlapped at multiple times and on a number of projects. Most memorable for me was also our most recent service together, on an international consensus committee charged with making recommendations on human applications of heritable genome editing in the aftermath of the announcement of the birth of gene-edited twins in 2018.

The International Commission on the Clinical Use of Human Germline Genome Editing was convened in 2019 to address concerns that the international community lacked sufficiently clear direction around the responsible uses of heritable gene editing, and we were among the few members from North America.

Bartha and I found ourselves in frequent discussions, inside and outside meetings of the commission, as the two of us were seen by our fellow committee members as the card-carrying bioethicists among the group. That led to comparing notes about our charge, and about how our fellow members were articulating arguments or sometimes just making assertions about the ethics and policy questions at the core of our charge. We quickly realized that we saw the issues in similar ways, though Bartha from her purchase in law and mine in applied ethics. We saw the challenge in making recommendations intended to apply across international boundaries given the diversity of existing laws, regulatory regimes, and institutional policies and practices relevant to uses of gene editing techniques in humans. Adding to the challenges was the recognition that important societal differences would also influence the acceptability of the uses of genome editing, let alone the acceptability of harmonized policies for such a novel and emerging technology.

I followed Bartha's lead in doing our best to infuse the discussions of the meetings with clarity, realpolitik, and importantly, humility—the last being trademark Bartha. The report reflects that focus, including clarity and detail about what conditions needed to be met for competent regulatory oversight, setting the bar clearly. Again, trademark Bartha.

As I think about this experience, I'm struck by how much I cherish her insights and her approach, and most notably her style. Clear, focused, drawing the discussion back to important foundational issues, always in ways that help reach consensus. We need more like her.

VIGNETTE

The Magic Tin: Cookies, Policy, Ethics, and Mentorship

Rosario Isasi

"Scientists have labs and algorithms, but those of us in the 'ELSI' (Ethical, Legal and Social Issues) community have only words."[1] During her vast trajectory, Bartha proved that she didn't only have words, but also a steadfast determination to deliver actionable results. For her, capacity building in the ELSI field was a vital foundation for scientific innovation, and so, she became a force in building the next generations of scholars. For almost 14 years, I was one of those mentees who "grew up" professionally in an environment sustained by an ethos of integrity and collegiality, while surrounded by a magic tin, always filled with cookies and sweets to transform Montreal's most bitter winter days into sunny ones.

While globetrotting the world together, I discovered Bartha's wonderful talent as a storyteller and learnt about the intricacies of policymaking. Bartha is a pioneer in comparative policy; her rich scholarship demonstrates the complexities of developing robust, interoperable, ethical and policy frameworks in vast fields such as genetics, regenerative medicine, public health, and many others.[2] We always cherished explaining how policy is developed through complex processes which seek to reflect historical, cultural, and political environments.

One of my fondest memories is walking with Bartha in some part of the world, while discussing the meaning and effects of a given policy. We would often stop at historical sites while we reflected on whether the given policy was effective in aligning their ethos with their desired objectives, or if it was anticipatory enough to resist the challenges of evolving science and societies. With a cup of coffee (or maybe wine, depending on the time of day), we were

1 Bartha M Knoppers, 'Does policy grow on trees?' (2014) 15 BMC Medical Ethics 87.

2 Rosario M Isasi and Bartha M Knoppers, 'Mind the gap: policy approaches to embryonic stem cell and cloning research in 50 countries' (2006) 13 European Journal of Health Law 9; Rosario M Isasi and Bartha M Knoppers, 'Beyond the permissibility of embryonic and stem cell research: substantive requirements and procedural safeguards' (2006) 21 Human Reproduction 2474; Rosario Isasi, Erika Kleiderman, and Bartha M Knoppers, 'Editing policy to fit the genome?' (2016) 351 Science 337.

 | DOI:10.1163/9789004688544_023

delighted in finding commonalities and inconsistencies, and imagining how harmonization would one day be the norm. Those dialogues will often end drifting to talks about art, music, food, and life, because Bartha's knowledge is not restricted to the confines of the ethics and policy world. I always brought up the issue of fashion and she always carved time for me to indulge in some "shopping therapy." Bartha's most painful memory of me might be the one when I kindly suggested to her—like a rampant virus—the impetus to be more fashionable, which ended up us in Singapore spending beyond the modest means of scholars.

Bartha's legacy is not only in the generations of people she mentored, but also in real life. Her work paved the way for rich scholarly work promoting ELSI integration and championing comparative policy studies.

The first week of January we always had lunch at the brasserie Chez Alexandre in Montreal to discuss our "action plan" for the year. And, at those lunches, we always ended up with a little glass of champagne to make a wish: may the "dream drawer" be empty and the "grants drawer" full! As with the flowers she loves, the seeds she planted continue to grow and make a substantial impact for individuals, families, communities, and society at large. That has certainly been the case for me.

The gratitude tin is full.

CHAPTER 8

Population-Based Genome-Wide Testing in Babies: Newborn Screening or Mission Creep?

Jan M. Friedman

1 Introduction

The development and implementation of population-based newborn screening for serious preventable or treatable diseases of infancy was one of the most successful public health interventions of the twentieth century.[1] The success of newborn screening results from its ability to reduce serious lifelong disease or disability by the early recognition and treatment of conditions like phenylketonuria (PKU) and severe combined immunodeficiency disease in healthy-appearing infants. Initially begun in the 1960s for one very rare genetic disease, PKU, population-based newborn screening has since been expanded to include many other genetic diseases, as well as some conditions like congenital hypothyroidism or critical congenital heart defects that can have heterogenous or complex causes.

Over the past 10–15 years, genome-wide (exome or genome) sequencing has emerged as a first-tier test for genetic disease, facilitating a diagnosis in 30–50% of patients suspected to have such a condition.[2] Genome-wide sequencing is especially valuable in newborn infants because many serious genetic disorders present at or soon after birth, and the diagnostic precision offered by genome-wide sequencing may provide information that is critically

1 Beth A Tarini, 'The current revolution in newborn screening: new technology, old controversies' (2007) 161 Archives of Pediatrics & Adolescent Medicine 767; Ram Koppaka and Domestic CDC Public Health Achievements Team, 'Ten great public health achievements — United States, 2001–2010' (2021) 60 MMWR: Morbidity and Mortality Weekly Report 619.

2 Siddharth Srivastava and others, 'Meta-analysis and multidisciplinary consensus statement: exome sequencing is a first-tier clinical diagnostic test for individuals with neurodevelopmental disorders' (2019) 21 Genetics in Medicine 2413; Ontario Health (Quality), 'Genome-wide sequencing for unexplained developmental disabilities or multiple congenital anomalies: a health technology assessment' (2020) 20 Ontario Health Technology Assessment Series 1; Kristen M Wigby and others, 'Evidence review and considerations for use of first line genome sequencing to diagnose rare genetic disorders' (2024) 9 npj Genomic Medicine 15.

important in immediate clinical management.[3] The clear value of genome-wide sequencing in infants with clinical features of a genetic disease has raised the possibility of using this technology for population-based screening of healthy newborn infants for hundreds or thousands of genetic conditions that cannot be detected with current newborn screening methods.

Professor Bartha Knoppers is an international leader in ethical, legal, and public policy research regarding genomic newborn sequencing.[4] She has been writing and speaking incisively on newborn screening, genetic testing, and legal and ethical considerations regarding children's health generally for more than 30 years.[5]

2 Potential Benefits and Concerns Raised by Population-Based Genomic Newborn Screening

The purpose of newborn screening is to detect potentially fatal or disabling conditions in newborns as early as possible, often before the infant displays any signs or symptoms of a disease or condition. Such

3 Stephen F Kingsmore and F Sessions Cole, 'The role of genome sequencing in neonatal intensive care units' (2022) 23 Annual Review of Genomics and Human Genetics 427; Michael Muriello, 'Exome and whole genome sequencing in the neonatal intensive care unit' (2022) 49 Clinics in Perinatology 167; Stephen F Kingsmore, Russell Nofsinger, and Kasia Ellsworth, 'Rapid genomic sequencing for genetic disease diagnosis and therapy in intensive care units: a review' (2024) 9 npj Genomic Medicine 17.

4 Bartha M Knoppers and others, 'Whole-genome sequencing in newborn screening programs' (2014) 6 Science Translational Medicine 229cm2; Heidi Carmen Howard and others, 'Whole-genome sequencing in newborn screening? A statement on the continued importance of targeted approaches in newborn screening programmes' (2015) 23 European Journal of Human Genetics 1593; Karine Sénécal and others, 'Genome-based newborn screening: a conceptual analysis of the best interests of the child standard' (2015) 12 Personalized Medicine 439; Pascal Borry, Karine Sénécal, and Bartha Maria Knoppers, 'Do it yourself newborn screening' (2016) 170 JAMA Pediatrics 523; Jan M Friedman and others, 'Genomic newborn screening: public health policy considerations and recommendations' (2017) 10 BMC Medical Genomics 9; Vasiliki Rahimzadeh and others, 'Exome/genome-wide testing in newborn screening: a proportionate path forward' (2022) 13 Frontiers in Genetics 865400.

5 Claude M Laberge and Bartha Maria Knoppers, 'Newborn genetic screening: ethical and social considerations for the nineties' (1991) 2 Journal international de bioethique 5; Bartha M Knoppers and Mark A Rothstein, 'Panel on legal issues in genetic testing' (1993) Suppl B Journal of Insurance Medicine 263; Bartha M Knoppers, 'Confidentiality in genetic testing: legal and ethical issues in an international context' (1993) 12 Medicine and Law 573; Bartha Maria Knoppers, 'Donor insemination: children as in concreto or in abstracto subjects of rights?' (1993) 12 Politics and the Life Sciences 182; Bartha Maria Knoppers, 'Genetic testing: a comparative view' (1993) 8 Forum for Applied Research and Public Policy 26.

early detection allows treatment to begin immediately, which reduces or even eliminates the effects of the condition.[6]

Although newborn screening has expanded to include more than 30 rare diseases in some jurisdictions,[7] even the largest population-based newborn screening programs include only a tiny fraction of all treatable genetic disorders.[8] In contrast, sequencing the DNA from a small drop of blood obtained by pricking a baby's heel can identify genetic variants that are predictive of disease in dozens to hundreds (panel sequencing) or thousands (exome or genome sequencing) of additional genes. Most gene panel tests are currently performed by sequencing an individual's entire exome or genome and selecting only a small subset of the genes for bioinformatics analysis; limiting the analysis in this way makes interpretation of the results easier but is usually less sensitive than analyzing the entire exome or genome for disease-causing variants.

A population-based genomic newborn screening program to detect serious genetic conditions can be evaluated using standard public health criteria for assessing the value of disease screening. The Wilson-Jungner criteria[9] have been used for this purpose for more than 50 years (Box 1), although some experts now favour updated criteria that better reflect current circumstances (Box 2).[10]

Genomic newborn screening for any purpose raises several important clinical and ethical issues. One issue is the confusion that results from using DNA

6 Eunice Kennedy Shriver National Institute of Child Health and Human Development, 'What Is the Purpose of Newborn Screening?', available at: https://www.nichd.nih.gov/health/topics/newborn/conditioninfo/purpose.

7 Marci K Sontag and others, 'Infants with congenital disorders identified through newborn screening - United States, 2015-2017' (2020) 69 MMWR: Morbidity and Mortality Weekly Report 1265; J Gerard Loeber and others, 'Neonatal screening in Europe revisited: an ISNS perspective on the current state and developments since 2010' (2021) 7 International Journal of Neonatal Screening 15; Si Ding and Lianshu Han, 'Newborn screening for genetic disorders: current status and prospects for the future' (2022) 6 Pediatric investigation 291.

8 Zornitza Stark and Richard H Scott, 'Genomic newborn screening for rare diseases' (2023) 24 Nature Reviews Genetics 755.

9 James Maxwell Glover Wilson and Gunnar Jungner, 'Principles and practice of screening for disease' (1968), available at: http://apps.who.int/iris/bitstream/10665/37650/1/WHO_PHP_34.pdf.

10 Mark J Dobrow and others, 'Consolidated principles for screening based on a systematic review and consensus process' (2018) 190 CMAJ: Canadian Medical Association journal E422.

Box 1: Wilson-Jungner principles of screening for early disease detection[11]

- The condition sought should be an important health problem.
- There should be an accepted treatment for patients with recognized disease.
- Facilities for diagnosis and treatment should be available.
- There should be a recognizable latent or early symptomatic stage.
- There should be a suitable test or examination.
- The test should be acceptable to the population.
- The natural history of the condition, including development from latent to declared disease, should be adequately understood. There should be an agreed policy on whom to treat as patients. The cost of case-finding (including diagnosis and treatment of patients diagnosed) should be economically balanced in relation to possible expenditure on medical care as a whole. Case-finding should be a continuing process and not a "once and for all" project.

Box 2: Consolidated principles for screening[12]

- The epidemiology of the disease or condition should be adequately understood, and the disease or condition should be an important health problem.
- The epidemiology of the disease or condition should be adequately understood, and the disease or condition should be an important health problem.
- The natural history of the disease or condition should be adequately understood, the disease or condition is well-defined, and there should be a detectable preclinical phase.
- The target population for screening should be clearly defined, identifiable and able to be reached.
- Screening test performance should be appropriate for the purpose, with all key components specific to the test being accurate and reliable or reproducible. The test should be acceptable to the target population and it should be possible to perform or administer it safely, affordably and efficiently.
- Screening test results should be clearly interpretable and determinate to allow identification of the screening participants who should (and should not) be offered diagnostic testing and other posts-screening care.

11 Wilson and Jungner (n 9).

12 Dobrow and others (n 10).

- There should be an agreed-on course of action for screening participants with positive screening test results that involves diagnostic testing, treatment or intervention, and follow-up care that will modify the natural history and clinical pathway for the disease or condition; that is available, accessible and acceptable to those affected; and that results in improved outcomes. The burden of testing on all participants should be understood and acceptable, and the effect of false-positive and false-negative tests should be minimal.
- There should be adequate existing infrastructure, or a clear plan to develop adequate infrastructure, that is appropriate to the setting to allow for timely access to all components of the screening program.
- All components of the screening program should be coordinated and, where possible, integrated with the broader healthcare system (including a formal system to inform, counsel, refer and manage the treatment of screening participants) to optimize care continuity and ensure no screening participant is neglected.
- All components of the screening program should be clinically, socially and ethically acceptable to screening participants, health professionals and society, and there should be effective methods for providing screening participants with informed choice, promoting their autonomy and protecting their rights.
- The expected range and magnitude of benefits and harms for screening participants and society should be clearly defined and acceptable, and supported by existing high-quality scientific evidence (or addressed by ongoing studies) that indicates that the overall benefit of the screening program outweighs its potential harms.
- An economic evaluation of the screening program, using a health system or societal perspective, should be conducted (or a clear plan to conduct an economic evaluation) to assess the full costs and effects of implementing, operating and sustaining the screening program while clearly considering the opportunity costs and effect of allocating resources to other potential non-screening alternatives for managing the disease or condition.
- The screening program should have clear goals or objectives that are explicitly linked to program planning, monitoring, evaluating and reporting activities, with dedicated information systems and funding, to ensure ongoing quality control and achievement of performance targets.

sequencing for population screening of healthy individuals rather than as a means of genotyping patients who are suspected of having a genetic disease (Box 1, #8; Box 2, #3 and #6; Box 3, #1 and #2). Genome, exome, and gene panel sequencing are first-tier clinical tests, but they are not diagnostic of genetic disease per se.[13] Genome-wide sequencing is a highly-accurate way to detect genetic alterations (so-called "pathogenic" or "likely pathogenic" variants) that may be associated with the occurrence of a genetic disease *under some circumstances*. For example, a child who inherits a pathogenic *CFTR* p.Phe508del (ΔF508) allele from her father will have the disease cystic fibrosis *only* if she also inherits a disease-causing *CFTR* allele from her mother.

Exome and genome sequencing can determine genotypes very accurately, but the ability of the genetic changes found to predict a resulting phenotype varies by disease, gene, genetic variant, and the person's prior probability of having that genetic condition. For example, some forms of autosomal dominant intellectual disability, like that associated with *ARID1B* loss-of-function variants, are characterized by incomplete penetrance and variable expressivity.[14] A 5-year-old child with an *ARID1B* loss-of-function variant, severe developmental delay, and clinical features of Coffin-Siris syndrome is likely to have *ARID1B*-associated intellectual disability, while her 35-year-old father who is intellectually normal and has no dysmorphic features is not, even if both carry the same "likely pathogenic" *ARID1B* allele.

Estimating a healthy newborn's risk for a rare genetic disease is often difficult because our understanding of the functional consequences of many variants is incomplete, and our knowledge about the penetrance, natural history, and range of clinical manifestations of many conditions is limited[15] (Box 1, #7

13 Jan M Friedman, Kenneth Lyons Jones, and John C Carey, 'Exome sequencing and clinical diagnosis' (2020) 324 JAMA 627; Nina B Gold, Allan Nadel, and Robert C Green, 'Ready or not, genomic screening of fetuses is already here' (2024) 26 Genetics in Medicine 101008.

14 H Hilger Ropers and Thomas Wienker, 'Penetrance of pathogenic mutations in haploinsufficient genes for intellectual disability and related disorders' (2015) 58 European Journal of Medical Genetics 715.

15 Friedman and others (n 4); Jill Hagenkord and others, 'Design and reporting considerations for genetic screening tests' (2020) 22 The Journal of Molecular Diagnostics 599; Harvey L Levy, 'Ethical and psychosocial implications of genomic newborn screening' (2021) 7 International Journal of Neonatal Screening 2; Audrey C Woerner and others, 'The use of whole genome and exome sequencing for newborn screening: challenges and opportunities for population health' (2021) 9 Frontiers in Pediatrics 663752; Rahimzadeh and others (n 4); Robert C Green and others, 'Actionability of unanticipated monogenic disease risks in newborn genomic screening: findings from the BabySeq Project' (2023) 110 American Journal of Human Genetics 1034; Giancarlo la Marca and others, 'Current state and innovations in newborn screening: continuing to do good and avoid harm' (2023) 9 International Journal of Neonatal Screening 15; Luca Brunelli, Heeju Sohn, and Amy Brower, 'Newborn sequencing is only part of the solution for better child health' (2023) 25 The Lancet Regional Health - Americas 100581; Rachel Horton and others, 'Challenges of using whole genome sequencing in population newborn screening' (2024) 384 BMJ e077060.

and Box 2, #2; Box 3, #2). Moreover, there is usually no other laboratory test or imaging study that can reliably establish the clinical diagnosis of a genetic disease in an asymptomatic child. Recognizing false positive and false negative newborn screening results for many rare genetic diseases may only be possible after the children have been followed clinically for many years (Box 2, #4 and #5).[16]

Many authors have emphasized the need for clinical assessment and long-term follow-up of "screen-positive" infants to estimate actual diagnostic rates, sensitivity, and specificity of genomic newborn screening.[17]

Theoretical discussions of genomic newborn screening often focus on sequencing all of the protein coding genes (i.e. the exome) or the entire genome, but the function of most human genes is unknown, and sequencing them would be of no immediate value.[18] Consequently, almost all concrete proposals and pilot projects for genomic newborn screening involve bioinformatics analysis of only a panel of genes, usually just a few hundred, that are known to be associated with serious Mendelian diseases that may occur in young children and are clinically "actionable." For example, the National Health Service in England has undertaken the Generation Study, a pilot project that is using genome sequencing with analysis limited to a selected set of genes to screen at least 100,000 newborn infants for hundreds of rare, treatable genetic diseases that are likely to become symptomatic prior to age 5 years.[19] The genes being analyzed have been selected because they meet four major principles of population screening (Box 3).

Analyzing only a subset of genes facilitates interpretation of the sequencing data and focuses the screening on important health problems (Box 1, #1 and #8; Box 2, #1 and #3), but choosing the best subset of genes to test is difficult.

---

16 Chanjuan Hao and others, 'Newborn screening with targeted sequencing: a multi-center investigation and a pilot clinical study in China' (2022) 49 Journal of Genetics and Genomics 13; Horton and others (n 15); Dale L Bodian and others, 'Utility of whole-genome sequencing for detection of newborn screening disorders in a population cohort of 1,696 neonates' (2016) 18 Genetics in Medicine 221; Levy (n 15); Stephen F Kingsmore and others, 'A genome sequencing system for universal newborn screening, diagnosis, and precision medicine for severe genetic diseases' (2022) 109 American Journal of Human Genetics 1605; Ting Chen and others, 'Genomic sequencing as a first-tier screening test and outcomes of newborn screening' (2023) 6 JAMA Network Open e2331162; Gold, Nadel, and Green (n 13).

17 Bodian and others (n 16); Levy (n 15); Hao and others (n 16); Kingsmore and others (n 16); Chen and others (n 16); Gold, Nadel, and Green (n 13); Horton and others (n 15).

18 João J Rocha and others, 'Functional unknomics: systematic screening of conserved genes of unknown function' (2023) 21 PLOS Biology e3002222.

19 Horton and others (n 15).

Box 3: Principles used to decide which genes to include in the UK's Generation Study genomic newborn screening pilot project[20]

- There is strong evidence the variant(s) causes the condition and can be reliably detected.
- A high proportion of individuals who have the genetic variant(s) would be expected to have debilitating symptoms if the condition is undiagnosed.
- Early or pre-symptomatic intervention for the condition has been shown to lead to substantially improved outcomes in children compared with intervention after symptom onset.
- Conditions screened for are only those for which the interventions are equitably accessible.

Several gene lists have been proposed for newborn screening;[21] but there is no consensus on which genes should be included. Downie and associates[22] recently compared six lists of genes that have been suggested for genomic newborn screening. Of a total of 1,279 genes on one or more of these lists, only 55 (4.3%) were included on all six lists. Similarly, a survey of 238 clinical or laboratory geneticists found that only 25 (3.8%) of 649 genes associated with potentially-treatable genetic diseases were recommended for inclusion in newborn screening by 85% or more of the respondents.[23] This diversity of opinion probably reflects current limitations of our knowledge of the penetrance, natural history, and variability of clinical expression of many rare genetic diseases (Box 1, #7; Box 2, #2), as well as lack of agreement about what constitutes clinical "actionability" and whether pre-symptomatic diagnosis and treatment are beneficial for these conditions[24] (Box 1, #2; Box 2, #6 and #12).

20 Horton and others (n 15).

21 Ozge Ceyhan-Birsoy and others, 'A curated gene list for reporting results of newborn genomic sequencing' (2017) 19 Genetics in Medicine 809; Stephen F Kingsmore, 'Dispatches from Biotech beginning BeginNGS: rapid newborn genome sequencing to end the diagnostic and therapeutic odyssey' (2022) 190 American Journal of Medical Genetics Part C: Seminars in Medical Genetics 243; Kingsmore and others (n 16).

22 Lilian Downie and others, 'Gene selection for genomic newborn screening: moving towards consensus?' (2024) Genetics in Medicine 101077.

23 Nina B Gold and others, 'Perspectives of rare disease experts on newborn genome sequencing' (2023) 6 JAMA Network Open e2312231.

24 ibid.

3 Mission Creep?

Exome and genome sequencing are powerful and informative technologies that provide information on all protein-coding genes, not just those that are targeted for analysis. Genome sequencing also provides information on millions of single nucleotide polymorphisms (SNPs) in every individual. SNPs are genetic markers that can be used to predict one's risk of developing common adult-onset diseases, to assess genetic contributions to normal traits like height, and to determine ancestry. The availability of all of this additional genetic information has led to suggestions that the results of newborn genome-wide sequencing be used for many purposes besides the generally accepted goal of current newborn screening programs—to detect potentially fatal or disabling conditions in infants and provide immediate treatment to prevent or reduce serious disease manifestations.[25] Thus, it has been suggested that genomic newborn screening might be used to:

1. **Short-cut the diagnostic odyssey in children who subsequently develop symptoms of genetic disease.** Bioinformatics re-analysis of the genomic data obtained at birth could be performed rapidly without having to undertake diagnostic genome-wide sequencing if symptoms of a genetic disease appear later in life.
2. **Inform the family of the likelihood that an infant will develop a genetic disease for which no effective treatment currently exists.** This would enable the family to prepare for the consequences of the child developing this disease later in life or to take advantage of future preventative or therapeutic interventions that may become available.
3. **Offer risk stratification for common diseases of later life.** This would help healthcare providers offer better guidance regarding lifestyle, diet, career choice, etc. during childhood, when such interventions might be most effective.

---

25 Jeffrey R Botkin, 'Assessing the new criteria for newborn screening' (2009) 19 Health Matrix 163; Jonathan S Berg and others, 'Newborn sequencing in genomic medicine and public health' (2017) 139 Pediatrics e20162252; Jorune Balciuniene and others, 'At-risk genomic findings for pediatric-onset disorders from genome sequencing vs medically actionable gene panel in proactive screening of newborns and children' (2023) 6 JAMA Network Open e2326445; Bryant Furlow, 'Newborn genome screening in the USA: early steps on a challenging path' (2023) 7 The Lancet Child and Adolescent Health 231; Stark and Scott (n 8); Danya F Vears and others, 'Are we ready for whole population genomic sequencing of asymptomatic newborns?' (2023) 16 Pharmacogenomics and Personalized Medicine 681.

4. **Provide preemptive pharmacogenomic testing.** Many pharmacogenetic variants that influence the efficacy or risk of adverse effects of drug treatments used in childhood could be identified by genomic newborn sequencing. In order to benefit the child, this information would have to be maintained in the medical record and made available to any physician who might consider treating the child with a relevant drug in the future.
5. **Test for heterozygous carrier status for recessive diseases.** Genome-wide sequencing can provide information on carrier status for thousands of serious autosomal or X-linked recessive diseases, but being a carrier for most of these conditions has no implications for the health of the individual. Carrier status may, however, be important for future reproductive decision making if the individual's partner is found to be a heterozygous carrier for one or more of the same diseases.
6. **Provide information for parents and other family members regarding their risks for developing a serious genetic disease.** Identifying a genetic variant in a gene like *BRCA2* or *PKP2* that is unlikely to cause disease in children but can influence clinical management in adults may trigger cascade testing that has important health consequences for the baby's parents and other relatives.
7. **Provide information for parents and other family members about their reproductive risks.** Genetic counselling should be available to the parents of any baby who is found to have a serious genetic disease on genomic newborn screening, but cascade testing of the parents for carrier status could also be offered if the infant is found to be a heterozygous carrier for a serious recessive disease.
8. **Promote research to improve our understanding of genetics and genomics.** Following infants who are diagnosed with a genetic disease through newborn screening is essential to determining the value of this program as a public health intervention. In addition, long-term studies of the health status, growth, and development of "screen-negative" as well as "screen-positive" infants is needed to establish the clinical utility of population-based genomic newborn screening and to improve our knowledge of the penetrance, natural history, and range of clinical expression of rare genetic diseases.

These proposed benefits all require data obtained through genome-wide sequencing of newborn infants, so the proposals are all subject to the concerns raised in the previous section regarding the clinical validity and clinical utility of genomic testing. In addition, these extended uses of genomic data are also subject to limitations imposed by our incomplete knowledge of penetrance, natural history, and clinical variability of the manifestations, uncertainty about the effectiveness of available treatments, etc.

One of the most important reasons that many conventional newborn screening programs have been successful is that they are universal—every baby born within the jurisdiction is offered, and almost all receive, newborn screening.[26] An important factor in achieving universal coverage is thought to be the use of implied parental consent for newborn screening—all parents are assumed to want this screening to benefit their baby because of the severity of the diseases included and the urgency and effectiveness of available treatment.[27] In some countries, a streamlined verbal consent for newborn screening is also obtained from the mother. In other countries, the parents are told that they can "opt-out" of newborn screening if they object to it, but the system is usually designed to assure that almost every infant receives "Baby's First Test."[28]

The assumption of benefit to all infants may also apply to newborn screening for other genetic diseases that meet standard public health criteria for screening[29] (Table 8.1, first row), and implied consent may also suffice for these conditions. However, genomic newborn screening to achieve the extended benefits listed above do *not* meet standard public health disease screening criteria and are very likely to require explicit parental consent for screening[30] (Table 8.1). Moreover, many of the extended benefits of genomic newborn screening cannot be achieved without long-term storage of the baby's genomic data (Table 8.1), which itself raises a number of legal and ethical concerns,[31] including: Who is responsible for maintaining these data for many years? Who is responsible for assuring the privacy and security of these data? Who should have access to these data in the future? Only the child? The child's physicians? Members of the child's immediate family? Other relatives? The legal system? The criminal justice system? Insurance companies? Potential employers? Scientific or medical researchers?

---

26 Friedman and others (n 4); Robert J Currier, 'Newborn screening is on a collision course with public health ethics' (2022) 8 International Journal of Neonatal Screening 51; Stark and Scott (n 8).

27 Friedman and others (n 4); Currier (n 26); Stark and Scott (n 8).

28 'Baby's First Test', available at: https://www.babysfirsttest.org/.

29 Wilson and Jungner (n 9); Dobrow and others (n 10).

30 Currier (n 26); Ute Spiekerkoetter and others, 'Genomic newborn screening: are we entering a new era of screening?' (2023) 46 Journal of Inherited Metabolic Disease 778; Stark and Scott (n 8).

31 Berg and others (n 25); Friedman and others (n 4); Woerner and others (n 15); Spiekerkoetter and others (n 30); Horton and others (n 15).

TABLE 8.1 Consequences of mission-based and extended genomic newborn screening

Proposed beneficial uses of genomic newborn screening data	Explicit consent	Long-term genomic data storage	Benefit to child
Detect serious genetic disease in infants and provide immediate effective treatment	Probably not required	Not necessary	Direct
Short-cut the diagnostic odyssey	Required	Required	Contingent
Inform the family of the likelihood that an infant will develop a genetic disease for which no effective treatment currently exists	Required	Not necessary	Contingent
Offer risk stratification for common diseases of later life	Required	May be necessary	Contingent
Provide preemptive pharmacogenomic testing	Required	Required	Contingent
Test for heterozygous carrier status for recessive diseases	Required	Not necessary	Contingent
Provide information for parents and other family members regarding their risks for developing a serious genetic disease	Required	May be necessary	Indirect
Provide information for parents and other family members about their reproductive risks	Required	May be necessary	Indirect
Promote research	Required	May be necessary	None

Long-term storage of data obtained through genomic newborn screening would require explicit parental consent in most jurisdictions[32] and might also require re-consent of the individual who was tested at birth for continued storage beyond the age of majority.[33] Although genomic newborn screening can be done without long-term storage of genomic data, this issue preoccupies many commentators. The idea that maintaining an individual's genome sequence in his electronic medical record or some other central repository is of substantial benefit to him and other family members is based on the assumption that

32 Currier (n 26); Stark and Scott (n 8).

33 Kenneth D Mandl and others, 'Newborn screening program practices in the United States: notification, research, and consent' (2002) 109 Pediatrics 269; Leslie G Biesecker and others, 'Should all babies have their genome sequenced at birth?' (2021) BMJ n2679; Furlow (n 25).

sequencing a person's genome when the data are actually needed is difficult and very expensive. This is no longer true, and if genome sequencing were cheap enough for universal genomic newborn screening to be practical, repeat sequencing when clinically indicated would probably be less expensive and more informative than storing a baby's genomic data safely and securely for many years. Most, if not all, of the extended benefits suggested for genomic newborn screening that require long-term storage of the baby's genomic data can be obtained by just-in-time sequencing of a blood or saliva sample from the concerned individual or family member(s) when the need or desire for the information arises, obviating many of the ethical issues that have been raised about having to store genomic newborn screening data.[34]

Of the proposed beneficial uses of universal genomic newborn screening data listed in Table 8.1, only detecting a potentially fatal or disabling disease in an infant and providing immediate treatment to prevent or reduce the disorder's serious manifestations directly benefits every child who is tested. Many of the other proposed benefits are contingent upon additional factors that are uncommon in the population as a whole—e.g. short-cutting the diagnostic odyssey only benefits those who subsequently develop symptoms of a genetic disease and preemptive pharmacogenomic testing only benefits children who require a treatment that may be affected by pharmacogenetic variation at some point in the future.

Other possible uses of genomic data obtained through newborn screening do *not* directly benefit the child who is tested but may provide an indirect benefit by helping to improve the health or well-being of other family members. However, these benefits could all be obtained by performing genomic screening directly on the other family members, who, if they are adults, can consent to the testing themselves. Genomic screening of adults who wish to have such testing would eliminate the ethical concerns raised by proxy consent in an infant for procedures that do not directly benefit her and by using the child instrumentally to benefit others.[35]

4 A Public Health Perspective: Genomic Newborn Screening as an Enhancement of Conventional Newborn Screening

Implementing genome-wide sequencing (or sequencing of a selected panel of genes) in every newborn infant would raise some important health policy

34 Berg and others (n 25); Friedman and others (n 4); Woerner and others (n 15); Rahimzadeh and others (n 4); Horton and others (n 15).

35 Rahimzadeh and others (n 4).

issues, many of which Professor Knoppers has explored through international and human rights lenses. One issue is that the screening tests, no matter how they are done, are only a small part of a newborn screening program. Genome sequencing can be performed on the small filter paper samples that are currently being collected on every baby for newborn screening. However, these samples must be processed and analyzed in a completely different way than the tests for inborn errors of metabolism or endocrine disorders included in most current newborn screening programs. Once "screen positive" infants are found, the family (or in some programs, the responsible health-care professional) must be notified and the child recalled for further evaluation, which may require additional testing and specialist assessments that differ for different diseases. The infant must then be treated if necessary and followed clinically to determine disease onset or progression, observe for complications and beneficial or adverse effects of treatment, and provide other necessary services such as genetic counselling for the family. Appropriate follow-up and treatment need to be available for every disease for which newborn screening is being performed, and the necessary services should be provided to every infant who screens positive in order for the program to succeed.[36] Access and affordability of such services are likely to be more difficult in jurisdictions without comprehensive universal healthcare systems.

It is important to emphasize that the follow-up and treatment needed for genomic newborn screening are largely in addition to services that are currently in place for other forms of newborn screening.[37] Even for conditions that are already part of current newborn screening programs, additional resources will be needed because some infants who screen positive by current testing methods are not detected by genome sequencing and vice versa.[38] Adding genomic testing to existing universal newborn screening programs will increase the overall cost of those programs substantially, even if the cost of the sequencing itself is small.

---

36 Tarini (n 1); Bridget Wilcken, 'Newborn screening: how are we travelling, and where should we be going?' (2011) 34 Journal of Inherited Metabolic Disease 569; la Marca and others (n 15); Stark and Scott (n 8).

37 Friedman and others (n 4); Levy (n 15); Rahimzadeh and others (n 4); Spiekerkoetter and others (n 30).

38 Bodian and others (n 16); Aashish N Adhikari and others, 'The role of exome sequencing in newborn screening for inborn errors of metabolism' (2020) 26 Nature Medicine 1392; Tamara S Roman and others, 'Genomic sequencing for newborn screening: results of the NC NEXUS Project' (2020) 107 American Journal of Human Genetics 596; Monica H Wojcik and others, 'Discordant results between conventional newborn screening and genomic sequencing in the BabySeq Project' (2021) 23 Genetics in Medicine 1372; Hao and others (n 16).

Cost-effectiveness, which is an important consideration for all public health interventions, has not yet been demonstrated for population-based genomic newborn screening for any disease.[39] However, cost-effectiveness has been shown for population-based newborn screening for Severe Combined Immunodeficiency and Spinal Muscular Atrophy,[40] two conditions that can be identified by doing special DNA tests (not genome-wide sequencing) on newborn blood spots.

Implementation of genomic newborn screening before it has been shown to be cost-effective and to meet other standard public health criteria[41] risks damaging or loss of the current wide-spread public and political support for universal newborn screening.[42] Several large-scale pilot studies of genomic newborn screening are currently underway,[43] and it is important that the results of these studies be obtained and analyzed in a manner that permits accurate assessment of the sensitivity and specificity of genomic newborn screening for serious genetic diseases, the clinical utility of pre-symptomatic diagnosis and intervention, cost-effectiveness, and the overall net benefit to children.[44]

5 Conclusions

Most of the concerns regarding population-based genomic newborn screening that Professor Knoppers and others have raised can be avoided by limiting the

39 Friedman and others (n 4); Stark and Scott (n 8); Vears and others (n 25).

40 Yao Ding and others, 'Cost-effectiveness/cost-benefit analysis of newborn screening for severe combined immune deficiency in Washington state' (2016) 172 The Journal of Pediatrics 127; Sophy TF Shih and others, 'Newborn screening for spinal muscular atrophy with disease-modifying therapies: a cost-effectiveness analysis' (2021) 92 Journal of Neurology, Neurosurgery & Psychiatry 1296; Sophy TF Shih and others, 'Modelling the cost-effectiveness and budget impact of a newborn screening program for spinal muscular atrophy and severe combined immunodeficiency' (2022) 8 International Journal of Neonatal Screening 45; Diana Weidlich and others, 'Cost-effectiveness of newborn screening for spinal muscular atrophy in England' (2023) 12 Neurology and Therapy 1205; Tamara Dangouloff and others, 'Cost-effectiveness of spinal muscular atrophy newborn screening based on real-world data in Belgium' (2024) 34 Neuromuscular Disorders 61.

41 Wilson and Jungner (n 9); Dobrow and others (n 10).

42 Levy (n 15); Rahimzadeh and others (n 4).

43 Stark and Scott (n 8); Spiekerkoetter and others (n 30).

44 Friedman and others (n 4); Josephine Johnston and others, 'Sequencing newborns: a call for nuanced use of genomic technologies' (2018) 48 Hastings Center Report S2; Hagenkord and others (n 15); Rahimzadeh and others (n 4); Stark and Scott (n 8); Spiekerkoetter and others (n 30).

program to screening for serious diseases that can be ameliorated effectively in asymptomatic or very mildly symptomatic infants and by avoiding long-term storage of individually identifiable genomic data. If we implement universal genomic newborn screening in a manner that meets standard public health guidelines[45] (Box 1-3) and resist the temptation to exploit this powerful new technology for other purposes that have not been shown to have clinical benefit or utility, we are likely to maximize the benefits and minimize the risks for the children who are screened.

45 Wilson and Jungner (n 9); Dobrow and others (n 10); Horton and others (n 15).

VIGNETTE

BMK's Garden: Helping Us Bloom and Grow

Nadine Thorsen

When taking in the beauty of a flourishing garden, we often do not consider the expertise, knowledge, and skill of the talented gardener who tended to it. They seek a deeper understanding of the symbiotic relationship of all elements that make up a garden and with that, they work hard to watch it blossom and they take great pride in the fruits of their labour. I have had the privilege to witness and take part in Bartha's flourishing garden over a decade.

BMK has committed both to her scholarship of furthering science to improve human health and to fostering a strong, supportive community, both at the Centre of Genomics of Policy and more widely in her networks. She has planted the seeds to grow a workspace that fosters the importance of caring deeply for each individual, no matter what title, or position. She has a talent for seeing the potential in people, providing them with trust, autonomy and the opportunities they need to bloom and grow. This can be said about my time at the CGP—by putting her faith in my decision making abilities, she has empowered me to navigate by using my creativity when faced with challenges. She leads with grace when faced with varieties of challenging situations especially the more bureaucratic ones—nothing shakes BMK.

You can always find time during the day in which Bartha's door is open. No matter how busy she is, you have her full attention; she makes you feel seen, heard, and valued. Her tiny paper agenda is packed to the brim, but she will always make space. This presence, this ability to be fully there for others, is a rare and precious gift in a leader.

What truly sets Bartha apart is her capacity to appreciate each person for who they are and to manifest this in countless ways, large and small. She makes a point to celebrate milestones in people's lives: birthdays, weddings, baby showers, graduations, and so on. These celebrations of fully acknowledging them demonstrates that she sees people as whole human beings, not just employees. Cards are circulated, gift bags are filled, flowers are ordered, and bubbly is popped to mark these special occasions. From the "pet corner" (a collection of pictures of the team' pets), to the ever-present cookie jar, to artwork, to filling the office with holiday decorations, to the plants that brighten each room, Bartha filled the space with her special touch that communicates the value she sees in creating a symbiotic atmosphere. Each gesture, seemingly small, has a profound impact on the morale and the sense of community.

We mark this occasion to celebrate Bartha's creation of a beautiful garden. One that will continue to bloom and grow for seasons to come..

VIGNETTE

Bartha and Me

Rose-Marie Hozyan

This story begins in 1994, when the beautiful and distinguished Me Bartha Maria Knoppers[1] came to work as a consultant at McMaster Meighen (now known as Borden Ladner Gervais), and introduced everyone to the new field of "genetics and ethics" in law. I could never have guessed how my life was about to change.

It wasn't long before Bartha became highly sought after by those working in the medical field. While there was a buzz in all the McGill University teaching hospitals, she and I quickly developed a kinship and became somewhat of a dynamic duo!

As word continued to spread, many pharmaceutical companies requested her expertise. Everyone wanted to hear what Bartha had to say, even Pope John Paul II.

Suddenly, Bartha found herself travelling all around the world attending meetings and speaking at conferences. I was riding the wave with her, travelling through her itineraries. Life with Bartha was the equivalent to riding on a high-speed train and there was no stopping her. I tried very hard to teach her the word "No," but all attempts proved to be unsuccessful. She was very determined and possessed a strong work ethic. To add to the thrill of it all, everyone wanted to either work with or for Bartha. This was because she always made time for anyone who came knocking on her door. To the young, she was inspiring, caring, and an invaluable mentor. She built the Centre de recherche en droit public (CRPD) family at the Université de Montréal and, in 2009, they all followed her over the mountain to McGill University to start the Centre of Genomics and Policy (CGP), just like the Von Trapp family in the Sound of Music.

At the CGP, Bartha's days were always filled with back-to-back meetings. They would start in the early morning and flowed well into the afternoons. On some occasions, meetings would be followed by her running home to pack a suitcase for the next adventure, often in Europe. It was a running joke that she lived somewhere in the middle of the Atlantic, somewhere between EST and

1 "Maître" (Me) is a French honorific used for the law professions (e.g. solicitors, notaries).

DOI:10.1163/9789004688544_026

CEST time. It was the only plausible explanation for her being able to keep the jetlag under control. What was also amazing is that she had the carry-on luggage system down packed: one small suitcase for as long as it took, and she always looked amazing! Most importantly were all the colleagues she met throughout her travels—many of whom are now life-long friends.

Even with all this going on, she never missed celebrating any of the holidays. The office was always decorated in full style. Halloween, Christmas, and Easter made the spotlight, and there were always chocolates, cupcakes, and cookies for everyone to enjoy. Staff events were also a priority for her, summer barbeque picnics in her backyard—family style, which was important to her.

As I look back on the last 30 years, I can truly say that it has been an absolute pleasure working for Bartha. Though the high-speed train of Bartha's professional career has come to somewhat of a halt, I thank her for the great ride it's been and know that life has many more adventures in store for us both. I will forever cherish the memories we have made and look forward to the ones we have yet to make. If Bartha has taught me anything it is that you should not wait for the great moments in life; make each of the moments in your life great.

Eidelweiss, Edelweiss,
Every morning you greet me,
In rain and snow, sunshine bright,
You looked happy to meet me.

Blossoms of tulips,
May you bloom and grow,
Bloom and grow forever,

Eidelweiss, Eidelweiss
Bless our Bartha forever.

CHAPTER 9

A Human Rights Lens to Understanding the Concept of "Serious" Genetic Conditions

Erika Kleiderman and Vardit Ravitsky

1 Introduction

The late Professor Dorothy Wertz and Professor Bartha Knoppers first considered the concept of "serious" genetic conditions in a 2002 article summarizing the findings of an international survey of 1,264 practicing genetics professionals.[1] They set out to a) understand how qualifiers such as "serious" and "grave" were being interpreted as gateway criteria for access to reproductive genomic technologies and gene therapies; and b) assess genetics professionals' acceptance of various approaches used to circumscribe their professional judgements about seriousness in these contexts. Respondents were asked to list three genetic conditions they considered: a) lethal, b) serious but not lethal, and c) not serious. Respondents listed a total of 537 genetic conditions with substantial overlap between categories. In total, 51 genetic conditions appeared in all three categories. There was general agreement among respondents that precedence ought to be given to the patient as the decision maker, over laws, hospital ethics committees, national ethics committees, individual doctors, or lists developed by professional associations. Therefore, if the seriousness threshold is to be used, Wertz and Knoppers argue that the concept "must be qualified to include the judgement of the patient and physician, with the patient making the final, and one hopes, informed, decision" (p. 35).[2] Their findings highlighted the challenges of defining the seriousness threshold and evidenced the myriad ways that practicing genetics professionals from around the world invoked the concept within their particular legal and policy contexts.[3] One possible reason for the lack of consensus in definition and use of the seriousness threshold stems, in part, from differences between biomedical definitions of disease or its clinical manifestations, and the

1 Dorothy C Wertz and Bartha Maria Knoppers, 'Serious genetic disorders: can or should they be defined?' (2002) 108 American Journal of Medical Genetics 29.

2 ibid.

3 ibid.

lived patient experience.[4] Wertz and Knoppers also highlighted the important role of socio-economic factors (e.g. availability and affordability of treatments) in perceptions of what would be considered "serious".[5] Such socio-economic factors are commonly overlooked, they argued, when considered alongside biomedical factors. However, little has been written since on this issue.

The seriousness of genetic conditions has been most explored in the context of abortion and preimplantation genetic testing (PGT), notably in Australia and the United Kingdom.[6] The most commonly used qualifiers in laws, policies, and regulations for a condition, disease, or disability include "serious," "severe," and "grave."[7] This seriousness threshold has also been the focus of sustained parliamentary debates in some countries, given that the threat of "serious" disability is an essential legislative criterion for access to abortion and PGT.[8] Yet, few (if any) legislators and regulatory bodies have defined the conceptual scope of seriousness as it relates to genetic testing and reproductive services.

Professors Wertz and Knoppers were one of the first to identify this conceptual gap in definition and responsibility, and their work served as the starting point for our current work on further unpacking the concept and delineating what elements or factors ought to be considered when discussing seriousness so as to foster a common understanding in how we think about the concept.[9] This veil of interpretative uncertainty[10] has proven to be problematic, particularly when seriousness is used as a filter or threshold for permissibility or access to emerging genomic technologies that could improve health, such as human genome editing. There is general agreement that early onset, life threatening conditions are "serious," and this agreement is most pronounced at the extremes of the spectrum of diseases.[11] Yet, most genetic conditions do not fall at the extremities, they are not always clear-cut, and the determination

4 Erika Kleiderman, Vardit Ravitsky, and Bartha Maria Knoppers, 'The "serious" factor in germline modification' (2019) 45 Journal of Medical Ethics 508.

5 Wertz and Knoppers (n 1).

6 Isabel Karpin and Kristin Savell, *Perfecting Pregnancy: Law, Disability, and the Future of Reproduction* (Cambridge University Press 2012).

7 ibid.

8 ibid.

9 Kleiderman, Ravitsky, and Knoppers (n 4); Erika Kleiderman and others, 'Unpacking the notion of "serious" genetic conditions: towards implementation in reproductive decision-making?' (2024) European Journal of Human Genetics, doi: 10.1038/s41431-024-01681-0.

10 Karpin and Savell (n 6).

11 Wertz and Knoppers (n 1); Kristin Savell and Isabel Karpin, 'The meaning of "serious disability" in the legal regulation of prenatal and neonatal decision-making' (2008) 16 Journal of Law and Medicine 233.

of seriousness will depend on contextual elements, including a person's circumstances and their lived experience.

The law's specification of seriousness as a threshold to justify or restrict the use of or access to a given genomic technology is premised on the assumption that there is a shared understanding of the concept and that it can be given meaning.[12] It has been argued that the inability to provide a specific definition or account of "serious" may be intentional and render it a valuable regulatory tool, given the seeming preference to defer its appraisal or application to healthcare providers.[13] Alternatively, the creation of lists or a stringent definition of seriousness could constrain both healthcare providers' professional discretion, as well as the patient's autonomy.[14] Therefore, a balance must be struck between biomedical definitions or objective criteria and contextual elements as they relate to a given person as we move towards further unpacking seriousness.

The broader community of genetics professionals have agreed that albeit helpful, a fixed definition of "serious" is likely not the solution given its inherent subjectivity and socio-historical contingency.[15] However, there is value in trying to operationalize seriousness, as it provides a useful starting point for discussions between clinicians and patients as well as among policymakers.[16] To advance operationalization, agreeing on a set of core dimensions and procedural elements that ought to be considered in the appraisal of seriousness is an important first step.[17] As we have argued elsewhere, this can serve as a conceptual tool for mapping the contours of the concept and for ensuring a more coherent and consistent process for understanding the seriousness of a genetic condition across contexts.[18]

How society conceives of health and disease is foundational for understanding seriousness and is highly consequential for policy.[19] We therefore explored two conceptual approaches, objectivism and constructivism, for how seriousness relates to health and disease:

12 Karpin and Savell (n 6).
13 ibid.
14 ibid; Savell and Karpin (n 11).
15 Kleiderman, Ravitsky, and Knoppers (n 4); Karpin and Savell (n 6); Savell and Karpin (n 11); Wertz and Knoppers (n 1).
16 Karpin and Savell (n 6); Kleiderman, Ravitsky, and Knoppers (n 4).
17 Kleiderman and others (n 9).
18 ibid.
19 Kleiderman, Ravitsky, and Knoppers (n 4).

> Rather than relying solely on a biomedical objectivist approach for understanding the concepts of 'health' and 'disease', socioeconomic and cultural contexts should be considered, as suggested by the constructivist approach, since they provide a more appropriate basis on which the notion of 'serious' can be framed and elaborated. The integration of these two approaches would be more nuanced and culturally sensitive and would also align with the goals of human rights. We have focused on both the promotion of the right to science and the right to the highest attainable health. These rights provide a legally actionable focus and represent common, internationally agreed on values that can in turn help guide the development of national regulatory approaches.[19] Thus, human rights may provide a more universal and legitimate foundation on which the governance of 'serious', 'health' and 'disease' [...] can be built.[20]

The excerpt above, inspired by the early work of Professors Wertz and Knoppers, premises our broader aim in this chapter, which is to argue for how a human rights-based approach, in combination with objectivist and constructivist perspectives of health and disease, can strengthen and help inform the appraisal of seriousness. Such an approach can also encourage a common understanding of the elements and various features of seriousness in the context of access to emerging genomic technologies. We begin by presenting key objectivist and constructivist accounts of health and disease, as well as their shortcomings. We then discuss human rights-based approaches, specifically focusing on the right to the highest attainable standard of health and the right to science. We conclude that a human rights-based approach to conceptualizing seriousness best integrates both objectivist and constructivist ways of thinking. It uniquely captures, in our view, the interplay between objective, quantifiable elements and the inextricable contextual or subjective elements of a genetic condition for a more actionable consideration of seriousness.

2 Objectivist and Constructivist Accounts of Health and Disease

Theories of health can be: a) positive (i.e. explain what health is and how one can experience reduced health) or negative (i.e. explain what disease is and perceive health as the absence of disease); b) evaluative (i.e. health is understood by assessing evaluative concepts or language, such as harmful, beneficial,

20 ibid, 4.

bad, good, etc.) or non-evaluative (i.e. purely descriptive account of health); and c) objective (i.e. health or disease are based on objective facts beyond a person's experience) or subjective (i.e. how a person experiences health or disease).[21] Both objectivist and constructivist perspectives provide conceptual lenses through which relevant dimensions and factors related to the seriousness of a genetic condition can be further understood and contextualized.[22]

2.1 *The Objectivist Approach*[23]

Christopher Boorse proposed one of the most influential objectivist accounts of health and disease, known as the function-based theory.[24] For Boorse, "the human body comprises organ systems that have natural functions from which they can depart in many ways. Some of these departures from normal functioning are harmless or beneficial, but others are not. The latter are 'diseases'".[25] Put plainly, a disease is a malfunction of normal or statistically typical human biological processes.[26] In this sense, for something to be considered a disease involves "both a claim about the abnormal functioning of some bodily system and a judgement that the resulting abnormality is a bad one;"[27] whereas health is understood as species-typical functioning (i.e. normal human functioning).[28] Therefore, an organism is functioning normally provided it can "accomplish its basic biological goals of survival and reproduction at a level that is statistically typical for age- and sex-matched members of its species."[29]

---

21 Elizabeth Barnes, 'Theories of Health' in Elizabeth Barnes (ed), *Health Problems: Philosophical Puzzles about the Nature of Health* (Oxford University Press 2023).

22 We note that this chapter does not provide an exhaustive overview of all objectivist and constructivist accounts of health, but rather focuses on the more influential or key accounts. For a complete overview of such accounts and theories of health, readers are invited to consult Barnes (n 21).

23 The literature also refers to this approach as naturalism.

24 Christopher Boorse, 'On the distinction between disease and illness' (1975) 5 Philosophy & Public Affairs 49; Christopher Boorse, 'A Rebuttal on Health' in James M Humber and Robert F Almeder (eds), *What Is Disease?* (Humana Press 1997); Christopher Boorse, 'A second rebuttal on health' (2014) 39 The Journal of Medicine and Philosophy: A Forum for Bioethics and Philosophy of Medicine 683.

25 Dominic Murphy, 'Concepts of Disease and Health' in Edward N Zalta (ed), *The Stanford Encyclopedia of Philosophy* (Spring 2021, Metaphysics Research Lab, Stanford University 2021), available at: https://plato.stanford.edu/archives/spr2021/entries/health-disease/.

26 Christopher Boorse, 'Health as a theoretical concept' (1977) 44 Philosophy of Science 542.

27 Murphy (n 25).

28 ibid.; József Kovács, 'The concept of health and disease' (1998) 1 Medicine, Health Care, and Philosophy 31; Norman Daniels, 'Normal functioning and the treatment-enhancement distinction' (2000) 9 Cambridge Quarterly of Healthcare Ethics 309; Boorse (n 26).

29 Barnes (n 21), 23.

Generally, the line between health and disease, for objectivists, is rather uncontroversial as these concepts are grounded in biological facts of the human body (i.e. a purely biomedical conception). Thus, health and disease are considered objective, non-evaluative, and generally value-neutral.[30] However, a challenge for Boorse's function-based accounts is that "not all 'abnormal' functioning is pathological (nor is it obvious that all pathological functioning is abnormal)."[31] Theories of health centered on organ functionality do not account for differences between abnormality and pathology, given that many pathologies do not lead to early death or prevent reproduction.[32] Scholars have also argued that accounts based on species-typical functioning cannot fully capture what is "bad" about a condition given their lack of normativity.[33]

Therefore, framing seriousness through an objectivist lens renders its qualification rather narrow and leaves little room for incorporating behavioural, psychological, or socio-cultural factors.[34] For example, list-based approaches allow for objective, quantifiable filters through which to consider genetic conditions[35] but are also criticized for limiting access to emerging genomic technologies given the focus on the purely biomedical aspects or clinical manifestations of a genetic condition.[36]

Although objectivism can insufficiently account for contextual elements of health and disease, some proponents recognize that there is more to the concept of disease than purely biological malfunction, even if this type of biological malfunction is a necessary condition.[37] In this sense, some objectivists

30 Kleiderman, Ravitsky, and Knoppers (n 4); Robert M Sade, 'A theory of health and disease: the objectivist-subjectivist dichotomy' (1995) 20 The Journal of Medicine and Philosophy 513; Murphy (n 25); Daniels (n 28); Boorse (n 26); Barnes (n 21).

31 Barnes (n 21), 21.

32 ibid.

33 Quill R Kukla, 'What counts as a disease, and why does it matter?' (2022) 2 The Journal of Philosophy of Disability 130; Robert L Spitzer and Jean Endicott, 'Medical and mental disorder: proposed definition and criteria' (2018) 176 Annales Médico-psychologiques, revue psychiatrique 656; Jerome C Wakefield, 'The concept of mental disorder: on the boundary between biological facts and social values' (1992) 47 American Psychologist 373; Elselijn Kingma, 'Paracetamol, poison, and polio: why Boorse's account of function fails to distinguish health and disease' (2010) 61 The British Journal for the Philosophy of Science 241.

34 Kleiderman, Ravitsky, and Knoppers (n 4); Kovács (n 28); Albert Farre and Tim Rapley, 'The new old (and old new) medical model: four decades navigating the biomedical and psychosocial understandings of health and illness' (2017) 5 Healthcare 88.

35 Kleiderman, Ravitsky, and Knoppers (n 4); Human Fertilisation and Embryology Authority (HFEA), 'PGT-M Conditions', available at: https://www.hfea.gov.uk/pgt-m-conditions/.

36 Kleiderman, Ravitsky, and Knoppers (n 4).

37 Murphy (n 25); Dominic Murphy, *Psychiatry in the Scientific Image* (MIT Press 2006); Havi Carel, 'Can I be ill and happy?' (2007) 35 Philosophia 95; Daniel M Hausman, 'Is an

admit that a biological judgement must be made, but that a person's lived experience should also be considered[38] in a hybrid blend of objectivist and constructivist accounts. An example of such a hybrid account is Jerome Wakefield's selected function theory of health (harmful dysfunction), which he defines as "an effect of the organ or mechanism that enters into an explanation of the existence, structure, or activity of the organ or mechanism."[39] For Wakefield, a dysfunction implies "an unfulfilled function, that is, a failure of some mechanism in the organism to perform its function."[40] Therefore, for a condition to be pathological, harmful dysfunction is necessary, wherein harm is not limited to an objective assessment but includes the goals and values of society (i.e. a normative component is needed).[41] Such a hybrid approach would indeed integrate both objective and subjective elements and thus more appropriately capture the nuances and intricacies for determining the seriousness of a genetic condition.

2.2 *The Constructivist Approach*

According to constructivism, there is "no natural, objectively definable set of human malfunctions that cause disease."[42] Constructivists integrate norms, values, and human judgements in how health and disease are framed.[43] Using a constructivist lens, disease is not solely defined by objective biological malfunction, but the subjective reality of human experience must also be considered. The World Health Organization (WHO) exemplifies a constructivist account of health given that it defines health as a "state of complete physical, mental and social well-being and not merely the absence of disease or infirmity."[44] Yet, the WHO definition is not without its critics for lacking specificity and medicalizing social problems.[45]

Ethical and legal boundaries are socially constructed. They vary across societies and cultures and evolve over time.[46] Generally, such boundaries are

overdose of paracetamol bad for one's health?' (2011) 62 The British Journal for the Philosophy of Science 657.

38 Murphy (n 25).

39 Wakefield (n 33), 382.

40 ibid., 381.

41 Barnes (n 21); Kukla (n 33).

42 Murphy (n 25).

43 Daniels (n 28); Farre and Rapley (n 34).

44 World Health Organization, 'Constitution of the World Health Organization' (1946), 1, available at: https://www.who.int/about/accountability/governance/constitution.

45 Kleiderman, Ravitsky, and Knoppers (n 4); Kovács (n 28).

46 Kovács (n 28); Daniels (n 28).

created to facilitate classification and guide decision-making. Through a constructivist lens, it is not that the bodily processes are objectively malfunctioning, but rather that they diverge from the socially constructed notion of human nature and are labeled "abnormal."[47] Therefore, individual interests must also play an integral role in determining whether something is a disease according to constructivists.[48]

Two influential constructivist theorists of health include Lennart Nordenfelt and Sridhar Venkatapuram, who place normative significance on wellbeing. Nordenfelt proposes a holistic or praxis-oriented concept of health whereby "the bodily and mental state of a person [is] such that he or she has a second-order ability to realize his or her vital goals, given standard or otherwise accepted circumstances."[49] More specifically, health is tied to achieving one's aims, wants, and desires.[50] Therefore, for Nordenfelt, a person has a disease if, and only if, they have "at least one organ or mental faculty which is involved in such a state or process as tends to reduce the health (in the praxis sense)" of the person.[51] Building on Nordenfelt's theory, Venkatapuram argues that health should be "a person's ability to achieve or exercise a cluster of basic human activities or capabilities."[52] In his account, health is "a metacapability—it is the physical and mental ability to access the other capabilities (relationships, projects, play, artistic endeavour, etc.) that together make up human flourishing."[53] Both Nordenfelt and Venkatapuram's theories can, however, be critiqued in light of "healthism," or the "tendency to over-value and over-moralize health—to treat it as more central and more primary than it often is, and thus to be too zealous in its pursuit and too critical of behaviors that don't promote it."[54] It is important to consider not only health as valuable, but other factors that may at times be contradictory or conflict with health.[55]

Another set of constructivist accounts—social constructionists—view disease as contingent on collective normative judgements.[56] Tristram Englehart,

47 Murphy (n 25).

48 ibid.

49 Lennart Nordenfelt, 'Functions and health: towards a praxis-oriented concept of health' (2018) 13 Biological Theory 10, 16.

50 Barnes (n 21).

51 Nordenfelt (n 49).

52 Sridhar Venkatapuram, 'Health, vital goals, and central human capabilities' (2013) 27 Bioethics 271, 272.

53 Barnes (n 21), 49–50.

54 ibid., 50–51.

55 ibid.

56 ibid.

Jr. argues, for example, that a disease is “a category constructed from the social norms and practices of medical institutions (and perhaps our social norms and practices in responding to these institutions).”[57] As such, something is a disease if it can be treated according to the practices of medicine.[58] The challenge, however, is that such an approach would make it almost impossible to accept that society and medical institutions may be wrong about what is considered a disease or treated as such.[59]

These accounts of health reveal that the boundaries between objectivism and constructivism are blurred. Scholars recognize a general need to consider “both human values and biological phenomena” when attempting to conceptualize health and disease.[60] Rather, theoretical distinctions can be drawn based on what aspects of health each account prioritizes. For example, objectivists emphasize biological malfunctioning or departures from species-typical functioning, whereas constructivists prioritize the subjective lived experience of individuals before considering underlying biological malfunctions.[61]

Therefore, objectivist and constructivist accounts of health and disease provide a basis for defining, categorizing, exploring, and mapping the seriousness of a genetic condition.[62] In this way, they serve as interpretive theories that assist in describing and translating systems of meanings.[63] This translation is particularly important as concepts of health and disease have implications for individuals, society, and policy.[64] Moreover, it is clear from the literature that arriving at a common understanding of seriousness in genetics will require both objectivist and constructivist considerations of health and disease that integrate medical, social, cultural, or personal contexts.[65]

---

57 ibid., 55.

58 H Tristram Engelhardt, ‘The disease of masturbation: values and the concept of disease’ (1974) 48 Bulletin of the History of Medicine 234.

59 Barnes (n 21); Kukla (n 33).

60 Murphy (n 25).

61 ibid.

62 Jane Ritchie and Liz Spencer, ‘Qualitative Data Analysis for Applied Policy Research’ in Alan Bryman and Robert G Burgess (eds), *Analyzing Qualitative Data* (Routledge 1994); Mita Giacomini, ‘Theory Matters in Qualitative Health Research’ in Ivy Bourgeault, Robert Dingwall, and Raymond De Vries (eds), *The SAGE Handbook of Qualitative Methods in Health Research* (SAGE Publications Ltd 2010).

63 Ritchie and Spencer (n 62); Giacomini (n 62).

64 Kleiderman, Ravitsky, and Knoppers (n 4).

65 ibid; Murphy (n 25).

3 A Human Rights-Based Approach

As the chapters and vignettes in this volume demonstrate, Professor Knoppers is a pioneer and thought leader in the field of law, ethics, and genomics and has explored ethical and legal themes of emerging technologies for decades. Her scholarship advanced a human rights framework in genetics/genomics such that emerging technologies can move "beyond risk-focused principles and policies to a framework that views genomic and clinical databases as global public goods […] that must be respected, protected, and promoted, and that draws a roadmap for conducting collaborative genome science in an ethically responsible, solidaristic manner."[66] She clarifies in her scholarship how human rights can promote core values such as justice, equity, solidarity, empowerment, and transparency. She furthermore framed innovative discussions of the right to science and the right to the highest attainable standard of health, most notably in global genomic and clinical data sharing.[67] Professor Knoppers' influence on human-rights based policy guidance is evident, for example, in the Global Alliance for Genomics and Health's (GA4GH) Framework for Responsible Sharing of Genomic and Health-Related Data, and its accompanying policies.[68] Her career-long work and interest in the ethics and law of assisted reproductive technologies also prioritized international principles of human rights, including the rights of the child and the rights of future generations, which were novel applications at the time.[69]

Human rights are universal, interdependent, and indivisible.[70] Central to all human rights is the legal and ethical principle of human dignity, which is

66 Bartha M Knoppers and others, 'A human rights approach to an international code of conduct for genomic and clinical data sharing' (2014) 133 Human Genetics 895, 901.

67 ibid; Bartha Maria Knoppers and Adrian Mark Thorogood, 'Ethics and big data in health' (2017) 4 Current Opinion in Systems Biology 53; Jennifer Salerno and others, 'Ethics, big data and computing in epidemiology and public health' (2017) 27 Annals of Epidemiology 297; Rumiana Yotova and Bartha M Knoppers, 'The right to benefit from science and its implications for genomic data sharing' (2020) 31 European Journal of International Law 665.

68 Bartha Maria Knoppers, 'Framework for responsible sharing of genomic and health-related data' (2014) 8 The HUGO Journal 1.

69 Bartha M Knoppers and Sonia LeBris, 'Recent advances in medically assisted conception: legal, ethical and social issues' (1991) 17 American Journal of Law & Medicine 329; Bartha Maria Knoppers and Erika Kleiderman, 'Heritable genome editing: who speaks for "future" children?' (2019) 2 The CRISPR Journal 285.

70 Yvonne Donders and Monika Plozza, 'Look before you leap: states' prevention and anticipation duties under the right to science' (2024) 28 The International Journal of Human Rights 354.

essential to sustaining balance between the protection of individual rights and freedoms and the broader, collective interests of humanity.[71] Human rights are "protected by international treaties that create binding legal commitments for the States that ratify them."[72] These state parties have an obligation to incorporate their international obligations to respect, protect, and fulfill their rights into domestic laws and enforce them.[73] Yet, how each state party fulfills their obligations varies.

Human rights are used as "a set of internationally recognized legal norms and established practices" and guide human rights-based approaches to policy and practice.[74] Human rights-based approaches integrate universality (all humans possess rights), equity (common goods and services are distributed fairly), and comprehensiveness (systematic and inclusive considerations).[75] Therefore, a human rights-based approach to policy and practice in genomics relies on shared international norms and values to guide technology governance, development, and translation.[76] Human rights approaches also underscore "domestic law and relevant concerns about fairness, social justice, and non-discrimination to individuals and society likely to be affected."[77]

Framed by the Universal Declaration on Human Rights (UDHR, 1948)[78] and subsequent binding international treaties such as the International Covenant

---

71 Britta C van Beers, 'Rewriting the human genome, rewriting human rights law? Human rights, human dignity, and human germline modification in the CRISPR era' (2020) 7 Journal of Law and the Biosciences 1; Rumiana Yotova, 'Regulating genome editing under international human rights law' (2020) 69 International & Comparative Law Quarterly 653.

72 Molly K Land and Jay D Aronson, 'The promise and peril of human rights technology' in Jay D Aronson and Molly K Land (eds), *New Technologies for Human Rights Law and Practice* (Cambridge University Press 2018), 4.

73 ibid; Rumiana Yotova, 'Anticipatory duties under the human right to science and international biomedical law' (2024) 28 The International Journal of Human Rights 397.

74 Land and Aronson (n 72), 3.

75 ibid; Armando De Negri Filho and Victoria J Furio, 'A human rights approach to quality of life and health: applications to public health programming' (2008) 10 Health and Human Rights 93.

76 Leifan Wang, Xiaohui Liang, and Weiwen Zhang, 'Genome editing and human rights: implications of the UNGPs' (2022) 4 Biosafety and Health 386; Andrea Boggio and others, 'The human right to science and the regulation of human germline engineering' (2019) 2 The CRISPR Journal 134.

77 Wang, Liang, and Zhang (n 76), 388.

78 General Assembly United Nations, 'Universal Declaration of Human Rights' (1948), available at: https://www.un.org/en/about-us/universal-declaration-of-human-rights.

on Economic, Social and Cultural Rights (ICESCR, 1966),[79] an international human rights-based approach may be a useful lens through which to consider concepts such as health and disease generally, and seriousness in genomics, specifically.[80] A human rights-based approach to health is advantageous given its legally enforceable mechanisms and universal scope.[81] It also establishes a baseline expectation of human dignity from which to harmonize technology governance.[82] This approach can be expanded to influence and shape both the right to the highest attainable standard of health and the right to science given evolving societal perceptions and challenges, as well as increased knowledge and experience with disruptive genomic technologies.[83]

3.1 *The Right to the Highest Attainable Standard of Health*

The right to the highest attainable standard of health (hereafter "right to health") was first articulated in the Constitution of the World Health Organization (1946) as "the enjoyment of the highest attainable standard of health."[84] The Constitution recognized the right to health as "one of the fundamental rights of every human being without distinction of race, religion, political belief, economic or social condition."[85] It was subsequently reaffirmed as a fundamental economic, social, and cultural human right under many international and national human rights instruments and treaties. Article 12 of the ICESCR recognizes "the right of everyone to the enjoyment of the highest attainable standard of physical and mental health."[86] In its General Comment No. 14 on Article 12 of ICESCR, the Office of the High Commissioner of Human Rights enumerated essential elements of the right to health, most notably

79 United Nations Human Rights Office of the High Commissioner, 'International Covenant on Economic, Social and Cultural Rights' (1966), available at: https://www.ohchr.org/en/instruments-mechanisms/instruments/international-covenant-economic-social-and-cultural-rights.

80 Kleiderman, Ravitsky, and Knoppers (n 4).

81 ibid; Knoppers and others (n 66).

82 Kleiderman, Ravitsky, and Knoppers (n 4); Knoppers and others (n 66); Leslie London, 'What is a human-rights based approach to health and does it matter?' (2008) 10 Health and Human Rights 65; Audrey Chapman and Jessica Wyndham, 'A human right to science' (2013) 340 Science 1291.

83 Kleiderman, Ravitsky, and Knoppers (n 4).

84 World Health Organization (n 44).

85 ibid.

86 United Nations Human Rights Office of the High Commissioner, 'International Covenant on Economic, Social and Cultural Rights' (n 79).

related to availability, accessibility, acceptability, and quality.[87] Article 24 of the Convention on the Rights of the Child (1989) extends equal rights to health for children.[88] Article 25 of the Convention on the Rights of Persons with Disabilities (2006) recognizes that persons with disabilities have the right to "the enjoyment of the highest attainable standard of health without discrimination on the basis of disability."[89]

It is important to note that the right to health does not imply the right to be healthy.[90] Health is both a medical and cultural concept with ties to "deeply held cultural [and religious] values and ideas about life, death, disease, suffering and healing."[91] Various factors can influence a person's health, such as education, income, food, housing, access to potable water and adequate sanitation, behaviour, and environment.[92] It entails numerous elements such as maternal health, child health, access to essential drugs and is concerned with equitable access and health services for the most vulnerable in society.[93] Therefore, the right to health includes the right to healthcare but also extends to the underlying determinants of health.[94] The right to health also contains both freedoms (right to be free from discrimination) and entitlements (right to primary healthcare).[95]

---

87 United Nations Human Rights Office of the High Commissioner, 'E/C.12/2000/4: General Comment No. 14 on the Highest Attainable Standard of Health, The Committee on Economic, Social and Cultural Rights' (2000), available at: https://www.ohchr.org/en/documents/general-comments-and-recommendations/ec1220004-general-comment-no-14-highest-attainable.

88 United Nations Human Rights Office of the High Commissioner, 'Convention on the Rights of the Child' (1989), available at: https://www.ohchr.org/en/instruments-mechanisms/instruments/convention-rights-child.

89 United Nations Human Rights Office of the High Commissioner, 'Convention on the Rights of Persons with Disabilities' (2006), available at: https://www.ohchr.org/en/instruments-mechanisms/instruments/convention-rights-persons-disabilities.

90 Yvonne M Donders, 'Exploring the cultural dimensions of the right to the highest attainable standard of health' (2015) 18 Potchefstroom Electronic Law Journal/Potchefstroomse Elektroniese Regsblad 179.

91 ibid., 181.

92 ibid; Paul Hunt, 'The Human right to the highest attainable standard of health: new opportunities and challenges' (2006) 100 Transactions of The Royal Society of Tropical Medicine and Hygiene 603.

93 Hunt (n 92); Paul Hunt and Gunilla Backman, 'Health systems and the right to the highest attainable standard of health' (2008) 10 Health and Human Rights 81.

94 Donders (n 90); Hunt (n 92).

95 Donders (n 90); Hunt (n 92).

Operationalizing the right to health is progressive and subject to available resources.[96] States that embed the right to health into existing healthcare systems generally have three key objectives: "to promote — the right to health as a fundamental human right; to clarify the scope of the right to health; and to identify good practices for the operationalization of the right to health at community, national and international levels."[97] From a normative perspective, the right to health encourages health policymakers to "devote special attention to the vulnerable and disadvantaged, enhance community participation, ensure that health interventions strengthen health systems, and so on."[98] The right to health is "the only perspective that is both underpinned by universally recognized moral values and reinforced by legal obligations."[99]

Insofar as the right to health is a fundamental human right, it can help clarify the normative and practice-based ethics of access to emerging genomic technologies for patients and families. Therefore, if we frame certain genetic conditions as "serious," the right to health may be useful in determining who has legitimate claims to the technology and for ensuring access for those most likely to benefit from it.[100] The need to integrate contextual elements into our common understanding of seriousness reinforces why relational dimensions of the right to health—and the right to access technologies that advance the highest attainable level of health—should be considered. As argued elsewhere,[101] we recognize that such contextual factors may be weighted differently across jurisdictions, depending on cultural and religious values, as well as resource availability. Relying on a human rights-based approach means that both the right to health and the right to science impart on risk-benefit analyses when applied to emerging genomic technologies. It could "shift our focus from avoiding risks to protecting opportunities,"[102] which would foster scientific advancement, promote health, improve quality of life, and reduce financial burdens associated with healthcare.[103]

---

96 Kleiderman, Ravitsky, and Knoppers (n 4); Hunt (n 92).

97 Hunt (n 92), 604–605.

98 ibid., 104.

99 Hunt and Backman (n 93), 90.

100 Kleiderman, Ravitsky, and Knoppers (n 4).

101 Kleiderman and others (n 9).

102 Eric T Juengst, 'Crowdsourcing the moral limits of human gene editing?' (2017) 47 Hastings Center Report 15, 21.

103 Kleiderman, Ravitsky, and Knoppers (n 4).

3.2 *The Right to Science*

Initially recognized in the 1940s, under Article 27(1) of the UDHR (1948): "everyone has the right freely to participate in the cultural life of the community, to enjoy the arts and to share in scientific advancement and its benefits", this right and its obligations have in large part remained dormant.[104] The rationale behind the right was that science—a recognized and protected "cultural activity able to produce 'benefits' for humanity"[105]—"should be guaranteed as a human right to an independent participatory good, a good requiring a strong institutional and normative structure" and creating collective duties and responsibilities for the actors involved.[106]

The participatory dimension of the right to science is important, as it protects science as a public good and considers both individual and collective interests in its creation.[107] One way to capture the participatory dimension of the right to science is through "equal participation in the information, deliberation and decision over issues of anticipation of both the beneficial and adverse effects of science."[108] Scientists in the UK[109] and Australia[110] demonstrated the power of meaningful public participation and deliberation in a series of citizen juries on human genome editing. Public engagement methods for advancing policy research on emerging technologies can "shape both the scientific enterprise and scientific progress and the resulting benefits of scientific progress."[111] Such an approach "promotes procedural justice—fairness and inclusion, as well as respect for autonomy—by incorporating those impacted into the process."[112] It is essential in democracies as it helps capture both common and dissenting views, while fostering transparency and understanding.[113] It is only through

104 United Nations (n 78).

105 Andrea Boggio, 'The right to participate in and enjoy the benefits of scientific progress and its applications: a conceptual map' (2021) 34 New York International Law Review 43, 49.

106 Samantha Besson, 'Anticipation under the human right to science: concepts, stakes and specificities' (2024) 28 The International Journal of Human Rights 293, 295.

107 ibid.

108 ibid., 300.

109 University of Cambridge, 'Should we allow genome editing of human embryos?' (University of Cambridge, 28 February 2023), available at: https://www.cam.ac.uk/stories/citizens-jury.

110 Dianne Nicol and others, *Genome Editing: Formulating an Australian Community Response: Report to Decision Makers, Stakeholders, and Members of the Public* (University of Tasmania 2022).

111 Boggio (n 105), 77.

112 Jodi Halpern and others, 'Societal and ethical impacts of germline genome editing: how can we secure human rights?' (2019) 2 The CRISPR Journal 293, 294.

113 ibid.

the realization of the right to science that the participation in and access to the benefits of scientific progress can be experienced.[114] Therefore, the benefits of science, as a kind of public good, must reach beyond the enterprise itself and be shared with the greater public community or collective, both at a national and global level.[115] Like the participatory spirit of citizen juries for human genome editing, the qualification of "serious" requires multi-stakeholder input (e.g. healthcare providers, genetic counsellors, policymakers, and patients and their families).[116]

However, some have argued that the right to science has devolved into nothing more than a passive right with the progressive individualization of science.[117] In 1966, the right "to enjoy the benefits of scientific progress and its applications"[118] was enshrined in Article 15(1)(b) of the ICESCR. Given the legally binding nature of the ICESCR for all 165 signatories, obligations to realize the right to benefit from science were further outlined in Article 15. In 1975, the right to benefit from science was codified in Article 6 of the UN Declaration on the Use of Scientific and Technological Progress in the Interests of Peace and for the Benefit of Mankind (1975):

> All States shall take measures to extend the benefits of science and technology to all strata of the population and to protect them, both socially and materially, from possible harmful effects of the misuse of scientific and technological developments, including their misuse to infringe upon the rights of the individual or of the group, particularly with regard to respect for privacy and the protection of the human personality and its physical and intellectual integrity.[119]

The right to science can be interpreted to protect a cluster of rights. These rights include the right to participate in science, the right to access science and enjoy its benefits, the freedom to pursue scientific discovery, and the right to

114 Boggio (n 105).

115 ibid; Besson (n 106).

116 Kleiderman, Ravitsky, and Knoppers (n 4).

117 Besson (n 106).

118 United Nations Human Rights Office of the High Commissioner, 'International Covenant on Economic, Social and Cultural Rights' (n 79).

119 United Nations Human Rights Office of the High Commissioner, 'Declaration on the Use of Scientific and Technological Progress in the Interests of Peace and for the Benefit of Mankind', available at: https://www.ohchr.org/en/instruments-mechanisms/instruments/declaration-use-scientific-and-technological-progress-interests.

be protected against the adverse effects of scientific progress.[120] A distinction can be made between "the development of science itself, which should not be constrained, and the results and outcomes of science and technology, which should be directed towards human interests, such as peace, democracy, and international cooperation."[121] The abovementioned cluster of rights are interrelated but conceptually distinct.[122]

General Comment No. 25 on Article 15 of ICESCR, the Office of the High Commissioner of Human Rights states that unacceptable harm includes "harm to humans or to the environment that is: (a) threatening to human life or health; (b) serious and effectively irreversible; (c) inequitable to present or future generations; or (d) imposed without adequate consideration of the human rights of those affected."[123] Therefore, states have various obligations to ensure that these rights are fulfilled and protected, including the obligation to prevent harms caused by adverse effects of scientific progress, which may justify the limitation of certain dimensions of the right to science, like scientific freedom.[124] Given the various dimensions of the right to science, the "weighing and balancing of interests between the rights protected under the right to science: the right to benefit from scientific progress and its applications, the right to be protected from risks of harm of scientific progress and its applications, and, last but certainly not least, scientific freedom" is essential.[125]

Anticipatory duties and responsibilities are also applicable under the right to science.[126] States are mandated to act with due diligence to maximize the benefits of science, minimize any possible harms or adverse effects, and anticipate possible future harms.[127] States fulfill these duties through prevention and precaution, two legally enforceable duties first elaborated in international environmental law and have since become the strategy for coping with scientific uncertainties around harm.[128] Anticipatory duties are obligations of conduct (i.e. best effort obligations), which requires States to do their best to avoid

120 Donders and Plozza (n 70); Besson (n 106).

121 Donders and Plozza (n 70), 7.

122 Boggio (n 105).

123 United Nations Human Rights Office of the High Commissioner, 'E/C.12/GC/25: General Comment No. 25 on Article 15: Science and Economic, Social and Cultural Rights', 12 (2020), available at: https://www.ohchr.org/en/documents/general-comments-and-recommendations/general-comment-no-25-2020-article-15-science-and.

124 Donders and Plozza (n 70).

125 ibid., 10.

126 Besson (n 106); Donders and Plozza (n 70).

127 Yotova (n 73); Besson (n 106); Donders and Plozza (n 70).

128 Donders and Plozza (n 70); Besson (n 106).

foreseeable harms and mitigate risks, without the expectation that harms be completely prevented.[129]

Besson argues that "unlike most other human rights duties, the duties arising out of the right to science are collective duties, i.e. duties States and international institutions of jurisdiction bear together and not only concurrently."[130] This suggests that "human rights should fundamentally be understood as normative relationships that correspond to relationships of jurisdiction."[131] States have an obligation "to ensure non-discriminatory, fair and equitable access to the benefits of science and its applications in order to prevent present and future inequality in the enjoyment of fundamental rights."[132]

There is a complementary relationship between the human right to science and the promotion of the highest attainable standard of health, "as they work together to increase knowledge that can serve to decrease and prevent human suffering."[133] This relationship can serve as a basis for governments to weigh benefit sharing and competing interests around the promotion of scientific advancements so as to assess the impact on healthcare systems, while protecting access and reducing inequalities.[134] In recent decades, the pace and impacts of science have drastically changed, as well as the scale of investment in science. This results in faster developing scientific advances, particularly in genetics/genomics, that propose lasting or irreversible consequences, and pose higher risks and uncertainties given the possibility for effects to be passed on to future generations (e.g. human germline genome editing).[135] Scientific endeavours are also undertaken on a global scale. There has been a shift towards the privatization of science, thereby reducing the transparency and predictability of scientific projects, while also bringing more populations into closer proximity of experiencing science's adverse effects.[136] States are therefore expected to oversee the responsible conduct of both basic and pre-clinical research on emerging genomic technologies.[137] Here again, the rights to health and to benefit from science can be a useful "starting point for building

---

129 Besson (n 106); Yotova (n 73); Donders and Plozza (n 70).

130 Samantha Besson, 'Science without borders and the boundaries of human rights: who owes the human right to science?' (2015) 4 European Journal of Human Rights 462, 467.

131 ibid., 468.

132 Yotova (n 73), 398.

133 Kleiderman, Ravitsky, and Knoppers (n 4), 510.

134 ibid; Andrea Boggio and Calvin WL Ho, 'The human right to science and foundational technologies' (2018) 18 The American Journal of Bioethics 69.

135 Besson (n 106).

136 ibid.

137 Kleiderman, Ravitsky, and Knoppers (n 4).

international consensus on governing principles that promote responsible scientific and technological advancements,"[138] including qualifying the parameters and thresholds used (e.g. "serious"), whether technologies should move through the bench-to-bedside pathway, and who can ultimately access such technologies.

4 A Human Rights-Based Approach to Navigating Seriousness

As mentioned at the outset, seriousness is seen as an acceptable threshold that confers a sense of security regarding the limits and appropriate applications of emerging genomic technologies (i.e. that they will be used in an ethical and responsible manner and for legitimate purposes). Currently, most laws, regulations, and policies include a seriousness threshold to restrict the use of genomic technologies to a certain subset of "serious" genetic conditions. Similarly, "serious" is used to justify a right to access emerging genomic technologies that may have a higher degree of uncertainty and may initially be perceived as risky. Yet, these legal and policy instruments do not define or provide guidance regarding how the threshold ought to be applied or the notion qualified. This implies that it falls to healthcare providers to interpret what is a "serious" genetic condition. The few laws, regulations, and policies that attempt to provide some guidance will typically acknowledge the complexity of the concept of seriousness and the need to consider multiple contextual factors that take into account the patient's perceptions and lived experience, noting that it cannot be a purely medical determination. The legal and political dimensions of human rights can guide development of more robust governance frameworks that promote and delineate the parameters for the responsible translation of and access to emerging genomics technologies.[139]

As argued earlier, a purely objectivist view of disease as a "value-free objective concept," focused on biological dysfunction, is incomplete.[140] It lacks flexibility and fails to tell us anything about the lived experience of a genetic condition from a first-person perspective.[141] On the other hand, a purely constructivist view of disease as a subjective, socially-constructed concept,

138 Boggio and others (n 76), 141.
139 Knoppers and others (n 66).
140 Carel (n 37), 97.
141 ibid.

neglects certain underlying biological, genetic, and psychological factors.[142] Therefore, a hybrid of the two perspectives would provide a more appropriate basis to help inform our understanding of seriousness. A human rights-based approach offers such a lens through which both objectivism and constructivism can be considered in the aggregate, and allows us to integrate biological and environmental dimensions into the qualification of seriousness, as well as social values and lived experience. This interplay between the medical and experiential aspects of a genetic condition can provide a more actionable consideration of seriousness based on common, internationally agreed upon values.[143]

Emerging genomic technologies will be costly at the outset, which will create barriers to access.[144] Such technologies are often limited to "serious" genetic conditions. The use of "serious" provides justified limits of acceptability for the uses of a technology, as well as justifications for public funding or coverage for technological uses with the goal of promoting health and improving quality of life for future generations, where possible.[145] Therefore, to ensure equitable access to those most likely to benefit, a mechanism must be in place to determine who has the most urgent need and to provide a consistent and coherent appraisal of seriousness.

A common understanding of the factors that comprise the appraisal of seriousness can offer such a consistent and coherent consideration of the concept in clinical discussions and policy deliberations that are made for the betterment of humankind via the right to health and the right to science. Such a human rights-based approach encourages us to look at not only individual state parties, but also recognize the joint interests of all relevant parties (the state, the users, and the public) so as to ensure the realization of the right to health and the right to science.[146] Global calls for public engagement and deliberation offer people the opportunity to consider both potential benefits of scientific progress, as well as possible adverse effects, while bringing to light societal and cultural values and attitudes towards emerging genomic technologies.[147] Results from such public deliberations can help delineate what society considers a scientific benefit and can be used to inform future policymaking related

142 Kenneth S Kendler, Peter Zachar, and Carl Craver, 'What kinds of things are psychiatric disorders?' (2011) 41 Psychological Medicine 1143.

143 Kleiderman, Ravitsky, and Knoppers (n 4).

144 ibid; Boggio and Ho (n 134); 'The gene-therapy revolution risks stalling if we don't talk about drug pricing' (2023) 616 Nature 629.

145 Kleiderman, Ravitsky, and Knoppers (n 4).

146 ibid.

147 ibid.

to the assessment of a new genomic technology (i.e. balancing the benefits and risks), including how a seriousness threshold may factor in.[148] Thus, public engagement efforts can best support equitable and inclusive approaches to governing emerging genomic technologies, while ruling out otherwise contentious applications.[149]

Finally, although beyond the scope of this chapter, the rights of future generations should also be considered in the context of emerging genomic technologies. This legal construct—given the absence of a rights holder—captures the principle of intergenerational equity and requires States "to act with due diligence with respect to activities likely to affect future generations and prevent harm to them."[150] This anticipatory right originates and is commonly used in international environmental law and international biomedical law.[151] The rights of future generations are of particular relevance when discussing emerging genomic technologies that can have unforeseeable and irreversible consequences on future generations and the environment (e.g. human germline genome editing). This legal construct includes considerations around consent, long term follow-up, and intergenerational monitoring.[152]

5 Conclusion

A human rights-based approach to emerging genomic technologies has been at the heart of the influential scholarship of Professor Knoppers for decades. The right to health and the right to science are fundamental human rights and essential to any conversation around the ethical use and equitable access to emerging genomic technologies. In the case of framing certain genetic conditions as "serious," the complementary relationship between the right to health and the right to science may be useful in balancing the risks and uncertainties associated with emerging technologies with the potential to promote health and improve quality of life for those living with such genetic conditions. The relationship between the right to health and the right to science may also be useful in determining who has the most urgent claim to the use of emerging genomic technologies, while reducing burdens and costs associated with

148 ibid.

149 ibid.

150 Yotova (n 71), 679.

151 Besson (n 106); Yotova (n 73).

152 Bryan Cwik, 'Designing ethical trials of germline gene editing' (2017) 377 The New England Journal of Medicine 1911; Knoppers and Kleiderman (n 69).

healthcare, so as to ensure equitable access for those most likely to benefit from specific technologies.

Indeed, one of Professor Knoppers' most significant contributions has been the emphasis on these specific rights, and a deep exploration of the ways in which they should be operationalized and implemented. With a focus on promoting the human or humanity in law, policy, and ethics, her work has significantly shaped the literature in this space. It has brought to light considerations around human dignity as the guiding principle for balancing the rights and interests of individuals and those of the broader collective. The importance of social justice—equitable access and a fair distribution of benefits—have also been a core focus of her work in ensuring a responsible path forward for emerging genomic technologies. Finally, her deep care for the protection and promotion of the rights of the child, as well as the rights of future generations, clearly demonstrates her desire to leave this world a little bit better than we found it.

VIGNETTE

Bartha M. Knoppers: Why Family Matters

Trudo Lemmens

Even many of those with "human" as a core component of their work or academic scholarship fail to appreciate the value and role of healthy and supportive human relations. This is perhaps even more common with academic leaders who are, as Bartha M. Knoppers has always been, exceptionally academically productive, deeply professionally engaged, broadly involved in national and international policy making, and successful in stimulating those around them to live up to their standards. Those of us who had the privilege to study and/or work with Bartha M. Knoppers, now Distinguished James McGill Professor Emerita—or short, Bartha for the friends—know how she stands for the opposite.

My professional career in health law and bioethics has from its very early years been intimately connected to Bartha. Under her guidance, I discovered many of the components of my early scholarship, a topic that was as new and trendy at the time as AI these days: ethical, environmental, economic, legal, social issues of genetics, or GE^{3}S as it became later known in Canada. A research contract with her research group at the Université de Montréal brought me to the topic of my doctoral dissertation at McGill University, for which she became, as external expert, my co-supervisor. And throughout my further career, I encountered her in the context of research projects or advisory committees, or I guessed Bartha's supportive influence when I was invited to join or chair a committee or task force.

But even though a professional context dominates our exchanges, the touching personal moments and conversations connected to professional encounters are what I remember the most. These encounters and experiences also helped me understand what has driven so much of Bartha's work over all these years, and her drive to support those around her and to help them thrive. I think of the times spent over lunch or dinner at conferences or in our respective homes, sharing experiences as parents, talking about a common friend struggling with illness or personal or professional setback, and just taking the time to appreciate the comfort and support of mutual friendship.

A moment where my personal and professional life directly intersected, in which Bartha played a key role, has become a most cherished family story. It captures so well her ability to prioritize even in the most serious professional moments what really matters in our lives.

When I defended my doctoral dissertation under Bartha's co-supervision, our two sons were 8 and 4 years old. I worked full-time from the second year of my doctorate, and in two different positions at the University of Toronto. My family endured at least two very intensive summers of doctoral drafting, when it occurred to me I better finish my dissertation before going up for tenure. We thought it was therefore even more fitting to turn the doctoral defence into a family experience. The plan was for my wife Pascale to come to the public defence with our oldest son while my mother-in-law would walk around with the youngest, and then bring him to the reception afterwards. The setting became even more familial when my brother-in-law showed up with one of his slightly older sons, to give him a flavour of academia. The two boys sat in the front row to the left, close to the examination committee members. As the defence progressed, the more they sank in their chairs and eventually fell asleep, shoulder to shoulder. While that was already unusual for a doctoral setting, the real highlight occurred just after I finished my 20-minute presentation.

In the midst of my response to the toughest question of the exam—an examiner was overall skeptical of using discrimination law in a core private law setting of insurance—the door flew open right in front of me, and my mother-in-law appeared with our four-year old at her hand. He yelled loudly "papa" and started waving enthusiastically. I stood there, uttering things that resembled an answer, but with my brain racing about how to deal with the situation, since my mother-in-law didn't immediately seem to realize the exam wasn't finished yet. The chair of the examining committee interrupted angrily: "The child is distracting the candidate! Can someone take care of this?" My wife took charge and left the room with him. Later, when it was eventually Bartha's turn to ask a final question, she took the occasion to put all of it in perspective. Before even formulating a question, she gave an exposé about the crucial contributions of family and loved ones to academic success. She thanked my family for having exposed their children to an academic event, found a way to turn even my youngest son's appearance at the hand of his grandmother into a meaningful happening, and convinced everyone this was all a celebration of the deeply human components of such events. Even the well-meaning but grumpy chair was clearly charmed by this lesson in how to place humanity and human relations at the core of our professional lives. And yes, there still was an academic question and discussion following that minilecture on life. But while I don't remember exactly that question, her intervention, which epitomizes Bartha's approach to life and work balance and to what really matters in our lives, remains engrained in the memory of all those who were there. Academia needs more Bartha Knoppers.

VIGNETTE

The Light Shines Back on You: Protégés of Bartha M. Knoppers

Judy Illes

There is a time at which the giants in our field of ethics—bio, biomedical, genomics, and neuroethics—can hardly be more celebrated in their illustrious careers than they have been already. They are winners of major distinctions and awards, medals and trophies, grants and contracts, and seats at the table with ministers and heads of state. At that point, it is the success of their protégés—trainees, and mentored researchers and collaborators—that come to matter.

Bartha has inspired and influenced two generations of leaders in the ethical and legal dimensions of the biosciences. Two with whom I am very familiar, and who exemplify Bartha's global and progressive vision for a bioethics anchored in concern for humanity, are remarkable women.

Vardit Ravitsky, PhD, is President and CEO of the Hastings Center, Professor of Bioethics at the Université de Montréal, and Senior Lecturer on Global Health and Social Medicine at Harvard University. As a mentored collaborator of Bartha, and distinguished bioethicist, Professor Ravitsky has navigated the complex ethical mazes of genetics, genomics, and novel technologies for modifying and editing the human condition. She was also instrumental in developing Canadian thinking on ethics and policy-making during the COVID-19 pandemic. Together with Bartha, other ethics experts, and me, Professor Ravitsky has been a driving force in an initiative to create a national bioethics body for Canada for the past three years.[1] Her passion for bioethics and commitment to this country are surpassed only by her ability to navigate and travel seamlessly between her co-primary locations in Ottawa, New York State, and Jerusalem.

1 Judy Illes and others 'Canadian ethicists recognize the critical importance of science and research' (The Conversation, 30 June 2021), available at: https://theconversation.com/canadian-ethicists-recognize-the-critical-importance-of-science-and-research-163204; Judy Illes and others, 'Re-Invigorating Notions of a Bioethics Council for Canada in a New Era of Biomedicine' in Maria do Céu Patrão Neves (ed) *The Kaleidoscope of Global Bioethics* (Conselho Nacional de Ética para as Ciências da Vida, 2023).

 | DOI:10.1163/9789004688544_029

Vasiliki (Vaso) Rahimzadeh, PhD is faculty in the Center for Medical Ethics and Health Policy at Baylor College of Medicine, and Bartha's former PhD student. Her research on the ethical, legal, and social issues of health data sharing across emerging computing environments has been influential in informing both data governance policy and practice across Canada, the United States, and internationally. Vaso was the first and only student observer at the Standing Committee on Ethics at the Canadian Institutes of Health Research (CIHR), a role to which she brought continuous insight and creative intelligence.

Two other colleagues are remarkable men who have centred the human in intellectual debates about the brain and the biosciences. Eric Racine, PhD, was a Research Assistant with Bartha at the Centre de Recherche en Droit Public at the Université de Montréal at the very beginning of his PhD. His efforts were focused on public engagement in population genomics research, an interest he pursues still deeply to this day. Eric, who shines light back on almost everyone's life he touches, is an internationally recognized bioethics researcher at the Institut de Recherches Cliniques de Montréal (IRCM), and holds joint appointments at both the Université de Montréal and McGill. He breathes life into everything ethics—pragmatic, living, neuro, and more.

Michael Beauvais is an SJD candidate at the Faculty of Law at the University of Toronto. With grace and determination, Michael led a major publication with Bartha and me in 2021 for the journal NeuroImage called "A marathon, not a sprint – Neuroimaging, open science and ethics."[2] I believe it is the first invited ethics piece of its kind in this journal that is highly influential for the world of brain imaging.

I hope that I, too, as an internationally recognized Canadian neuroscientist-neuroethicist, shine a little light on Bartha. Under Bartha's leadership, the Centre of Genomics and Policy (CGP) has been an institutional role model for Neuroethics Canada at the University of British Columbia (UBC), under my direction, for more than 15 years. CGP's caring, intellectually stimulating, and robust supportive environment are values and goals that we have embodied at UBC. On a personal note, as a role model, Bartha has taught me to bring the world of ethics to my own students, collaborators, colleagues, and the public, even when ethics is sometimes scorned or faced with skepticism and adversity in the harsh world of life sciences.

With deep vision and thoughtfulness, Bartha has taught us all the importance of responsibly stewarding our respective specializations within bioethics with unfailing energy and vigor.

---

2 Michael J S Beauvais, Bartha Maria Knoppers, and Judy Illes, 'A marathon, not a sprint - neuroimaging, Open Science and ethics' (2021) 236 NeuroImage 118041.

CHAPTER 10

Defining Best Interests: Challenges and Perspectives in Paediatric Ethics

Pascal Borry

1 Introduction

Parents bear both moral and legal responsibility for their children and are granted the authority to make decisions on their behalf. Public and private institutions likewise make decisions that affect children. The criterion of "best interests" has emerged as a central element and a guiding tool in ethical and legal discussions related to children in medicine, as evidenced in the academic literature[1] and national and international normative documents.[2] Throughout her career, Professor Bartha Knoppers has continuously called attention to medical, public health, and research ethics topics that affect minors. Over the last 15 years, I have had the privilege to collaborate with her on projects related to paediatric health, including ethical issues in neonatal screening,[3] direct-to-consumer genetic testing,[4] as well as anti-doping.[5]

---

1 Loretta M Kopelman, 'Using the best interests standard to decide whether to test children for untreatable, late-onset genetic diseases' (2007) 32 The Journal of Medicine and Philosophy 375; Els Geelen and others, 'Constructing "best interests": genetic testing of children in families with hypertrophic cardiomyopathy' (2011) 155A American Journal of Medical Genetics 1930; Mary Kay Pelias, 'Genetic testing of children for adult-onset diseases: is testing in the child's best interests?' (2006) 73 Mount Sinai Journal of Medicine 605.

2 United Nations Educational, Scientific and Cultural Organization (UNESCO), 'Universal Declaration on the Human Genome and Human Rights' (1997); European Union, 'Charter of Fundamental Rights of the European Union' (2000).

3 Heidi Carmen Howard and others, (2015) 'Whole-genome sequencing in newborn screening? A statement on the continued importance of targeted approaches in newborn screening programmes' (2015) 23 European Journal of Human Genetics 1593; Bartha M Knoppers and others, 'Whole-genome sequencing in newborn screening programs' (2014) 6 Science Translational Medicine 229cm2.

4 Pascal Borry and others, 'Anonymity 2.0: direct-to-consumer genetic testing and donor conception' (2014) 101 Fertility and Sterility 630; Heidi C Howard, Bartha Maria Knoppers, and Pascal Borry, 'Blurring lines: the research activities of direct-to-consumer genetic testing companies raise questions about consumers as research subjects' (2010) 11 EMBO Reports 579.

5 Erika Kleiderman and others, 'Doping controls and the "Mature Minor" elite athlete: towards clarification?' (2020) 12 International Journal of Sport Policy and Politics 179.

© PASCAL BORRY, 2025 | DOI:10.1163/9789004688544_030

Professor Knoppers has advocated throughout her work an inherently *human-centred* approach, focusing on what is most beneficial for the well-being and welfare of individuals and, in particular, children. She often articulated the need to find a delicate equilibrium between the child's best interests and welfare on the one hand, and on the other hand, recognizing other interests such as the child's burgeoning autonomy and self-determination with regard to their age and maturity. Professor Knoppers has been an active scholar and advocate. She has approached her work with the ambition to develop policies, tools, and approaches that benefit those most in need but often least able to voice this need themselves.

Humanity, as a concept or ethical theory, often involves a commitment to respecting and enhancing the dignity, rights, and inherent value of every individual. The best interests of the child (BIC) standard is the dominant ethical framework in paediatric medicine and bioethics. The BIC aligns with this humanity-focused perspective by ensuring that decisions and actions prioritize the human aspect, taking into account the unique needs, vulnerabilities, and rights of individuals. However, a persistent concern throughout the evolution of contemporary paediatric ethics relates to how the BIC should be defined and applied. In the academic literature, the BIC standard differs in its interpretation in many respects, but the major differences relate to what interests are emphasized and prioritized.[6] As demonstrated by Slater,[7] most theories of BIC are individualistic in their understanding of decision-making and centre a best-interest decision exclusively on the individual's self-regarding interests. Shah argues that invoking the BIC standard at a group level is confusing at best, a legal fiction at worst, and should not be applied to public health decisions.[8] She advances that using the BIC standard in the group context privileges utilitarianism in balancing competing interests.

In a joint publication[9] with Professor Knoppers, we recognized that the scope and significance of the BIC standard at a populational level is hard to characterize. We highlighted that tensions can emerge between the interests of children as a group and the best interests of a particular child. Nevertheless, we clearly acknowledged that the rights of the child, as articulated in the 1989 United Nations Convention on the Rights of the Child (CRC), should remain a

6 Erica K Salter, 'Deciding for a child: a comprehensive analysis of the best interest standard' (2012) 33 Theoretical Medicine and Bioethics 179, 184.

7 ibid.

8 Seema Shah, 'Does research with children violate the best interests standard? An empirical and conceptual analysis' (2012) 8 Northwestern Journal of Law and Social Policy 121.

9 Karine Sénécal and others, 'Genome-based newborn screening: a conceptual analysis of the best interests of the child standard' (2015) 12 Personalized Medicine 439.

primary consideration in public health endeavours such as screening programs, and by extension in decisions affecting minors. Although the specific interpretation of the BIC is challenging, its legal and ethical significance cannot be ignored. The CRC is a crucial document that enshrines BIC standard in Article 3. Article 3 stipulates that in all actions concerning children, whether undertaken by public or private social welfare institutions, courts of law, administrative authorities, or legislative bodies, the best interests of the child shall be a primary consideration. As comes clear through Professor Knoppers' analysis,[10] the interpretation of Article 3 necessitates a nuanced approach and careful attention to language. The term "a" primary suggests that factors other than the BIC principle are considered when institutions, authorities, or administrations act. Article 3 describes the BIC indeed as "a" primary rather than "the" primary consideration. The BIC should be among the first aspects to be considered and should carry substantial weight in all decisions affecting children. It is not the exclusive consideration, however, as children have other protected rights. For example, Article 12 states that all "States Parties shall assure to the child who is capable of forming his or her own views the right to express those views freely in all matters affecting the child, the views of the child being given due weight in accordance with the age and maturity of the child."[11]

As Professor Knoppers and colleagues[12] pointed out, in a General Comment published by the United Nations Committee on the Rights of the Child addressing the interpretation of Article 3, the BIC principle applies decidedly to children not only as individual children, but also as a group or constituency.[13] Unquestionably, the BIC concept must be considered in legislative measures, policies, and programs for children, including in public health decisions that affect children.

This chapter discusses the applications of and intersections between the BIC and paediatric health, genetics, and research. Linking Professor Knoppers'

10 Ma'n H Zawati, David Parry, and Bartha Maria Knoppers, 'The best interests of the child and the return of results in genetic research: international comparative perspectives' (2014) 15 BMC Medical Ethics 1.

11 United Nations, 'Convention on the Rights of the Child', available at: https://www.ohchr.org/en/instruments-mechanisms/instruments/convention-rights-child.

12 Zawati, Parry, and Knoppers (n 10).

13 United Nations Committee on the Rights of the Child (CRC), 'CRC General Comment No. 7 (2005): Implementing Child Rights in Early Childhood' CRC/C/GC/7/Rev.1 (2006), available at: http://www.refworld.org/docid/460bc5a62.html; United Nations Committee on the Rights of the Child (CRC), 'CRC General Comment No. 14 (2013) on the right of the child to have his or her best interests taken as a primary consideration (art. 3, para. 1)' CRC/C/GC/14 (2013), available at: http://www.refworld.org/docid/51a84b5e4.html.

scholarship and the BIC as a guiding principle, I discuss newborn screening, the storage of newborn blood spots, and paediatric data sharing.

2 The Best Interest of the Child and Newborn Screening

Traditional newborn screening (NBS) programs limit testing for conditions in which their natural histories are well understood, require immediate medical intervention in order to prevent serious and permanent illness, and treatment is available. Traditional NBS is therefore justified from a public health standpoint because it reduces morbidity and mortality by detecting and treating diseases at the early stages of newborn life. The clinical utility of NBS programs is globally recognized but inconsistently implemented. NBS programs are usually state-mandated, requiring support from local governments and available resources and also operate on a presumed consent basis in view of the best interests of the child. That is, parental consent to heal-prick a newborn for screening purposes is given by default unless the parents explicitly opt out.

Whole-genome sequencing presents new opportunities to expand the early detection of more diseases with genetic etiology. It has since created high expectations in the context of newborn screening and a possible paradigm shift in this public health program. In a document for the European Society of Human Genetics, we described this tension in the following way:

> Will we use new sequencing technologies as a tool to answer focused clinical questions or will we use it to sequence entire genomes in order to return a set of results at birth and as a pure data and information generator, much of which can be analyzed and returned throughout a person's lifetime? The first approach raises differences in scale but is amenable to our current forms of analysis such as cost effectiveness and evaluation of population health programmes and so on. The second approach is partially based on an assumption that personalized medicine based on analysis of the genome is a potential reality, desirable and an effective use of scarce health-care resources.[14]

Professor Knoppers has emphasized many times that the availability of whole-genome sequencing might affect the purposes and practices of population screening programs such as newborn screening and that "any change

14 Howard and others (n 3).

in the goals of NBS programs should be discussed carefully and should represent the best interests of the child."[15] She has often emphasized that the fundamental goal of NBS is to benefit the infant.[16] This means that the responsible use of genome sequencing within a public health program such as NBS should not be technology-driven, but rather evaluated on the basis of its public health potential. As a consequence, a primary justification for implementing whole-genome sequencing as a newborn screening tool should be the health interests of the child.[17]

Professor Knoppers has consistently positioned NBS clearly as a part of the professional, paediatric standard of care and remains critical of any expansion that would undermine the primary aim of newborn screening. Given the additional ethical, legal, and social consequences that whole-genome sequencing raises, she has frequently cautioned against rapid expansion of sequencing-based NBS programs which could drive parents to refuse screening altogether.[18] She warned that such developments would not be in the best interests of the child, and advocated that "mandatory screening with a targeted list can remain in place for disorders for which genomic knowledge could directly benefit the infant during childhood."[19] In this light, it remains crucial to continue to develop genomic education of healthcare professionals and parents and to promote public trust in healthcare programs such as NBS and to maximize participation rates as the main focus of NBS should always be the identification and treatment of the asymptomatic, at-risk newborn.

Already in 2009 discussions took place about reporting reproductive information through newborn screening, and Professor Knoppers emphasized the importance of defending the essence of newborn screening and the best interest of the infant. As formulated in this commentary:

> Reproductive benefits are assuming elevated prominence in expanded newborn screening panels without sufficient clarity regarding how, or even whether, these should be pursued. Given the historic mandatory or implied-consent structure of newborn screening programmes, providing reproductive risk information as a primary benefit of newborn screening overturns the traditional hierarchy of benefits for public screening

15 Knoppers and others (n 3).

16 Karine Sénécal, Brigid Unim, and Bartha Maria Knoppers, 'Newborn screening programs: next generation ethical and social issues' (2018) 2 OBM Genetics 1.

17 Howard and others (n 3).

18 Vasiliki Rahimzadeh and others, 'Exome/genome-wide testing in newborn screening: a proportionate path forward' (2022) 13 Frontiers in Genetics 865400.

19 Knoppers and others (n 3).

> interventions. Alternatively, reproductive benefit could remain a secondary goal of newborn screening within the existing implied-consent or mandatory systems but with the inclusion of an additional choice specific to receiving this information. Unless a preference-sensitive decision making process for receiving reproductive risk information is incorporated, we argue that pursuing reproductive benefit through newborn screening programmes is not appropriate and may be best achieved through traditional antenatal screening programmes.[20]

For the same reason, Professor Knoppers encouraged professional and governmental agencies to develop frameworks, standards, and consensus documents. Through the Public Population Project in Genomics and Society (P³G), among others, she developed consensus among subject matter experts in paediatric research and care. Her policy development initiatives on the use of WGS in paediatrics are valid today:

> Now is the time to: 1) reach an international consensus based on public health ethics and law, as well as evidence-based outcomes; and 2) distinguish the use of WGS in the clinical/research setting from that of public health programs. It is also important to better understand the potential risks and benefits of sequencing newborns in public health, by studying for example its psychosocial risks for family dynamics over time. Although the public health benefit of newborn screening programs is irrefutable, psychosocial aspects, equity and programmatic challenges need to be addressed, to say nothing of quality assurance. How to ensure we act in the best interests of all newborns in shaping the international paediatric norms for the next 50 years?[21]

3 The Best Interest of the Child and Storing Newborn Blood Spots

Newborn dried blood spots are generally stored in public health laboratories in order to enable screening, re-testing, postmortem analysis, or for laboratory audit/quality control. The storage of dried blood spots for these purposes is not particularly controversial. Consent for such uses is usually considered implied since they support the primary purpose of the initial collection, namely

20 Yvonne Bombard and others, 'The expansion of newborn screening: is reproductive benefit an appropriate pursuit?' (2009) 10 Nature Reviews Genetics 666.

21 Sénécal, Unim, and Knoppers (n 16).

screening for various disorders. However, storing newborn screening blood spots for purposes unrelated to clinical care is hotly debated and Professor Knoppers soon realized that there was "an urgent need to develop policies that address the issue of dried blood spot storage, secondary use and the ensuing ethical, legal, and social dilemmas."[22]

In particular, these dried blood samples represent a valuable resource for research, public health surveillance, and sometimes for non-medical purposes (e.g. identifying disaster victims). Chief among the "dilemmas" that concerned Professor Knoppers were privacy and confidentiality. Immediately following birth is a particularly vulnerable and chaotic time for parents and thus not ideal to approach for consent to storage and other uses. It is unclear whether parents can distinguish the clinical from research purposes for storage. Parental views on retaining and using screening samples are mixed and there is no uniform length of time for storage.[23]

Dr Denise Avard and Professor Knoppers emphasized several times the importance of dried blood spot cards in facilitating epidemiological research, the improvement of healthcare services, and a better identification of individuals in need of preventive treatment or services. However, they considered it crucial that those initiatives would never undermine "public confidence in the value of newborn screening purposes per se."[24] Therefore, they advocated several times the importance of introducing regulatory policies and security measures to regulate the length of sample retention and access to identifiable samples. Moreover, they emphasized the need for increased transparency, the development of governance models, and improvement of informed consent requirements. In sum:

> There is a need to come up with better ways of respecting and balancing individual rights with the common good of public health. If NBS are to be treated as biobanks, parents should at a minimum be notified of storage and of research practices and given the opportunity to opt-out. It is of utmost importance however, that such notification does not affect the participation of parents in the newborn screening programme itself – a

22 Linda Kharaboyan, Denise Avard, and Bartha Maria Knoppers, 'Storing newborn blood spots: modern controversies' (2004) 32 Journal of Law, Medicine & Ethics 741.

23 Denise Avard and Bartha Maria Knoppers, 'Research and Public Health Surveillance Using Newborn Bloodspots in Canada' in Bartha Maria Knoppers (ed), *Genomics and Public Health: Legal and Socio-Ethical Perspectives* (Martinus Nijhoff Publishers 2007); Robin Z Hayeems, 'Using newborn screening bloodspots for research: public preferences for policy options' (2016) 137 Pediatrics e20154143.

24 Kharaboyan, Avard, and Knoppers (n 22).

public health programme in the best interest of the at-risk, asymptomatic newborn.[25]

4 The Best Interest of the Child and Paediatric Data Sharing

In the rapidly advancing field of biomedical research, characterized by increasing data-intensive and collaborative research,[26] the sharing of data, including genomics and health-related information, is crucial for scientific progress and its subsequent benefits.[27] However, children are often excluded from data sharing initiatives, particularly in genomics, due to concerns about the sensitivity of genomic information, consent-related issues, and the risk of re-identification.[28]

While international research ethics guidelines acknowledge that children are a vulnerable class of research participants and need special protections, Professor Knoppers has repeatedly underscored that overly protective policies can hinder potential health benefits for children in the long term.[29] The best interests of the child standard has two functions here. On the one hand, the BIC standard is protective; research ethics principles require a favourable risk-benefit ratio and an overall protection from harm and coercion in research.[30] On the other hand, the BIC standard is promotional; it enables children's inclusion in research necessary to advance understanding of paediatric diseases and conditions. As expressed in a 2019 article by Dalpé, Thorogood, and Knoppers,

> The ethical principle of distributive justice calls for making high-quality health care available for all populations, including vulnerable groups. The inclusion of children and decisionally vulnerable adults is often considered necessary in both clinical trials and discovery research to provide evidence-based health care. There are concerns that exclusion of children from research may give rise to a lack of paediatric-specific therapies

25 Bartha Maria Knoppers, Denise Avard, and Karine Sénécal, 'Newborn screening programmes: emerging biobanks?' (2012) 21 Norsk Epidemiologi 166.

26 Kym M Boycott and others, 'International cooperation to enable the diagnosis of all rare genetic diseases' (2017) 100 American Journal of Human Genetics 695.

27 Bartha M Knoppers and others, 'A human rights approach to an international code of conduct for genomic and clinical data sharing' (2014) 133 Human Genetics 895.

28 Vasiliki Rahimzadeh and others, 'Key implications of data sharing in pediatric genomics' (2018) 172 JAMA Pediatrics 476.

29 Michael JS Beauvais and Bartha Maria Knoppers, 'Coming out to play: privacy, data protection, children's health, and COVID-19 research' (2021) 12 Frontiers in Genetics 659027.

30 ibid.

> and impact on the standard of care. In order to further develop safe and effective therapies specific to children, there is a need to improve their participation in biomedical research and this, take into account an appropriate level of protection.[31]

Recognizing the unique health needs of minors and the distinct etiologies of childhood diseases, Professor Knoppers and colleagues argue that restricting paediatric data sharing can impede important research for both current and future paediatric patients.[32] Professor Knoppers played a major role in calling for greater sharing of children's genomic and related health data as a result. She advocated for a proportionate balance between protecting children and promoting scientific discovery. The challenges in sharing paediatric data, including ethical and legal considerations, have prompted the development of frameworks such as the Key Implications for Data Sharing (KIDS) by the Global Alliance for Genomics and Health (GA4GH) in 2018.[33] KIDS provides policy points to guide responsible decision-making in paediatric genomics data sharing, addressing aspects like the involvement of minors, parental consent, balancing benefits and risks, and data protection.

As children become capable of developing their views, they should have the opportunity to express them, and their level of participation in such decisions should increase with maturity. The UN Committee on the Rights of the Child (UN Committee) considers the right to be heard as a fundamental principle guiding the interpretation and implementation of all other children's rights. Article 12 of the CRC furnishes this right, emphasizing the child's capacity to express views freely in all matters affecting them, with due consideration to their age and maturity. While the CRC does not mention data sharing explicitly, Article 12 can be interpreted to mean that children should be actively involved in age-appropriate ways in the decision-making processes related to genomic and clinical data sharing.[34] While full legal consent may not be possible until a child reaches the age of majority, obtaining assent should be common practice when appropriate and feasible. Assent procedures should provide child-friendly explanations of the nature, purpose, and implications of data sharing

---

31 Gratien Dalpé, Adrian Thorogood, and Bartha Maria Knoppers, 'A tale of two capacities: including children and decisionally vulnerable adults in biomedical research' (2019) 10 Frontiers in Genetics 289.

32 Dimitri Patrinos and others, 'Sharing and safeguarding pediatric data' (2022) 13 Frontiers in Genetics 872586.

33 Vasiliki Rahimzadeh and others, 'Key implications of data sharing in pediatric genomics' (2018) 172 JAMA Pediatrics 476.

34 Rahimzadeh and others (n 28).

aligned with the child's level of understanding.[35] Of course, it is acknowledged that assent for data sharing might not always be feasible, particularly for neonates, developmentally immature children, or those with severe cognitive disabilities that limit comprehension and full participation in discussions.

In many circumstances, recontacting children once they become adults respects their autonomy.[36] This is often possible in a context where researchers have ongoing communication with the research participants, but might not be proportionate or feasible in every research context or study. Professor Knoppers and colleagues considered the circumstances around recontact, positing:

> The issue of recontacting participants of pediatric research when they reach the age of majority is important for several reasons. Among them, longitudinal studies and studies of large population cohorts are becoming more common. In addition, data are being stored for longer durations and increasingly shared in larger data sets. This is especially true with the recent emphasis on biobanks that collect and store (sometimes indefinitely) genomic and phenotypic data from medical records and tissue samples. Adolescents are unique stakeholders in this "recontact to consent" debate by virtue of their de facto increasing capacity to understand the risks and benefits of the research in which they are enrolled, or by virtue of being legally presumed capable of doing so at a certain age. Recontact to consent at the age of majority could be seen as the extension of the recognition that consent is a continuing process. According to this principle, when participants acquire the capacity to consent, they have the right to decide either to continue taking part or to withdraw their parents' proxy consent.[37]

Parental authority for children sunsets at the age of majority, typically 18 years in most jurisdictions. The transition in decision-making from the once-child to the now-adult is a gradual process, aligned with the child's increasing capacity to guide their own development, leading to a natural diminishment of parental responsibilities. Consequently, researchers engaged in genomic studies must be cognizant of this shifting dynamic, acknowledging the increasing autonomy of the child in decision-making processes. It becomes imperative

35 Patrinos and others (n 32).

36 Bartha Maria Knoppers and others, 'Recontacting pediatric research participants for consent when they reach the age of majority' (2016) 38 IRB: Ethics and Human Research 1.

37 ibid.

for researchers to implement measures that safeguard and respect the growing autonomy of the child, particularly where it is developmentally appropriate to do so.

5 Conclusion

In one of her articles, Professor Knoppers referred in her conclusion to Charles Dickens and to the fact that the noisiest authorities of any era will insist it be received in the "superlative degree of comparison only."[38] That article was a lesson in leaving room for sensitivity to diverse physical, relational, and cognitive dimensions of vulnerability. Through her whole academic career, Professor Knoppers has endorsed a humanity-driven approach with attention to context and proportionality. The best interests standard and humanity share common ground in their emphasis on individual well-being, dignity, rights, and ethical decision-making. The best interests standard, particularly in the context of children, is a humanist approach at its core. It reflects a commitment to respect the unique needs and vulnerabilities of individuals while promoting their overall welfare.

The BIC has served the test of time as a guiding principle for navigating an evolving ethical, legal, social, and political landscapes into which children are brought. The emergence of whole-genome sequencing prompts careful consideration of its integration into NBS programs, with a persistent emphasis on the fundamental goal of benefiting the infant. The storage of newborn blood spots presents ethical dilemmas, especially concerning secondary uses unrelated to the initial screening, advocating for regulatory policies, transparency, and improved informed consent to strike a delicate balance between individual rights and public health interests. In the realm of paediatric data sharing, the BIC standard has both protection and promotional functions. The challenges of balancing the child's rights with data sharing imperatives have led to the development of frameworks like KIDS that too proportionately balance the special protections for children with opportunities to benefit from scientific progress by sharing their data. Charles Dickens' protagonist, Oliver Twist, stepped forward and asked: "Please, sir, I want some more." The contributions of Professor Knoppers will continue to impact the field and continue to benefit those who need it most, in particular infants.

38 Dalpé, Thorogood, and Knoppers (n 31).

VIGNETTE

Mentorship and Gratitude: A Thank You to Professor Knoppers

Dimitri Patrinos

Professor Knoppers truly embodies the meaning and spirit of mentorship. Her guidance, advice, and encouragement over the years that I have known her have helped to shape me both personally and professionally. I count myself very fortunate to have had the privilege to know and learn from her and to count her among my mentors. I am therefore very honoured to be able to provide my personal tribute to her in this collection.

When I first met Professor Knoppers in 2019, I was finishing my Juris Doctor at the Université de Montréal and had just been hired as a research assistant at the Centre of Genomics and Policy at McGill University. I was thankful to be part of her team at the Centre and even more thankful to have been given the opportunity to work with her directly on many projects. I am especially grateful to have worked with Professor Knoppers on her cherished paediatrics projects. She has long been passionate about children's rights, and I am happy to have helped her in the development of ethical "tools" to help further children's health rights through research.

Working with Professor Knoppers has been one of the most formative experiences of my life so far. Coming in with very little prior academic experience, I learned so much about research and academic writing. Her comments and "scribbles" on the rough drafts of our papers have been among my greatest learning moments. I am grateful to have learned from the example Professor Knoppers has set as a scholar. Her passion and dedication to her work are truly inspiring. As a current doctoral student, Professor Knoppers' example has been a great motivation for me during this transitory and intellectually challenging (yet stimulating) time.

I am also very grateful for the advice, help, and encouragement Professor Knoppers has given me over the years. She has always been available to speak with me and let me "pull up a chair" in her office. When I first expressed interest in applying for doctoral studies in law, she was incredibly supportive and encouraging, volunteering her time to help read and improve my research proposal and giving me the confidence to go ahead with this new endeavour.

 | DOI:10.1163/9789004688544_031

Whenever I needed a letter of recommendation, I knew I could always count on her generosity and support.

Most importantly, however, Professor Knoppers has encouraged me to find my own academic path and voice. Forging one's own path is a challenging yet crucial aspect of the beginning stage of one's academic journey. Professor Knoppers' advice and encouragement, as well as the model she has created through her scholarship and teaching, have taken on new meaning and importance for me as I embark on this career in academia. For this, I will always be grateful.

VIGNETTE

Shining Bright: A Journey of Illumination, Influence, and Inspiration

Amalia M. Issa

Where do you even begin to capture the essence of Bartha Maria Knoppers, or simply BMK as so many know her? Let's start with her name. "Bartha," of Germanic origin, means the "bright one." And let me tell you, she lives up to that name in every way possible. Her brightness has touched lives all over the world, not just in Canada or the US.

There are so many aspects to her brilliance. BMK's intellectual luminosity shines through her groundbreaking research on the legal, ethical, and social dimensions of genetics, genomics, and biotechnology. Her extensive body of work, comprising numerous publications, presentations, policies, and guidelines, is a testament to her unparalleled expertise. As a dedicated educator, BMK's light has illuminated the minds of students at the Université de Montréal and McGill University through years of courses and seminars. Bartha's transformative influence is evident in the lasting impressions left on those fortunate enough to cross paths with "Professor Knoppers." Her teachings, often distilled into memorable "Knopperisms," are legendary. In the words of BMK herself, the journey with her is always "onward and upward," a mantra embraced by all who have had the privilege of knowing and collaborating with her.

If you were to tally up all the scientists, lawyers, ethicists, and other experts that Bartha has mentored over the years, you'd have enough people to fill a whole city! It's no surprise that she has been recognized with awards like being named a Great Montrealer, receiving the Order of Canada, and more recently the Lifetime Achievement Award from the Canadian Bioethics Society. Bartha has guided numerous individuals to success in their careers, ensuring that her light will illuminate academic fields for generations to come across esteemed universities in Canada, the US, and Europe.

Bartha never wavers in her principles or her commitment to humanity and the dignity of human persons. Her relentless service on Task Forces and Advisory Boards, along with her impassioned speeches on responsible genomic data sharing and the right to benefit from science, have resonated with audiences worldwide.

DOI:10.1163/9789004688544_032

Stemming from Bartha's deep roots as the daughter of a minister, her strong and abiding faith is always shining brightly in all her interactions. Bartha's exceptional ability to seamlessly integrate her life, family, and work in an authentic manner sets her apart in a league of her own. I have learned a lot from her about how to better live an integrated life.

Bartha's brightness extends to her keen appreciation for beauty. If you're lucky enough to travel with Bartha or bump into her at a conference overseas, get ready to be surrounded by beauty (not to mention adventure!) right away. She'll probably be the first one to suggest checking out a museum, taking a stroll through the picturesque streets, or marvelling at the breathtaking river views or the flowers, all the while chatting about everything from life to art to current events and the latest research in global genomics.

Bartha is truly an exceptional friend who always makes time for lunch and chats at Chez Alexandre, her beloved dining spot in Montreal. Plus, she somehow manages to reply to all her emails herself, and in record time, even though she gets bombarded with hundreds every day, signing each one simply as "BMK."

CHAPTER 11

"Beyond the Moral Appeals of Bioethics:" International Human Rights Law as the Basis for the International Governance in the Biomedical Science

Andrea Boggio and Rumiana Yotova

1 Introduction[1]

Concerns for human dignity and the need to orient scientific progress toward the welfare of humanity have been central to Professor Knoppers' scholarly and policy work throughout her career, as the essays collected in this volume demonstrate. Her contributions to the international governance of biomedical science are "humanistic" in nature, in the sense that progress in biomedicine is anchored in human dignity and ensuring that governance enables science to progress responsibly, in a manner respectful of human rights, and produces scientific knowledge whose applications benefit humanity. Professor Knoppers tirelessly worked to move beyond trendy governance debates, instead finding deeper, normative anchoring for responsible science and innovation in the existing framework of international law. The cornerstones of this framework are human dignity, Article 27 of the Universal Declaration of Human Rights[2] and the codification of the right to benefit from science in Article 15 of the International Covenant on Economic, Social and Cultural Rights.[3]

In this chapter, we revisit Professor Knoppers' progressive journey in contributing to the international governance of biomedical science, highlighting her pioneering efforts to anchor a humanistic governance approach in international law. Our analysis uncovers a reliance on international law from the beginning of her work on international governance with a gradual integration

1 The quote in the chapter title comes from Bartha Maria Knoppers, 'Framework for responsible sharing of genomic and health-related data' (2014) 8 The HUGO Journal 3.

2 Universal Declaration of Human Rights (adopted 10 December 1948 UNGA Res 217 A(III) (UDHR) art 27.

3 International Covenant on Economic, Social and Cultural Rights (adopted 16 December 1966, entered into force 3 January 1976) 999 UNTS 171 (ICESCR) art 15.

 | DOI:10.1163/9789004688544_033

of human rights. This path, which we think is necessary to anchor international governance in biomedical science "beyond the moral appeals of bioethics," is a testament to the evolving nature of her understanding, consistently driven by pragmatism and clarity about the objectives of governance but also by a deeply idealistic humanistic approach. Professor Knoppers' contributions to the governance of the human genome, including human gene editing and data sharing, which we have had the privilege to contribute to, exemplify this intellectual trajectory.[4]

The chapter is divided into three sections. First, we look at how Professor Knoppers has used international legal concepts to ground governance frameworks in medicine and biomedical research. There, we revisit her early work on conceptualizing the human genome as the common heritage of humanity and her subsequent use of the concept of global public goods and of the right to benefit from science as foundations for governance. Next, we turn to a policy area in which her efforts to ground governance in international law have been particularly effective and impactful: germline gene editing. There, we identify the most important contributions of Professor Knoppers and point to the critical questions highlighted by her intellectual trajectory. Finally, we conclude with an assessment of the status of international human rights law as the basis for the international governance of biomedical science.

2 Anchoring Humanistic Governance of the Biomedical Science in International Law

A theme that runs throughout Professor Knoppers' scholarly and policy work is a commitment to a humanistic approach in the governance of biomedical science grounded in international law. As highlighted by other chapters in this volume, Professor Knoppers has defined responsible governance of the biosciences in relation to human welfare and the recognition of human dignity and human rights. As a legal scholar, she understood the value of anchoring governance to legal concepts and principles as a more politically and conceptually stable source of authority than bioethical frameworks. In this section, we provide an overview and analysis of her intellectual path in advocating for the use

4 Rumiana Yotova and Bartha M Knoppers, 'The right to benefit from science and its implications for genomic data sharing' (2020) 31 European Journal of International Law 665; Andrea Boggio and others, 'The human right to science and the regulation of human germline engineering' (2019) 2 The CRISPR Journal 134.

of legal concepts in the international governance of biomedical science. We identify three phases of this path and discuss each in turn.

2.1 *The Common Heritage of Humankind*

An early mobilization of international law to support a humanistic approach to governance was the idea of applying the international law concept of the "common heritage of humankind" to the human genome. Until then, scholars had only used the concept in the context of the law of the sea, outer space law, and cultural heritage law.[5] This progressive use of a concept alien to the governance of biomedical science came in 1991[6] in reaction to a 1982 Recommendation on Genetic Engineering adopted by the Council of Europe. The instrument indicated that Member States needed to recognize "a right to a *genetic inheritance* which has not been artificially interfered with, except in accordance with certain principles which are recognized as being fully compatible with respect for human rights (as, for example, in the field of therapeutic applications)."[7] The Council of Europe identified the normative basis of this right to genetic inheritance in "the rights to life and to human dignity protected by Articles 2 and 3 of the European Convention on Human Rights[, which] imply the right to inherit a genetic pattern which has not been artificially changed."[8]

Puzzled by the vagueness of the Council of Europe's Recommendation but also interested in better understanding the role of "inheritance" and "human dignity" in relation to the development of genomic knowledge and therapies, Professor Knoppers aptly raised a fundamental question: "… we must determine what genetic heritage is. Does it mean the collective gene pool or the individual genome?"[9] The answer to these questions came from suggesting

---

5 See e.g. United Nations Convention on the Law of the Sea (adopted 10 December 1982, entered into force 16 November 1994) 1833 UNTS 3 (UNCLOS) Part XI 'The Area' 3; United Nations Treaty on Principles Governing the Activities of States in the Exploration and Use of Outer Space, including the Moon and Other Celestial Bodies (adopted on 19 December 1966, entered into force on 10 October 1967) 610 UNTS 205 (Outer Space Treaty) art I; UNESCO Convention for the Protection of Cultural Property in the Event of Armed Conflict (adopted 14 May 1954, entered into force 7 August 1956) 249 UNTS 240, preamble and art 1.

6 Bartha Maria Knoppers, *Human Dignity and Genetic Heritage: Study Paper* (Law Reform Commission of Canada 1991).

7 Council of Europe, Recommendation 934 on Genetic engineering (1982) para 7.b (emphasis added). The Council of Europe also asserted a requirement that 'gene therapy must not be used or experimented with except with the free and informed consent of the person(s) concerned, or in cases of experiment with embryos, fetuses or minors with the free and informed consent of the parent(s) or legal guardian(s).' See ibid para 4.d.

8 ibid., para 4.a.

9 Knoppers (n 6) 2.

that the human genome needed to be recognized as a "common heritage of humankind." Such a legal concept permitted the connection of genetic heritage to "the recognition of the dignity of each person, and of humanity as a whole"[10] and to advocate for "medically oriented principles of respect for human life."[11] It also meant advocating for approaching scientific progress (knowledge and its applications) in genomics as a public good freely accessible by all.[12]

Professor Knoppers' ideas found an international audience when she was appointed to the Legal Commission of the International Bioethics Committee (IBC), which had been charged with drafting the text of the Declaration on the Human Genome and Human Rights, subsequently adopted by UNESCO in 1997. As acknowledged by the Chair of the IBC,[13] Professor Knoppers was instrumental in shaping the thinking of the Committee and including "common heritage of humanity" language in the draft of the Declaration. The IBC embraced the humanistic framework ideated by Professor Knoppers, as noted in the Report of the Fourth Meeting of the Legal Commission of the IBC, held in Paris on April 27, 1994:

> The outline declaration, by proclaiming the human genome, common heritage of humanity, aims to stress that humankind has a particular responsibility with regard to the human genome as one of the elements that make up the identity of each of us and indeed the identity of humankind itself. The concept therefore applies to all the expressions of the human genome – past, present and future –, which are the source of diversity and of the potential for genetic evolution.[14]

The IBC conceptualized humanity "as a subject of international law, with rights and responsibilities towards itself and future generations"[15] and stressed humanity's collective obligation to "safeguard its common heritage—natural and cultural, tangible and intangible, intellectual and genetic"[16] and "moral solidarity."[17]

---

10 ibid., 4.

11 ibid.

12 UNESCO, *Birth of the Universal Declaration on the Human Genome and Human Rights* (Division of the Ethics of Science and Technology of UNESCO 1999) 59 (Fifth Meeting of the Legal Commission of the IBC, 25 September 1995).

13 ibid. 53 (Fourth Meeting of Legal Commission of the IBC, 27 April 1994).

14 ibid. 54.

15 ibid.

16 ibid., 61 (Sixth Meeting of Legal Commission of the IBC (Paris, 25 January 1996).

17 28 C/Resolution 0.12, Medium-Term Strategy for 1996–2001, reaffirming "the urgent need to strengthen the moral solidarity of mankind in order to safeguard its common heritage – natural and cultural, tangible and intangible, intellectual and genetic."

Unfortunately, the text approved by Member States contained a watered-down version of what had been developed by the drafting committee. The concept of "common heritage of humanity" appears in Article 1, which reads:

> The human genome underlies the fundamental unity of all members of the human family, as well as the recognition of their inherent dignity and diversity. *In a symbolic sense*, it is the heritage of humanity.[18]

The text does not qualify heritage as "common" and does not clearly frame it as a *legal* concept. Rather, it settles for a murkier, less compelling "symbolic sense." A quarter-century later, it is still unclear what to make of the "symbolic sense" or, indeed, what the legal implications, if any, of qualifying the human genome as the heritage of humanity may be. The provisions on solidarity and co-operation are worded in hortatory language and relegated to Section E on Solidarity and International Co-operation, which appears after the articles on the "rights of the persons concerned," research on the human genome, and the "conditions for the exercise of scientific activity." Section E opens with Article 17, which reads:

> States *should* respect and promote the practice of solidarity towards individuals, families and population groups who are particularly vulnerable to or affected by disease or disability of a genetic character. They *should* foster, inter alia, research on the identification, prevention and treatment of genetically based and genetically influenced diseases, in particular rare as well as endemic diseases which affect large numbers of the world's population.[19]

The questions regarding the human genome as the heritage of humanity and of solidarity in relation to genetic technologies and diseases have become ever more pressing with the advances in biomedical science, particularly the development of big genomic data and genome editing. If the human genome forms part of the common heritage regime, then it is subject to equitable access, freedom of scientific research, benefit-sharing of any scientific and even technological advances, and any interference with it ought to be done for peaceful purposes and the benefit of humanity.[20] It is hoped that law and policymakers

---

18 UNESCO Declaration on the Human Genome and Human Rights (1997), art 1 (emphasis added).

19 ibid., art 17 (emphasis added).

20 Yotova and Knoppers (n 4), 686 et seq; Rumiana Yotova, 'Regulating genome editing under international human rights law' (2020) 69 International and Comparative Law Quarterly 653, 676–680.

will revisit these issues when designing an international regime for the governance of the human genome and related technological applications in the future.

2.2 *Science as a Global Public Good*

The Declaration's structure and text proved influential and set the tone for the years to come. The lack of traction of the "heritage of humanity" as a legal construct to define the status of the human genome as an individual and collective "good" did not deter Professor Knoppers from pushing her commitment to a humanistic approach to its governance. In the years that followed the UNESCO Declaration, the greatest demands for innovation in governance came from the data-intensive research and the associated research infrastructure, which emerged in the aftermath of the mapping of the human genome and the explosion of digital capabilities. These developments prompted renewed interest in the proper balance between collecting and sharing genomic health data with appropriate individual safeguards. In this phase, Professor Knoppers anchored her humanistic approach to the concept of science as a *global public good*. This approach is most evident in her work for the Human Genome Organization (HUGO)[21] and in her advice to the Organisation for Economic Co-operation and Development (OECD).[22]

Prompted by the emergence of population-level genomic sequencing technologies, the HUGO Statements "gradually recognized the 'public good' of genetic databases, going so far as to characterize the human genome as 'part of the common heritage of humanity' in 2000."[23] They reflected "an increasing recognition of public ethical concerns, with a shift of focus from individual to communal interests,"[24] exemplified by the growing relevance of reciprocity and solidarity. In these statements, reciprocity was "reconceived as an exchange with communities, rather than individuals, in order to promote participation where research promised no immediate personal benefits. The principles of

21 Professor Knoppers was first Chair (1996–2004) and then Member (2012–2016) of HUGO's International Ethics Committee.

22 Professor Knoppers was part of the Advisory Expert Group for the Development of an OECD Draft Recommendation on the Use of Personal Data (2015–16). Her contribution to drafting the World Medical Association's Declaration of Taipei on health databases and biobanks must also be acknowledged, the first ethical principle of which provides that "Research and other Health Databases and Biobanks related activities should contribute to the benefit of society, in particular public health objectives." See World Medical Association, 'WMA Declaration of Taipei on Ethical Considerations regarding Health Databases and Biobanks' (2002, rev. 2016), para 8.

23 Bartha Maria Knoppers, Adrian Thorogood, and Ruth Chadwick, 'The Human Genome Organisation: towards next-generation ethics' (2013) 5 Genome Medicine 38.

24 ibid.

solidarity, citizenry and universality emerged," Professor Knoppers and colleagues note, "respectively fostering responsibility towards the health of others together with individual choice, public engagement with research, and acknowledgement of the human genome as a *public good*."[25]

During the same decade, Professor Knoppers also contributed to drafting the Recommendation of the OECD Council on Health Data Governance, published in 2017.[26] Its preamble prominently features the recognition "that access to, and the processing of, personal health data can serve health-related public interests and bring significant benefits to individuals and society"[27] and "that achieving these benefits requires the careful development and application of robust, context appropriate, privacy protective health data governance frameworks that require the identification and management of privacy and security risks."[28] The first recommendation listed on the instrument is "that governments establish and implement a national health data governance framework to encourage the availability and use of personal health data to serve health-related public interest purposes while promoting the protection of privacy, personal health data and data security."[29]

This approach had weaker ties to international law than her previous work. Professor Knoppers appealed to the ideas of Enlightenment political philosopher David Hume. In her words, "humanity as a whole should be the beneficiary of global public goods."[30] Professor Knoppers adds, "[t]he qualifying mark of a global public good is that it meets the needs of present generations without jeopardizing those of future generations."[31] Interestingly, valuing science as a public good is at the heart of the recognition of the right to benefit from science.[32] This link will be explicitly made only in the third phase of her work, arguing that:

> Together, the concepts of the "common heritage of humanity" and the "global public goods" have furthered the emergence of collaborative

25 ibid. (emphasis added).

26 OECD, *Recommendation of the OECD Council on Health Data Governance* (2017).

27 ibid 3.

28 ibid.

29 ibid., 4.

30 Bartha Maria Knoppers, 'Of genomics and public health: building public "goods"?' (2005) 173 CMAJ: Canadian Medical Association Journal 1185.

31 ibid.

32 Lea Shaver, 'The right to science and culture' (2010) 1 Wisconsin Law Review 121 (2010) 121; Samantha Besson, 'Anticipation under the human right to science: concepts, stakes and specificities' (2024) 28 The International Journal of Human Rights 293; Cesare PR Romano and Andrea Boggio, *The Human Right to Science: History, Development, and Normative Content* (Oxford University Press 2024).

> genomic science focusing on international data sharing to build what has been termed the "genome commons." These genome commons have sought the establishment of "a global knowledge resource for the advancement of science," where "all human genomic sequence information, generated by centres funded for large-scale human sequencing, should be freely available and in the public domain in order to encourage research and development and to maximize its benefit to society."[33]

While related to the common heritage of humanity, the concept of global public goods emphasizes first and foremost the free and open access to the global good and, in the second place, its use in a way that benefits society and the international community as a whole. It leaves open the question as to whether this should be done through benefit-sharing or in other ways.

2.3 *The Right to Benefit from Science*

In the third phase, Professor Knoppers has linked her humanistic approach to the governance of biomedical science to the right to benefit from science. This lesser-known human right is undergoing a renaissance after being brought out of obscurity in 2009 as a result of the publication, under the auspices of UNESCO, of the Venice Statement on the right to enjoy the benefits of scientific progress and its applications.[34] Linking governance of the biomedical sciences permitted Professor Knoppers to anchor her commitment to the primacy of humanity and human dignity to the normative content of a specific human right. This permitted reinforcing a framework grounded on the concepts of the "common heritage of humanity" and global public goods by linking governance to specific entitlements and duties recognized in international law, a level of policy governance closer to the practice in the biomedical field than that offered by the general concepts of "common heritage of humanity" and "global public goods." As such, this constitutes a step forward in specifying the content of a humanistic governance of the biomedical sciences. Her exemplary

---

33 Yotova and Knoppers (n 4), 687.

34 UNESCO, The Right to Enjoy the Benefits of Scientific Progress and its Applications (UNESCO 2009) (Venice Statement). Before the publication of the Venice Statement, very few international human rights scholars had tackled its normative content. See Richard Pierre Claude, *Science in the Service of Human Rights* (University of Pennsylvania Press 2002); Christian Starck, 'Freedom of scientific research and its restrictions in German constitutional law' (2006) 39 Israel Law Review 110; Yvonne Donders and Vladimir Volodin (eds), *Human Rights in Education, Science and Culture: Legal Developments and Challenges* (Ashgate 2007); Audrey R Chapman, 'Towards an understanding of the right to enjoy the benefits of scientific progress and its applications' (2009) 8 Journal of Human Rights 1.

contributions during this phase include co-founding the Global Alliance for Genomics and Health (GA4GH)[35] and her work on genome editing, including her most recent contribution as a member of the International Commission for the Clinical Use of Human Germline Genome Editing and its 2020 report on heritable human genome editing.[36]

Grounded in human rights law, the GA4GH Framework[37] aims at "activating the human rights of everyone to share in scientific advancement and its benefits, as well as from the protection of the moral and material interests resulting from scientific production."[38] In its Preamble, the framework recognizes the centrality of the "human" in sharing health data. "[R]esponsible sharing of human genomic and health-related data, including personal health data and other types of data that may have predictive power in relation to health ... ensures continued progress in our understanding of human health and wellbeing."[39] The instrument adds that responsible sharing "highlights, and is guided by, Article 27 of the 1948 Universal Declaration of Human Rights,"[40] which reads:

> Article 27 guarantees the rights of every individual in the world "to share in scientific advancement and its benefits" (including to freely engage in responsible scientific inquiry), and at the same time "to the protection of the moral and material interests resulting from any scientific ... production of which [a person] is the author."[41]

The GA4GH Framework articulates how the human rights of various stakeholders inform its governance principles and:

> ... interprets the right of all people to share in the benefits of scientific progress and its applications as being the duty of data producers and

35 Professor Knoppers co-founded (2013) and co-chaired the Regulatory and Ethics Working Group (and then entitled Work Stream) of the GA4GH (2013–2019). Since 2022, she has been a Member of its Board of Directors.

36 National Academy of Sciences, National Academy of Medicine, the Royal Society, *Heritable Genome Editing,' Report of the International Commission for the Clinical Use of Human Germline Genome Editing* (The National Academy Press 2020) 158.

37 Knoppers (n 1).

38 Bartha M Knoppers and others, 'A human rights approach to an international code of conduct for genomic and clinical data sharing' (2014) 133 Human Genetics 895; Bartha Maria Knoppers and others, 'Responsible processing and sharing of genomic data: bringing health technologies industries to the table' (2023) 23 The American Journal of Bioethics 33.

39 Knoppers (n 1), para 1.

40 ibid., para 3.

41 ibid.

> users to engage in responsible scientific inquiry and to access and share genomic and health-related data across the translation continuum, from basic research through practical applications. It recognizes the rights of data producers and users to be recognized for their contributions to research, balanced by the rights of those who donate their data. In addition to being founded on the right of all citizens in all countries to the benefits of the advancements of science, and on the right of attribution of scientists, it also reinforces the right of scientific freedom.[42]

Invoking the right to science creates the conditions for expanding the governance horizon by explicitly connecting knowledge production (research) with the fruits of that production (applications). To this end, the GAAGH Framework notes that:

> The challenges raised by international, collaborative research require a principled but nevertheless practical Framework that brings together regulators, funders, patient groups, information technologists, industry, publishers, and research consortia to share principles about data exchange.[43]

Professor Knoppers' influence in introducing a human rights-based approach to human germline editing can be seen in the Report of the International Commission for the Clinical Use of Human Germline Genome Editing, of which she was a member. The Report emphasized "[t]he need to develop governance approaches to encompass [human heritable genome editing] provides a potential opportunity to use and develop the content of internationally recognized human rights to influence future laws, policies, and regulatory responses around [human heritable genome editing,]" while recognizing that:

> However, the possibility of using human rights to frame, delimit, or expand concepts such as the freedom to conduct scientific research, the right of everyone to benefit from scientific advances, the right of children to the highest attainable standard of health, or even the rights of future generations has not yet been discussed by international bodies deliberating on [human heritable genome editing].[44]

---

42 ibid., para 4.

43 ibid.

44 National Academy of Sciences (n 36), 158.

Indeed, framing and clarifying the scope and consequences of the application of these substantive human rights to health data sharing and human genome editing is an important avenue for future work whose foundations were laid by Professor Knoppers.

3 Germline Editing and the Rights of Future Generations

A theme of Professor Knoppers' work worth exploring more in detail is the rights of future generations in the context of germline gene editing. A humanistic approach to biomedical sciences stresses the importance of considering the rights of future generations when engaging in germline editing.[45] These so-called rights lie at the crossroads of her human rights-based approach to genome editing and her common heritage and global public goods-based approach to the human genome and biomedical science.

Professor Knoppers and colleagues see the concept of the rights of future generations as a bridge between the best interests of the child with their rights to life and to health on the one side, and unborn children on the other vis-a-vis the concept of the "best interest of future children."[46] She uses this latter concept as an argument in favour of therapeutic germline editing and raises the possibility of intergenerational monitoring of its consequences, provided such editing is done in accordance with human rights.[47] Professor Knoppers aptly acknowledges that there might be a tension between the individual aspects of the rights of children, understood as an "individual good" and the collective aspects of the rights of future generations as an expression of the common good.[48] These strands in Professor Knoppers's work invite further disentangling and elaboration.

One question that arises concerns the character of the so-called rights of future generations and their relationship with human rights. Another question concerns the relationship between the rights of future generations and the right to benefit from science, including the ways in which the two reinforce each other or come into tension. This relationship can be illustrated through the case study of germline editing. Third, there is the issue concerning the

45 See Bartha Maria Knoppers and Erika Kleiderman, 'Heritable genome editing: who speaks for future children?' (2019) 2 CRISPR Journal 285; Erika Kleiderman, Minh Thu Nguyen, and Bartha Maria Knoppers, 'Of the rights and best interests of future generations' (2020) 20 The American Journal of Bioethics 38.

46 Knoppers and Kleiderman (n 45), 286.

47 ibid., 288.

48 Kleiderman, Nguyen, and Knoppers (n 45), 40.

implications of the rights of future generations and the right to benefit from science for germline editing.

On a conceptual level, the idea of "future generations" can be seen as implicit in the concept of "humanity," which consists of both present and future generations, as well as of individuals, communities, and other collectives. The future generations are also implicit in the concept of the "human" in its present and future form. The idea of the "humane" human underpins the obligation of present generations to engage in inter-generational equity through burden sharing so as to prevent harm to future generations.

Turning to the first question, human rights can be seen as entitlements of individuals and sometimes collectives against the State that are innate in all humans by virtue of their human dignity and, more fundamentally, of being "human" and part of "humanity." In contrast, the rights of future generations cannot be understood as an entitlement because they have no real beneficiary, right-holder, or even a representative. These rights are thus better understood not as a form of human rights for future humans, but as a form of inter-generational equity which entails burden-sharing by the present generations and whose obligation-holders are both States and more generally, the present generation of humanity. The rights of future generations are not "rights"; rather, they are imperfect obligations without a correlative right holder. They impose anticipatory duties on their obligation holders to act with due diligence to prevent harm to the well-being and physical existence of future generations, as well as not to compromise their human dignity and their ability to enjoy basic human rights, including the right to life, the right to health and indeed the right to benefit from science.[49] In this way, the rights of future generations are a forward-looking concept that reflects long-term prevention of harm and preservation of benefits over the course of numerous generations.

The concept of the rights of future generations finds expression in several international soft-law instruments, including in biomedicine rather than in international human rights treaties. These soft law instruments clarify the relationship between the rights of future generations and science and technology to a limited extent and are entirely silent on the relationship between the rights of future generations and human rights. For instance, the UNESCO Declaration on Bioethics and Human Rights recommends that States give due regard to the impact of life sciences on future generations.[50] According to the UN Declara-

49 Rumiana Yotova, 'Anticipatory duties under the human right to science and international biomedical law' (2023) 28 International Journal of Human Rights 397.

50 UNESCO Declaration on Bioethics and Human Rights (2006) art 16 (Protecting future generations).

tion on the Responsibilities of the Present Generations Towards Future Generations, in the field of human genetics, the rights of future generations entail a basic obligation to ensure that scientific and technological progress does not impair or compromise the preservation of the human species.[51] UNESCO declarations in the field provide a mix of obligations and recommendations to give due regard to the impact of life sciences on the rights of future generations so as not only to safeguard them but also to benefit them.[52] The Preamble of the Oviedo Convention emphasizes the beneficence aspects of the obligation in requiring "that progress in biology and medicine should be used for the benefit of present and future generations."[53] The Universal Declaration on Bioethics and Human Rights defines as one of its objectives the dual obligation to safeguard and promote the rights of present and future generations.[54] The UN Declaration on the Rights of Future Generations requires that "[t]he present generations have the responsibility of ensuring that the needs and interests of present and future generations are fully safeguarded."[55] At a minimum, the present generations *should* strive to ensure the continuation of humankind with due respect for the dignity of the human person.[56] Based on these instruments, it can be concluded that States should make decisions in the field of biomedicine, including genetics, with due regard to the rights of future generations to prevent harm, preserve their existence, and maximize benefits.

Recent interpretations of human rights treaties shed some light on the relationship between human rights and the rights of future generations. For example, the UN Human Rights Committee conceptualizes the rights of future generations as entailing an obligation on States to take action to preserve future generations' ability to enjoy human rights, particularly the right to life.[57] This approach is balanced and convincing because it has a forward looking human rights focus aimed at preservation of rights without actually endowing the not yet in existence right-holders with them. The UN High Commissioner

51 UNESCO, Declaration on the Responsibilities of the Present Generations Towards Future Generations (1997), art 6 (Human genome and biodiversity).

52 UNESCO (n 50), art 16; UNESCO, Declaration on Science and the Use of Scientific Knowledge (1999), para 39.

53 Convention for the Protection of Human Rights and Fundamental Freedoms (European Convention on Human Rights, as amended) (ECHR) Preamble, para 1.

54 UNESCO (n 50), art 2 (g).

55 UNESCO (n 51), art. 1.

56 ibid., art. 3.

57 HRC, General Comment 36, Article 6: Right to Life, UN Doc CCPR/C/GC/36, 3 September 2019, para 62. See also *Teitiota v. New Zealand,* Communication No. 2728/2016, UN Doc CCPR/C/127/D/2728/2016, 23 September 2019, para 9.4.

on Human Rights adopted a slightly broader interpretation of the principle of intergenerational equity as placing "a duty on us to act as responsible stewards of our environment, and ensure that future generations can fulfil their human rights."[58] In the Reykjavik Declaration, the Member States of the Council of Europe boldly declared that the rights of future generations are equal to the rights of present generations in that they entail the full enjoyment of human rights.[59] While normatively appealing, the Council's declaration is more aspirational for the future development of the law than reflective of the current position of international law.

International and domestic courts, too, have started engaging with the rights of future generations. In particular, they have begun to helpfully clarify the relationship between the rights of future generations and human rights in the context of climate change. According to a recent judgment of the German Constitutional Court, the right to life and the right to health can give rise to "an objective duty to protect future generations."[60] The European Court of Human Rights framed the rights of future generations as "intergenerational burden-sharing, both in regard to different generations of those currently living and in regard to future generations."[61]

The Court reasoned:

> While the legal obligations arising for States under the Convention [ECHR] extend to those individuals currently alive who, at a given time, fall within the jurisdiction of a given Contracting Party, it is clear that future generations are likely to bear an increasingly severe burden of the consequences of present failures and omissions to combat climate change and that, at the same time, they have no possibility of participating in the relevant current decision-making processes.[62]

58 Michelle Bachelet, 'ONE UN Side event: SDG16 and realising the right to participate – empowering people as agents of more effective climate change' (9 December 2019), available at: https://www.ohchr.org/en/statements/2019/12/25th-session-conference-parties-one-un-side-event-sdg-16-and-realizing-right.

59 Declaration of the Fourth Summit of Heads of State and Government of the Council of Europe (Reykjavík, Iceland, 16–17 May 2023), Appendix V.

60 Order of the First Senate of 24 March 2021, 1 BvR 2656/18 DE:BVerfG:2021:rs20210324.1bvr265618, para 1.

61 *Case of Verein Klimaseniorinnen Schweiz and Others v Switzerland,* Application No 53600/20, ECtHR, Judgment, 9 April 2024, para 419 (sic).

62 ibid., para 420.

Notably, the Court clarified the responsibilities that the rights of future generations impose on States in the field of human rights:

> In view of the urgency of combating the adverse effects of climate change and the severity of its consequences, including the grave risk of their irreversibility, States should take adequate action notably through suitable general measures to secure not only the Convention rights of individuals who are currently affected by climate change, but also those individuals within their jurisdiction whose enjoyment of Convention rights may be severely and irreversibly affected in the future in the absence of timely action.[63]

The Court held that State measures "should, in the first place, be incorporated into a binding regulatory framework at the national level, followed by adequate implementation," and the margin of appreciation to be afforded to States is reduced as regards the setting of the requisite aims and objectives."[64]

Accordingly, it can be concluded that the rights of future generations require States to act with due diligence and adopt timely binding laws and other relevant measures to ensure that the enjoyment of fundamental human rights of future generations will not be severely and irreversibly affected. These rights include the right to life and the right to health but arguably also the right to benefit from science and its applications. While the threshold of risk to the enjoyment of these rights required to trigger the obligation to act today is very high, this is a welcome clarification of the "rights" of future generations in the context of human rights law, i.e. the right to enjoy fundamental rights in the future. The high threshold for action strikes a reasonable balance between the rights of present generations and their obligations towards the future ones.

This leads to the second question concerning the relationship between the rights of future generations and the right to benefit from science. The right to benefit from science is one of the fundamental economic, social, and cultural rights set out in the Universal Declaration of Human Rights[65] and the International Covenant of Economic, Social and Cultural Rights.[66] Indeed, General Comment 25 on the right to benefit from science defines "morally unacceptable harm" as including "harm to humans or the environment that is (a)

63 ibid., para 499.
64 ibid., para 549.
65 UDHR, art 27.
66 ICESCR, art 15.

threatening to human life or health, (b) serious and effectively irreversible, or (c) inequitable to present or future generations."[67]

Present generations and, in particular, States ought to ensure that the ability of future generations to benefit from science and its applications is not severely and irreversibly affected. Arguably, this would entail continuing to develop science and technologies humanely for the benefit of individuals and humankind as a whole, including its most vulnerable groups. Relatedly, it would also entail ensuring equitable access to science and its applications for the benefit of the different present generations and also the future ones. In the context of germline editing, this means its use for peaceful, therapeutic, and preventive purposes only, with full respect for human dignity and human rights so as not to exacerbate social inequalities but also to protect the right to life and the right to health of present and future generations. The rights of future generations also require States to regulate germline gene editing as a high-risk scientific and technological application that can significantly impact the rights of future generations. States should do so by taking into account the risk of harm and the benefits for future generations' existence, well-being, and rights when making decisions concerning both the legality and permitted applications of interventions in the human genome. This could entail conducting continuous impact assessments of the possible long-term consequences, risk monitoring, risk management, and constant re-evaluation when authorizing specific scientific and technological applications.[68]

Overall, Professor Knoppers work on the rights of future generations provides an important and much-needed link between the governance of the human genome as a common heritage of humanity and/or a global public good and the humanistic approach to biomedical science so as to ensure that any interventions in the human genome are done with due regard to human dignity and the ability of future generations to enjoy human rights.

4 A Path to Humanistic Governance

Professor Knoppers' work on international human rights as the necessary foundation for the governance of the human genome and of biomedical science is both visionary and timely in ensuring the humane development of science and its applications. She has opened avenues for future research but also for

67 UNCHR 'General comment No. 25 (2020) on article 15: science and economic, social and cultural rights,' UN Doc E/C.12/GC/25, para 56.

68 See Yotova (n 49).

policy and legislative work, including the development of international governance frameworks for the human genome, big genomic data, and technological applications based on human dignity and human rights, with due regard to the rights of future generations.

Anchoring global governance in biomedical science invites more normative work on foundational principles for human rights-based frameworks in this space, such as the common heritage regime made applicable to the human genome, the giving of equitable access to science and its applications as a global public good, and orienting germline editing endeavours towards the benefit of the individual, as well as the welfare of humanity as a whole with its present and future generations. Professor Knoppers' approach is pan-humanistic in that it embraces the rights, interests, and benefits of the individual, those of collectives, and of humanity as a whole. It transcends the present interests and concerns of the human and humanity to address those of the generations to come.

This conceptual work, however, is unfinished, as the case study on genome editing demonstrates. A human rights approach to biomedical sciences raises more novel questions than it answers that transcend the traditional bioethical approaches to biomedicine. Governing gene editing and genome knowledge are seemingly intractable problems that cannot be solved once and for all by morality or law. They evolve as new knowledge is produced, new applications come to life, humans evolve, and the planet around us changes. By anchoring the analysis to binding legal commitment and generally accepted global governance standards, Professor Knoppers situates the academic and policy discourse "beyond the moral appeals of bioethics." This is a path that Professor Knoppers has inaugurated and defined in her long and productive career. It is up to the next generation of academics, lawyers, and policymakers to pick up the baton and make good use of her ideas and wisdom.

VIGNETTE

A Memorable and Enjoyable 20 Years

Kazuto Kato

I have had the privilege of working with Bartha for more than twenty years. Starting with the Ethics Committee of the Human Genome Organization (HUGO), I was with her over the ensuing years for the International HapMap Project, the International Cancer Genome Consortium (ICGC), ELSI 2.0,[1] and the Global Alliance for Genomics and Health (GA4GH). This means, in other words, that I have been with her since the beginning of my work in the international ELSI community. I am so grateful to Bartha for teaching me so many things. They include how to be a good chairperson (she is amazing in enabling everyone in a meeting the time and space to speak comfortably, and yet finishes meetings *always* on time!) and how to be an equal partner with scientists. Bartha also gave me many opportunities to meet wonderful younger scholars (at that time, anyway!) such as Yann Joly, Rosario (Rosie) Isasi, and Edward (Ted) Dove.

One of my most memorable moments of Bartha was during an early project meeting of the HapMap project, which commenced in late 2002. Since the Project was aiming to analyze genomes of the four diverse populations of the world, the project needed to find a good way of labelling the populations. The ELSI group which Barth was leading thought that we should not oversimplify (nor overgeneralize) the labelling such as European, Asian, and African. This would avoid an impression that the Project was aiming to analyze racial differences of the genomes. In the meeting, the ELSI group (including me and Bartha) was seated in the back of the conference room. When a genetic researcher started to show slides of the preliminary data and spoke about the results of the analysis of "Asian samples" and then "African samples," Bartha suddenly stood up and shouted something along the lines of, "No, that is *not* what we are doing!" I do not remember exactly what she said, but I have a very clear and vivid memory of her standing up and expressing alarm to the scientist. Then the ELSI group proposed a more specific way of labelling the population, which led to the use of three-letter abbreviations such as YRI (Yoruba in Ibadan), CHB (Han Chinese in Beijing), JPT (Japanese in Tokyo), and CEU (Utah residents with Northern and Western European ancestry from the CEPH

1 Jane Kaye and others, 'ELSI 2.0 for genomics and society' (2012) 336 Science 673. ELSI stands for anticipating and addressing the ethical, legal, and social implications (ELSI) of scientific developments.

 DOI:10.1163/9789004688544_034

collection). This labelling system is still used in the human genetics research community all over the world and is a testament to Bartha's creative, sensitive, and intelligent mind—not to mention her ever-present desire to promote the "human" and human rights in ethics, law, and policy.

On many other occasions, such as at the ICGC and the various GA4GH meetings around the world (see Figure 1 below for a photo us in Beijing), Bartha skilfully showed her talent of convincing scientists and medical researchers of the importance of ELSI and the value of closely working together with ELSI scholars. She is cheerful all the time, yet determined enough in her insightful, well-informed views that she became a respected colleague of eminent researchers such as Francis Collins and Thomas Hudson. Through all of these experiences with Bartha, I learned that ELSI researchers can work effectively and collaboratively with leading scientists, and yet retain an ability to give constructive criticisms to enable more ethical (and ultimately, more socially valuable) scientific research. I utilize such skills every day in my work in the Japanese projects as well as in the international projects including the World Health Organization Technical Advisory Group on Genomics (WHO TAG-G).[2] I owe you so much and would like to thank you, Bartha!

FIGURE 1 Photo from ICGC Conference 9th Scientific Workshop (17-19 May 2014) in Beijing, China. Bartha Knoppers is centre and Kazuto Kato is at the right end. Photo courtesy of Kazuto Kato (reprinted with permission).

2 World Health Organization, 'Technical Advisory Group on Genomics (TAG-G)', available at: https://www.who.int/groups/technical-advisory-group-on-genomics-(tag-g).

VIGNETTE

Bartha Maria Knoppers: A Fantastic Woman!

Michèle Stanton-Jean

In 1997, during the fourth meeting of the International Bioethics Committee (IBC) of the United Nations Educational, Scientific and Cultural Organization (UNESCO), I had my first encounter with Bartha Maria Knoppers in Paris. As the Deputy Minister of Health Canada at that time, I was invited to attend the IBC session as a guest of UNESCO, where Canada was present to offer feedback on the draft Declaration on the Human Genome and Human Rights. Since I was not very familiar with the topic of bioethics, I was quite impressed with the calibre of the debates.

Bartha was a member of the IBC. During that meeting, she was one of the speakers on a panel on bioethics and women. Being myself one of the authors of *L'Histoire des femmes au Québec depuis quatre siècles*,[1] I was struck by the quality of her presentation. She raised all the right questions about the then status of women and all the work that was needed to give all women the autonomy they deserve and the right to determine their own destiny.

In 2005 she asked me to join her team at the Centre de recherche en droit public at the Université de Montréal. It is difficult to say "no" to Bartha. I accepted and worked there with her for a couple of years and was involved in many committees and meetings on ethical, legal, and social issues in human genetics. These included Quebec's population biobank, CARTaGENE, and the beginning of the International Institute for Research in Biomedical Ethics, a France-Quebec project, which she put in place with Dr Christian Hervé from the Paris Descartes University.

Bartha is a fantastic woman, full of scientific and pragmatic ideas on ways to deal with all the issues facing the field of human genetics. Bartha is also a team player, always ready to support and defend those who are working with her, always ready to celebrate your birthday, review a paper, or share a glass of wine to exchange views—but never forgetting when you must deliver the work that she has asked you to do.

When I met Bartha for the first time in Paris, she quoted in her presentation a famous French author, Georges Bernanos, who said, "We do not endure the future; we create it." This is what she has done throughout her career; she contributes to creating a better future in a world where science and technology developments are used for the benefit of humanity taking into account justice and ethics.

1 Le collectif Clio (Micheline Dumont, Michèle Jean, Marie Lavigne, and Jennifer Stoddart), *L'Histoire des femmes au Québec depuis quatre siècles* (Quinze 1982).

 | DOI:10.1163/9789004688544_035

CHAPTER 12

Persons, Genomes, and Populations

Ron Zimmern

1 Introduction

This chapter is an attempt to set out my thinking about the relationship between individuals and populations. The context is our increased understanding of the human genome and its architecture. It is designed to question certain aspects of the conventional wisdom that has guided us over the last fifty years or so; it is not intended to be a scientific or academic offering. It sets out my views on the issues that sit at the intersection of genomics, public health, epidemiology, and clinical medicine based on over fifty years of experience in the practice of medicine and public health. Professor Bartha Knoppers' interest in the importance of the "human" in genomics and bioethics has not been inconsiderable in helping to develop my thoughts; and it is her insistence of the role of the "human" that has resonated so well with my own views, particularly those that inform my understanding of the importance of the personal as well as that of the numerical.

Her own take on these matters has encompassed many aspects of genomics and public health practice. I shall single out just one of her concerns, which is that the genome and genetic information is a "common heritage of humanity;"[1] and that it should serve as a public good,[2] a public information resource that should be the subject of open communication. This thinking has been at the heart of many of her publications and has led to her insistence that we all have a right to benefit from science, an understanding that has profound implications for genetic data sharing. These ideas are essentially grounded in public health values. She expresses concerns, as do I, about the proper relationship between the individual "human" and the population with whom each individual shares that common heritage.

My own development and career pathway have also been an enormous influence in shaping this thinking. I trained first as a neurologist and then,

1 Rumiana Yotova and Bartha M Knoppers, 'The right to benefit from science and its implications for genomic data sharing' (2020) 31 European Journal of International Law 665.

2 Bartha Maria Knoppers, 'Of genomics and public health: building public "goods"?' (2005) 173 CMAJ: Canadian Medical Association Journal 1185.

after a degree in law, shifted to train in public health. Unlike most of my colleagues in that specialty, I have always seen the discipline to be best served by finding an appropriate balance between the needs of the population and those of the individual, rather than by solely concentrating on those of the population itself. The writings of Professor Geoffrey Rose have been a guiding light. His influence on my thoughts cannot be overestimated. Since 1997 my work has been directed solely at the public health and policy implications of advances in genomic science, and it is that intersection that has brought me so close to Professor Knoppers' own work. Her humanity, as everyone knows, shines through all that she does. Although a lawyer, her understanding of genomic science and epidemiological concepts is profound but, whatever the subject matter, affected individuals have always been foremost in her thoughts.

My starting point is to reflect on individuals and on populations, and to ask what the connection is between them. I do this by asserting premises.

First, I start with the rather obvious assertion that individuals are real, by which I mean that they have an existence of their own. They exist in the world in the same way as dogs, cats, and horses, or chairs, tables, buses, and cars. By contrast, populations are socially constructed. Their composition can be defined in whatever way I choose, ranging from more coherent constructs such as those born in China, resident in Sweden, live in a city, of male sex, or age 65 and above; to the less coherent such as those with beards, one leg, or who wear hats. Individuals are what they are. But I can define a population as I wish according to the attributes that I chose. Some of those attributes may have a biological reality such as sex, but others may not, such as residence in a particular country. How I choose to define a population will depend on the question that I wish to address and on the reason for so doing. The reason matters and can be, for example, political, moral, clinical, or scientific, among others. There is an essence in the nature of individuals which I cannot alter. By contrast, I am able to define the characteristics of a population.

By so saying, I do not intend to imply that to establish populations and to work with population groups or subgroups is not useful. It clearly is, as testified by the advances in epidemiology and the insights given by that discipline. It is rather to dispel the idea that populations have a reality in the same way that individuals have a reality. There is an essential element in the reality of individuals that is not present in populations. Margaret Thatcher captures this idea in these words:

> I think we have gone through a period when too many children and people have been given to understand 'I have a problem, it is the Government's job to cope with it!' or 'I have a problem, I will go and get a grant

> to cope with it!' 'I am homeless, the Government must house me!' and so *they are casting their problems on society and who is society? There is no such thing! There are individual men and women and there are families* and no government can do anything except through people and people look to themselves first.[3]

Thatcher was, of course, wrong to say that there was no such thing as society, but entirely correct in characterizing society, like populations, as not real in the same way that individuals are real. Populations and society are both nominalist concepts; they are socially constructed just as governments, the law, and money are socially constructed. Some have attempted to describe these as "social facts," a term first used by Durkheim and defined "as a thing originating in the institutions or culture of a society which affects the behaviour or attitudes of an individual member of that society."[4] These are not real in the sense that chairs, tables, dogs, and cats are real. But they are real in the sense that they interact with individuals. Growing up in one country rather than another, with a different culture and different laws, can have profound effects on individuals, just as individuals have the capacity to effect changes in law and culture within their society.

For these reasons, but also because biology and natural selection work through individuals, I suggest that the more important element of a population is not the population itself but the individuals that make up that population.

As a second premise, I emphasize that individuals differ one from another. They differ for at least two reasons: because their genomes are different from each other, and because their life experiences are different. All human traits, whether pathological or physiological, come about as a result of the interaction between the genome and the environment. Identical twins have the same genome but both in utero and after birth their environments differ. So there are differences between identical twins even though they have the same genome. There is no human trait that is not influenced by both environmental and genetic factors. Even in the so-called genetic disorders such as the haemoglobinopathies or cystic fibrosis, we can observe the phenomenon that geneticists call *expressivity* whereby mutations in the same gene can lead to different manifestations of the disease. Some of these differences will be due to the

3 Margaret Thatcher, 'Interview for 'Woman's Own' ("No Such Thing as Society")', in Margaret Thatcher Foundation: *Speeches, Interviews and Other Statements* (London 1987), available at: https://newlearningonline.com/new-learning/chapter-4/neoliberalism-more-recent-times/margaret-thatcher-theres-no-such-thing-as-society (emphasis added).

4 Émile Durkheim, *The Rules of Sociological Method* (SAGE Publications, Inc. 1986 [1895]).

exact variant in the gene which is mutated; others will be a result of other genetic variants in those individuals; and others still will be as a consequence of different environmental exposures. At the other end of the spectrum will be injuries such as being struck by lightning, which many would attest to being a purely environmental exposure or determinant with no genetic component. But it is well documented that genetic factors influence whether an individual prefers the outdoors and exercise; if so, they will have a higher risk than those whose personalities lead to a more indoor and sedentary lifestyle.

It is also the case that biology works through individuals and not populations. It is an individual's genomic architecture and her environmental milieu, be that the physical or biological, or the social and political, that shape that individual. The interaction of these external factors with the internal biology determine how that individual behaves, her physiology, and her liability to the development of disease. Even socio-political factors work through the individual's physiology—the cerebral cortex, the hypothalamus, the autonomic nervous system, and the orchestration of the hormones that may or may not be released—and through such mechanisms disease risk.

As a third premise, I state as a matter of historical fact that the practice of medicine—of diagnosis, treatment, and prognostication—has always been a relationship between two individuals: a physician and a patient. This has been so over the last four millennia. The point that I seek to discuss is not the nature of that relationship, nor the issues around paternalism and autonomy in the doctor-patient relationship, nor the complex issues of personal identity through space and time. It is purely and simply to emphasize that it is the individual patient that matters, and that advice given to a patient should be given on the basis of not just the generalities of her pathology, but of the physician's understanding of her *individual* values, wishes, and aspirations.

Over much of the last two millennia treatments were on the whole not very effective. It is only in recent decades that effective treatments have become available, and categorized to be effective or otherwise in groups of patients, a consequence of the use of clinical trials in determining the effectiveness of medicines. But until then, doctors prescribed for the individual patients and have been as much a therapeutic agent themselves as the medicines that they prescribe.[5] The illness of an individual is much more than the pathology that is its proximate cause. It encompasses the fears and the anxieties of anyone faced with illness and all physicians since Hippocrates have always understood this to be so. These are some of Hippocrates' quotes:

---

5 Michael Balint, *The Doctor, his Patient and the Illness* (Pitman Medical 1968).

> It is more important to know what sort of person has a disease than to know what sort of disease a person has.
>
> If we could give every individual the right amount of nourishment and exercise, not too little and not too much, we would have found the safest way to health.
>
> Whoever would study medicine aright must learn of the following subjects. First he must consider the effect of each of the seasons of the year and the differences between them. Secondly he must study the warm and the cold winds, both those which are common to every country and those peculiar to a particular locality. Lastly, the effect of water on health must not be forgotten.[6]

Such understanding is the understanding of the personal in the management of illness, the individual in the context of the environment. This is the "human" which lies at the heart of clinical practice.

Chinese medical practice, as Hippocrates, also recognizes the unique nature of every individual. Two individuals presenting with the same symptoms will be treated differently. Each is unique, as we now know from our understanding of genetic heterogeneity. Why then should it be expected that each will benefit from a uniform therapeutic that is based on symptomatology rather than an individually tailored regime based on the unique characteristics of the individual? The taking of a detailed history and the placing of patients in their environmental context—the food they eat, the climate they experience, the pollution in their atmosphere, their financial circumstances, their social interactions—define that individual and the context for how they should be managed: what medicines they should take and what outlook might be expected for their illness.[7]

These three premises that I advance—the reality of the individual as against socially constructed populations, the heterogeneity of individuals, and the personal nature of the clinical consultation—are the starting points of this chapter. They are assertions, I acknowledge, but assertions that can be supported by evidence, though I shall not attempt to set these out here. Rather, I seek to discuss four implications that arise from these three premises.

First, I shall consider some matters that concern the relationship between the practice of public health and the practice of clinical medicine. Second, I talk about some of the issues that arise from the heterogeneity of populations and the insights of Professor Rose and his two sets of distinctions—between

---

6 Hippocrates, available at: https://www.goodreads.com/author/quotes/248774.Hippocrates.

7 Wikipedia, 'Traditional Chinese medicine', available at: https://en.wikipedia.org/wiki/Traditional_Chinese_medicine.

population prevention and high risk prevention, and between the causes of incidence and the causes of cases. Third, I speak about my growing unease about the evidence-based medicine movement. Fourth and finally, I discuss the issue of personalization and the future of healthcare.

2 The Relationship between the Practice of Public Health and the Practice of Clinical Medicine

I was privileged to give the Milroy Lecture at the Royal College of Physicians in 2008, in which I declared:

> Public health practice in the twenty first century can no longer ignore the knowledge derived from genetic and molecular science; and that an understanding of the genetic, molecular and cellular mechanisms of disease will be as important to the public health community as an understanding of the social determinants of health.[8]

What I had in mind was the need for a public health approach which took on biological as well as environmental and social determinants of health. These I saw to be complementary and not in conflict one with the other; but because of the way in which biological and environmental factors interact, it seemed to me essential to have regard to both without favour for the one or the other. Sadly, most public health practitioners have not seen fit to incorporate biological determinants into their conventional paradigm, but rather to equate public health as a subject concerned only with the more distal determinants of health such as poverty, inequality, fiscal policy, smoking, alcohol, nutrition, sexual behaviour, or environmental pollution in air and water, rather than the more proximate biological determinants in the individual organism. This conceptualization of the field is damaging and short-sighted.

This split between the public health and the clinical approach was evident long before the genetic revolution. In 1991, Kerr White, Deputy Director at the Rockefeller Foundation, published his book, *Healing the Schism: Epidemiology, Medicine and the Public's Health*, in which he asserted that the two cultures "medicine" and "public health" seem to live in different, often unfriendly worlds.[9]

8 Ron Zimmern, 'Testing challenges: evaluation of novel diagnostics and molecular biomarkers' (2009) 1 Clinical Medicine: Journal of the Royal College of Physicians of London 68.

9 Kerr White, *Healing the Schism: Epidemiology, Medicine and the Public's Health* (Springer-Verlag 1991).

He traced the histories of Schools of Medicine and Schools of Public Health in the United States, and documented the decision of the Rockefeller Foundation to support the creation of Schools of Public Health, separate from Schools of Clinical Medicine. It was to this that he ascribed the development of the two cultures in the quote above and his solution was the development of the discipline of clinical epidemiology through the creation of the International Clinical Epidemiology Network (INCLEN). It is uncertain to what extent clinical epidemiology has contributed to the bringing together of medicine and public health; but it is quite clear that whereas clinicians have by and large have embraced the importance of these wider determinants in disease prevention, public health professionals (at least in the UK) have not on the whole sought to understand biological mechanisms of disease and their importance in preventing disease in populations. (It is important to exclude my academic colleagues from this wide generalization since most have an understanding of the interactions between the social and the biological.)

Even earlier, Professor Sir Douglas Black, in his Rock Carling Lecture in 1984, entitled *An Anthology of False Antitheses*, made much the same point.[10] He wrote about the distinction between individual and population, treatment and prevention, and hospital and community; he showed that all were, to him, false antitheses. Medicine in its entirety embraced *all* of these aspects and any attempt to separate them and to pit one against the other was false, pointless, and even detrimental to human health.

This distinction is mirrored in that between clinical science and epidemiology, a debate which has had an even longer history dating back to 19th century France. I am indebted to Raphael Scholl, whose PhD thesis in the Department of the History and Philosophy of Science at the University of Cambridge was entitled *Bridging the Gap between Populations and Individuals in the Philosophy of Medicine*.[11] He showed that, among other things, the distinction between individual and population as patients was a live subject debated at the French Academy in the 1820s. He writes:

> In nineteenth century France, a group of physicians and scientists argued that physicians' ability to judge disease progression and therapeutic success in individual patients was – contrary to widespread

10 Douglas Black, *An Anthology of False Antitheses* (Nuffield Trust 1984).

11 Raphael Scholl, *Bridging the Gap between Populations and Individuals in the Philosophy of Medicine* (PhD thesis, Department of History and Philosophy of Science, University of Cambridge 2022).

> believes – severely limited. They suggested that studies of entire groups of patients were needed to produce more reliable results.[12]

One of the physicians who expounded this was Pierre Charles Alexandre Louis, whose contribution to medicine was the development of the "numerical method", a forerunner to epidemiology, the clinical trial and evidence-based medicine. As Scholl writes:

> His opponents, such as the Montpellier pathologist B. J. I. Risueno d'Amador, disagreed: Group-level trials were unscientific, since they yielded mere probability instead of causal understanding. He judged knowledge of probabilities to be useless to medicine because it could not tell physicians how to treat the individual patient at hand.[13]

Since that time, epidemiology has grown from strength to strength but implicit in its study was an assumption of population homogeneity. As I wrote in a paper in 2011, emphasizing the importance of having regard to the diverse genetic architectures of individuals, and how epidemiology would need to change because of it:

> The study of epidemiology has been based on an implicit assumption of population homogeneity. This assumption has served us well for over 150 years [...] Our whole approach has been to apply interventions "to" a population; we frame the relationship between intervention and outcome in terms of the population as a whole. In contrast, we pay scant attention to the variation in the distribution of effect size of environmental determinants among and between individuals.
>
> The reality is that we are all different, genetically and because of our individual life experiences. The effect of interventions and the relationship between risk factors and disease will differ from one individual to another.[14]

These considerations speak to issues of generality and individuality. The epidemiologist and public health practitioner focus on the former, and are concerned about distal determinants of health and disease that are primarily

12 ibid., 6.

13 ibid., 8.

14 Ron Zimmern, 'Genomics and individuals in public health practice: are we luddites or can we meet the challenge?' (2011) 33 Journal of Public Health 477, 478.

social and environmental. The clinician focuses on the latter, and directs herself at the specific characteristics of that individual and at more proximate biological determinants.

3 The Heterogeneity of Populations

My second task is to discuss the insights of Professor Geoffrey Rose, an important contributor to these issues and known by students of public health and epidemiology for his distinction between population prevention and high risk prevention.[15] The latter relied on, for example, treating patients with high blood pressure using drugs; the former sought to lower the mean blood pressure of the entire population by reducing that population's sodium consumption. The Gaussian frequency distribution curve around the mean blood pressure of the high sodium population would shift to the left as the sodium consumption of that population was reduced. In so doing, the numbers of patients with high blood pressure would also be reduced, but many in the "normal" risk group would also benefit and the numbers with stroke or heart disease would be more greatly reduced than a strategy that just relied on treating those with clinically defined hypertension. It was clear that Rose regarded the two approaches as complementary, yet in my experience, there are many who seek to speak of these as being in tension, one with the other.

Far less well known was Rose's distinction between "causes of incidence" and "causes of cases," whereby the reasons for health differences across populations are different to those that could be cited for differences between individuals within the same population. By concentrating on the causal factors for an individual's blood pressure, one would miss those factors that were responsible for the average blood pressure in two populations. The broader approach was necessary for effective public health action. Yet in clinical practice, the physician would wish to know which of her patients might more accurately be a member of the subset of the population at one end of the Gaussian risk curve and which the other. An individual's genetic predisposition would be an important factor in placing the patient along the spectrum of disease risk; but equally important would be to understand the environments to which

15 Geoffrey Rose, 'Sick individuals and sick populations' (1985) 14 International Journal of Epidemiology 32; Hilary Burton and others, 'Time to revisit Geoffrey Rose: strategies for prevention in the genomic era' (2012) 9 Italian Journal of Public Health e8665.

that individual was exposed, and the periods across those individuals' lives at which the exposure took place.[16]

It is clear, using evidence dating from Richard Doll's work, that tobacco is a cause of lung cancer.[17] If we compare two populations, one comprising individuals who have never smoked and the other those smoking 60 cigarettes or more per day, the incidence of lung cancer in the smoking population will be much higher. Yet not all those who smoke over 60 cigarettes a day will develop lung cancer, and there are those who have never smoked who will. In a population comprising only heavy smokers, tobacco consumption would be regarded as part of the causal field, the context for which one might look to understand why even in that population it is only some individuals but not others who develop cancer. For those in that particular population, tobacco cannot be cited as a cause of who will develop lung cancer and who will not because all will have been so exposed. Tobacco is clearly a cause of lung cancer, but cannot be cited as such in that context. Other factors must be at play in determining the causes of cancer in those individuals.

These considerations enable one to understand that some of the causal factors that determine disease in the individual are likely to be different from one individual to another, given that populations are made up of diverse and heterogeneous individuals. Whereas sodium consumption is likely to be the most important determinant of a population's average blood pressure, it is likely to be seriously misleading to infer from this that sodium consumption is the sole or the most important determinant of an individual's blood pressure status, or that the reduction of an individual's sodium consumption will necessarily reduce (although it may do) in any clinical meaningful way that individual's blood pressure. The implications of acknowledging these considerations are tremendous.

4 The Evidence-Based Medicine Movement

These implications lead to my third concern, which is to raise serious questions about the evidence-based medicine movement, led by the late Dr David

16 Katherine Keyes and Sandro Galea, 'Population Health Science' in Katherine Keyes and Sandro Galea, *The Causes of Cases versus the Causes of Incidence* (Oxford University Press 2016).

17 Richard Doll and A Bradford Hill, 'Smoking and carcinoma of the lung' (1950) 2 British Medical Journal 739.

Sackett at McMaster University in Canada.[18] These ideas have had a growing influence on healthcare since the mid-1900s, especially in relation to the use of clinical trials as a guide to the treatment of individual patients. Epidemiology was in the early stages of development when I started my training in public health in the early 1980s. I had been taught that the results of epidemiological studies were best used to generate hypotheses that could be tested by scientists or for which the suggested causative mechanisms could be investigated. There was little suggestion at that time that their primary use should be to inform clinical decision-making. Observational studies, whether of case-control or cohort by design, sought to determine causes of incidence in the populations in which the studies were carried out. Well replicated studies had, for example, shown unequivocally that smoking raised the probability of developing lung cancer, and salt the probability of developing high blood pressure. In a similar vein, clinical trials were used to demonstrate the efficacy of a particular medicine against either a placebo or another medicine. Studies which showed a positive effect for the medicine being studied led to the view that the medicine was efficacious, or that it was more efficacious than the control medication.

The advocates of health promotion suggested that advice to patients and the prescription of medicine could be informed by such evidence; that for the first time in the history of medicine, preventive interventions could be based on science and on solid evidence rather than on the experience of individual physicians. Individuals were thus advised, even exhorted, to avoid certain behaviours such as smoking or salt consumption. The health promotion movement aimed to change the behaviour of individuals and was not content just to supply information for the individual to act on or not as they wished. Attempts to differentiate certain groups of individuals from other groups were said to "dilute" the health promotional message and were not encouraged. Scant attention was paid to the fact that for some individuals, these environmental agents probably did not do much by way of raising their individual disease risk, nor that avoiding them would lower it. The advice was given to all, and little regard was given, for example, to the fact that there were many with a particular determinant who would not develop the disease, and that some who were not so exposed would do so.

The situation was little different in the context of medicines for the treatment of illness. Patients with particular diseases were advised to take one drug rather than another based on clinical trial data. The demonstration of greater efficacy of a particular drug led to its use in all patients (unless there was some

18 See e.g. David Sackett, 'Evidence based medicine' (1997) 21 Seminars in Perinatology 3.

contraindication). A positive clinical trial result for a particular drug meant that it should be prescribed for all with that illness and likely to be effective. This assumption was made notwithstanding the evidence that, for all classes of drugs, the drug was only effective in a proportion of patients. In 2003, Dr Allen Roses, Vice President at GlaxoSmithKline, in part based on the work of Brian Spear, was quoted in *The Independent* as saying: "The vast majority of drugs - more than 90 per cent - only work in 30 or 50 per cent of the people," [...] "I wouldn't say that most drugs don't work. I would say that most drugs work in 30 to 50 per cent of people. Drugs out there on the market work, but they don't work in everybody."[19]

It is well understood that the taking of statins would on average reduce cholesterol levels by around 30 percent. But I have not seen any publication that sets out the frequency distribution of effect size of cholesterol reduction in the study population. It is unlikely, but possible, that these drugs reduce cholesterol by 60 percent in half the population and have zero effect in the other half. It is equally well known that individual patients with hypertension respond differentially to the class of anti-hypertensive drug that they are given. Whether to prescribe a diuretic, a beta blocker, a ACE inhibitor, and angiotensin II receptor blocker or a calcium channel blocker is now more often than not a matter of trial and error; in the future it may be biology that will inform the clinician as to the most suitable class of drug.

So while it is clear that on average those who take an "effective" medicine are more likely to be cured than those who do not, for each individual person, other factors will also play a part in determining the efficacy of that medication. It is also perhaps important to state explicitly that my skepticism about evidence-based medicine is targeted solely at its use in determining the management of individual patients or the giving of advice to individual citizens. Evidence is an important element in many other spheres such as public policy, the formulation of scientific hypotheses, and the efficacy of population-based interventions.

The study of the genetically determined variation in drug efficacy between individuals is the science of pharmacogenetics. It is not the purpose of this chapter to go further into this; rather it is to use pharmacogenetics as a lead into the discussion of personalized medicine: the idea—in terms of the

19 Allen Roses, 'Glaxo chief: our drugs do not work on most patients' (8 December 2003) *The Independent*, available at: https://www.independent.co.uk/news/science/glaxo-chief-our-drugs-do-not-work-on-most-patients-5508670.html. See also Brian Spear, Margo Heath-Chiozzi, and Jeffrey Huff, 'Clinical application of pharmacogenetics' (2001) 7 Trends in Molecular Medicine 201.

prediction of disease, its treatment, and its prognosis—that we can do better than to use just averages; that data will allow one to attribute at the level of the sub-population (if not the individual) the probability of developing a disease, the likelihood of treating it successfully, and the probability of dying from it. The personalization of medical care is a large and important subject that is now in the spotlight of health policy discussion and I will turn to it as my fourth topic for discussion.

5 The Personalization and the Future of Healthcare

The point that I have tried to make in the preceding paragraphs was the disconnect between epidemiological evidence, which is based on population averages, and health promotional based interventions, which are directed at the individual. I turn now to discuss a separate point, the difference between two public health approaches: the classical interventions directed at the environment, and the health promotional approach requiring individuals to make appropriate changes in their own lives. I also discuss the ethical differences between them.

The standard classical public health intervention was directed at the environment. There were laws to ensure cleaner air and mechanisms to provide clean water. Fluoride was added to drinking water and environmental health laws were promulgated for food premises. The list can be much longer. But central to all these interventions was that it did not involve the agency of the individual citizen. The citizen was of course affected by these measures, but it was not the choice or behaviour of the individual that determined whether or not the measure would be put in place. This was the model that informed the sanitary engineer of the 19th century, a dominant force in the practice of public health.

In the second half of the 20th century a new set of interventions emerged under the rubric of health promotion. Information was given to individual citizens who were exhorted to change their behaviour. Alcohol was bad and should only be taken in moderation; certain foods were considered healthy and others unhealthy; unprotected sex should not be encouraged; and as for smoking, it was an evil that should not be tolerated and nobody should take up the habit. The individual's own behaviour was the factor that would determine that person's exposure to the adverse factor. The public health intervention was not directed externally but directly at citizens who were in effect told what was good for them, and how they ought to behave. It involved human agency. The social engineer in the guise of the health promoter took the place of the sanitary engineer as the key public health worker, and her success was not determined by her effectiveness in getting the message across to citizens, leaving them to make an informed choice, but rather in her ability to effect behavioural change.

It is this requirement to effect change in the behaviour of citizens who might have wanted to act otherwise that I find disturbing; and it is this attempt to override the agency and free will of individual citizens that in my view plays a role in the removal of the "human" in the promotion of health. It is clearly the duty of states and their agents to provide the best and the latest advice about healthy behaviours to their citizens, but is it their role to force these behavioural choices on them? We live in a free society and whereas we might be encouraged to follow advice that will reduce our risk of disease, should we be pressured into so doing? Yet by ensuring that actual changes in behaviour was what the health promotion professional was urged to achieve, and that targets were based on such changes rather than just on the provision of information, suggests that social engineering was at work.

By making these comments I do not suggest that we go for some form of unbridled libertarianism. Our freedom to act needs to be constrained.[20] We should not condone action that leads to harm to others, or that raises the probability of such harm. But where harms are confined to the individual, state intervention should err on the side of information provision rather than behaviour change. It is absolutely right that our movements should be curtailed in the context of an epidemic if the evidence is that to do otherwise would lead to preventable illness or death. But for the state to seek to induce me to eat more healthily rather than just to advise me to do so is, at least for me, somewhat problematic.

This is not the place to set out in detail the role of "nudging" as a tool for promoting health. It is a huge subject worthy of detailed consideration. Suffice it to say that I am uncomfortable with its explicit use where the intention is to change the behaviour of the individual citizen, using it as an inducement that works at a subconscious level. Those who wish to market unhealthy products often use such techniques. Given that there is much evidence to show that human behaviour is irrational and susceptible to such subconscious inducements (inducements which would be considered unethical by health promoters), I am not persuaded that those who wish their citizens to be healthier should use the same unethical techniques. Cass Sunstein, in his book *The Ethics of Influence,* regards a nudge as one of many forms of influence to which

---

20 John Stuart Mill, *On Liberty* (Cambridge University Press 2011 [1859]).

we are all subjected in daily life.[21] He suggests that influences that promote our welfare, autonomy, and dignity to be a "good" nudge. The "bad" nudge is by contrast designed to promote the objectives of the nudger rather than those who are nudged.

I am not sure that I am convinced by his arguments. Even though these subconscious influences come at me from all directions, it is not necessarily the case that I should explicitly attempt to influence another person in this way, even in her best interests. It is the lack of honesty and transparency that concerns me. If, having been provided with the necessary information, I continue to wish to behave in what the health promoter believes, or even knows, to be undesirable for my health I, notwithstanding Sustein's arguments, continue to have some concern for such subconscious manipulation of my behaviour. I think that what is at stake here is that the nudger is not aware of my individual values. No matter how irrational it may appear to some, I may for my own personal reasons choose, entirely rationally, an unhealthy lifestyle. To be manipulated in this way, even for the best of reasons, is not something to which I can wholeheartedly support. Inducements that work at a conscious level seem to me to have greater ethical merit, such as offering cash or other explicit benefits to behave in a certain way. I am not competent to know whether such mechanisms are more or less effective than the "nudge" at the subconscious level, but such inducements have at least the merit of honesty and transparency.

What I set out above is of course, from a professional philosophical perspective, both superficial and naive. There are epistemological, ethical, and other complexities in the philosophy of free will and of intentionality which not only am I incompetent to explore, but which would involve a significant philosophical digression. Whether the citizen has a responsibility and a duty to stay healthy is another question that requires similar philosophical unpacking. But this must be left to others. Suffice it that I just make two points. First, that the attempted engineering of social behaviour is but one of the factors that might have contributed to the impression that the "human" in medical care has been disregarded. Second, that from a lay perspective, what I set out above does represent a point of view which, though philosophically unsophisticated, is not without a rational basis.

These same considerations do not apply to the standard classical public health interventions, because they are affected without having to act through the agency of the individual citizen. For sure every citizen is affected since laws apply to all; and clean water and clean air is available to all. But the intervention

21 Cass R Sunstein, *The Ethics of Influence: Government in the Age of Behavioral Science* (Cambridge University Press 2016).

was made by the state on our behalf after an accepted political and democratic process informed by the most up-to-date scientific evidence. Its legitimacy is grounded in the social contract made between the citizen and the state. The state imposes these measures on us because they are in part measures that no citizen can do individually, but in part also because their implementation has been subject to a significant degree of academic and political scrutiny, a democratic process, and agreed by most (if not all) to be an acceptable way to proceed.

The approach adopted by health promoters is undoubtedly a form of paternalism but, paradoxically during the same period, paternalism in the practice of clinical medicine was increasingly felt to be problematic. Doctors should no longer advise or tell the patient what was good for him or her. Patient autonomy was to be the foremost driver of the clinical interaction, and direct advice from the physician should be replaced by a process of joint decision-making wherein it became the duty of the doctor to provide the necessary information to enable patients to decide on the management of their medical condition. It is a great mystery to me what justification there can be for insisting on the primacy of patient autonomy in clinical care, yet being so vociferous in demanding change in health behaviour in the health promotion context. My concern is not that one should veer more towards paternalism or individual autonomy—that is another debate which I shall touch on later in this chapter—but the lack of coherence between the two approaches. What are the factors that justify this extreme move towards individual autonomy in the clinical encounter, yet approach the prevention of disease as a matter for which the state can be aggressively paternalistic?

6 Towards the Individualized Health Management of Patients

My fourth and final topic is personalized medicine and more generally healthcare in a context where it is now possible to individualize the management of patients. In part this has come about because the technology and the advances in understanding population heterogeneity have allowed it to do so. But more importantly, all health systems in the world are faced with a crisis due to rising demand and the need for financial restraint. The factors responsible for the demand are the demography of a rising elderly population, science and technology push, and rising patient expectations. Health services have been forced to reduce costs through piecemeal efficiency savings and managing demand, an accepted (but in my view not acceptable) euphemism for healthcare rationing. It is a reality and a tragic choice[22] that the demands of healthcare exceed the resources available for it. Health systems around the world are seeking solutions to address such an imbalance. Citizens may not have what they *wish* to have; their healthcare systems may only give them what they *need* to have. But the distinction between needs and wants is not entirely clear and may cynically be said to be the distinction between what I want and what the state thinks I should have. Of course, the assessment of a healthcare need is more evidence-based and objective than implied by such a view, but even then it can be said that this approach is one of the reasons for dissatisfaction for such systems and for the view that healthcare has been depersonalized.

One example will show this well. There is a considerable literature on what is termed *health needs assessment*. One version of this is that a health need is that which is first, common and prevalent and, second, a serious condition which can be shown through evidence to be effectively treated or managed.[23] Under such a paradigm health systems might judge diseases such as heart disease and cancer to be a significant health need since they are common conditions, serious, and with effective treatments. Much by way of health resources are directed at such conditions. Conditions such as dementia would not be considered a high priority because, though prevalent, there is no effective therapy; nor skin conditions such as lipomata or sebaceous cysts because, though eminently treatable, they are considered not to be serious. From a population perspective, the approach is defensible, but from the perspective of the individual citizen with a condition that is not as prevalent as heart disease, stroke, cancer, diabetes or some such, the approach is deeply unfair and discriminatory. Why should I be disadvantaged because I happen to have a relatively rare disorder such as systematic lupus erythematosus but not so if I have angina, colon cancer, or breast cancer?

And who is to decide whether a condition is serious or not? (See Kleiderman and Ravitsky's chapter in this volume for a more elaborate discussion on the question.) The population-based approach suggests that health systems should prioritize the common conditions that are also deemed to be serious. The utilitarian approach on which much of public health practice is based, while giving regard to individual or subjective feelings, does so only on some form of aggregate basis. It may be an acceptable philosophical basis on which to proceed when applied to the classical public health interventions, but when

---

22 Guido Calabresi and Philip Chase Bobbitt, *Tragic Choices* (W.W. Norton & Company 1978).

23 John Wright, Rhys Williams, and John Wilkinson, 'Development and importance of health needs assessment' (1998) 316 The BMJ 1310.

it is used as the basis for resource allocation for clinical services, much injustice can be caused. The clinical encounter that is at the heart of the doctor-patient relationship has, in my view, been much neglected in recent years and is most likely a significant factor in the discontent of patients and citizens and for the lack of humanity in health service provision. It will need to be addressed if we are to make more human the systems of healthcare in which the practice of medicine is located.

Additionally, the classical public health approaches directed at structural and environmental determinants of health and generalized health-promotion messages and programs designed to prevent disease have only been partially successful. This "one size fits all" mentality has taken no account of population heterogeneity. Many have argued that we must think in terms of a sustainable system of healthcare that will require first, a radical change in service organization a part of which is a greater shift from hospital to community; second, a shift from the treatment of established disease to early diagnosis and prevention; and third, the empowerment of citizens to take greater responsibility for their own health.

In relation to these three sets of changes, the eminent American biologist Leroy Hood argues cogently that the "find it and fix it" approach of conventional medicine will not do as we move into the 21st century; rather, we must move towards a paradigm of "scientific wellness" where through the use of genomics, the deep phenotyping of all citizens, digital measurements, and the use of AI for their analysis, we try to keep ourselves consistently well as we move through life. The goal would be his "P4 medicine": predict, prevent, personalize, and participate, and a shift in emphasis from illness to wellness. I myself, in speaking about public health genomics, have emphasized the new drivers of demography, science, technology, the environment, and globalization as the impetus for genomic and biomedical science and digital science, and the crystallization of autonomy and individualism as core values of our 21st century society as significant drivers of the personalized medicine movement.

The "wellness" on which Hood is so focused is discussed in this way in his book:

> Healthcare should target the maintenance and enhancement of wellness. It should prioritise preventing diseases over fighting them once they have arrived. It should centre on the principle of keeping us in tip top condition to live healthy lives in the long run.[24]

---

24 Leroy Hood and Nathan Price, *The Age of Scientific Wellness: Why the Future of Medicine Is Personalized, Predictive, Data-Rich, and in Your Hands* (Belknap Press 2023), 50.

And to get there will require that we are informed about:

> [...] the various interlocking biological systems in our bodies [...] The measurement of wellness we should be collecting – the genome, phenome and digital measurements of health – are far more detailed and subtle than how we feel.[25]

This implies, he says, that we must have knowledge and understanding of both our genome and our lifestyle choices and life history; that medicine should be more data rich, systems driven and powered by artificial intelligence; and that its aims should be to eliminate chronic disease and to focus on healthy ageing.

The cardiologist and scientist Eric Topol, in his book, *The Creative Destruction of Medicine*, makes similar points, envisaging that the new medicine will come about as a result of the *superconvergence* of genomics, imaging, wireless sensors, information systems, mobile connectivity, the internet, social networking, and increased computing power and a data universe.[26] All these are different ways of describing a future known by the varying terms precision medicine, P4 medicine, stratified medicine, and personalized medicine. I have in the past suggested that we use these terms interchangeably to refer to an approach which: (a) treats individuals as whole persons and empowers them to take greater responsibility for their own health, (b) determines their individual biological characteristics and risk, and (c) manages their care in accordance with those characteristics and with their individual values. Yet in reality, apart from the term "personalized medicine" (which is the one that I favour), the others either neglect or give scant emphasis to treating individuals as persons or to furthering their empowerment. Rather, they focus on the biological and the technical aspects of the individual, on data, and the power that may emerge from their analysis.

The individual is placed at the centre of healthcare only to the extent that the data about that individual can be used to distinguish her from other individuals. These other terms fail to encompass and pay scant attention, if any at all, to the values, aspirations, emotions, likes and dislikes, hopes and fears, motivations and preferences, or any of the other characteristics that are associated with our being human. They neglect the more intangible aspects, the spiritual dimension, of our humanity, preferring to concentrate on the biological. And it is for this reason that I prefer to use the term, *personal*, which I

25 ibid., 50

26 Eric Topol, *The Creative Destruction of Medicine: How the Digital Revolution Will Create Better Health Care* (Basic Books 2012).

envisage in my mind as a dumbbell at one end of which is concentrated all that should be know about that person's biology, but at the other the individual's subjective world, the world that is the person from her own perspective and that of her friends, family, and community. A system of personalized medicine will only be acceptable if we concentrate on both ends of that dumbbell rather than just on its scientific limb. And it is that other end of the dumbbell that speaks to Professor Knoppers' long-standing concern about the "human" in genomics and bioethics.

This conception of the personal is the main focus of discussion in some circles, though given little attention in those inhabited by Hood, Topol, or the genomics communities that champion precision medicine. The Personalised Care Institute in the United Kingdom is an example of those that use the word "*personalized*" in a somewhat different manner.[27] It is a virtual organization that seeks "to equip health and care professionals with the knowledge, skills and confidence to help patients get more involved in decisions about their care;" and defines personalized care as that which "gives patients more control and choice when it comes to the way their care is planned and delivered, taking into account individual needs, preferences and circumstances." It tells us that ultimately patients want:

1. to be treated as a whole person by professionals they trust;
2. to be involved in decisions about their health and care;
3. to be supported to manage their own health and well being, through health coaching, access to self-management programs and to peer support in the community; and
4. their care to feel co-ordinated

and that when patients are involved in decisions about their treatment, there is research evidence that shows that outcomes and patient satisfaction are better. What ties this conception of the personal to that of those who champion precision medicine is the emphasis on the individualization of healthcare, away from the *one-size-fits-all* paradigm to which we have all been so accustomed.

It comes close to returning us to the point that I made at the start of this chapter, that the practice of medicine has "always been a relationship between two individuals, a physician and a patient." Modern healthcare is perhaps less reliant on that relationship than it did in the past, but if we replace *physician* by the *team of professionals* delivering that care, the relationship still applies. It applies but perhaps less effectively because the relationship and bond between two individuals is itself therapeutic. The knowledge that one is being cared for

27 Personalised Care Institute, available at: https://www.personalisedcareinstitute.org.uk.

by a skilled individual in whom one has trust has important consequences. Trust is an ingredient that must not be overlooked in healthcare. Whereas one is able to have trust in a team, it is not the same as trust in an individual, and perhaps it is not surprising that there are individuals in the team with whom the patient develops a bond in preference to other individuals in that team.

This trust encompasses the concept of patient autonomy, of the view that the physician's relationship with the patient is based on the respect the physician has for the patient as an individual with her own values, wishes, and aspirations, and the need to take those into consideration. This is entirely right and proper and the development of shared care as the way medicine should be practised today has been emphasized as the basis of how we should proceed. But this emphasis on the autonomy of the patient is, in my view, not entirely without problems. It is the law that any attempt by the physician to treat the patient without her consent is a battery on the patient even if the consequence of not so treating is that the patient dies. I do not speak here of the situation in which the patient wishes to die but that where the patient wishes to be treated and to recover. This one-sided emphasis on autonomy, without considering the other values in medical ethics discourse, namely beneficence and non-maleficence, can be problematic. This emphasis on autonomy came about in part because of the realization that there was a power imbalance between the doctor and the patient which needed to be rectified. The paternalism that was the hallmark of past medical practice was seen as something undesirable that needed to be eradicated. And to the extent that there were arrogant physicians who had no regard to the views of their patients, the balance had to be redressed.

My concern is that it has now gone too far the other way.[28] We seek medical care when we have a problem with our health, just as we seek legal advice or financial advice from lawyers and accountants. Yet we do not, in these other examples, regard the advice that they give paternalistic. Assuming that we are dealing with competent professionals, they give the best advice that is known to them, but we do not demonize their advice as something that disregards our autonomy. Why should it be different in the case of medical advice? I am not convinced of arguments that it should. The assessment of the patient's (or client's) values and wishes and attention to their dignity should be at the core of every professional interaction, but this does not need to extend to embracing the negotiation of advice which may not be optimum for the patient's

28 Edmund Pellegrino and David Thomasma, *For the Patient's Good: The Restoration of Beneficence in Health Care* (Oxford University Press 1988).

(or client's) situation. The principle of autonomy of course dictates that he or she may not accept it. But that is entirely reasonable and proper.

The distinction that I make is between (a) the giving of advice or the management of the patient that takes into account the wishes and values of the patient and has regard to her dignity, from (b) that which suggests that a compromise between what the patient wants and what the professional recommends as the optimum way for treating the patient. Is it really in the patient's interest that her views and the physician's are given similar weight? I engage with a professional because that professional will know more than I do about the matter for which I seek advice. If I know as much I would not need that advice, so why then does the pejorative adjective of paternalism apply in my consultation with doctors? And is this wholesale move towards the autonomy of patients without consideration for their well being something that is in the interests of patients?

7 Concluding Thoughts

This discussion about autonomy and paternalism is somewhat of a digression. The main point that I want stress in this chapter is that healthcare has been always and should continue to be rooted in a personal relationship between the professional and the citizen, and that the practice of guidelines-based medicine, and of a one-size-fits-all approach, is at the heart of the discontent with modern healthcare. The future of healthcare lies in the greater personalization of healthcare. It is only by taking such a route that it will restore to the citizen her humanity in her interaction with healthcare, its professionals, and its institutions. But the result that we desire will only result if the personalization embraces the dumbbell approach, one that demands both a greater understanding of the citizen's biological individuality and her values and wishes. To go just down the road of precision medicine will continue the path of dehumanization that resulted from a generalized approach, but for a different reason. To concentrate entirely on the wishes and values of the patient with no scientific understanding of her individual biology will be equally unsatisfactory, the consequence of which will be no more than a variant of the one-size-fits-all approach coupled with greater humanity.

These are but general thoughts that may or may not be of interest to readers. They seek to question received views in modern medical practice, not because I suggest that what I advocate should be the norm, but to understand why these received views should persist as the standard paradigm. If there are generalized threads that run through these thoughts, they are that we should pay greater attention to the distinction and the relationship between populations and individuals, and between the biological and the personal—pleas that Professor Knoppers has also long championed.

Medicine has benefited hugely from science and in particular the genomic revolution, but has it done so at the expense of the "human"? And what can be done to restore the "human" to the centre of medical practice?

VIGNETTE

Bartha, CGP, and the McGill Genome Centre

Mark Lathrop

I write this in honour of Bartha Knoppers, who has had a seminal impact on how human genomics has evolved over the last four decades, and on how I and other genome scientists pursue our research in this field. Like my own, Bartha's career has spanned the genomics era, starting from initial efforts in the 1980s to develop a complete map of DNA variants in the human genome and to positionally clone the genes responsible for Mendelian genetic disorders, followed by the international Human Genome Project effort that gave the first sequence of the human genome by 2002, through to the on-going consolidation of these efforts to provide genome-based medicine.

Having early recognized that these advances would have profound societal impacts, Bartha has applied legal rigour, policy insights, and genetic knowledge to sharpen scientific and public insight into these. Primarily trained and working in Canada, but with strong links to Europe and the US, she has shaped the international legal and governance frameworks that guide the worldwide collaborative initiatives that are now fundamental to genomics research. Her work in the 1980s and 1990s led to her inclusion in the NIH working group for the Ethics, Legal, and Societal Issues (ELSI) for genomics, which played a key role in setting the agenda for research in the area over more than two decades. Her important policy contributions have continued to this day as illustrated, for example, in co-authoring the 2020 report on Human Germline Genome Editing, commissioned by the Royal Society (UK), the National Academy of Sciences (US), and the National Academy of Medicine (US).[1]

The practical impact of ELSI research has been a central motif that distinguishes much of Bartha's work. In the early 2000s, in collaboration with Professor Claude Laberge, she initiated the Québec CARTaGENE health cohort study,[2] which pioneered principles of public consent and data access

1 International Commission on the Clinical Use of Human Germline Genome Editing, *Heritable Human Genome Editing* (National Academy of Medicine, National Academy of Sciences, and the Royal Society 2020).

2 Philip Awadalla and others, 'Cohort profile of the CARTaGENE study: Quebec's population-based biobank for public health and personalized genomics' (2013) 42 International Journal of Epidemiology 1285.

 | DOI:10.1163/9789004688544_037

and informed many other on-going cohort projects. The Public Population Project in Genomics and Society (P³G),[3] founded by Bartha in 2004, was a ground-breaking initiative bringing together experts from the different disciplines with a commitment to information sharing and supporting researchers to improve the health of people around the world. P³G is a precursor to the Global Alliance for Genomics and Health (GA4GH),[4] which Bartha co-founded in 2013, and which now unites more than 500 organizations from around the world in the common purpose of advancing accessible genomics for the benefit of all.

Bartha joined McGill University in 2009, where she established the Centre for Genomics and Policy (CGP).[5] The CGP quickly emerged as the predominant centre worldwide for this area of research. Closely associated with the McGill Genome Centre,[6] which has greatly benefited from its expertise, the CGP is unique in integrating social and policy research directly with molecular genetics and genomics.

The CGP is, of course, just one of Bartha's many legacies that will continue to propel the agenda of public benefit from genomics for the current and future generations. The field of human genetics owes her a tremendous debt of gratitude.

---

3 Sylvie Ouellette and Anne Marie Tassé, 'P3G—10 years of toolbuilding: From the population biobank to the clinic' (2014) 3 Applied & Translational Genomics 36.

4 Global Alliance for Genomics and Health, available at: https://www.ga4gh.org/.

5 Centre of Genomics and Policy, available at: https://www.genomicsandpolicy.org/.

6 McGill Genome Centre, available at: https://www.mcgillgenomecentre.ca/.

VIGNETTE

Bartha's Presence

Ubaka Ogbogu

Presence: "the fact or condition of being present."[1]

Present: "constituting the one actually involved, at hand, or being considered."[2]

we dance in the hallways of life
to the steady but joyous beats
of those who cheer us on

∴

I don't remember the precise moment I first met Bartha. It is not because I forgot. There is nothing forgettable about any meeting with Bartha. Rather, it is that I do not need or want to because it feels like Bartha has always been there. One thing that defines Bartha for me through her various outsized roles in the health law and policy community—whether as icon, leader, convener, sage, mentor, and colleague—is presence. Bartha is present. She is always there for me and countless others, both professionally and personally.

Whatever that moment of first meeting was, she multiplied it in countless ways. Over drinks in Leuven and dinner in Berlin. At numerous workshops, meetings, and conferences. In reference letters and recommendations that lifted me and many others higher and higher. Through research collaborations and co-authorships. A quiet chat and words of encouragement. Sharp wit and laughter. Grace, poise, and a killer fashion sense. Always there, always giving of her immense knowledge, intelligence, and charm.

In a chapter written in 2008 and entitled, "Policymaking and Poetry," Bartha, writing about policy evolution in relation to science and biotechnology, observed:

1 Merriam-Webster Dictionary.
2 ibid.

> The patterns of policymaking in biotechnology follow a similar pattern to decolonization through artistic efforts. First, there is repugnance at the emergence of scientific breakthroughs, then protest, then acceptance... then hopefully dynamic policy built on principles and vision—a creation that sincerely speaks to the individual and so to the universal.[3]

This observation is not just poignant and true, it is the only one I have read that captures an entire world of affairs so completely and in ways that feel both poetic and real. It could have only come from someone who truly sees and cares about people, ideas, and places, and about how these things interact and move through time. From someone who is present.

---

3 Bartha Maria Knoppers, 'Policymaking and Poetry' in Sean Caulfield and Timothy Caulfield (eds), *Imagining Science: Art, Science and Social Change* (University of Alberta Press 2008).

CHAPTER 13

Human Diversity, Equity, and Bartha Maria Knoppers

Henry T. Greely

I first remember meeting Professor Bartha Maria Knoppers in mid-October 1995 in Bethesda, Maryland (USA), where I worked as her (unpaid) typist. She was a member of the Ethics Committee of the Human Genome Organization (HUGO), which was meeting there. One of the topics they discussed was the Human Genome Diversity Project (HGDP), for which I was providing ethics advice.[1] I had made a presentation to the Committee about the HGDP. It had not been met with unanimous acclaim, though I do remember thinking Professor Knoppers' questions were fair, and good. But at some point that afternoon, she was trying urgently to write a summary of the meeting. I don't remember the details, but, although it was in the very early days of laptop computers, I had my laptop with me. And I was a good typist. (It's always useful, I think, to have a marketable skill to fall back upon.) I volunteered to help her by typing and found myself transcribing her excellent sentences and perfect paragraphs, albeit with occasional editorial suggestions. If I recall correctly, the statement was not entirely complimentary to the HGDP, but the potential conflict didn't bother her, or me. We just did the work. And became fast friends.

Almost thirty years later, we are still fast friends. And Professor Knoppers still "does the work." That work has been vast in quantity and in scope, but the themes of humanness and equity recur frequently, often in the context of genomics. This chapter, in accordance with the theme of this Festschrift honouring her academic career, explores the mutual relevance of those terms in her work. How do genes affect our concepts of "human," either as a noun (a "human being") or as an adjective ("human" DNA)? What does equity mean with respect to genomes, which are different in every person but (until very

1 A good discussion of the HGDP and especially its ethical dimensions through 1996 can be found in Henry T Greely, 'The Ethics of the Human Genome Diversity Project: The North American Regional Committee's Proposed Model Ethical Protocol' in Bartha Maria Knoppers (ed) *Human DNA: Law and Policy: International and Comparative Perspectives* (Kluwer Law International 1997).

© HENRY T. GREELY, 2025 | DOI:10.1163/9789004688544_039

recently) "made" by all our ancestors, the environments they faced, and chance? And how does her work illuminate these questions?

This chapter will start with a brief review of the incredible scope of Professor Knoppers' work. It will then discuss her positions about human genetic diversity as they relate to equity, pushing critically at some of them. It will end by discussing her views on equity in human genetic diversity in the context of her views on human cultural diversity, and what that kind of diversity means for universal bioethical guidelines, rules, or laws.

1 Professor Knoppers' Work

I want to begin with a brief discussion of Professor Knoppers' work. While it is covered in great detail across the chapters of this book, I also need to talk about it. The combination of incredulity and awe her record inspires in me permeates everything I think and write about her.

It was surprisingly hard to find a comprehensive curriculum vitae or bibliography for her, but, according to Wikipedia, the repository of all facts, many of which are true, "Prof. Knoppers has published over 565 peer-reviewed articles, over 117 book chapters and 38 books."[2] The editors of this book provided me with a master CV for her, dated January 2024. Looking at its beginnings is illuminating.

Professor Knoppers received her bachelor's degree in French and English Literature from McMaster University in 1972 and her master's degree in comparative literature from the University of Alberta in 1974. (To me the most unexpected item in her CV was her master's thesis: "Towards a National Caribbean Literature: The Poetry of Aimé Césaire and Derek Walcott.")

In 1978, the same year she received the first of her two law degrees from McGill University (in common law), she published her first two articles: "The 'Legitimization' of Artificial Insemination: Promise or Problem?"[3] and "Les notions d'autorisation et de consentement dans le contrat médical."[4]

2 Wikipedia, Bartha Knoppers, https://en.wikipedia.org/wiki/Bartha_Knoppers, last accessed on May 22, 2024.

3 Bartha Maria Knoppers, 'The "legitimization" of artificial insemination: promise or problem?" (1978) 1 Family Law Review 108.

4 Bartha Maria Knoppers, 'Les notions d'autorisation et de consentement dans le contrat médical' (1978) 19 Cahiers de Droit 893 ["The ideas of authorization and consent in the medical contract", my translation.]

Two things stand out to me about her two earliest articles. The first is her resolute internationalism. From the beginning she published in both French and English. Yes, by itself that might not be too surprising for a law student at McGill (not only a law school in Quebec, but one that proudly teaches in both English and French), yet it is consistent with the international approach she has taken throughout her career. Perhaps it stems from growing up in the Netherlands, Canada, and the United States, but Professor Knoppers is the least nationalistic person I know (which resonates with her occasional call for a "global" passport!). Although in recent years most of her work has been published in English, French publications continue, as, more importantly, does her emphasis on international law, organizations, and committees.

The second is the breadth of her topics. One paper is on a bread-and-butter legal issue, albeit one with ethical overtones. The second is about a new reproductive technology, and not just about the technology but about its reception in society, its "legitimization." In the last few years, she has published on the international human right to science, ethical issues in precision oncology, tensions between the European Union's General Data Protection Regulation (GDPR) and a biomedical data commons, children's right to health, cancer risk screening, legal regulation of genetic counselors in Canada, and more. They all do revolve around health, and more closely around genetics and health, but across a broad swath of issues.

She was a student for another seven years after her first articles appeared, with diplomas and degrees from the Sorbonne (in civil law in 1979), from Cambridge (in legal studies in 1981), McGill again (civil law, in 1982), and finally her Doctorate of Laws from the Sorbonne (1985). But while a student, she published 10 more articles, five in French and five in English, on reproduction, on medical information, and on hospital ethics committees, among other things. And she wrote two theses and co-authored two books. She has been incredibly prolific, in part because she started early.

In some ways more impressive than the list of her publications is the list of her committee and board memberships. I count 29 on-going memberships and over 135 past ones, many as a co-chair, chair, founder, or president. Having served on or interacted with several of those groups, I am in awe of Professor Knoppers' work ethic, concentration, and, especially, patience. She is the perfect committee leader, gracefully herding cats of all sizes and shapes. I want now to examine her work, largely in her leadership roles, in two main respects: the tensions between access and equity in human genome research and the roles for global guidelines or international law in the biosciences.

2 Genetic Diversity and Equity

2.1 *The HGDP*

2.1.1 Background

My first encounter with Professor Knoppers involved the intersection of two themes found throughout much of her work: human genetic diversity and equity. From 1992 I had been involved in the then-new HGDP. That Project can be said to have started in 1991 with a "Call for a Survey of Worldwide Human Genetic Diversity," published in October 1991.[5] The call was a result of discussions among a group of population geneticists, including prominently Luca Cavalli-Sforza, Allan Wilson (who tragically died in July 1991, before the HGDP was fully launched), Marcus Feldman, Mary-Claire King, Bob Cook-Deegan, and Walter Bodmer. Its initial goal was to collect fifty samples, in the form of cell lines made from white blood cells, from 500 human populations around the world, with a special emphasis on population groups that were small and viewed as in danger of disappearing.

The HGDP was often confused with the slightly older Human Genome Project (HGP), founded in 1990, but the two were quite different. The HGP's goal was to create a complete sequence of all of the base pairs "the human genome," about 3.2 billion As, Ts, Cs, and Gs. The HGDP was based on the fact that, in 1991, there were over 5 billion different human genomes, one for each living person. (It's over 8 billion today.)

The HGP was fueled by the interest in medical advances from understanding the human genome. The HGDP disclaimed any efforts at searching for medical value but sought to better understand the evolution and history of our species.

The HGP was funded heavily by the US National Institutes of Health and Department of Energy, with substantial contributions from public and private funders in the United Kingdom, Canada, the European Union, Japan, China, and other countries. During its life, from 1990 through 2003, its total budget was about $3 billion. The HGDP received almost no funding, with grants of a few hundred thousand dollars from the US National Science Foundation.

The HGP was declared completed in 2003 with the announcement of a (largely) complete human genome. The HGDP effectively was completed in April 2002 with the announcement of the creation of the HGDP/CEPH cell line panel, containing more than 1,000 cell lines from 51 populations around the

5 Luigi Luca Cavalli-Sforza and others, 'Call for a worldwide survey of human genetic diversity: A vanishing opportunity for the Human Genome Project' (1991) 11 Genomics 490.

world.[6] The HGDP as a project collected no further DNA, but those cell lines have been widely used in research for more than 20 years and remain available to qualified researchers.

I had become involved in the HGDP in 1992 when two of its leaders, Luca Cavalli-Sforza and Marcus Feldman, invited me to lunch at the Stanford Faculty Club to discuss some of its ethical and legal issues. Soon I was actively involved in providing advice to the Project, becoming a member of its North American Regional Committee and chair of that Committee's "ELSI" (ethical, legal, and social implications) Committee.

2.1.2 The HUGO Ethics Committee and the HGDP

Meanwhile, Professor Knoppers had become involved in the HUGO Ethics Committee. HUGO is an international, non-governmental organization of scientists and scholars founded in 1989 to promote international genomic activities, possibly through serving as a coordinating body for various national efforts. She joined its International Ethics Committee in 1995, but she came to HUGO with a substantial background in genetics issues. Her first publication on genetics was an article in 1985, followed quickly by a flood of articles and book chapters.

She also had substantial advisory and committee experience on genetic topics. From 1983 she had served as a legal advisor and research associate for the Quebec Network of Genetic Medicine. In 1988 she became a legal advisor to the Canadian College of Genetic Medicine on genetic testing of ova and sperm donors. By 1993 she had become a member of the Social Issues Committee of the American Society of Human Genetics; the Canadian Genome Analysis and Technology Program; the then joint NIH/Department of Energy ethical, legal, and social issues committee; and a World Health Organization Scientific Group on the Human Genome Project.

Perhaps most importantly, in 1993 she became one of the first members of the newly formed UNESCO International Bioethics Committee. In that position, she was deeply engaged in the long process of the formulation and eventual adoption in November 1997 of the UNESCO's Universal Declaration on the Human Genome and Human Rights. (She and I may have met in April 1984 at a Paris meeting of the International Bioethics Committee where I made a presentation about the ethics of HGDP; she seems very likely to have been there, but I do not remember whether she was or not.)

6 Howard M Cann and others, 'A human genome diversity cell line panel' (2002) 296 Science 261.

On October 13 through 15, 1995, the HUGO Ethics Committee met in Bethesda, Maryland, at least in part to consider ethical issues raised by the HGP and the HGDP. At that point, the Committee had a "discussion document" on principled conduct of genetic research, which it considered at that meeting, in addition to hearing from some speakers on the issues. I attended at least the portions relevant to the HGDP. I was accompanied by Dr Kenneth Kidd, who talked about the science, while I discussed the ethical and legal issues, particularly those raised by the (then in draft) Proposed Model Ethical Protocol for Collecting DNA Samples, developed and ultimately adopted by the North American Regional Committee of the HGDP.[7] I made a presentation about the Model Protocol and answered questions about it. And, as the session ended, I ended up volunteering (or possibly "being volunteered") as Professor Knoppers' typist for a report on the session.

Eight days after the end of the Bethesda meeting, on October 23, the journal Genomics received a submission from Professor Knoppers, Marie Hirtle, and Sébastien Lormeau, entitled "Ethical Issues in International Collaborative Research on the Human Genome: The HGP and the HGDP."[8] This article was accepted on March 5, 1996, and published as a "Special Feature" on June 1, 1996 (back when "published" meant "on paper"). The Guidelines it contained had just been adopted by the HUGO Council as HUGO's Code of Ethics on March 21, 1996. The article and the Guidelines focused on ten principles, all helpfully starting with the letter "C": Competence, Communication, Consultation, Consent, Choice, Confidentiality, Collaboration, Conflict of Interest, Compensation, and Continual Review.

2.1.3 Professor Knoppers' Views

The 1990s saw the production of a vast number of declarations, guidelines, principles, protocols, and other documents, created by global organizations or individual projects, aimed at ensuring that human genome research was done ethically. Professor Knoppers was involved in many, although by no means all, of them. And, in most of those efforts, her voice was that of a member of a committee, or a drafter, or even a chair—but not a solo statement of her own views. And yet the positions she endorsed, in a wide range of documents for

7 North American Regional Committee, Human Genome Diversity Project, 'Proposed model ethical protocol for collecting DNA samples' (1997) 33 Houston Law Review 1431.

8 Bartha Maria Knoppers, Marie Hirtle, and Sébastien Lormeau, 'Ethical issues in international collaborative research on the human genome: the HGP and the HGDP' (1996) 34 Genomics 272.

varying groups, were largely consistent even though the number of principles or the terms for them may have changed.

The 1996 HUGO Statement was the adoption of the report of the HUGO Ethics Committee, which Professor Knoppers chaired. It is a good place to see some of her consistent themes, particularly when read in conjunction with the paper she co-authored in Genomics about these issues, which included the HUGO Statement as an appendix.[9] The Statement says:

> [...] the HUGO-ELSI Committee bases its recommendations on the following four principles
>
> 1. Recognition that the human genome is part of the common heritage of humanity;
> 2. Adherence to international norms of human rights;
> 3. Respect for the values, traditions, culture and integrity of participants; and
> 4. Acceptance and upholding of human dignity and freedom.[10]

It then notes five concerns raised by human genome research, with a focus on the HGP and the HGDP:

1. Fear genome research could lead to discrimination against and stigmatization of individuals and groups and be misused to promote racism;
2. Loss of access to discoveries for research purposes, especially through patenting and commercialization;
3. Reduction of human beings to their DNA sequences and attribution of social and other human problems to genetic causes;
4. Lack of respect for the values, traditions, and integrity of populations, families, and individuals; and
5. Inadequate engagement of the scientific community with the public in the planning and conduct of genetic research.[11]

The Statement then launches into its "Ten Cs". All of this had been expanded upon, in discussion and to some extent in scope, by the analysis in the article to which it is an appendix. That article put to one side questions of eventual possible misuse of genetic information and instead looked specifically at issues of sampling. It examined questions about recruitment, consent, confidentiality and access (to both genetic materials and information), compensation and commercialization, and patents.

9 ibid.

10 ibid., 279.

11 ibid.

So, what does all this say about Professor Knoppers' position on "equity"? Equity is a notoriously slippery term, derived ultimately from the Latin noun "*aequus*," for "even, just, equal"[12] or "even, fair."[13] Most of the positions taken by the HUGO Statement speak to issues other than equity. A constant theme is the need to deal in a *fair* way with people, to use appropriate procedures. These include the requirements to *communicate* with research participants in ways they can understand, to *consult* with them about their cultural norms that could affect this kind of research, to act only with their free and informed *consent*, to respect their *choices*, to protect the *confidentiality* of their contributions (of material and of information), and to both reveal and review potential *conflicts* of interests.

One of the problems with equity is that it not only requires treating like cases the same, but treating unlike cases differently in light of their relevant variation. It is in this respect that Professor Knoppers' view might be questioned.

A core tension in genetic research about human genetics revolves around the facts that humans are not, in fact, very diverse genetically—but that diversity is much of what we want to study. Medically, it is the ways in which different versions of "the same" DNA lead to different diseases, conditions, risks, or protections. For human evolution and history, it is how minor differences can be used to trace the movements and the intertwining branching of our species. (And now, with ancient DNA, we can also look at our related species, gone but in some cases having left us DNA, in remains or in the sequences of living *Homo sapiens*, that can be used to bring some light into our mutual connections.) Genetically we are all (almost) identical, but we mainly discuss those small differences.

And a similar problem affects us when we look at actual people, in themselves and in their groups. To believers in universal human rights, we all share a common humanity which demands equal rights and dignity. But when we look around our world, we see great differences, in treatment and in power, between different kinds or different groups of humans. Those differences may mean that treating all groups alike is, in some contexts in today's world, just not fair.

The first of the listed principles on which the Committee's recommendation was based is "Recognition that the human genome is part of the common heritage of humanity." A year later, this position was incorporated, in somewhat different language, in Article 1 of UNESCO's Universal Declaration on the

12 Online Etymology Dictionary, 'Equity', available at: https://www.etymonline.com/word/equity.

13 Oxford English Dictionary, 'Equity', available at: https://doi.org/10.1093/OED/1084315931.

Human Genome and Human Rights (which Professor Knoppers was closely involved in developing): "The human genome underlies the fundamental unity of all members of the human family, as well as the recognition of their inherent dignity and diversity. In a symbolic sense, it is the heritage of humanity.[14] Although the exact meaning of "common heritage of mankind," in the context of the human genome (even without the added complication of its "symbolic" sense in the UNESCO Declaration) and elsewhere, continues to be debated, its general thrust clearly opposes private ownership or control over the genome.

The HUGO Statement states that "*collaboration* between individuals, populations, and researchers and between programs in the free flow, access, and exchange of information is essential not only to scientific progress but for the present or future benefit of all participants." It also says, "undue inducement through *compensation* for individual participants, families, and populations should be prohibited." It modifies that ban, however, by "agreements with individuals, families, groups, communities, or populations that foresee technology transfer, local training, joint ventures, provision of healthcare or of information infrastructures, reimbursement of costs, or the possible use of a percentage of any royalties for humanitarian purposes." The compensation issues are explored further in the article's discussion of "compensation and commerciality." The article, but not the Statement, also discusses patenting genetic information.

The Statement, and the accompanying article, want to treat all people who provide DNA samples the same, as altruistic actors who are contributing, as they *should*, to a global effort that will benefit everyone. But everyone is not the same, either as individuals or as groups. One difference is that very few individuals have "something" in their DNA that is both extraordinary and important. But more groups, whether genetically related families, villages, or ethnic groups, do have variations in their DNA that may have some scientific or commercial value. The Statement and accompanying article do not just say that such people "should" make a voluntary contribution for the common good, but that any contribution they make must be on such a basis, unless it is one of a limited number of approved kinds of compensation: "agreements with individuals, families, groups, communities, or populations that foresee *technology transfer, local training, joint ventures, provision of health care or of information infrastructures, reimbursement of costs,* or the *possible use of a percentage of any royalties for humanitarian purposes*" (emphasis added).

14 Professor Knoppers had been working with this idea several years earlier. See Bartha Maria Knoppers, *Human Dignity and Genetic Heritage: Study Paper* (Law Reform Commission of Canada 1991).

That seems a nice, ethical resolution, but is it ethically required? And is it ethically required from all people, or peoples, not all of whom are situated similarly? Should a family ravaged by genetic disease, whose ill fortune holds a key for scientific advances—and commercial profit—not be allowed to get some payment? It is well and good to consider the genome "the common heritage of mankind" (even though only symbolically), but for such people, the "common heritage" gave them an uncommon curse.

But, undoubtedly because of my work with the HGDP, which faced a barrage of criticism from organizations interested in the rights of indigenous peoples, for me the genome issues had special meaning in the context of dispossessed and discriminated against populations, which include many indigenous groups in various parts of the world. When the activists in those groups said, "you've stolen our land and our culture and now you want to take our genes," the critique resonated.

It did not, at that time, lead me to call for full rights for populations to negotiate whatever deals they wished with those seeking DNA samples. The Protocol calls some kinds of benefits especially appropriate. These include technology transfer, to populations where it would be helpful,[15] and, subject to a lot of considerations, medical services.[16] They also included money—subject to a variety of caveats, the Model Protocol said that "there is no inherent reason why researchers cannot make an appropriate payment to the community or to individual donors for their participation in the HGFP, as compensation for the time that participation has taken."[17] These benefits were all in the context of compensation for the costs and inconveniences of participating, but the Protocol went beyond that, saying that should the HGDP's work lead to the development of some commercially valuable products, some "fair share" of the proceeds would be returned to participating communities.[18] "[T]he Committee intends to establish a system of contractual protection of the population's interest, through the population's choice of its own control, control by a charitable third party, such as UNESCO, or a fixed-percentage royalty."[19]

These provisions went beyond the HUGO Statement, but, because of the short life of the HGDP, the direct compensation for time and hassle was rarely made and the royalty plan was never implemented. But the National American Regional Committee did make another commitment to groups, as groups,

15 Proposed Model Ethical Protocol (n 7), 1454–55.

16 ibid., 1456–61.

17 ibid., 1454.

18 ibid., 1466–68.

19 ibid., at 1468.

that went beyond the HUGO Statement. It called for "group consent." When the research concerns not just individuals but individuals who are sampled because they are part of a population, we argued that not just the individuals but the population, through whatever mechanisms were appropriate for it, should have to consent for the research to take place. This grant of, or recognition of, the power to say "no" in some ways was more important than issues of compensation. It would provide the group, through its internal mechanisms, with the ability to negotiate terms as the power to say "no" and make it stick is the power to negotiate.

The Knoppers article discusses the HGDP's group consent concept and neither accepts nor rejects it. The Statement takes broad but unclear position: "[I]nformed decisions to *consent* to participate can be individual, familial, or at the level of communities and populations."

The argument for compensation, including flat out payment, for human DNA samples is not a simple one. On the one hand, those found to have a particular, important genetic variation did nothing to create it and it almost certainly could have been found in other people. Paying for DNA is one form of "commodifying" human biology, something that is widely, though not universally, shunned.[20] Group consent opens a host of difficult questions about the defining of "groups" and the identification of their culturally or legally relevant governing structures.[21] In the late 1990s and early 2000s, the issue of group consent was discussed widely and generally rejected, at least by the governments and projects that would have had to implement it. But the arguments continue, pushed in part through newly aggressive advocates of indigenous sovereignty. These are not now largely focusing on human DNA samples but on

20 Issues of "commodification" of human body parts have been discussed for decades or centuries, including questions of ownership of blood, organs for transplantation, and human corpses. See Margaret Radin, *Contested Commodities* (Harvard University Press 1996) (general discussion of ethical limits of "commodification"). In the genomics context, this has arisen most often in questions of patenting human genomic information, a question that produced a great deal of discussion. In 2013, the US Supreme Court ruled that unaltered human DNA sequences could not be patented as "compositions of matter. See *Association for Molecular Pathology* v *Myriad Genetics*, 569 US 576 (2013). Somewhat ironically, most of the world rejected that position and continues to allow these gene patents. The overall effects of that decision, and the debate that focused on it, remain unclear. See Jacob S Sherkow, Robert Cook-Deegan, and Henry T Greely, 'The *Myriad* decision at 10' (2024) 25 Annual Review of Genomics and Human Genetics 397. For a more general discussion on patents issues, see Jacob S Sherkow and Henry T Greely, 'The history of patenting genetic material' (2015) 49 Annual Review of Genetics 161.

21 See Henry T Greely, 'The control of genetic research: involving the groups between' (1997) 33 Houston Law Review 1397.

samples from non-human organisms found in the home areas of indigenous peoples, and in some cases preserved or modified by them.

This does not mean that Professor Knoppers' views on equity and genome diversity were wrong, but it does mean that they can be contested in ways that her work from the mid-1990s did not explore. Does she still hold them now, nearly 30 years later? Much has changed, but for reasons discussed in the last section of this chapter, I suspect she does.

2.1.4 A Brief Coda: One Year Later in Montreal

Professor Knoppers returned to this general subject in early September 1996, having organized the First International Conference on DNA Sampling & Human Genetic Research: Ethical, Legal, and Policy Aspects. The Conference proceedings became a book of 455 pages, with 40 chapters from the speakers.[22] By this time, the HGDP had been branded by its opponents as "The Vampire Project." The meeting was opened by the Governor General of Canada and demonstrations had been announced. Cavalli-Sforza, a stately Italian gentleman, at that point over 74 years old, was viewed as a possible target of abuse and so, to his amusement (and mine), Professor Knoppers hired a bodyguard for him for the duration of the conference, a former boxer. The bodyguard's services turned out not to be needed, but, as I recall, he and Luca got along very well.

2.2 *Another Side of Genetic Diversity and Equity*

That tricky concept of equity appears in another context with regard to human genomic diversity and in this context, Professor Knoppers has strongly urged the importance of a different kind of equity. In the now half century or so of analyzing at least some human genomes—and the more than 20 years of producing whole human genome sequences—a vastly disproportionate number of the genomes analyzed or sequenced have come from a relatively small set of humans: the roughly one-sixth with ancestry largely from Europe.[23] More DNA sampling and analysis from the majority of the world's population would not only increase scientific knowledge about human genomics, but would open more widely the advantages of medical genomics, not yet enormous but not trivial, to those populations.

22 Knoppers, *Human DNA* (n 1).

23 Alicia R Martin and others, 'Clinical use of current polygenic risk scores may exacerbate health disparities' (2019) 51 Nature Genetics 584 (see especially Figure 1); see also Editorial, 'Genetics for all' (2019) 51 Nature Genetics 579.

Commitments to diversity, equity, inclusion, and justice (DEIJ) have proliferated in academic and in science in the last five years, brought into high profile by racial tensions and the Black Lives Matter movement in the US "DEI" and "JEDI" committees have become on the one hand commonplace and, on the other, intensely controversial. (Some American states have banned such diversity efforts in public universities.) Professor Knoppers' commitment to this predates its recent explosion of interest. In her case, it is firmly rooted, I believe, in her view that science should benefit everyone, not just those in privileged positions. It is part of her vision of one, global, humanity, a humanity that science ill serves if it ignores most of its members.

This commitment to broad inclusiveness (one form of equity) can be seen in at least two of the international projects in which Professor Knoppers has taken leading roles: the Global Alliance for Genomics and Health (GA4GH) and the Human Cell Atlas (HCA).

2.2.1 The GA4GH

In 2013, Professor Knoppers was a co-founder of the GA4GH, co-chaired the effort's Regulatory and Ethics Working Group (and later called the Regulatory and Ethics Work Stream) for its first seven years, and remains a member of the Board of Directors of the GA4GH, Inc. (a non-profit Canadian corporation that is the legal entity for the Alliance).

The Alliance's main goal is to create a global information resource for genetic data.

> GA4GH aims to build a secure "internet of genomics." Authorised researchers and clinicians will easily search the globe's genomic and related data— while the human rights of people who share their data stay fully protected.
>
> The GA4GH community develops free, open-source products that make it simple and safe to request, access, and study data stored anywhere. GA4GH products help organisations become effective data stewards.[24]

Professor Knoppers set out the project's principles in a 2014 article.[25] The Framework she laid out was intended to guide "responsible sharing of human genomic and health-related data," with particular reference to "the human

---

24 GA4GH, 'About us', available at: https://www.ga4gh.org/about-us/.

25 Bartha Maria Knoppers, 'Framework for responsible sharing of genomic and health-related data' (2014) 8 The HUGO Journal 3.

rights of privacy, non-discrimination and procedural fairness." And it was a *legal* framework, not just an ethical one.

> The value of this Framework is that it: offers political and legal dimensions that reach beyond the moral appeals of bioethics and provides a more robust governance framework for genomic and health-related data sharing; speaks to groups and institutions, not just individuals; stresses the progressive realization of duties; and urges action by governments, industry, funders, publishers, and researchers to create an international environment for responsibly sharing data.[26]

GA4GH has been alive to the need for diversity. In May 2020, GA4GH launched an Equity, Diversity, and Inclusion Advisory Group. Its webpage says:

> [P]eople of Asian, African, Latino, Middle Eastern, Oceanic, and other Indigenous or non-European ancestries appear in a small percentage of genomic studies—despite making up most of the global population. Women and people from many marginalised groups are underrepresented among scientists and engineers. Individuals from countries of low- and middle-incomes, or where the primary language is not English, hold comparatively few positions in genomic initiatives.
>
> GA4GH recognises that systemic barriers prevent these and other groups from participating fully in the genomics community. Towards eliminating barriers, the EDI Advisory Group works to institute a culture of equity, diversity, and inclusion across GA4GH, intentionally engaging a wide range of voices in goal setting and leadership opportunities.[27]

2.2.2 The HCA

The HCA is yet another global project that bears the Professor Knoppers imprint. Launched in 2016, the HCA "is mapping all cell types in the healthy body, across time from development to adulthood, and eventually to old age."[28] Professor Knoppers serves on the Organizing Committee, which governs the Project, and on the ethics working group, which she has co-chaired. The HCA also has an equity working group; the leaders of the two working groups,

26 ibid.

27 GA4GH, 'EDI Advisory Group', available at: https://www.ga4gh.org/about-us/edi-advisory-group/.

28 Human Cell Atlas, 'About the Human Cell Atlas, available at: https://www.humancellatlas.org/learn-more/#event-launch-of-the-human-cell-atlas.

including Professor Knoppers, published a letter in Nature stating "we aim to ensure that data are generated from and by individuals who represent diversity in gender, age, geography, ethnicity and socio-economic status."[29] HCA representatives have published more details about the HCA's commitments to equity, very broadly speaking, and its awareness of systemic inequities in global science in a powerful piece, written at least partially in response to the Black Lives Matter movement in the US.[30]

3 The Push for International Law and Standards Versus Human Cultural Diversity

In 2019, following a "think tank" on legal boundaries and the "human" in humanity Professor Knoppers and I hosted, the two of us wrote a policy forum piece in Science, entitled "Biotechnologies Nibbling at the Legal 'Human.'"[31] We surveyed new developments in human biology and medicine and asked what they meant for the law's definition of human. We wrote that:

> Although it may be tempting to think that these new developments require us to reconsider the time-honored legal definitions of humans, living humans, or human tissue, we suggest that current legal dualisms can be applied in ways that provide adequate flexibility to allow weighing the many issues that surround developments in genetics, neurosciences, and cellular bioengineering and challenge how we legally define what is "human."[32]

We argued that using the word, and the concept, "substantially" would be helpful. People who have lost important human features—limbs, memories, cognition—are substantially human; rats with some human neurons in their brains are not. We recognized that such a slippery word would not satisfy everyone and that it would not lead to universally consistent applications, but in a biological world where rigid borders and inviolable definitions are increasingly disappearing, it seemed to us the best way forward. We both recognized

---

29 Partha Majumder and others, 'How to ensure the Human Cell Atlas benefits humanity' (2022) 605 Nature 30.

30 Partha P Majumder, Musa M Mhlanga, and Alex K Shalek, 'The Human Cell Atlas and equity: lessons learned' (2020) 26 Nature Medicine 1509.

31 Bartha Maria Knoppers and Henry T Greely, 'Biotechnologies nibbling at the legal "human"' (2019) 366 Science 1455.

32 ibid.

that there is diversity in ways of being human, but there is some fuzzy core of substantial humanness.

And yet, more broadly, I think we do disagree on some consequences, at least, of being human. Professor Knoppers is—in her own background, in her feelings, and in her logic—an internationalist. She spends enormous amounts of her highly valuable time on international or global committees, projects, and documents, often in situations where my patience would rapidly disappear, but hers does not. She believes in universal human rights that apply to everyone and in resources, like the human genome, that should be accessible to everyone. We may not all take the same positions on important issues, but, to some extent at least, I believe Professor Knoppers thinks we *should*. But many humanly created entities "live" in the space between global "humanity" and 8 billion individual human beings—different countries, religions, laws, cultures, with many different positions on these issues. I do not mean to suggest that she does not respect those differences, or does not take pleasure in them, but, it seems to me, those groups are not of fundamental importance in her views.

To call this a fixed position, or even a philosophy, would be unfair. I think of it as a leitmotif, a tendency, a bias, or a filter, in how she sees and reacts to the world—as a world primarily made up of one humanity. We all have such predispositions in how we see the world. How much they come from our environments, our cultures, our experiences, the willed results of our cognition, or even (maybe, to some extent) our genes certainly is not clear to me. I suspect personalities play a role, perhaps along the lines of Isaiah Berlin's famous essay "The Hedgehog and the Fox" ("a fox knows many things, but a hedgehog knows one big thing," taken from ancient Greek poet Archilocus)[33] or the often-recognized differences between lumpers and splitters.[34]

Professor Knoppers is entirely too sophisticated and subtle thinker to be all of one or all of the other, but I think she leans toward one big theme: global humanity. I, on the other hand, sophisticated and subtle or not so much, am much more of a fox. I look at the world and its 8 billion people and see myriad, intersecting, reinforcing, and conflicting groups that have at least somewhat different values.[35] I have trouble with the concept of universal human rights (except in the positivist examples of mutually agreed upon treaties), though I

33 Isaiah Berlin, 'The Hedgehog and the Fox' in Henry Hardy and Aileen Kelly (eds), *Russian Thinkers* (Viking 1978).

34 Wikipedia, 'Lumpers and splitters', available at: https://en.wikipedia.org/wiki/Lumpers_and_splitters.

35 I even included the words "the Groups Between" in the title of one of my articles on the ethics of the HGDP: see Greely (n 21).

will confess to trouble with the concept that they do not exist. And the idea that all humans can, should, or will be guided by, or treated according to, universal precepts seems to me both normatively and, even more, practically unlikely.

Let me provide an example that may illustrate what I think are my differences from Professor Knoppers. She has in recent years been a strong proponent of the international human right to science. This actually *is* a right created (or recognized?) by treaties, including a brief mention in Article 27 of the Universal Declaration of Human Rights. (I know about this human right only because Professor Knoppers and others organized a conference on it at the Brocher Foundation on the outskirts of Geneva in December 2022, to which I was invited and for which I, eventually, wrote an article.)[36]

The Universal Declaration is largely aspirational; it was to be turned into legal binding obligations in the subsequent conventions and commitments. The International Covenant on Economic, Social and Cultural Rights ("ICESCR") was one of the first two such treaties; the International Covenant on Civil and Political Rights was the other. Both entered into force in 1976, 28 (long) years after the Universal Declaration and 22 years after drafts of both were presented to the United Nations' General Assembly. The ICESCR has been ratified by over 170 countries. (The US signed it but has not ratified it and thus is not bound by it.)

Article 15 of the ICESCR has four subparts, two of which are particularly relevant:

> 1. The States Parties to the present Covenant recognize the right of everyone:
>
>   …
>
>   a. To enjoy the benefits of scientific progress and its applications;
>   b. To benefit from the protection of the moral and material interests resulting from any scientific, literary, or artistic production of which he is the author.
>
>   …
>
> 2. The States Parties to the present Covenant undertake to respect the freedom indispensable for scientific research and creative activity.

In 1975 the General Assembly addressed the human right to science separately, in the "Declaration on the Use of Scientific and Technological Progress in the

36 Henry T Greely, 'Implementing the human right to science in neuroscience' (2024) Journal of Law and the Biosciences lsae011.

Interest of Peace and for the Benefit of Mankind."[37] Section Six of this document added a commitment for states to avoid misuse of science:

> All States shall take measures to extend the benefits of science and technology to all strata of the population *and to protect them, both socially and materially, from possible harmful effects* of the misuse of scientific and technological developments, including their misuse to infringe upon the rights of the individual or of the group, particularly with regard to respect for privacy and the protection of the human personality and its physical and intellectual integrity. [emphasis added]

The international human right to science had been largely ignored from the adoption of the ICESCR until the last decade or so. Since then, a small group of academics have been writing about it, often urging it as a means to protect science from often ill-informed attacks. Professor Knoppers has played a leading role in that endeavour, not least through co-organizing the Brocher conference and the subsequent special issues of the Journal of Law and the Biosciences and The International Journal of Human Rights that came out of it. In her view, more understanding and application of the human right to science will both force governments to provide access to (good) science to their people and compel them to give scientists broad freedom in scientific efforts.

I was asked to talk about, and write about, the human right to science in the context of neuroscience. I did so, but with considerably more skepticism than I think Professor Knoppers would have hoped. Apart from a general bias against international legal regimes that lack strong, or even moderate, enforcement mechanisms, it seemed to me that the human right to science contains too many potentially conflicting provisions. It tells member states they must "respect the freedom indispensable for scientific research," that they must protect populations from the misuse of science, that they must protect the rights of inventors, but that they must take measures to "extend the benefits of science" to all "strata of the population." It seems to me that different countries will inevitably interpret those somewhat conflicting duties in different ways, especially given the lack of serious teeth to the right.

So, is Professor Knoppers right, and the human right to science should provide a strong tool for protecting and extending science, or am I right, that it is too ambiguous, broad, and weak to do much? I think the best answer to the question is "yes." Both are aspects of the truth, just seen from different

37 UN General Assembly, Charter of Economic Rights and Duties of States: Resolution / Adopted by the General Assembly, 17 December 1984, A/RES/39/163.

vantages. And both, I argue, are necessary. It makes me feel uncomfortable to describe Professor Knoppers—with extraordinary committee skills, great patience, a knack for bringing conversations back to the crucial points, and an indefatigable appetite to "do the work," as a dreamer. But I do think her aspirations aim very high. And I'm not entirely happy describing myself as stuck in the muddy details, unable to discern the road through the potholes, but that might not be (entirely?) unfair.

In the event, progress needs both dreamers and nitpickers. Professor Knoppers encompasses, in her visions and in her work, both strands but with a crucial tilt toward the ideal. And that is just one of the many reasons that she has been such an effective and important force in the exploration of ethical and legal issues raised by the biosciences, *and* in the creation and implementation of ways to deal, fairly and effectively, with them.

4 Conclusion

Professor Knoppers is not only a force of nature, but a good friend. I want to close with my favorite memory of her.

It was August 2006 and I was in Toulouse, France, attending a symposium of the Institut international de recerche en éthique biomédical, organized by (of course) Professor Knoppers. The symposium's title was "Biological Material and Electronic Data: Much Ado About Nothing?"[38] Professor Knoppers and I were having lunch with two other speakers, and friends, Tim Caulfield from the University of Alberta and Eric Meslin, then at the University of Indiana and from 2016 until recently the President of the Council of Canadian Academies. We were in a small restaurant in an old part of Toulouse; it was a sleepy weekday in August and the place was only half full.

The four of us were having a very good time, talking at about 1.6 kilometers a minute, at least occasionally (I suspect) about bioethics, but laughing constantly ... until we were kicked out. Another customer (we were pretty certain we knew which one) had complained that we were too noisy—we were having too much fun. Now, to be fair, the manager seemed a little apologetic and only

38 The symposium produced a book, edited by Professor Knoppers and Christian Hervé, and published in a bilingual edition as Bartha Maria Knoppers and Christian Hervé (eds), *Matériel biologique et informatisation: beaucoup de bruit pour rien?/Biological Material and Electronic Data: Much Ado About Nothing?* (Les Études Hospitalières 2006). It included a chapter from me I rather liked: Henry T Greely, 'Electronic Transfer of Medical Records in Clinical Care and Research: An Irresistible Force Meets a Moveable Object' at 35–50.

asked us to move to a table the waiter set up for us just outside the door. And we stayed there for a good long time, talking and laughing more, now with the added topic of being ejected from a restaurant for laughing too much.

And that's my favorite picture of Professor Bartha Maria Knoppers, PhD, OC, OQ, AdE, FRSC, FCAHS, an irresistible analyst of ethical problems, an immovable defender of human rights—and, on occasion, an unquenchable laugher! Our field, our world, and, very much, myself are better for her presence.

VIGNETTE

Human Dignity at the Crossroads of Law and Science

Patrick A. Molinari

I've known Bartha for almost forty years. For more than half of that period, from 1985 to 2009, we were both professors at the Université de Montréal's Faculty of Law, sharing complementary areas of interest.

On her arrival at the Faculty of Law, Bartha, who had been recruited as a professor of civil and family law, quickly demonstrated her willingness to focus her research and teaching activities on the legal and ethical issues surrounding biotechnology. The tenacity with which she deployed her scientific and professional initiatives from the outset of her academic career will have been the most powerful predictor of her exceptional contribution to the advancement of knowledge.

In many respects, Bartha reproduced in the rather traditional environment of law schools a research model inspired by scientific faculties. She set up research teams made up of researchers from many disciplines, graduate students, and partners from many institutions, both national and international. She has thus created, and above all directed, a veritable research enterprise, an expression that I use here in the highest sense and with the utmost admiration.

What's more—and not always sufficiently emphasized in the context of Bartha's career—is how many trainees who were at one time on the research teams she led now occupy leading positions in Quebec and Canadian society as well as internationally. Bartha's scientific and social leadership goes far beyond her own accomplishments and must be recognized for the significant contribution she has made to the next generation of researchers and experts she has trained and inspired.

Bartha is a humanist. This is the strongest impression that emerges from her work, publications, and public interventions. This quality, whether innate or acquired, guides her reflections on the development of public policy in the fields of genetics, health data management, and population health more generally. At the intersection of law, ethics, and science, these reflections are always centered on respect for the human person and the imperative of protecting human dignity.

DOI:10.1163/9789004688544_040

What stands out most persistently is Bartha's personality forged from a complex amalgam of austerity and casualness. Over the years and at the many events we have attended, I've been able to observe this duality in her personality. Bartha has a natural disposition for good humour and epicureanism, and anyone who has heard Bartha's scintillating laughter would agree. I think I even remember seeing Bartha, probably a long time ago, elegantly lighting a small cigar—obviously Dutch—and holding a glass of champagne in her other hand.

VIGNETTE

A Tribute to Bartha

Graeme Laurie

It is a common feature of the significant relationships in our lives that we vividly recall the first time we encountered someone. This is very true of my experience of Bartha, albeit on that occasion I was in the audience when she presented at the Human Genome Organization (HUGO) annual meeting in Edinburgh in 2001. I had come specifically to the conference to hear Bartha. Not only was I not disappointed, but a veil was lifted from my eyes as to what academia can be. The phenomenon of examining the ethical, legal, and social issues (ELSI) of genetics and genomics was coming into its own at that time, but those of us working in the field always faced the same dilemma: how do we get scientists to take seriously the ethico-social implications of their research in a manner that both brings their research findings to the public domain in a responsible way and which engages with the ELSI issues in a timely fashion?

So much ELSI work has had the unenviable role of playing bolt on to the "serious science." Bartha completely rejects this normative framing. Her work with HUGO stands as testament to that fact and my own experiences of working with her in subsequent years have taught me more than I could ever hope to know about how we can bring the learnings of the ethico-legal ivory tower to the real world, and particular to the scientific world and the public domain.

Bartha has been the driving force behind innumerable successful collaborations between the sciences, the social sciences, and humanities. These have brought the policy implications of academic research to the fore and turned them into tangible realities. I have been privileged to work with Bartha on a number of such projects, and my enduring impression has always been the same: it is difficult to say "no" to Bartha! She represents a unique blend of outstanding academic credentials with a "can do" attitude and talent for fostering productive interdisciplinary interactions.

But I have discovered her secret: her unrelenting sociability. Every meeting organized by Bartha leads to unforgettable stories about the excellent social time that was had by all. This kind of social brokering is priceless and no one delivers like Bartha.

On this point, I want to end with my own (failed) attempt to be hospitable to Bartha. On the occasion of her first visit to my home in Edinburgh, I prided myself on being able to offer her any tipple of her choosing (having diligently

DOI:10.1163/9789004688544_041

stocked my bar beforehand). Imagine my dismay when Bartha requested … a sherry. The one thing I had *not* thought of! But, after a frantic search of the drinks cupboard, I was able to source the Christmas trifle sherry which, abashedly, I served to Bartha with sincere apologies. In characteristic *bonhomie* style Bartha not only graciously accepted but requested a second sherry! We need more Barthas in academia and in public policy—the world is immeasurably better as a result.

CHAPTER 14

Families through the Lens of Genomics: Obligation or Consideration?

Ellen Wright Clayton

Professor Knoppers has an enormous heart and a strong belief that people should care for each other. She also has a deep conviction that genetic information can often be crucial for a person's healthcare. These positions underlie some of the major themes in her enormously influential and far-reaching oeuvre. The first and more elemental is that humans, and indeed all of creation, are connected to each other.[1] Truly, no human is an island. The discussion that follows focuses on one aspect of connection—sharing test results with adult relatives.[2]

1 Intrafamilial Communication

This theme of connection leads Professor Knoppers to argue that people are ethically obligated to inform their at-risk relatives about adverse genetic test results and that the relatives have an ethical claim to this information. In this regard, she is laser-focused on the potential benefit that family members could receive from having this information. She rejects the notion that individual autonomy is sufficient to allow individuals who receive genetic results to decide whether and with which family members to share genetic information, arguing instead that obligations among family members arise from notions of mutuality, reciprocity, the duty of rescue, and the idea that genetic information is family property.[3] Indeed, Professor Knoppers asserts that functional families

1 Bartha Maria Knoppers, 'Human genetics: parental, professional and political responsibility' (1993) 1 Health Law Journal 13; Bartha Maria Knoppers and Ruth Chadwick, 'Human genetic research: emerging trends in ethics' (2005) 6 Nature Reviews Genetics 75.

2 Decisions about testing and sharing genetic information with minors is beyond the scope of this essay.

3 Lee Black and others, 'Intrafamilial disclosure of risk for hereditary breast and ovarian cancer: points to consider' (2013) 4 Journal of Community Genetics 203; Bartha Maria Knoppers and others, 'HUGO Ethics Committee Statement on DNA sampling: control and access' (1998) 11 Genetic Resources 43; Bartha Maria Knoppers, 'Genetic information and the family: are we our brother's keeper?' (2002) 20 Trends in Biotechnology 85; Bartha Maria Knoppers and

© ELLEN WRIGHT CLAYTON, 2025 | DOI:10.1163/9789004688544_042 will share genetic information and that failure to do so means that families are dysfunctional.[4] Beginning at the turn of the millennium,[5] many commentators have joined her in arguing that genetic information should be shared with and belongs to at-risk relatives.[6]

Yet in light of her conception of families, it is particularly intriguing that Professor Knoppers begins one of her seminal articles, "Towards a reconstruction of the 'genetic family': New principles?,"[7] with the following epigraph from Jane Austen's insightful novel *Pride and Prejudice*: "Nobody who has not been in the interior of the family can say what the difficulties of any individual of that family may be." This citation suggests that other factors may need to be considered in deciding how to respond to individuals' decisions about whether and how to share information with family members. The discussion that follows draws upon the empirical literature to illustrate common themes of what people say and do with respect to sharing genetic information.

1.1 *Intrafamilial Communication Following Clinical Genetic Testing*

Several things are striking about what is known about intrafamilial communication of genetic risk information. One is that numerous researchers have asked people what they *think* they would do with genetic test results. In many of these investigations, the researchers study responses of people in the general population who are not currently facing these issues.[8] Most people who

---

Kristina Kekesi-Lafrance, 'The genetic family as patient?' (2020) 6 The American Journal of Bioethics 77; Gillian Nycum, Denise Avard, and Bartha Maria Knoppers, 'Factors influencing intrafamilial communication of hereditary breast and ovarian cancer genetic information' (2009) 17 European Journal of Human Genetics 872; Gillian Nycum, Bartha Maria Knoppers, and Denise Avard, 'Intra-familial obligations to communicate genetic risk information: what foundations? What forms?' (2009) 3 McGill Journal of Law & Health 21; Bartha Maria Knoppers, 'Towards a reconstruction of the "genetic family": new principles?' (1998) 49 International Digest of Health Legislation 241.

4 Knoppers, 'Genetic information' (n 3).

5 David J Doukas and Jessica W Berg, 'The family covenant and genetic testing' (2001) 1 American Journal of Bioethics 2.

6 Deborah R Gordon and Barbara A Koenig, '"If relatives inherited the gene, they should inherit the data." Bringing the family into the room where bioethics happens' (2022) 41 New Genetics and Society 23; Madison K Kilbride, 'Genetic privacy, disease prevention, and the principle of rescue' (2018) 48 Hastings Center Report 10; Álvaro Mendes and others, 'Communication of information about genetic risks: putting families at the center' (2018) 57 Family Process 836.

7 Bartha Maria Knoppers, 'Towards a reconstruction' (n 3).

8 Amber M Aeilts and others, 'BRCAShare—Assessment of an animated digital message for intrafamilial communication of pathogenic variant positive test results: a feasibility study' (2023) 32 Journal of Genetic Counseling 475; Marisa Greenberg and Rachel A Smith, 'Support seeking or familial obligation: an investigation of motives for disclosing genetic test results' (2016) 31 Health Communication 668.

have a strong family history or are personally affected by a disorder—in these studies almost always heritable cancer—avow a sense of obligation to their relatives.[9] Even so, they report that they plan to tell some but notably, not all of their relatives.[10]

Even people who have previously undergone genetic testing report being swayed in the decision about sharing their genetic results by how close they feel to their relatives.[11] Lafrenière and colleagues identified several factors that influence whether and how women share their testing results for BRCA1/2 variants with family, including their own characteristics and those of their relatives, family culture, closeness of connections, and the larger sociolegal contexts.[12] Some women in the study worried that genetic risk information may impede their relatives' ability to obtain health insurance, an ongoing concern in the United States despite the enactment of the Genetic Information Nondiscrimination Act.[13] Women also expressed concern that the relative may be otherwise preoccupied with life events, such as upcoming weddings or family deaths, which makes them hesitate to share at the time. And sometimes, the proband may be overwhelmed by the results or other events in their own life that may supersede their communicating with family.

Although some research into what families *actually* do following clinical genetic testing was done in the early 2000s,[14] there has been remarkably little investigation since that time into what families *actually* do following clinical genetic testing. Here as well, researchers to date have focused on highly

9 Marleah Dean and others, 'Sharing genetic test results with family members of BRCA, PALB2, CHEK2, and ATM carriers' (2021) 104 Patient Education and Counseling 720; Greenberg and Smith (n 8).

10 Greenberg and Smith (n 8); Kelsey Stuttgen Finn and others, 'Factors that influence intent to share genetic information related to cancer risk with family members' (2021) 26 Journal of Health Communication 545; Carolyn Winskill and others, 'Predictors of women's intentions to communicate updated genetic test results to immediate and extended family members' (2023) 26 Public Health Genomics 24.

11 Mel Wiseman, Caroline Dancyger, and Susan Michie, 'Communicating genetic risk information within families: a review' (2010) 9 Familial Cancer 691.

12 Darquise Lafrenière and others, 'Family communication following BRCA1/2 genetic testing: a close look at the process' (2013) 22 Journal of Genetic Counseling 323.

13 Public Law 110-233, enacted 21 May 2008.

14 Terri Blase and others, 'Sharing GJB2/GJB6 genetic test information with family members' (2007) 16 Journal of Genetic Counseling 313; Chanita Hughes and others, 'All in the family: evaluation of the process and content of sisters' communication about BRCA1 and BRCA2 genetic test results' (2002) 107 American Journal of Medical Genetics 143; Kim Chivers Seymour and others, 'What facilitates or impedes family communication following genetic testing for cancer risk? A systematic review and meta-synthesis of primary qualitative research' (2010) 19 Journal of Genetic Counseling 330.

penetrant dominant variants, particularly those affecting heritable cancer predisposition, which loom large in the mind of the public. Most of these studies involve few patients (if sample size is reported at all). A recent systematic literature review of decision making following clinical genetic testing and information sharing among family dyads found only 15 studies across the world.[15] Most of these studies focused on reproductive genetic testing, which is ethically and, in many states in the US, legally fraught. Only five studies focused on information sharing, four of which investigated sharing only with first and second-degree relatives (e.g. at-risk adult relatives) which remains the group most commonly discussed in the literature on obligations of family sharing. A different systematic review identified myriad barriers to talking with relatives, including demographic factors, knowledge deficits, and an array of attitudes, emotional responses, and beliefs of the patient.[16] Dean and colleagues recently found patients who had received pathogenic variants in cancer predisposition genes were often motivated by a sense of obligation, but an unspecified number were deterred by fear of their relatives' reactions, the challenge of conveying complex information, and lack of closeness, which led some not to share.[17]

1.2 *Intrafamilial Communication Following Research Genetic Testing*

Far more work has been done in recent years exploring whether and how research participants share research results they receive with their relatives. The focus on the research setting has doubtless been spurred by several factors. One is the ongoing debate about whether to return research results at all,[18] and if so, what results ought to be returned—primary and/or secondary findings,[19]

---

15 Wai Ki Law and others, 'Decision-making about genetic health information among family dyads: a systematic literature review' (2022) 16 Health Psychology Review 414.

16 Swetha Srinivasan and others, 'Barriers and facilitators for cascade testing in genetic conditions: a systematic review' (2020) 28 European Journal of Human Genetics 1631.

17 Dean and others (n 9); see also Vasiliki Rahimzadeh and others, 'To disclose, or not to disclose? context matters' (2015) 23 European Journal of Human Genetics 279; Jennifer M Taber and others, 'Prevalence and correlates of receiving and sharing high-penetrance cancer genetic test results: findings from the Health Information National Trends Survey' (2015) 18 Public Health Genomics 67.

18 Susan M Wolf and Robert C Green, 'Return of results in genomic research using large-scale or whole genome sequencing: toward a new normal' (2023) 24 Annual Review of Genomics and Human Genetics 393.

19 Rachel S Purvis and others, 'First do no harm: ethical concerns of health researchers that discourage the sharing of results with research participants' (2020) 11 AJOB Empirical Bioethics 104; Danya F Vears and others, 'Return of individual research results from genomic research: a systematic review of stakeholder perspectives' (2021) 16 PloS One e0258646; Adrian Thorogood, Gratien Dalpé, and Bartha Maria Knoppers, 'Return of individual

and more recently, reinterpretation of genetic results over time.[20] Another question is how to return results to the participants themselves, which can be particularly challenging when the investigator is not the participant's care provider.[21] Investigators in these translational studies are already examining how participants receive results and what they do in response, which provides a platform for examining intrafamilial sharing as well.

1.2.1 What Research Participants Say They Would Do about Sharing Their Results

Even though many people participate in research in order to help their families and even though they often feel that they have the responsibility to share results,[22] studies to date show that participants do not always plan to share genetic test results with their relatives and often do not do so.[23] Here as well, a number of studies have asked what people think they would do about informing family members about concerning genetic research results. One particularly intriguing study conducted focus groups with African American, Hispanic, and American Indian/Alaska Native participants to explore their willingness to share research results with relatives.[24] The participants generally thought relatives should know for their future care, but that relatives should have the right to refuse receiving these results, noting that refusal is itself contested.[25] These respondents nonetheless wanted control over whether and how recipients were told, either because they thought it would be hard for investigators to find relatives or more often because the participants saw themselves as the

genomic research results: are laws and policies keeping step? (2019) 27 European Journal of Human Genetics 535.

20 Paul S Appelbaum and others, 'Practical considerations for reinterpretation of individual genetic variants' (2023) 25 Genetics in Medicine 100801; Jonathan M Davis, Lynne Yao, and Barbara E Bierer, 'Protecting pregnant women with substance use disorders and their neonates participating in research' (2019) 322 JAMA 609.

21 Ellen Wright Clayton and others, 'Studying the impact of translational genomic research: lessons from eMERGE' (2023) 110 American Journal of Human Genetics 1021.

22 Sarah D Madrid and others, '"A gift to my family for their future": attitudes about genetic research participation' (2022) 25 Public Health Genomics 98.

23 LM (Leonie) van den Heuvel and others, 'How to inform relatives at risk of hereditary diseases? A mixed-methods systematic review on patient attitudes' (2019) 28 Journal of Genetic Counseling 1042.

24 Xuan Zhu and others, 'Perspectives regarding family disclosure of genetic research results in three racial and ethnic minority populations' (2020) 11 Journal of Community Genetics 433.

25 See e.g. Claire Murphy and others, 'The right not to know: non-disclosure of primary genetic test results and genetic counselors' response' (2024) 33 Journal of Genetic Counseling 875.

gatekeepers for the information. Factors that they thought would influence their decision to disclose included blood relationship, emotional closeness, how they saw their relative's ability to deal with the information, and risk of stigmatization.

1.2.2 Sharing After Return of Actual Research Results

Observational studies support this complexity in sharing research results. The eMERGE (Electronic Medical Record and Genomics) Network,[26] which has focused on understanding the impact of returning genetic test results, has been a particularly rich source of information. In a recent article by Wynn and colleagues, which focused on this issue, the investigators surveyed recipients of pathogenic predominantly dominant, actionable disorders in the third phase of eMERGE.[27] Only a third of the respondents told all their first-degree relatives about their results, while 4% had not told anyone, including their healthcare provider. Participants who received results from a genetics provider were more likely to talk with family than those who learned some other way.[28] More than two-thirds of those who disclosed their results cited a sense of obligation or a desire to help, while more than a third declined to share saying that their at-risk relative was too young. Another 25% declined, citing a lack of a relationship with the relative.[29] Investigators in the Clinical Sequencing Exploratory Research consortium also reported challenges in having participants share information with families.[30]

In light of these challenges in reaching relatives,[31] much attention has been devoted to developing strategies to facilitate intra-family communication within families in both the clinical and research settings. Common strategies

---

26 eMERGE Consortium, 'eMERGE Publications: 2007–2022', available at: https://emerge-network.org/publications/.

27 Julia Wynn and others, 'Do research participants share genomic screening results with family members?' (2022) 31 Journal of Genetic Counseling 447.

28 Clayton and others (n 21).

29 Deborah J Bowen and others, 'What improves the likelihood of people receiving genetic test results communicating to their families about genetic risk?' (2021) 104 Patient Education and Counseling 726.

30 Julia Wynn and others, 'Clinical providers' experiences with returning results from genomic sequencing: an interview study' (2018) 11 BMC Medical Genomics 45; see also Mary B Daly and others, 'Communicating genetic test results within the family: is it lost in translation? A survey of relatives in the randomized six-step study' (2016) 15 Familial Cancer 697.

31 Rachel Schwiter and others, 'How can we reach at-risk relatives? Efforts to enhance communication and cascade testing uptake: a mini-review' (2018) 6 Current Genetic Medicine Reports 21.

include patient letters or other information materials as well as inviting referrals.[32] Recently, Schmidlen and colleagues described developing a chatbot that patients could agree to be shared with relatives in MyCode®.[33] While slightly more than half of probands consented to its use, only about one quarter of the recipients of the chatbot completed it. In a different study, Dean and colleagues suggested, based on their assessment of factors that promote and discourage family sharing, that family information letters should provide specific information about predisposing variants while making clear that results could change in light of research.[34]

2 Role of Healthcare Providers

2.1 *What Probands Want from Clinicians and Investigators*

People varied widely in what role they would like for healthcare providers to play in providing information for relatives. Some wanted to control what clinicians did.[35] Many wanted support from clinicians in sharing results,[36] ranging from providing written materials to share[37] to having face-to-face meetings with relatives. And some wanted clinicians to reach out directly to relatives, but even then usually only after the proband made contact first.[38]

2.2 *The Debate about What Clinicians May and Should Do*

As noted above, most people do share at least some results with their relatives and often welcome support for their providers. Clinicians and researchers clearly should help their patients and participants discuss results with their at-risk relatives. In addition, much effort has been going into giving probands the tools to do this, and many providers devote much time to talking with and seeing these relatives either as individual referrals or in group meetings.

32 Kelly A McClellan and others, 'Exploring resources for intrafamilial communication of cancer genetic risk: we still need to talk' (2013) European Journal of Human Genetics 903.

33 Tara Schmidlen and others, 'Use of a chatbot to increase uptake of cascade genetic testing' (2022) 31 Journal of Genetic Counseling 1219.

34 Dean and others (n 9).

35 Zhu and others (n 24).

36 van den Heuvel and others (n 23).

37 Dean and others (n 9).

38 Nora B Henrikson and others, '"It would be so much easier": health system-led genetic risk notification—feasibility and acceptability of cascade screening in an integrated system' (2019) 10 Journal of Community Genetics 461.

A burning question for the professional community for years has been whether clinicians are ever ethically warranted and/or legally permitted to inform their patient's relatives over the patient's objections.[39] Informed by her commitment to family obligations and her desire that all receive the benefits of advances in genetics, over her career, Professor Knoppers has become an increasingly strong proponent of providers' conveying information to relatives even over their patients' objections at least in some circumstances.[40] Many other commentators[41] and professional organizations agree.[42] In countless meetings and conversations over the years, clinicians and investigators have expressed moral distress when their patients and research participants decline to share results with their relatives or refuse to permit these professionals to do so. They reason that genetic information can be enormously valuable and in some cases lifesaving when shared at clinically actionable times.

Yet there are powerful ethical and legal reasons why clinicians and investigators should hesitate before overriding patients' and participants' objections to sharing.[43] The millenia-old obligation of confidentiality, which is foundational to the clinician-patient relationship and for which the law provides significant protection, is a primary reason. Yet, early on, a few courts in the United States evinced a desire to ensure that family members receive genetic risk information. In one prominent case, a court in New Jersey in 1996 held that a physician had a duty to tell a child about the heritable cancer that affected her father,

---

39 Kenneth Offit and others, 'The "duty to warn" a patient's family members about hereditary disease risks (2004) 292 JAMA 1469; Susan M Wolf and others, 'Returning a research participant's genomic results to relatives: analysis and recommendations' (2015) 43 Journal of Law, Medicine & Ethics 440; Wolf and Green (n 18); ASHG, 'ASHG statement. Professional disclosure of familial genetic information. The American Society of Human Genetics Social Issues Subcommittee on Familial Disclosure' (1998) 62 The American Journal of Human Genetics 474.

40 Black and others (n 3); Knoppers, 'Towards a reconstruction (n 3); Knoppers and Kekesi-Lafrance (n 3); Mireille Lacroix and others, 'Should physicians warn patients' relatives of genetic risks?' (2008) 178 CMAJ: Canadian Medical Association Journal 593; Knoppers, 'Genetic information and the family' (n 3).

41 Offit and others (n 39), Edward S Dove and others, 'Familial genetic risks: how can we better navigate patient confidentiality and appropriate risk disclosure to relatives?' (2019) 45 Journal of Medical Ethics 504; Wolf and others (n 39); Wolf and Green (n 18).

42 ASHG statement (n 39).

43 Dov Fox, Emily Spencer, and Ali Torkamani, 'Returning results to family members: professional duties in genomics research in the United States' (2018) 38 Journal of Legal Medicine 201; Jane E Zebrac and others, 'Comparing the attitudes of physicians and non-physicians toward communicating a patient's BRCA1 mutation to a first-degree relative against a patient's wishes' (2022) 13 Journal of Community Genetics 403.

which she ultimately developed decades later.[44] This ruling elicited much criticism.[45] The New Jersey state legislature later passed a law limiting the scope of that decision.[46] In a more narrowly reasoned case, the Florida Supreme Court in 1995 held that while the physician had a duty to tell his patient that she had a heritable cancer and what it meant for her relatives, he had no direct duty to the patient's at-risk daughter and hence no liability when the daughter subsequently developed the same disease.[47] Notably, neither case addressed confidentiality at any length or whether the patients had objected at all.

These cases, which focused on risk notification, have been largely superseded in the United States by the enactment of the Privacy Rule of the Health Insurance Portability and Accountability Act (HIPAA), which provides that a physician can share information with family members only about the patient's care or payment and only so long as the patient does not object.[48] The Office of Civil Rights, which enforces HIPAA, states that physicians can share genetic information with clinicians caring for their family members, but again only so long as the patient had not objected.[49] Given the legal impact of objections, physicians who wish to tell relatives should inform their patients about their plan and give them a choice. Moreover, HIPAA does not preempt more privacy protective state laws, which can be challenging given the potpourri of these statutes in the US.[50] These provisions of the HIPAA Privacy Rule, which protect patient privacy and confidentiality, have led to heated debates about when, if ever, it is legally permissible in the United States to warn family members about their genetic risk over the probands' objection in the United States.[51]

---

44 *Safer* v *Pack*, 677 A.2d 1188 (NJ App Div 1996).

45 See e.g. Ellen Wright Clayton, 'What should the law say about disclosure of genetic information to relatives?' (1998) 1 Journal of Health Care Law & Policy 373; Angela Liang, 'Argument against a physician's duty to warn for genetic conditions: the conflicts created by Safer v. Estate of Pack' [1998] 1 Journal of Health Care Law & Policy 437; Kristin E Schleiter, 'A physician's duty to warn third parties of hereditary risk' (2009) 11 The Virtual Mentor: VM 697.

46 N.J. STAT. ANN. § 10:5–47 (a)(6) (2001).

47 *Pate* v *Threlkel*, 661 So.2d 278 (Fla 1995)

48 45 CFR § 164.510 (2024).

49 US Department of Health and Human Services, 'Modifications to the HIPAA Privacy, Security, Enforcement and Breach Notification Rules Under the Health Information Technology and Economic and Clinical Health Act and the Genetic Information Nondiscrimination Act; Other Modifications to the HIPAA Rules; Final Rule', 78 Fed. Reg. 5566–5702, 5668 (2013).

50 See e.g. Ellen Wright Clayton and others, 'The law of genetic privacy: applications, implications, and limitations' (2019) 6 Journal of Law and the Biosciences 1.

51 Mark A Rothstein, 'Reconsidering the duty to warn genetically at-risk relatives' (2018) 20 Genetics in Medicine 285; Sonia Suter, 'Legal challenges in genetics, including duty

ABC v St George's Healthcare NHS Trust & Ors,[52] a case from the United Kingdom (and England specifically), is probably the most visible case in this century that concerns warning family members about genetic risk. In her carefully reasoned opinion for the High Court, Justice Amanda Yip concluded that in the distinctive facts of that case, it was "fair, just, and reasonable" to require the defendant forensic psychiatrist to consider whether the interest of the claimant, who was then pregnant and also a patient of the forensic psychiatrist, in learning about her father's Huntington's disease despite his stringent objection, in order to justify violating the father's and the public's interest in confidentiality. The Court specifically pointed out the importance of the existing therapeutic relationship between the forensic psychiatrist and the claimant and the clear foreseeability of harm in finding that a duty to consider whether to balance the claimant's interest in receiving the information against the patient's and the public's interest in confidentiality could exist in this case. Justice Yip made clear that her decision was very narrow, emphasizing that she was finding neither "a free-standing duty of disclosure nor … a broad duty of care owed to all relatives in respect of genetic information." And, ultimately, the Court concluded that there was no breach of duty in this case, given medical opinion and that causation had not been demonstrated, and given insufficient evidence that the claimant would have terminated her pregnancy but for the breach of such a duty owed to her.

3 Conclusion

There are many reasons why sharing genetic test results with at-risk relatives can be desirable. Sharing information within families offers the possibility of benefit to relatives who may be able to intervene in their own health. Indeed, cascade testing leading to healthcare intervention is often essential to demonstrate cost effectiveness of genetic testing.[53] And it often pains clinicians when their patients' relatives do not receive this information.

to warn and genetic discrimination' (2020)10 Cold Spring Harbor Perspectives in Medicine a036665. See also Clayton (n 45) (potential tort liability pre-HIPAA). But see Nora B Henrikson and others, 'What guidance does HIPAA offer to providers considering familial risk notification and cascade genetic testing?' (2020) 7 Journal of Law and Biosciences lsaa071.

52 *ABC* v *St George's Healthcare NHS Trust* [2020] EWHC 455 (QB).

53 Gregory F Guzauska and others, 'Population genomic screening for three common hereditary conditions: a cost-effectiveness analysis' (2023) 176 Annals of Internal Medicine 585.

But using terms such as "obligation" to describe what patients, research participants, clinicians, and investigators should do may claim too much. Research consistently shows that information sharing often is not the only issue at stake even for people who receive highly penetrant, medically actionable genetic test results. They can have competing personal interests, other obligations of care, as well as various levels of social connection with their kin. Surely, these human factors, to which Professor Knoppers so aptly alluded in her reference to Jane Austen, must be taken into account, especially when test results have less immediate clinical impact. In addition, breaching patient confidentiality is not to be done lightly given its importance to healthcare, especially since disclosure is at least arguably illegal. In light of all this complexity within families and in healthcare, might we honour Professor Knoppers' powerful advocacy of the importance of genetic connection and care in families more fully by making a more modest claim that probands should seriously consider sharing genetic test results with at-risk relatives, and that clinicians and researchers should prioritize addressing probands' concerns while encouraging and assisting probands in their efforts?

VIGNETTE

Bartha: An Exemplary Academic

David Townend

Like everyone who has had the privilege of working with Bartha, I have many happy memories of extremely engaging and fruitful collaborations. Not least, I remember very fondly a seminar that we ran together at the Brocher Foundation, just outside of Geneva, on data sharing in medical research. Of course, the conviviality that attended those two days on the shores of Lac Léman is a strong part of the memory, but the most important part was that the meeting had only two short papers at the start of the proceedings. The rest of the time was spent in roundtable discussion of the issues. It wasn't a parade of prepared positions declared via PowerPoint slides or typed-up papers; rather, it was an opportunity to find solutions to intractable problems through respectful and open-minded academic dialogue, and it resulted in a high-quality peer-review journal article.

There are two aspects that are at the heart of what makes Bartha not only a great academic, but an inspirational leader. First, there is her extraordinary energy and commitment to making the governance and regulation of science and medicine work. Bartha is brilliant in her command of the substance of the legal (and ethical) problems in making research in new and emerging health fields work for people, and in making academe work to find solutions. She has a commitment to balancing the different legitimate interests and needs in play in any problem situation without losing sight of the enormous potential that new research in genetics, medicine, and health might bring to individuals and communities. She is fully immersed in the detail not only of the law, but of the science. She is an inquisitive academic, always asking "why?", without fear of not knowing. She brings such enormous energy to that, and to the organizing of the debate; her ability and energy to bring people together, to make them focus, and to produce results in so many projects and fora is astonishing. These aspects of her contribution would already make her one of the great academics in our field, but there is a second aspect that makes her one of the great academic leaders, "full stop."

And that is that Bartha is one of the most generous people in academia and in policymaking. She sees potential in others and shares opportunities like no other; Bartha draws people into her work and encourages them with kindness and compassion. And there is always laughter and hospitality. The conversation continues, wide-ranging—yes, about the issues at hand, but about so many things beyond—into the evenings at conferences and meetings, often over favourite tipples. She embodies the true spirit of University and academe, and her humanity is what defines her as an exemplary academic, colleague, and friend.

VIGNETTE

Climbing Every Mountain: Bartha Maria's Melody of Mentorship

Nicole Palmour

My first introduction to Bartha Maria Knoppers was barely a year after I started my PhD studies at McGill University. I submitted an abstract to the Third International DNA Sampling Conference, which was to be held in Montreal in September 2002. Selected presentations would be published in a post-conference book. Bartha's group, then situated at the University of Montreal, was organizing the conference, abstract selection, manuscript collection, and editing. I was fortunate to have my abstract selected to be presented.

I admit to having been intimidated. This was my first international conference and Bartha was a close colleague and friend with my primary PhD supervisor, Dr Kathleen Glass. I *so* wanted to do a good job. Ultimately, I learned much from the experience, both in terms of preparation for an international presentation, and drafting the accompanying manuscript for publication.

The highlight, however, was Bartha's presentation. Little did I know that watching Bartha at the conference was only the beginning of my journey. I remember being captivated by her commanding presence and her presentation that seamlessly connected images with ideas.

I should note that I had just completed a MSc in Forensic Psychology, and had been accepted in the Department of Human Genetics to do an interdisciplinary PhD with two supervisors. Interdisciplinary work is all the rage now, but 22 years ago it was unusual. I proposed exploring the "Forensic Applications of Molecular Genetics: Ethical and Policy Issues," which meant I was integrating ethics, law, forensic genetics, and policy all in one thesis.

As fascinated as I was by the thesis, I kept having niggling thoughts of, "Where will this go? What will I do when this is completed? What kind of job does a thesis like this lead to?"

It was at this conference that I had my "Aha!" moment. Watching this dynamic woman, hosting an international DNA conference, carving the path forward for other women, in two fields dominated by men—genetics and law. I thought to myself at the time, "This is my path forward."

It wasn't until 10 years after the conference that I would realize the vision I had. I was hired by the Centre of Genomics and Policy, at that point situated at

 | DOI:10.1163/9789004688544_044

McGill; Bartha and Denise Avard welcomed me in with open arms, and it felt like home. By this time Bartha was fully in her stride as Director of the Centre, with a dedicated multidisciplinary team tackling challenges at the interface of medicine, law, and public policy.

I never tire of watching Bartha grappling with a complex problem, as she drills down to the foundational components, breaking down issues so that they are understandable yet nuanced. Then she recombines the components, building back such that each component has a raison d'être and is "interoperable." As a mentor of young scholars, I've watched her subtle and not-so-subtle promotion and nudging of students to present, write, and apply for funding. I smile as she asks questions designed to spark curiosity, share ideas, and inspire others to pick up where she's left off. I am proud to be one of many to build on her legacy.

CHAPTER 15

Whither Consent in Clinical Genetics?

Susan E. Wallace

1 Introduction

I well remember my first day of work at the Centre de recherche en droit public (CRDP), Université de Montréal (UdeM), in April 2007. Professor Bartha Maria Knoppers asked me and my colleague, Stephanie Lazor (at the time a law student at McGill University), to find text in consent forms from Public Population Project in Genomics (P^{3}G) Consortium member studies that indicated a specific action or category of information, such as the risks of participation or how samples and data would be stored. The results would be used to create best practice guidelines and consent tools. Stephanie was better at the beginning than me. Fortunately, I quickly improved as reviewing consent forms and creating model templates was an activity I would be repeating in the future. It is through these reviews that I have come to agree with the position that there is no consensus as to what constitutes *informed* consent and what precise information is needed to help a person reach *being informed* so that consent as such can be achieved. However, model (or generic) consent tools can be one way to help with the often complex consent process.

In this chapter, I will trace the important part tool creation has had in better enabling the sharing of genomic and other information for research and in clinical care. I will argue that determining the context where consent is needed is one of the best ways to help narrow down the elements that might be included to highlight the key, specific issues that are important for an individual to understand. It can be especially important when distinguishing between consent for participating in medical research and consent for clinical care as both have many similarities but also different requirements and processes.

Professor Knoppers has been a leader in this area, from the early days of population biobanking and moving into using whole-genome sequencing (WGS) data for diagnosis and treatment. Based on her compassion for people and intellect, she has spread her wealth of knowledge and insight across disciplines across the world. Consent tools are only one of her contributions, and I am grateful for the opportunities I have had and people I have met through working with these tools over the years. They can be seen as a gift of communication, a way to better allow people to understand their choices in what

DOI:10.1163/9789004688544_045

are often complex and unsettling situations. I know, from discussions with peers, the literature, and the fact that this approach is still being used today, that consent tools continue to be a useful resource through which researchers can tackle the evolving contexts in which consent is needed. They are also one tangible indication of Professor Knoppers' firm belief in the right of everyone to benefit from medical and genetic discoveries. As she wrote, "The unique and private genetic 'me' is discovered through the study and comprehension of the human 'us'."[1]

2 Background

The term "informed consent" appeared in the 1950s, with ethical, philosophical, and legal discussions arising in the 1970s.[2] Whistleblowers, such as Maurice Pappworth[3] and Henry Beecher,[4] brought to light what we now see as unethical practice in research. The histories of the Nuremberg Trials, Tuskegee Study, and the Cartwright Inquiry into the 1966 Proposal (*Carcinoma in situ*) study remind us of the horrors that can result from biomedical research without independent oversight, ethical review and, one might say, a sense of common decency.[5] These and other revelations, published by concerned academics, reporters, and patients, brought unethical practices to light, resulting in new regulations, processes, laws, and practices to ensure that the research participant's welfare takes priority over the research question. This shift from researchers to participants has also been echoed in clinical care. Traditionally, the doctor-patient relationship was sufficient, where a one-to-one conversation would provide the opportunity for the clinician to give information to the patient and then receive consent to conduct treatment. Now, as illustrated by

1 Bartha Maria Knoppers and Michael JS Beauvais, 'Three decades of genetic privacy: a metaphoric journey' (2021) 30 Human Molecular Genetics R156.

2 Tom L Beauchamp, 'Informed consent: its history, meaning, and present challenges' (2011) 20 Cambridge Quarterly of Healthcare Ethics 515.

3 Maurice H Pappworth, '"Human guinea pigs"—a history' (1990) 301 BMJ 1456.

4 Henry K Beecher, 'Ethics and clinical research' (1966) 274 New England Journal of Medicine 1354.

5 Committee of Inquiry into Allegations Concerning the Treatment of Cervical Cancer at National Women's Hospital and into Other Related Matters, *The Report of the Committee of Inquiry into Allegations Concerning the Treatment of Cervical Cancer at National Women's Hospital and into other related matters* (GPO Auckland, 1988), available at: https://www.nsu.govt.nz/health-professionals/national-cervical-screening-programme/legislation/cervical-screening-inquiry-0; David J Rothman, *Strangers at the Bedside: A History of How Law and Bioethics Transformed Medical Decision Making* (Basic Books 1991).

recent United Kingdom (UK) law (and other countries' laws), patients can, and do, demand more.

Montgomery v Lanarkshire Health Board[6] is a relatively recent UK court case where this shift is clearly exemplified. Briefly,[7] when Mrs Montgomery gave birth to her son, there were complications. The baby was large, and his shoulders were caught in the vaginal canal during delivery. With great difficulty, he was born vaginally, but suffered from cerebral palsy due to loss of oxygen. Her clinician had recognized the possible risks to the mother and foetus but decided that these could be managed during birth. Therefore, the clinician did not offer the option of a caesarean section, as she did not believe it would be in Mrs Montgomery's best interests. However, Mrs Montgomery was informed that during the birth, if there were complications, a caesarean section could be carried out. Mrs Montgomery brought a claim of negligence against clinicians and sought damages on behalf of her son. The lower court heard that with a caesarean section Mrs Montgomery's son would have been born without injury. On appeal to the Supreme Court, the Court agreed that, had she been told of the possible complications, Mrs Montgomery would probably have elected, before delivery, to have a caesarean section and in consequence, damages were awarded.

The findings of the case have had a major influence in the UK on the process of informed consent in clinical care. The decision showed that it is no longer sufficient for patients to simply rely on their clinician to take a course of action on their behalf. The judges noted that,

> …[T]he doctor's advisory role involves *dialogue*, the aim of which is to ensure that the patient understands the seriousness of her condition, and the anticipated benefits and risks of the proposed treatment and any reasonable alternatives, so that she is then in a position to make an informed decision. This role will only be performed effectively if the information provided is *comprehensible*. The doctor's duty is not therefore fulfilled by bombarding the patient with technical information which she cannot reasonably be expected to grasp, let alone by routinely demanding her signature on a consent form.[8] (emphasis added)

6 *Montgomery v Lanarkshire Health Board* [2015] UKSC 11.

7 For a more detailed analysis and additional articles, see Rob Heywood and José Miola, 'The changing face of pre-operative medical disclosure: placing the patient at the heart of the matter' (2017) 133 Law Quarterly Review 296.

8 *Montgomery* (n 6), [90].

However, as Coggan and Miola write, it is a bit more complex than simply leaving the decision to the patient:

> There is an assumption that if a doctor lists the risks inherent in a procedure and then allows the patient to make her own choice based on that, her decision is rendered autonomous. This combination of autonomy and liberty may, at first glance, be seen as logically harmonious. ... Yet the two concepts can combine to cancel each other out, particularly if they are used in an unsophisticated form and without another key to autonomous decision-making; *effective communication*. While disclosure of relevant information is part of serving autonomy, it is not in itself enough. Other factors such as the patient understanding the information must also exist.[9] (emphasis added)

The informed consent process in a clinical setting is dialogue; the clinicians communicate the potential risks and benefits to a patient and help them come to a decision. There is a balance between the professional knowledge and experience of the clinician with the needs and wants of the patient. In day-to-day healthcare, this is not a straightforward process as communication skills and levels of understanding vary across individuals. In the lower court ruling, Mrs Montgomery lost the judgment, as it was decided, among other reasons, that her questioning about the risks of the vaginal delivery "...had been of a general nature only. Unlike specific questioning, general concerns set no obvious parameters for a required response."[10] This clearly puts the onus on the patient, who is not a learned medical professional, to have the expertise to be able to ask these specific questions. The judgment was overturned as the Supreme Court agreed that had she been given the information she needed, she would have had sufficient information to decide on a caesarean section.

So we see that communication and discussion of pertinent information is vital in consent to medical treatment. In a clinical setting, this exchange of information comes as part of the physical doctor-patient discussion and via words on a patient information sheet and consent form. But clinical medicine is changing with the introduction of genomics. The adding of a person's genetic information into treatment decisions adds an additional complexity and can make it even more difficult for an uninformed person to make an informed decision. No one can truly "understand" how they might react if they were to

9 John Coggon and José Miola, 'Automony, liberty, and medical decision-making' (2011) 70 The Cambridge Law Journal 523.

10 *Montgomery* (n 6), [33].

receive information about a condition that might not affect them for years, or not at all, or how a diagnosis might affect their current and future biological family members. True informed consent cannot exist. However, just as a parent tries to explain to a child why looking both ways is a good idea before crossing a road, we can do our utmost to explain to patients and participants, as best we can, the implications of being involved in research or treatment based on genomic data.

Professor Knoppers and colleagues have for many years been looking for the concepts and words that are contextually important for informed consent in the setting of genomics research. Tools based on best practice have been one way of sharing this knowledge. Tools developed in the research setting have provided a solid base on which tools for clinical genomics are now being developed.

3 Developing Consent Tools for Genomic Research

The approach to identifying the core elements for consent can be quite straightforward. First, one needs to ask oneself, for example:

1. What is it we want/need to do? (e.g. clinical care, a research study)
2. Who is doing this and where? (e.g. at a local hospital, creating an international research biobank)
3. Who/what is being recruited to participate? (e.g. patients, participants, datasets)
4. What are our obligations? (e.g. legal, ethical, practical)
5. What do we want to achieve? (e.g. clinical care, interrogating a dataset)
6. What do we need/want to tell our potential recruits in order for them to want to join?

Once these and other determinations have been made, one can examine existing consent materials, administrative, and legal documents, and examples of best practice to create a list of core elements one believes are needed for a consent form and patient information sheet (PIS). Using these, model consent materials can be created that can be amended to fix the local context. Simple? Maybe, but perhaps not when the research study involves gathering data from studies in multiple countries internationally, with differences in cultural attitudes, languages, and legal and administrative structures. Adding the processing of personal data such as demographic information and medical history, then whole-genome sequencing data, only adds to the complexity. However, if the goal is to share data for common good, these complexities need to be faced and overcome. One of the abiding principles that Professor Knoppers has followed over the years, as pertains to data and consent, has been that good quality data should be available to all for the good of all.[11] We know from the success of research studies worldwide that people are willing and happy for their data to be used in the advancement of medical knowledge and treatment. But, they want to be asked first, with the information they need and in a way they can understand, and they want to work with people and organizations that they trust.[12] Keeping consent materials and processes based on best practice and understandable, informative, and trustworthy has, and continues to be, the aim inspired in me by Professor Knoppers.

One of the important collaborative initiatives that Professor Knoppers spearheaded to further the legal and ethical sharing of research data was the P³G Consortium.[13] Established in 2004 and funded in 2007 by Genome Canada and Génome Québec, the aim of P³G was clear: "[b]uilding on the successful models of international collaboration…, the Public Population Project in Genomics (P³G) is dedicated to building a worldwide collaborative infrastructure, including a repository of tools and information (the P³G International Observatory), so as to foster interoperability between studies in human population genomics."[14] One of these tools would be a model consent template for population research biobanking. It was recognized by this time that to find meaningful associations between genes and disease, genes and environments, and between sets of genes, a large quantity of high quality biospecimens and their associated annotated data were needed.[15] These resources were defined as, "…usually longitudinal in nature, having] specific governance structures and may serve one or more large projects comparing phenotypic and genotypic information over time as well as receive requests for access for individual research projects."[16] Sharing across these national and international resources was one answer; however, many legal, ethical, cultural, and procedural hurdles stood in the way. P³G was a leader in developing tools to help to promote data sharing, whether nationally or internationally. Consent was, of course,

11 Bartha Knoppers, 'Framework for responsible sharing of genomic and health-related data' (2014) 8 The HUGO Journal 3.

12 Susan E Wallace and José Miola, 'Adding dynamic consent to a longitudinal cohort study: a qualitative study of EXCEED participant perspectives' (2021) 22 BMC Medical Ethics 12.

13 Bartha Maria Knoppers and others, 'The Public Population Project in Genomics (P3G): a proof of concept?' (2008) 16 European Journal of Human Genetics 664.

14 ibid.

15 George Davey Smith and others, 'Genetic epidemiology and public health: hope, hype and future prospects' (2005) 366 The Lancet 1484.

16 Bartha Maria Knoppers, 'Consent revisited: points to consider' (2005) 13 Health Law Review 33.

one important aspect to enable that sharing. As we wrote at the time, "[v]ariation across resources regarding consent policies and information provided in consent materials could hinder efforts to make genomic data available to researchers."[17] A model template, created and used by P^{3}G member resources, would help to *harmonize* consent practices to allow easier data sharing and foster public trust in biobanking.[18]

While population biobanking was in its infancy, by April 2009 P^{3}G had over thirty member projects. Those initial consent forms that Stephanie and I reviewed were from some of the founding members of P^{3}G. Fourteen studies contributed their consent forms and participant information sheets for our work, of which twelve were part of our analysis (others arrived late or were not available in English).[19] By going through them, we found clauses falling into five general categories: access, consent, commercialization, confidentiality, and governance. We created a "model information pamphlet" that included all the areas that were considered important by our members and followed agreed ethical standards. Once the materials were prepared, we presented them to the P^{3}G representatives and agreement was reached. Each study was assumed to be following their own local legal requirements; it was always clear that we could not interfere in this area, but we could help to ensure that the consent could be acceptable in most areas across those local settings.

The tools we created were a resource to be used as needed. As there was no requirement for any studies to use the P^{3}G model, it is difficult to judge success. However, we used this process again in a research study with specific expected outcomes. Professor Knoppers chaired the Ethics Committee for the International Cancer Genome Consortium (ICGC). With the goal, "…[t]o coordinate the generation of comprehensive catalogues of genomic abnormalities (somatic mutations) in tumours in 50 different cancer types and/or subtypes that are of clinical and societal importance across the globe,"[20] it was vital that member-study consent materials asked for and had gained consent for the elements needed for data to be collected, deposited, analyzed, and shared. It was decided that consent templates, built on the core bioethical elements agreed

---

17 Susan Wallace, Stephanie Lazor, and Bartha Maria Knoppers, 'Consent and population genomics: the creation of generic tools' (2009) 31 IRB: Ethics & Human Research 15.

18 Susan Wallace and Bartha Maria Knoppers, 'The Role of P3G in Encouraging Public Trust in Biobanks', in Peter Dabrock, Jochen Taupitz, and Jens Ried (eds), *Trust in Biobanking: Dealing with Ethical, Legal and Social Issues in an Emerging Field of Biotechnology* (Springer 2012).

19 Wallace, Lazor, and Knoppers (n 17).

20 The International Cancer Genome Consortium, 'International network of cancer genome projects' (2010) 464 Nature 993.

by the ICGC members, would be a useful tool. The consent template process was similar as with P^{3}G, but the complexity and stakes were much higher because data had to be shared for the study to succeed.

Reaching a consensus on the core bioethical elements of ICGC (elements required to be in all consent materials in order to participate)[21] required considerable negotiation. Genetics did add an additional layer of complexity for ICGC; there was extensive discussion about how to inform participants that the cancer samples they donated might be sequenced and this information added to the database, but these were still the early days of large-scale exome and whole-genome sequencing and not all laboratories had the equipment and experience to do these analyses.[22] It was debated whether data should be more available to commercial companies (it was) or whether results would be returned to individuals (they were not). Reviewing the consent forms from the ICGC-member countries also raised many questions. They were initially reviewed to create the model consents, but in doing so we found that the language was not as specific as we felt was needed. For example, very few consent forms at the time had a provision in place to enable data to cross regional or international borders, and if language were included, often it was so vague that it could be interpreted in various ways. This was actually a new type of endeavour; I reviewed numerous consents at this time and many studies had not envisaged sharing data with other countries, let alone within their own to other institutions or regions. It is an interesting ethical question as to whether a potential participant in a research study, on reading that their data will be shared "with investigators at other institutions conducting studies with our research team," would really understand that to mean international data sharing. As this was crucial, the ICGC Executive decided that they needed to confirm with all the principal investigators of ICGC member-studies that consent was in place to share internationally.[23] Principal investigators did confirm, but some did decide to revise their consents. One research study reconsented a large proportion of its participants.[24]

Model consent materials can help harmonize, but they can also teach. One study representative told us that their ethics review board was very appreciative of the model template, "as it helped them to understand the aims and structure of the ICGC and the requirements of local participation."[25] The ICGC consent materials

21 ibid.

22 This, of course, has now changed, and laboratories now conduct sequencing onsite.

23 Susan E Wallace and Bartha Maria Knoppers, 'Harmonised consent in international research consortia: an impossible dream?' (2011) 7 Genomics, Society and Policy 35.

24 Personal communication with the author.

25 ibid.

were not mandated (although some studies did adapt the templates for their own use). Their true importance, I would argue, was that they opened the door to a conversation as to what information was key to enabling individuals around the world to understand what it meant to participate in this study. While the countries all had differing cultural attributes and legal requirements, one could begin to "drill down" to the heart of what needed to be in the consent conversation at the data collection level. If Professor Tom Hudson, who led ICGC for many years, could speak to each of the millions of people who were being asked to contribute data to the study, what would he be asked and what would he say? Whether it be a large-scale, multi-national, biomedical research study or a consultation with one's local general practitioner, it comes down to the consent conversation. Of course, having this conversation is more difficult in biomedical research because contributing, for example, to a research database that will not provide individual benefit and where the results will not be known for many years, is very different from having personal clinical treatment.

4 Adding Genetics into the Consent Conversation

Our knowledge of genetics and their link to human health has developed rapidly over the last century. The link between cancer and chromosomes was first reported in 1902 and Morgan reported that genes were located on chromosomes in 1910.[26] Once the structure of DNA was discovered in 1953 and as new technologies were developed, individual genes were discovered and mapped and sequenced.[27] Genetic laboratory testing for diagnostic purposes began to be developed in the second half of the 20th century. In the pre-genomics era, "...genetic testing was an iterative process in which a clinician created a differential diagnosis, began by testing the one or two genes most likely to yield a diagnosis, and then testing other genes if the prior test was negative."[28] In the early 2000s, the cost of genome sequencing technologies was falling rapidly[29] and, with the wealth of data becoming available through research studies and biobanking resources, it was clear that determining the genetic basis of diseases and conditions would be key to introducing the era of personalized medicine.

26 Asude Alpman Durmaz and others, 'Evolution of genetic techniques: past, present, and beyond' (2015) 2015 Biomed Research International 461524.

27 Clare Turnbull and others, 'The 100 000 Genomes Project: bringing whole genome sequencing to the NHS' (2018) 361 BMJ k1687.

28 Shannon Rego and others, 'Informed consent in the genomics era' (2020) 10 Cold Spring Harbor Perspectives in Medicine 8.

29 Turnbull and others (n 27).

The 2010 ICGC marker paper noted:

> Given the tremendous potential for relatively low-cost genomic sequencing to reveal clinically useful information, we anticipate that in the not so distant future, partial or full cancer genomes will routinely be sequenced as part of the clinical evaluation of cancer patients and as part of their continuing clinical management.[30]

Only a decade later, the promise of tailoring oncological treatment based on sequence data is coming true.[31] Now that sequencing costs have diminished, the aim in some countries, such as the UK, is to bring sequencing into mainstream clinical care.

In 2015, Genomics England launched the 100,000 Genomes Project, designed to create a resource of whole-genome data collected from patients in two specific categories: those diagnosed with cancer and with rare inherited disease.[32] Both areas have benefited greatly from advances in genomics.[33] Although there were already many cancer-specific diagnostic tests, research has shown that cancers were not organ or tissue specific and this could change therapeutic practice and clinical trial design.[34] With the falling cost of sequencing, it was now more attractive to have a "…single all-encompassing test".[35] For those with rare diseases, in 2022 it was reported that there were over 300,000 million people suffer from a rare disease worldwide; by 2022, over 4,000 rare diseases had been discovered.[36] For Genomics England, "[s]equencing of the coding regions of all 20,000 genes by whole exome or genome sequencing eliminates reliance on the clinical hypothesis to select which genes to test and … enabled diagnoses of many previously unsolved cases."[37]

As the ICGC model consent materials benefited the cancer community, the rare disease community has created its own set of materials under the auspices

---

30 The International Cancer Genome Consortium (n 19).

31 Raffaella Casolino and others, 'Interpreting and integrating genomic tests results in clinical cancer care: overview and practical guidance' (2024) 74 CA: A Cancer Journal for Clinicians 264.

32 Turnbull and others (n 27).

33 Daniela Heim and others, 'Cancer beyond organ and tissue specificity: next-generation-sequencing gene mutation data reveal complex genetic similarities across major cancers' (2014) 135 International Journal of Cancer 2362; Lucia Monaco and others, 'Research on rare diseases: ten years of progress and challenges at IRDiRC' (2022) 21 Nature Reviews Drug Discovery 319.

34 Heim and others (n 33).

35 Turnbull and others (n 27).

36 Monaco and others (n 33).

37 Turnbull and others (n 26).

of the International Rare Diseases Research Consortium (IRDiRC)[38] and the Global Alliance for Genomics and Health (GA4GH).[39] As more data became available through, for example, sequencing studies and the efforts of patient communities, it became clearer that these data needed to be shared effectively throughout the scientific community.[40]

> To maximize the impact of these initiatives in contributing substantive amounts of quality data for research use, practical model consent clauses are essential to enhance data interoperability as well as to meet the informational needs of participants, ensure proper ethical and legal use of data sources and participants' overall protection.[41]

Rare disease research introduces new complexities to the consent process. Nguyen and colleagues note specific issues that must be addressed in rare disease consent materials that other research studies might not need.[42] As most rare diseases appear in childhood, there is a need to recruit children and family members to increase the likelihood of finding a genetic marker. Also, "[p]articular phenotypes of rare disease patients often require the collection and sharing of audiovisual data (e.g., facial images, videos, etc.) [and] the use of machine learning procedures for data phenotyping." Finally, because there is a scarcity of rare disease patients, genetic "matchmaking" can be used and this needs to be explained to potential participants. Dyke and colleagues note that there are two scenarios for matchmaking:

> 1) to assist the clinician in trying to find a match with a similar case elsewhere in the world to facilitate interpretation of findings and ultimately provide a diagnosis (and similarly to enable their discovery by other clinicians with similar patients); and 2) to enable exploratory research into the causes, development or treatment of rare diseases.[43]

The first may require identification of the individual, which raises privacy issues, but also raises the possibility of direct clinical benefit for the patient and their family. It also raises the issue of return of individual results, or

---

38 International Rare Diseases Research Consortium, available at: https://irdirc.org/.

39 Global Alliance for Genomics and Health, available at: https://www.ga4gh.org/.

40 Minh Thu Nguyen and others, 'Model consent clauses for rare disease research' (2019) 20 BMC Medical Ethics 55.

41 ibid.

42 ibid.

43 Stephanie OM Dyke and others, '"Matching" consent to purpose: the example of the Matchmaker Exchange' (2017) 38 Human Mutation 1281.

secondary findings,[44] a sometimes-controversial issue in the research setting, but an everyday occurrence in the clinical setting. The IRDiRC/GA4GH model consent clauses detail the core elements that should be included in consents and provide sample clauses that can be adapted to the local context.[45]

Tool development to encourage data sharing is one of the key activities of GA4GH.[46] GA4GH is a multi-partner organization, bringing together individual and Driver Projects (funded studies that follow GA4GH policies and use their tools as exemplars.) Professor Knoppers has been highly influential over the years with GA4GH. As one of its founding members she led the work on the GA4GH Framework for Responsible Sharing of Genomic and Health-Related Data.[47] She was a Chair of the GA4GH Regulatory and Ethics Working Group (and then called Work Stream) for many years, during which time a consent policy for GA4GH was created,[48] along with a consent toolkit[49] which continues to grow as science moves in new directions and new tools are needed.

One of these newer tools was designed and written to support clinicians in consenting patients and participants for genomic testing. Rego and others note that some of the clinical team "…may be less familiar with genetics and the complexities of informed consent for genomic sequencing."[50] Clinical genetic testing does introduce psychological and social risks that are not usually present in treatment not involving genomics.

> …[T]he risk of anxiety or stress related to pre-symptomatic knowledge that one may develop genetic condition for which there may not be any treatments or preventive measures, and the potential risk of stigma or discrimination due to such a genetic test result. The familial nature of genetic information also presents unique risks.[51]

---

44 Bartha Maria Knoppers, Ma'n H Zawati, and Karine Senecal, 'Return of genetic testing results in the era of whole-genome sequencing' (2015) 16 Nature Reviews Genetics 553.

45 Nguyen and others (n 40).

46 Heidi L Rehm and others, 'GA4GH: international policies and standards for data sharing across genomic research and healthcare' (2021) 1 Cell Genomics 2.

47 Knoppers (n 11).

48 GA4GH, 'Consent Policy' (version 2.0, 2010), available at: https://www.ga4gh.org/document/consent-policy-v2/.

49 GA4GH, 'Consent Tools', available at: https://www.ga4gh.org/document/archived-consent-tools/.

50 Rego and others (n 28).

51 ibid.

These potential risks will be detailed in consent forms, but also in one-to-one discussions so that individuals can better understand often complex investigations with unknown outcomes. Genetic counsellors work closely with other clinicians to discuss the potential issues with patients, answer questions, and provide professional guidance. But now, as sequencing technologies seek to become more integrated into the clinic, the process becomes much more uncertain for all parties. Instead of testing genes step-by-step in order to reach a diagnosis, a person's whole genome can be swiftly sequenced and examined for diagnostic purposes. While this allows for a rapid exclusion of possibilities, it does provide so much data that communication becomes difficult. As Patch and Middleton note, this forces the consent conversation to move from before testing takes place,

> ...[T]o where the main body of information about the genetic test result occurs post-test as opposed to pre-test. Once a genetic result is known there becomes a need to have a conversation about the relevance of this to treatment and clinical decision making within the pathway of resolving a medical issue, rather than a personal decision about the desirability and consequences of obtaining genetic information.[52]

However, the pre-test consent conversation is still important for the potentially at-risk, those who may be pre-disposed to get ill in the future. This points to one of the many uncertainties: even though my genes may pre-dispose me to a condition, does this mean I will suffer from it? If so, when and to what extreme? These can be the unknowns that raise a person's levels of anxiety about their, and perhaps their family's, future. The next question is: how do clinicians ensure their patients are informed sufficiently to enable them to make a decision when asked to consent?

> The consent conversation for a genomic test is multi-faceted. It should cover: the implications of the result, both for the individual patient and also their family (with a recognition that patients are expected to inform their relatives about their result so that they can seek out their own testing where relevant); the types of result that may come back from the laboratory (i.e. pathogenic, uncertain or benign) and what each of these will mean in terms of future risk and disease management and plans for genomic data storage, protection and sharing.[53]

52 Christine Patch and Anna Middleton, 'Genetic counselling in the era of genomic medicine' (2018) 126 British Medical Bulletin 27.

53 ibid.

Responding to the need for tools to help, Professor Knoppers and the GA4GH Consent Task Team developed Clinical Genomics Consent Clauses.[54] These clauses were created to be used in consent materials aimed at adults and mature minors. The process for creating these clauses is similar to the other GA4GH consent clauses. However, as with rare diseases, there were specific differences:

> For instance, the medical care environment mandates returning clinical actionable results. There is also the need to specifically require explicit permission for participation in ongoing research or for recontact for future research. In short, these adjustments reflect the fact that genomic testing decisions are taken at the same time as other clinical care ones. As genomic testing becomes a natural part of the clinical care pathway, authorization forms must be adapted to current medical practices and fit both the needs of the patient and healthcare providers.[55]

This integration into the clinical care pathway is well on its way. In the UK, the success of the 1000,000 Genome Project has now led to plans for the UK Genomics Medicine Service, which has the aim, "to be the first national health care system to offer whole-genome sequencing as part of routine care."[56] As part of the service, a single national testing directory will enable more informed diagnoses for those with cancer and rare diseases and enable better matching of people with therapeutics and interventions. It will begin with projects such as to embed the implementation of familial hypercholesterolemia (FH) services in primary care and reviewing the equity of access to genomic testing.[57] Those involved with the formation of the Service note there will be challenges in the areas of consent, as it is a key requirement, in amongst all the other time pressures and demands placed on them.

> Robust consent pathways need to be drawn up and disseminated with clear guidance on who should and can take consent, and educational initiatives to ensure clinicians taking consent feel equipped to do so. …A workforce shortage already looms in genetic counselling and will need

54 GA4GH, 'Clinical genomics consents' (2022), available at: https://ga4gh.org/document/clinical-genomic-consent-clauses/.

55 ibid.

56 National Health Service (NHS) England, 'NHS Genomics Medicine Service', available at: https://www.england.nhs.uk/genomics/nhs-genomic-med-service/.

57 Julia Robinson, 'Everything you need to know about the NHS Genomic Medicine Service' (2022) 308 Pharmaceutical Journal 7962.

to be addressed by increased training of individuals confident in taking consent and able to train others.[58]

5 Conclusion

The changes in how we study and treat people has moved the way we think about consent in a kind of circle. First, there was a conversation between a clinician and a patient. But then research involving human experimentation expanded hugely and, "…lost its intimate and directly therapeutic nature."[59] Rothman argues that, in the United States after World War II, research moved a "…cottage industry" and "…therapeutic in intent" to one where, "…researchers and subjects were more likely to be strangers to each other, with no necessary sense of shared purpose or objective."[60] This new approach, exemplified by multi-study international research projects, has highlighted this distance between those who will benefit and those who make that benefit possible, together with all of the unknowns between. This has often made it difficult to know what people needed to be told to fully inform them as to what their participation in research might mean. Now the results of some of those research studies are being brought back into the treatment room. Clinical genomics brings the consent conversation back to something more intimate, but it also brings with it the complexities of unknown future outcomes and the stresses that that brings. "Hybrid" consent forms, asking consent for clinical investigations, while also asking for consent for participation in research, are seen as positive way to encourage greater participation in clinical trials,[61] but can also be seen as being unduly coercive[62] and possibly confusing. Added to this is the need to explain the governance mechanisms involved in, for example, data sharing, privacy, confidentiality, legal protections, and ethics review that are put in place to guard against the horrors of the past. As Professor Knoppers said in 2005 and which is still true today, "the increasing complexity of choices

58 Katie Snape, Sarah Wedderburn, and Julian Barwell, 'The new Genomic Medicine Service and implications for patients' (2019) 19 Clinical Medicine 273.

59 Rothman (n 5).

60 ibid.

61 Amina Chaouch and others, 'Informed consent for whole genome sequencing in mainstream clinics: logical constraints and possible solutions' (2024) 32 European Journal of Human Genetics 260.

62 Sandi Dheensa and others, 'Towards a national genomics medicine service: the challenges facing clinical-research hybrid practices and the case of the 100 000 genomes project' (2018) 44 Journal of Medical Ethics 397.

and issues, and the legalistic nature of informed 'choice' and the consent 'process' could undermine the very act of communication and consensualism so necessary to ethically sound research."[63] It is not surprising that while many of us work very hard to write the perfect consent form, studies have shown that people do not read them thoroughly, or if they do, not well enough to properly remember what they read.[64]

Several years ago, a friend rang me one day to say he had been invited to participate in UK Biobank and wanted to know a bit more. At the time I sat on the independent Ethics and Governance Council and so launched into what Biobank was about and especially the safeguards in place to ensure that his data would be protected while being used to advance medical research. He interrupted me at one point and said, "that's all very well and good, but what I want to know is who's running it?" I replied that it had several sponsors, but the major ones were the Wellcome Trust and the Medical Research Council. He said, "that's fine, I don't need to hear anymore, *I trust them*." So he signed up. We need consent forms, information sheets, and the consent discussions. But we also need that trust because the perfect consent form does not exist.

One of the core foundation principles, espoused by Professor Knoppers and drawn from the GA4GH Framework for Responsible Sharing of Genomic and Health-Related Data, is that following best practice will foster trust, integrity, and reciprocity.[65] Materials built on best practice principles can guide and train researchers and clinicians in good consent practice. Then the resulting consent conversation, whether it takes place on-line, on paper, or in person, can provide the information needed to build and support a place of trust, where the patient or participant trusts in the clinicians, researchers, and institutions asking for that consent and can make their decision accordingly. It is by building this trust that clinicians and researchers show their integrity, encouraging reciprocity and participation. It is a virtuous circle, along which the flow of (consented) biomedical research data will continue to be used for the benefit of all.

This concept, "for the benefit of all," and its meaning in the context of consent, consent tools, and Professor Knoppers, can be seen in practical terms. It can mean working internationally sharing with researchers and clinicians

63 Knoppers (n 16).

64 Mary Dixon-Woods and others, 'Beyond "misunderstanding": written information and decisions about taking part in a genetic epidemiology study' (2007) 65 Social Science & Medicine 2212; Simon Paul Jenkins, Melanie J Calvert, and Heather Draper, 'Potential research participants' use of information during the consent process: a qualitative pilot study of patients enrolled in a clinical trial' (2020) 15 PLoS One e0234388.

65 Knoppers (n 11).

across the world tools to support and improve their consent practices. It can also be seen as working in and with many different disciplines (e.g. biobanking, rare disease research, law, clinical practice.) But I have learned that it is more than that and I am grateful for this lesson. "Benefit for all" exemplifies Professor Knoppers' core belief in people and that everyone deserves the best treatment, both as a person and as a patient or participant. This is ethical; this is treating people with dignity. This is Professor Bartha Maria Knoppers.

VIGNETTE

Bartha's True Legacy

Jasper A. Bovenberg

Both rooted in the Netherlands, Bartha and I have a common heritage. Next to a pair of wooden shoes, we have inherited the values, faith, and, above all, the spirit—which liberated our ancestors from tyranny and which is still reflected in the steel glass windows of the Academy Building of Leiden University—of letting your conscience prevail over compliance.

We share certain pleasures as well. Apart from going to the opera, visiting exotic places, and community singing over dinner, writing with Bartha is among the most enjoyable things. Of the various papers I have had the pleasure to co-author with Bartha, one stands out.[1] It is distinguished not because a high-brow journal published it, or because it was the fruit of a five-year research effort. Nor does the paper stand out because it summarized the state of the art in some subspecialist legal domain, or detailed the laws of all the countries involved in an international science consortium (Human Genome Organization, HapMap, Human Cell Atlas). It also doesn't stand out because it proposed a new law (*"Bad cases make bad laws, Jasper"*), suggested a novel IP policy, or cheer-led the next mega project in biomedicine. It did none of the above.

In fact, this joint paper did the opposite. It stood out because we wrote it in one day, and not as legal scholars, but as human beings. We did not defend the right to science, but underscored the sanctity of human life. Rather than deferring to its powers, we humbly acknowledged the limitations of the law. Instead of promoting new policies, we took note of their futility (*"Good intentions pave the way to hell, Jasper"*). And on the back of its potential for good, we pointed at the intrinsic shortcomings of medicine. We submitted in the paper that, in the end, to be truly human, none of us can hide behind laws imposed by others, ethics committee approvals, mandates imposed by governments, or behind product authorizations issued by regulatory agencies. To be truly human, we argued, we cannot have others supplant our personal responsibility and

1 Jasper A Bovenberg and Bartha M Knoppers, 'Embryos, Justice, and Personal Responsibility' (29 November 2018) Project Syndicate, available at: https://www1.project-syndicate.org/commentary/human-embryo-research-ethics-review-committees-by-jasper-a--bovenberg-and-bartha-m-knoppers-2018-11.

 | DOI:10.1163/9789004688544_046

we cannot outsource our moral obligations towards our fellow humans and humanity.

We worryingly live in a time where legal fundamentals, such as informed consent, the sanctity of the human genome, respect for bodily autonomy, freedom of speech and conscience, and the rights of children have been violated. Novel products have been marketed and imposed, on healthy populations, without proper safety checks such as for their genotoxicity and carcinogicity, and without liability, and where millions take to the streets to celebrate their right to choose to kill unborn life. We are also living in a time where a new European regulation proposes to turn Hippocrates' time-tested obligation of medical secrecy upside down, by confiscating personal medical records for use by the state and industry "to boost the data economy." And where the word "dignity" is, literally, struck through in a proposed amendment to the draft WHO pandemic treaty. Precisely in such concerning times, our joint paper still rings true, because it puts first and foremost that all humans, whether citizens, scientists, funders, supervisors, donors, patients, or parents, are, ultimately, personally answerable to his or her moral conscience.

This one paper, "Ethics, Embryo's and Personal Responsibility," showed so well Bartha's true heritage: to protect the human being, not so much in, but rather before law, policy, and medicine.

VIGNETTE

Thoughts about Bartha and Her Work

Eva Winkler

I had the great pleasure of getting to know Bartha in the early days of policy work for Global Alliance for Genomics and Health (GA4GH) and the International Cancer Genome Consortium (ICGC). We had been working on a framework that would enable the responsible sharing of human genomic data. It was very exemplary of the value and type of policy work by Bartha—based on a human rights approach, integrating bioethical principles, and offering both political and legal dimensions. The Framework for Responsible Sharing of Genomic and Health-Related Data, as it became known, would later come to serve as the reference point for all other specific policies in GA4GH, but also a blueprint for genomics projects around the world.

Bartha has pioneered this new way of policy work and research—generating *consensus* around genomics health policy with representatives from a wide array of different countries and cultures. Certainly, it takes more than the legal and genomics expertise to be successful in this endeavour; it is above all a testament to her charming way of bringing people together and listening to their diverse arguments and viewpoints that makes consensus building from such different countries and cultures possible. However, this would still not be enough. The third gift is her concise and stringent way of moderating a working group so that a policy is ultimately created. And not only that, but that it will then be published and accessible to scientists as a multi-authored paper. At first it just sounds like a lot of work, deliberation, and persuasion, but it is also an art—perhaps that of the wise statesperson!

I have also come to personally appreciate Bartha's wisdom—for example, that it is a blessing to have animal companions in the house when the children grow up and need some distance from their parents. You can also discuss opera and concert halls with her and learn how to keep life manageable with long-distance flights. Her broad interests and curiosity make her a dear colleague way beyond her professional life.

Her mission, in GA4GH, ICGC, and so many other endeavours, "enabling research in a responsible way," was not aspirational only. Rather, Bartha's work has also made this a reality for many important research initiatives and research oversight internationally.

At a time when problems are becoming increasingly complex and interconnected, science needs to better explain itself and make it clear that it is working to solve these problems for the benefit of people—for this, the work on trustworthy governance and oversight cannot be overestimated.

CHAPTER 16

Securing the "Human" in the Generalization of Risk Stratification Algorithms through the Human Right to Science

Calvin Wai-Loon Ho

1 Introduction

The human right "to share in scientific advancement and its benefits" in Article 27(1) of the Universal Declaration of Human Rights (UDHR) is premised on the belief that science should be an institutionalized and public enterprise.[1] It is less clear what public good(s) should be advanced by science, even as adverse effects stemming from scientific advancement became all too apparent at the end of the Second World War. Since that time, the relationship between the human institution of law and science has been at times tense, often varied and increasingly complex. Perhaps owing to the instrumentalization of science for commercial and political ends typically through legal mechanisms and processes, legal interventions are generally unwelcome by researchers, or are at best tolerated. In more recent history, earlier concerns among researchers over the potentially stifling effect of ethical governance (and related regulatory provisions) of research involving human participants is illustrative.[2] Some time ago, John Dewey reminded us that science and its application in technology represent human attempts to grapple with problems that range from simple to super-wicked.[3] More crucially, science and technology are forms of human inquiry that need democracy to thrive.

Over the past three decades, the scholarship of Professor Bartha Maria Knoppers has bridged the epistemic divide between law and science through the explication of what a democratic environment should look like from a human rights perspective. She was among the first thought leaders to identify

1 Audrey R Chapman, 'Towards an understanding of the right to enjoy the benefits of scientific progress and its applications' (2009) 8 Journal of Human Rights 1.

2 George Silberman and Katherine L Kahn, 'Burdens on research imposed by institutional review boards: the state of the evidence and its implications for regulatory reform' (2011) 89 The Milbank Quarterly 599.

3 John Dewey, 'Science and Society' in Jo Ann Boydston (ed), *John Dewey: The Later Works, 1925–1953* (Southern Illinois University Press 1985).

DOI:10.1163/9789004688544_048

complementarity between genomic science and human rights, particularly with public- or social goods-focused human rights and "solidarity rights" that include the recognition of the human genome (at the species level) as the common heritage of humankind.[4] The cosmopolitan comparative law methodology that she led in development has become a mainstream mode of academic and policy inquiry.[5] Not surprisingly, she has steered the development of science policies across the globe through leadership roles in leading scientific research enterprises and through advisory roles to policymakers in Canada, Singapore, and elsewhere. For her tireless advocacy for science as a shared human enterprise and for clarity of laws and policies to support its development, Professor Knoppers has received many accolades, including the Lifetime Achievement Award from the Canadian Bioethics Society in May 2021.[6] To state the obvious, it is well beyond the scope of this chapter to fully recognize the immense intellectual and policy legacies of Professor Knoppers. My project here is more modest. I seek only to show how she has made a distinct contribution to the rejuvenation of academic and policy interest in the human right to science (HRS) and inspired a new generation of scholars across different disciplines.

In the section that follows, I first explain the core obligations of the HRS and how Professor Knoppers' scholarship has helped to implement it in the context of biomedical research. I draw on discussions during a workshop Professor Knoppers co-organized at the Brocher Foundation in November 2022,[7] and my publication that followed as an output from that meeting.[8] I also show how Professor Knoppers has applied the HRS to her policy work on data governance, which demonstrates how a rights-based approach could anchor scientific research as a fundamentally human-centred and public-spirited endeavour. Following this, I then consider how Professor Knoppers and her colleagues have applied the HRS to identify normative and regulatory

4 Bartha Maria Knoppers, *Human Dignity and Genetic Heritage: A Study Paper prepared for the Law Reform Commission of Canada* (Law Reform Commission of Canada 1991), available at: http://www.lareau-legal.ca/Human.pdf.

5 Rosario M Isasi and Bartha Maria Knoppers, 'Mind the gap: policy approaches to embryonic stem cell and cloning research in 50 years' (2006) 13 European Journal of Health Law 9.

6 Faculty of Medicine and Health Sciences, 'Bartha Maria Knoppers receives Lifetime Achievement Award' (McGill University, 9 June 2021), available at: https://healthenews.mcgill.ca/bartha-maria-knoppers-receives-lifetime-achievement-award/.

7 Fondation Brocher, 'November 29 – December 1, 2022, Brocher Workshop on the Human Right to Science with a focus on Health', available at: https://www.brocher.ch/en/events/423/expert-workshop-on-the-right-to-science/.

8 Calvin WL Ho, 'Implementing the human right to science in the regulatory governance of artificial intelligence in healthcare' (2023) 10 Journal of Law and the Biosciences lsad026.

challenges in the use of artificial intelligence (AI) or machine learning (ML) software to generate polygenic risk scores (PRS, to be explained below). In the penultimate section of the chapter, I focus on a specific concern emerging in the regulation of PRS software (PRSS) as a medical device, and explain what characteristics and features regulators and regulatory interventions should have within a rights-based paradigm.

2 Human Right to Science

Although the HRS is recognized in Article 27 of the UDHR,[9] and Article 15 of the International Covenant on Economic, Social and Cultural Rights (ICESCR),[10] its substantive content and relevance to practical challenges have been relatively obscure compared to other human rights, like the right to health. It was not until 2009 that an expert statement on the HRS was published by UNESCO.[11] Among the different actions that were taken by UN bodies to explain the HRS from that time, it is the General Comment of the Committee on Economic, Social and Cultural Rights of the United Nations (UNCESCR) that now provides the most comprehensive official account of the HRS. Established in 1985 to implement the ICESCR, general comments of the UNCESCR are regarded as the official interpretation of the UN on the nature of economic, social, and cultural rights (ESCR) and their justiciability in terms of the principles, standards, and procedural rules that apply.[12] For the purposes of this chapter, the UNCESCR's articulation of the core (or minimum) content of the HRS and the core (or minimum) obligations of states in this connection is most pertinent.[13]

9 United Nations (General Assembly), Universal declaration of human rights (217 [III] A). Paris (1948), available at: https://www.un.org/en/about-us/universal-declaration-of-human-rights.

10 United Nations (General Assembly), International Covenant on Economic, Social, and Cultural Rights, Treaty Series 999 (December): 171 (1966), available at: https://www.refworld.org/docid/3ae6b36c0.html.

11 United Nations Educational, Scientific and Cultural Organizations (UNESCO), *The Right to Enjoy the Benefits of Scientific Progress and its Applications* (UNESCO 2009).

12 Helen Keller and Leena Grover, 'General Comments of the Human Rights Committee and Their Legitimacy' in Helen Keller and Geir Ulfstein (eds), *UN Human Rights Treaty Bodies: Law and Legitimacy* (Cambridge University Press 2012).

13 Committee on Economic, Social and Cultural Rights of the United Nations Economic and Social Council, *General comment No. 25 (2020) on science and economic, social and cultural rights (article 15(1)(b), (2), (3) and (4) of the International Covenant on Economic, Social and Cultural Rights)*, E/C.12/GC25, 30 April 2020, available at: https://tbinternet

As it explains, the following features must be present in order for the HRS to enable everyone to: (i) enjoy the benefits of scientific progress and it application; (ii) participate in science as part of cultural (or creative) life (hence inclusive of "citizen science"); (iii) benefit from the protection of the moral and material interests resulting from any scientific, literary, or artistic production for the inventor or author; (iv) enjoy freedom indispensable for scientific research and creative activity; and (v) take steps for the conservation, development, and diffusion of science.

Professor Knoppers has been instrumental in explaining what the HRS means for emerging medical technologies and how it applies to their development. As she and her collaborators explain, the HRS has at least three essential rights in implementation: first, the right of everyone to benefit from and contribute to scientific and technological progress (or the HRS in the public interest sense); second, the right of scientists, for instance, to do research and push forward science and technology (or the HRS in a technical sense); and third, countries' duty to provide an enabling environment (or the HRS in a governance sense).[14] The "benefits" to which the HRS relates is not limited to the material results of scientific research (e.g. a medical device) or to the data and scientific knowledge derived from the research, but also to the role of science in forming critical and responsible citizens who are able to participate fully in a democratic society.[15] As a cultural phenomenon, science presents a reality that is based on what it defines as rational and natural. Its values are reflected in what a society recognizes as fact and how members of a society understand themselves to be human. The effects of science on human life and social relations are thereby vast and profound, but its epistemic authority is neither absolute nor unconditional. To benefit from science, society and its constituents must be willing to defer to the various forms of expertise that give expression to scientific knowledge (e.g. in technology and in medicine). From this vantage point, the HRS is concerned with governing science as a form of power that shapes behaviour and influences choice.

.ohchr.org/_layouts/15/treatybodyexternal/Download.aspx?symbolno=E%2fC.12%2fGC%2f25&Lang=en.

14 Rumiana Yotova and Bartha Maria Knoppers, 'The right to benefit from science and its implications for genomic data sharing' (2020) 31 European Journal of International Law 665.

15 Article 27 of the Universal Declaration of Human Rights is noted to be especially relevant as it articulates the right of all individuals to freely participate in the cultural life of the community, to enjoy the arts and to share in scientific advancement and its benefits. United Nations (n 9), paragraphs 3 and 10.

A prominent theme that runs across Professor Knoppers' oeuvre is the core content and obligations of the HRS in its governance sense, or what has been described as the "right for people to have a legislative and policy framework adopted and implemented which aims at making the benefits of scientific progress available and accessible—both through encouraging new scientific discoveries and through removing barriers for existing scientific knowledge to be used for public benefit."[16] In this connection, the UNCESCR indicates that states have to implement, as a matter of priority, core obligations that include:[17] (a) developing a participatory national framework law on the HRS (with specification of legal remedies in case of violations) and implementing a participatory national strategy or action plan for the realization of the HRS; (b) ensuring access to those applications of scientific progress that are critical to the enjoyment of the right to health and other ESCR; (c) ensuring that (in allocation of public resources) priority is given to research in areas where there is the greatest need for scientific progress in health and the well-being of the population, especially with regards to vulnerable and marginalized groups; (d) ensuing that health professionals are properly trained in using and applying modern technologies resulting from scientific progress; and (e) fostering the development of international contacts and cooperation in the scientific field. While every reasonable effort must be made to implement the core obligations of the HRS using the maximum of its available resources (individually and through international assistance and cooperation), the UNCESCR reminds all states that they are also to take into account the *totality of the rights* enshrined in the ICESCR.[18] The right to participate in and to enjoy the benefits of scientific progress in the HRS may constitute an essential tool for the realization of other ESCR.[19]

The UNCESCR emphasizes progressive realization of ESCR by linking immediate measures with prospective ones.[20] For medical technologies in general,

16 Leslie London, Helen Cox, and Fons Coomans, 'Multidrug-resistant TB: implementing the right to health through the right to enjoy the benefits of scientific progress' (2016) 18 Health and Human Rights 25, 28. The United Nations Human Rights Office of the High Commissioner (UNHRC) explains this as "an environment that promotes the conservation, development and diffusion of science and technology, and the freedom indispensable for scientific research". See UNHRC, 'The right to benefit from scientific progress and its applications', available at: https://www.ohchr.org/en/special-procedures/sr-cultural-rights/right-benefit-scientific-progress-and-its-applications.

17 Committee on Economic, Social and Cultural Rights of the United Nations Economic and Social Council (n 13), adapted from paragraph 52.

18 ibid., [51].

19 ibid., [63].

20 ibid., [67–76].

states have a duty to make available and accessible to all persons (and especially to the most vulnerable) all the best available applications of scientific progress necessary to enjoy the highest attainable standard of health.[21] It follows that medical devices that are safe and effective should be prioritized in national health plans in order to make the best use of available resources for the fulfilment of ESCRs. There is also an obligation for states to promote scientific research, to create new medical applications, and make them accessible and affordable to everyone, especially the most vulnerable.[22] Where some scientific research presents health-related risks, states are required to mitigate these risks through careful application of the precautionary principle and the protection of participants in scientific research. More specifically, states should make every effort to ensure that "medical treatments ... are evidence-based, and that the risks involved have been properly evaluated and communicated in a clear and transparent manner, so that patients can provide properly informed consent."[23]

Here, Professor Knoppers and her colleagues crucially highlighted that while informed consent requirements are important, scientific research could be impeded if access to research materials and data are limited or altogether precluded. By linking the HRS with the right to health, states should ensure that all individuals are supported through clear laws and policies to engage constructively with the epistemic resources of science in order to attain the health goals that they value as socially embedded members of a community. Requirements such as informed consent should not be rigidly applied but must be responsive to wider communal needs as the ends should neither be simply technological advancement nor purely a health indicator. Often, the lack of clarity in laws and policies result in misalignment of values and interests that ultimately detract from ends that benefit persons and their communities. This also means that laws and policies must be refined over time through democratic processes, which in turn reflects the progressive realization of the ideals of both rights.

In this vein, Professor Knoppers and colleagues explain how a robust governance regime composed of laws and regulations that are (ideally) clear and responsive can help to anticipate harms and balance different (and at times competing) normative commitments. These commitments include the right of individuals to be informed of their involvement in research, to be protected from potential harm and to benefit, and the freedom of researchers to carry

21 ibid., [70].
22 ibid., [67].
23 ibid., [71].

out scientific activities for the common good and to be recognized for their endeavours. Ultimately, scientifically informed limits that state parties impose can never be pre-emptive of science, since these limits must be balanced against the freedom of scientists to conduct research and to benefit from their research, as well as general welfare in a democratic society.[24]

Inspired by Professor Knoppers, a group of scholars applied the HRS-approach to compare regulations in 18 jurisdictions governing the use of CRISPR in human germline engineering compared to the HRS.[25] To meet the standards and obligations of the HRS, state parties must, among other things, respect the freedom of scientists that is indispensable for scientific research and help to realize the right of everyone to benefit from scientific and technological progress. The essence of this comparative work is clearly and succinctly set out by Professor Knoppers with the editors of the edited monograph in an article published in a journal that is dedicated to the gene-editing technology:

> Scientific *freedom* and the right to benefit from *scientific* and technological progress are not absolute rights and can be restricted. However, states that intend to do so must conform with the conditions set by Article 4 of the ICESCR, according to which restrictions must be determined "by law," by "compatible with the nature of these rights," and "solely [intended] to promote the general welfare in a democratic society."... In our judgment, vagueness and obsolescence make many regulatory frameworks fail to meet the requirements set by Article 4 of the ICESCR. We believe that in regulating heritable gene editing, legislative measures must guarantee, as a default, scientists' freedom to use CRISPR, any other gene-editing tools that might be invented in the future, to create and modify human gametes and embryos, and identify reasonable opportunities for translational pathways of therapies to cure heritable genetic disorders. Limitations must be spelled out in statutory and regulatory instruments that are sufficiently clear to allow scientists to regulate their conduct based on those provisions. Obsolescence raises issues of whether restrictions are truly aimed to protect the "general welfare in a democratic society," considering they were envisioned, debated, and democratically adopted before the CRISPR revolution, that is, before we possessed the actual

---

24 Andrea Boggio and others, 'The human right to science and the regulation of human germline engineering' (2019) 2 The CRISPR Journal 134, 136.

25 Andrea Boggio, Jessica Almqvist, and Cesare PR Romano (eds), *Human Germline Genome Modification and the Right to Science: A Comparative Study of National Laws and Policies* (Cambridge University Press 2020).

> technological capacity to engage in germline engineering. At a minimum, the restrictions on basic research on germline cells must be revisited through engaging democratic debates of some form (legislative debates, public discussions, expert consultations, referenda) considering the state of evolving technology.[26]

With focus on policy application, a blueprint has been proposed in the form of a rights-based international code of conduct for genomic and clinical data sharing.[27] As the authors explain, sharing genomic and clinical data is essential for more accurate disease classification based on molecular profiles to enable tailored effective treatments, interventions, and models for prevention, and to realize the promises of precision medicine more broadly. While the need for data sharing is clear, they observe that current data sharing models and policies are not working as effectively as once anticipated. Obstacles include lack of policy harmonization, lack of structural support, legal and ethical hurdles, and different cultural and behavioural impediments. The proposed new rights-based framework seeks to overcome these challenges by embedding science in social and political life through implementing a co-regulatory system that builds synergy across the self-regulatory codes of ethics of genomic researchers and clinicians, and to foster responsible genomic research by offering stronger protection in the three critical areas of privacy, anti-discrimination and fair access, and procedural fairness. Human rights commitments serve to reinforce the durable and communal features of ethical codes that apply to clinicians and researchers, while forging a common purpose across them.

Perhaps even more crucially, Professor Knoppers and colleagues make explicit that significant investment of policy attention and resources is necessary to establish a governance regime that is not only clear as to its normative and regulatory requirements, but also responsive to the needs of a diverse range of stakeholders, including researchers.[28] One of the most important contributions in this connection has been through the Global Alliance for Genomics and Health (GA4GH), of which Professor Knoppers was the Co-Chair of its Regulatory and Ethics Working Group (and then later called the Work Stream) from 2013 to 2019. She co-authored the Framework for Responsible Sharing of Genomic and Health Related Data, a guidance document that underlies one of (if not the) largest not-for-profit alliances that is dedicated to advance human

26 Boggio and others (n 24), 139–140.

27 Bartha M Knoppers and others, 'A human rights approach to an international code of conduct for genomic and clinical data sharing' (2014) 133 Human Genetics 895.

28 Bartha Maria Knoppers, 'Does policy grow on trees?' (2014) 15 BMC Medical Ethics 87.

health through genomic data. This framework, along with accompanying policies on consent, privacy and security, accountability, ethics review recognition, and a data sharing lexicon, draw on the HRS to help realize the vision of facilitating data sharing in data intensive research to advance the common good.[29] The GA4GH's Accountability Policy, for instance, sets out a compliance mechanism that enables collective monitoring of data as a safeguard against misuse and responses that may be taken should this arise. It encourages all stakeholders with research data repositories to design governance regimes with consent mechanisms that allow data sharing, and recommends transparent policies and efficient processes to ensure the timely availability and quality of data. An overarching goal is to sustain trust among data providers, processors, and users that is ultimately linked to the right of all individuals to benefit from science. The crucial message bears repetition here. The HRS mandates states and non-state actors to establish a robust governance regime capable of mitigating risks and balancing the interests between the need for privacy on the part of individuals and the need for access to genetic and clinical data on the part of researchers.[30]

As richer genomic and health data in certain populations become available, there is growing interest among affected individuals, researchers, and healthcare providers in the potential use of such data to predict the likelihood of developing a specific condition or disease based on one's genetic makeup. One such tool that has been developed with the goal of preventing and more effectively treating serious diseases is PRS (to be explained in the next section). To enhance the accuracy and reliability of PRS, researchers are starting to use AI and ML techniques to generate PRS. To the best of my knowledge, Professor Knoppers and her colleagues are among first law and bioethics scholars to examine normative and regulatory challenges that are likely to arise in the confluence of PRS with AI or ML. In the sections that follow, I first illustrate how Professor Knoppers and her colleagues have applied HRS to identify normative and regulatory challenges in facilitating the development of AI/ML-based PRS software as a beneficial biomedical tool. I then focus on a specific concern that was raised in the regulation of such PRS software as a medical device, and

29 Bartha Maria Knoppers and Adrian Mark Thorogood, 'Ethics and Big Data in health' (2017) 4 Current Opinion in Systems Biology 53.

30 A similar message underscores the recommendations of the OECD on health data governance, in respect of which Professor Knoppers was a member of the drafting group. See OECD, Recommendation of the Council on Health Data Governance, OECD/LEGAL/0433 adopted on 13 December 2016, available at: https://legalinstruments.oecd.org/en/instruments/OECD-LEGAL-0433.

explain what characteristics and features regulators and regulatory interventions should have in order to be consistent with the HRS.

3 AI-Generated Polygenic Risk Scores

Risk stratification in healthcare and public health is expected to become more fine-grained as it increasingly leverages genetic and other data sources. The ability to better detect and predict disease progression could have a large impact on screening programs, even for monogenic variants like BRCA, where variant in a single gene has a very significant effect on that individual's predisposition to breast cancer. Here, Professor Knoppers and colleagues observe that mammographic breast screening programs for the general population are still mainly based on age (typically between 40 to 74 years) and conducted at different frequencies (e.g. every two years in the state of Victoria in Australia). This age-based approach does not take into account the heterogeneity of breast cancer subtypes, biological behaviour, and risk in the population, and would potentially miss fast growing tumours. As the data environment gains in breadth and depth over time, the ability to identify subgroups of individuals likely to have progressive tumours and to target screening to them, or to tailor the screening frequency and age based on their risk score could improve the efficiency of screening programs and reduce adverse consequences like unnecessary investigation, overdiagnosis, and overtreatment. Additionally, the ability to combine whole-genome sequencing (WGS) results with real-world clinical and socio-demographic data could enhance the prognostic value of ongoing risk stratification and classification for the screening and prevention of a range of illnesses, including cancer.

Unlike breast cancer, many diseases that we know of are polygenic disorders, which are caused by many genetic variants located throughout the whole genome, and by environmental and lifestyle factors. Related developments in large-scale research into small genetic variations (referred to as single nucleotide polymorphisms or SNPs) like genome-wide association studies (GWAS) show that most non-communicable disorders have a genetic component composed of a large number of genetic variants that each has a small effect on the disease risk.[31] It is against this technological backdrop that polygenic scores have emerged as a promising tool to support personalized risk level assessment. A polygenic score provides a single measure of the cumulative effect of

31 Cathryn M Lewis and Evangelos Vassos, 'Polygenic risk scores: From research tools to clinical instruments' (2020) 12 Genome Medicine 44.

multiple individually low-impact genetic changes, while a PRS is a weighted sum of several of the risk variants for a particular disease, and provides an estimate of that individual's genetic vulnerability to a trait or disease.[32] It is a tool that allows risk stratification based on variations in the individual's genotype profile in comparison with the relevant GWAS data.

A polygenic score is typically calculated based on input data and human-initiated methodologies that rely on clinical judgement to assess health risk, and could in principle be generated for any disease. More recently, ML techniques are being applied by multivariate algorithms to generate PRS using genetic and other health data from electronic health records. At the time of writing, the use of PRS has been most widely discussed in relation to cancer and coronary artery disease. The need for caution over how PRS is used in healthcare,[33] as well as its wider ethical and social implications,[34] have also been prominently featured. A concern, highlighted earlier on by Professor Knoppers and colleagues, relates to the seemingly intransigent obstacle of bias. If insufficient input data are available for individuals of an ancestry group, a risk stratification algorithm is likely to be less effective for that group than for the larger population. Some workarounds have been proposed to enable risk stratification algorithms to produce more accurate risk-estimates for a given population. These include the creation of separate PRS algorithms or risk stratification methodologies for individuals from distinct genetic ancestry groups, and the creation of a singular algorithm trained on holistic training data that are representative of diversity in genetic ancestry. Nevertheless, the variants that are currently used in generating PRS are established in GWAS, where over 95% of participants are European.[35] Consequently, PRS cannot be expected to have predictive accuracy when applied to people with non-European ancestry or to minority ethnic groups.

From a regulatory viewpoint, Professor Knoppers and colleagues invite us to consider if algorithms used to generate PRS should be regulated as a medical device in order to help ensure safety and effectiveness on the one hand, and facilitate the development of a rich and diverse data environment on the

32 Sowmiya Moorthie, Colin Mitchell, and Ofori Canacoo, 'Regulating polygenic score devices and tests' (PHG Foundation 2023), available at: https://www.phgfoundation.org/wp-content/uploads/2023/11/4-Regulating-polygenic-score-tests-and-devices.pdf.

33 Amit Sud and others, 'Realistic expectations are key to realising the benefits of polygenic scores' (2023) 380 The BMJ e073149.

34 Marie-Christine Fritzsche and others, 'Ethical layering in AI-driven polygenic risk scores – New complexities, new challenges' (2023) 14 Frontiers in Genetics 1098439.

35 Alicia R Martin and others, 'Clinical use of current polygenic risk scores may exacerbate health disparities' (2019) 51 Nature Genetics 583.

other. They caution that regulating PRS algorithms as a medical device would undermine the common good as it "impose[s] timelines, costs, and stringent and formal requirements concerning the clinical evaluation and safety and performance certifications on the manufacturer for the PRS to be placed in the market."[36] Two key challenges are highlighted in regulating PRS algorithms as medical devices.

First, PRS regulation as a medical device can cause uncertain, complicated, and/or costly collaboration or intellectual property development. While PRS could have a role in treatment response and in refining the penetrance of high-risk variants, the clinical utility of PRS is yet to be established.[37] For PRS to be used for individual diagnosis, prediction, and stratification, relative risks will need to be transformed to absolute risks. Due to limited diversity in GWAS data, current PRS has limited clinical applicability to minority ethnic groups and to non-European populations.[38] Improving the scientific validity, clinical utility, and clinical validity of PRS will require diverse genetic ancestry reflected in datasets used to generate PRS. Uncertain or burdensome regulatory frameworks may discourage collaboration, while increased regulatory hurdles could limit open and broad sharing of data associated with PRS and prompt proprietary attachment to PRS methodology and knowledge. Additionally, Professor Knoppers and her colleagues indicate that regulation may not be sufficiently responsive to dynamic changes in the risk profile of individuals, which depends on and changes with factors like age, environmental exposures, and illnesses. Should regulation be introduced, it will need to be sufficiently flexible for risk scores and methodology and calculations to adapt to the changes in order to provide an accurate risk assessment without having to obtain regulatory authorization. The conventional approach to medical device regulation does not offer this kind of flexibility.

Second, delaying PRS availability and limiting patient access to the technology may not be ethically defensible. Risk prediction models that incorporate PRS could potentially lead to better health outcomes by encouraging affected individuals to make simple changes in their lifestyles (see e.g. CanRisk).[39]

36 Bartha Maria Knoppers and others, 'Of screening, stratification, and scores' 11 (2021) 11 Journal of Personalized Medicine 736, 7.

37 Sud and others (n 33). See also Niall J Lennon and others, 'Selection, optimization and validation of ten chronic disease polygenic risk scores for clinical implementation in diverse US populations' (2024) 30 Nature Medicine 480

38 ibid.

39 Stephanie Archer and others, 'Exploring the barriers to and facilitators of implementing CanRisk in primary care: a qualitative thematic framework analysis' (2023) 73 The British Journal of General Practice e586.

Professor Knoppers and colleagues indicate that having access to such predictive models could potentially be beneficial if applied to a range of chronic conditions, but with the lack of diversity in datasets, ethnic minorities or under-represented populations are unlikely to benefit, and could even be harmed, from the utilization of such models.

In the section that follows, I illustrate how recent regulatory developments that apply to PRSS, like CanRisk, are broadly consistent with the foundational elements of the HRS as explicated by Professor Knoppers and her colleagues. Through legal regimes that regulate PRSS as a medical device, clear rules and policies enable patients to benefit (through participation) from constructive engagement with the epistemic resources of science, while enabling researchers to advance scientific knowledge. Through regulatory mechanisms that apply total product lifecycle supervision, device traceability, and transparency in surveillance (to be explained below), requirements like informed consent and safety of users are rendered more responsive to wider societal needs, including those of the scientific community. However, the risk-based approach adopted by these regimes do not adequately address machine- or deep-learning capability that a PRSS may have (also explained below) and other challenges associated with PRS that have been considered earlier. It is well beyond the scope of this chapter to explain how the HRS could help to address these challenges. The aim here is instead to show why the work of Professor Knoppers and her colleagues is groundbreaking in explaining how laws and policies should and could be refined over time through democratic processes, which in turn reflects the progressive realization of the HRS and other ESCR.

4 HRS Approach to Medical Device Regulation

The definition of medical device in most (if not all) jurisdictions is based on that developed by the Global Harmonization Task Force (GHTF), which states as follows:

> 'Medical device' means any instrument, apparatus, implement, machine, appliance, implant, reagent for in vitro use, software, material or other similar or related article, intended by the manufacturer to be used, alone or in combination, for human beings, for one or more of the specific medical purpose(s) of: diagnosis, prevention, monitoring, treatment or alleviation of disease,
>
> – diagnose, monitoring, treatment, alleviation of or compensation for an injury,

> – investigation, replacement, modification, or support of the anatomy or of a physiological process,
> – supporting or sustaining life,
> – control of conception,
> – disinfection of medical devices,
> – providing information by means of in vitro examination of specimens derived from the human body;
>
> and does not achieve its primary intended action by pharmacological, immunological or metabolic means, in or on the human body, but which may be assisted in its intended function by such means.[40]

It follows from this broad definition that a medical device may be classified as such based on its intended use and indications for use, degree of invasiveness, duration of use, and the risks and potential harms associated with their use. The classification system for medical devices developed by the GHTF is broadly risk-based in that only the potential harm to a patient or user (i.e. hazard) is reflected in the classification rules, but not the probability of harm.[41] The hazard presented by a medical device largely depends on its intended use and the technology it uses. In this respect, the classification rules consider whether the device: is life supporting or sustaining; is invasive and if so, to what extent and for how long; incorporates medicinal products, or human/animal tissues/cells; is an active medical device; delivers medicinal products, energy or radiation; could modify blood or other body fluids; is used in combination with another medical device.[42] By this approach, the risk profile of the device is regarded as quantifiable and relatively static, in the sense that its functions are stable and the outcomes are relatively clear and predictable for the indicated uses. A regulatory authority may take into account the probability that harm will occur by modifying the evidence requirements at the conformity assessment stage. In this connection, the regulator may consider the maturity of the technology, the number of adverse event reports for the device type, the length of experience that the manufacturer has with the device and the technology it embodies, and if the device user is a lay person.

40 Global Harmonization Task Force, *Definitions of the Terms 'Medical Device' and 'In Vitro Diagnostic* (IVD) *Medical Device'*, GHTF/SG1/N071:2012, 16 May 2012, Section 5.1. A definition is also provided for in vitro medical device (IVMD) which is intended for the in vitro examination of specimens derived from the human body. This type of device is not considered in this chapter as it is not relevant to PRS algorithms.

41 Global Harmonization Task Force, Principles of Medical Devices Classification (Revision of GHTF/SG1/N15:2006), 2 November 2012, GHTF/SG1/N77:2012.

42 ibid [5].

Under the GHTF's classification system, every medical device is assigned to one of four groups or classes. A device that is of low hazard (e.g. bandage) is classified as Class A. Since the extent of regulatory oversight is proportionate to the potential hazard that the device could cause, a Class A device is only subject to minimal regulatory requirements, if any. A Class B device (e.g. suction equipment) is of low to moderate level of hazard, and is subject to more regulatory control for assurance of safety and effectiveness. Moderate-to-high hazard device in Class C (e.g. lung ventilator) and high hazard device in Class D (e.g. heart valves) are subject to stringent regulatory scrutiny and oversight, and will generally require some proof of safety and effectiveness prior to market access. It is worth noting here that the GHTF indicates that regulatory requirements should not place "an unwarranted increase in the cost of regulatory compliance for either the manufacturer or … [Regulatory Authority], or delay market entry."[43] The types of regulatory control are specified by the GHTF in a separate document on conformity assessment as including the requirement for a manufacturer to apply an independently audited management system to the design and development process as well as to manufacturing; review by a regulatory authority or conformity assessment board of the manufacturer's summary technical documentation (e.g. clinical evidence) to verify conformity to all relevant essential principles prior to the device being placed on the market; and the manufacturer to undertake post-market evaluation and testing of marketed devices.[44]

The risk-based approach satisfies all three of the constituent rights under the HRS that Professor Knoppers and colleagues have identified.[45] It enables patients to benefit from and (through participation in clinical trials) contribute to scientific and technological progress. It also allows researchers and device developers to push the technology forward, and in grounding an enabling environment by, for instance, helping to align the expectations of developers and users. However, the risk-based classification scheme devised for medical devices is unlikely to adequately accommodate an adaptive PRSS using machine/deep learning. The IMDRF categorizes PRSS as an instance of software as a medical device (SaMD), which it defines as "software intended to be used for one or more medical purposes that perform these purposes

43 ibid.

44 Global Harmonization Task Force, Principles of Conformity Assessment for Medical Devices, 26 June 2006, GHTF/SG1/N40:2006.

45 Yotova and Knoppers (n 14); Boggio and others (n 24).

without being part of a hardware medical device."[46] It recognizes the complex clinical use environment that SaMD may be applied within and can raise or lower the potential to create situations hazardous to patients. Conditions that contribute to the complexity ranges from those that relate to the patient (e.g. disease progression), those arising from clinical care (e.g. clinical model applied to derive the output information and the level of clinical evidence available), and those that arise from the operation of the device (e.g. technological characteristics of the platform the software are intended to operate on), among others. Focused on intended use of SaMD to achieve particular clinical outcomes, risk characterization is abstracted to two factors:[47] (1) significance of the information provided by the SaMD to the healthcare decision; and (2) state of the healthcare situation or condition. Important considerations that do not influence the determination of the risk category of the SaMD (e.g. transparency of the inputs used, technological characteristics used by the SaMD, and more upstream considerations) are not included in this risk categorization framework. The intended use of the SaMD in clinical care may be significant in one of three ways: (i) to treat or to diagnose; (ii) to drive clinical management; or (iii) to inform clinical management.

The significance of an intended use is then associated with a healthcare situation or condition, that may be one of three states: (1) critical situation or condition; (2) serious situation or condition; and (3) non-serious situation or condition. As IMDRF also explains, every SaMD will have its own risk category according to its definition statement, even when it is interfaced with other SaMD, other hardware medical devices, or used as a module in a larger system.[48] Risk categorization thereby relies on "accurate and complete" SaMD definition statement from the manufacturer in the determination of the risk category by associating the significance of the information provided by the SaMD to the healthcare decision and the healthcare situation or condition.[49] These categories are in relative significance to each other, with the highest category being applicable to SaMD used across multiple healthcare situations or conditions. Put simply, the main components of risk for SaMD is its function

---

46 International Medical Device Regulators Forum, *Software as a Medical Device (SaMD): Key Definitions*, available at: https://www.imdrf.org/documents/software-medical-device-samd-key-definitions.

47 International Medical Device Regulators Forum (IMDRF), *"Software as a Medical Device": Possible Framework for Risk Categorization and Corresponding Considerations, IMDRF/SaMD WG/N12FINAL:2014*, paragraph 4, available at: http://www.imdrf.org/docs/imdrf/final/technical/imdrf-tech-140918-samd-framework-risk-categorization-141013.pdf.

48 ibid., 13–14, [7.1].

49 ibid.

and the severity of the disease. Consequently, a PRSS could be designated as high risk (i.e. categories III and IV in the IMDRF's 2014 guidance document) *if* it provides information used to diagnose or treat a disease *and if* the healthcare situation is serious or critical. By this rationale, a lower risk classification could apply to a PRSS if it is applied in a clinically safe context whereby the health-care situation would not be regarded as hazardous. The definition of SaMD has been adopted by all major scientific jurisdictions, along with characteristics that delineate a SaMD and the regulatory implications that follow. In Australia, for instance, the Therapeutic Goods Administration, which regulates medical devices, has issued new classificatory rules for SaMD that: (i) provide a diagnosis or screen for a disease or condition; (ii) monitor the state or progression of a disease or condition, or the parameters of a person with a disease or condition; (iii) specify or recommend a treatment or intervention; or (iv) provide therapy through the provision of information.[50]

Innovative regulatory changes followed in major scientific jurisdictions with the introduction of SaMD as a new regulated entity. I focus on three that are most pertinent to the HRS. First, regulatory responsiveness to change over the total product lifecycle is introduced. The regulatory principles proposed by the IMDRF sustain a risk-based approach but a total product/device lifecycle approach is now applied. This better accounts for device modifications through real-world learning and adaptation. Importantly, manufacturers are expected to have an appropriate level of control to manage changes during the lifecycle of the SaMD. IMDRF labels any modifications made throughout the lifecycle of the SaMD, including its maintenance phase, as "SaMD Changes."[51] Software maintenance is in turn defined in terms of four types of post-marketing modifications that could occur in the software lifecycle processes identified by the International Organization for Standardization,[52] namely:[53] (i) adaptive maintenance (modification performed to keep the software product usable in a changed or changing environment); (ii) perfective maintenance (modification to detect and correct latent faults in the software product before they are manifested as failures); (iii) corrective maintenance (reactive modification of a software product performed after delivery to correct discovered problems);

50 Therapeutic Goods Administration, Department of Health of the Australian Government, *Regulatory changes for software based medical devices*, Version 1.2, August 2021, available at: https://www.tga.gov.au/sites/default/files/regulatory-changes-software-based-medical-devices.pdf.

51 IMDRF (n 47) 22–23, [8.2].

52 International Organization of Standards, ISO/IEC 14764:2006 Software Engineering – Software Life Cycle Processes – Maintenance (2nd edn 2006).

53 IMDRF (n 47), 22.

and (iv) preventive maintenance (modification of a software product after delivery to detect and correct latent faults in the software product before they become operational faults).

When a manufacturer makes changes to SaMD that results in the change of the definition statement, the categorization of SaMD will need to be re-evaluated. As the IMDRF explains, change is inevitable since failures that arise may be due to errors, ambiguities, oversights or misinterpretation of the specification that the software is intended to satisfy, problems in writing code, inadequate testing, incorrect or unexpected usage of the software, or other unforeseen problems. A software change management process to ensure that the modified SaMD remains safe and of acceptable quality and performance will need to include considerations relating to:[54] (i) the socio-technical environment, or the SaMD's setting of use, typically characterized into spatial (e.g. locational), activity (e.g. workflows), social (e.g. responsibility), technological (e.g. devices, systems, data sources, and connections), and physical (e.g. ambient conditions) components; (ii) the technology and system environment, or the ecosystem where the SaMD operates, including installed systems, interconnections, and hardware platforms; and (iii) information security, which broadly relates to the preservation of confidentiality, integrity, and availability of information.

Second, traceability strengthens post-market surveillance. It is generally recognized that testing of software is insufficient to ensure safety in its operation. Safety features need to be built into the software at the design and development stages, and supported by quality management and post-marketing surveillance after the SaMD has been installed. Post-market surveillance includes monitoring, measurement, and analysis of quality data through logging and tracking of complaints, clearing technical issues, determining problem causes and actions to address, identify, collect, analyse, and report on critical quality characteristics of products developed. However, monitoring software quality alone does not guarantee that the objectives for a process are being achieved.[55] As a quality management system (QMS) requirement, the IMDRF states that maintenance activities should preserve the integrity of the SaMD without introducing new safety, effectiveness, performance and security hazards. It recommends that risk assessment, including considerations in relation

---

54 ibid., 22–27 [9].

55 International Medical Device Regulators Forum, *Software as a Medical Device (SaMD): Application of Quality Management System, IMDRF/SaMD WG/N23 FINAL:2015*, para. 7.5, available at: http://www.imdrf.org/docs/imdrf/final/technical/imdrf-tech-151002-samd-qms.pdf.

to patient safety and clinical environment and technology and systems environment, should be performed to determine if the changes affect the SaMD categorization and the core functionality of SaMD as set out in its definition statement.[56] Principles that underscore a QMS are set out as: (i) an organizational support structure to provide leadership, accountability and governance with adequate resources to assure the safety, effectiveness, and performance of the device;[57] (ii) lifecycle support processes that are scalable for the size of the organization and applied consistently across all realization and use processes (i.e. requirements management, design, development, verification and validation, deployment, maintenance, and decommissioning of the product);[58] and (iii) a set of realization and use processes that are scalable for the type of device and the size of the organization that take into account important elements required for assuring safety, effectiveness, and performance.[59] These principles are largely reflected in the more collaborative relationship between regulators and the developers and/or manufacturers of SaMD, but do not currently extend to patients and healthcare providers, as users.

In order to advance ML and to account for a wider range of actual uses that apply SaMD, regulatory governance will need to be more participatory in actively and meaningfully involving patients, healthcare providers, and other users or operators. The development of a tracking system for high-risk devices, which is based on the principles set out by the IMDRF on the establishment of a 'Unique Device Identification', points us in this direction.[60] Such a system of identification requires these devices to bear a unique identifier in human and machine-readable form in order to improve monitoring and tracking of these devices from the point of their manufacture to their use and eventual decommissioning.

Third, enhancing transparency is emphasized in the new regulatory proposal. Apart from initiatives like the Unique Device Identification systems, regulators in major AI-based medical devices jurisdictions also seek to enhance transparency by ensuring greater availability of information to patients, as well as in the public domain. In the EU, an implant card and information about an implantable device must be supplied to the patient in accordance

---

56 ibid., 26, [8.6].

57 ibid., 10-11, [6].

58 ibid., 12-18, [7].

59 ibid., 19-28, [8].

60 International Medical Device Regulators Forum, *Unique Device Identification System* (*UDI system*) *Application Guide*, available at: http://www.imdrf.org/docs/imdrf/final/consultations/imdrf-cons-udi-system-n48-180712.pdf.

with Article 18 of the MDR.[61] As a wider initiative, a comprehensive EU database (EUDAMED) on medical devices and certain post-marketing events (such as modifications or withdrawal of products) has been introduced. However, the EUDAMED database is currently only accessible by national competent authorities although a new version of the platform is being developed to serve multiple purposes that include product registration, collaborative arrangements with manufacturers, notification provision, and public dissemination of information.[62] Even with the innovative regulatory developments considered above, a number of challenges remain.[63] These include lack of clarity over the evidential threshold that is needed to meet clinical (for medical devices) or performance (for in vitro devices) evaluation, the extent of data that is required for verification and validation, the degree to which machine learning needs to fit with risk management elements of harmonized standards set out by the International Organization of Standards, the need for ML to be human interpretable, and the appropriate level of responsiveness to dynamic changes from machine learning. To meet these challenges, there will be growing reliance on the participation of patients, healthcare providers and caregivers in real-world conditions as existing SaMD apply machine learning capabilities, even as a greater number of diverse SaMD are introduced into clinical and ambulatory care. A rights-based approach that is centred on the HRS can help to address this deficiency and thereby steer regulatory and technological innovation forward.

5 Conclusion

Through the HRS, Professor Knoppers has shown us a vision of the democratic environment that science and technology require. As science and technology are also means by which we—as a species—understand and interact with our environment and are simultaneously shaped by it, they also signify the state of human civilization, particularly its ability to learn and to adapt. As she has

61 Regulation (EU) 2017/745 of the European Parliament and of the Council of 5 April 2017 on medical devices [2017] OJ L 117/1; and Regulation (EU) 2017/746 of the European Parliament and of the Council of 5 April 2017 on in vitro diagnostic medical devices [2017] OJ L 117/176.

62 European Commission, *European Database on Medical Devices* (EUDAMED), available at: https://ec.europa.eu/growth/sectors/medical-devices/new-regulations/eudamed_en.

63 Johan Ordish, Hannah Murfet, and Alison Hall, 'Algorithms as medical devices' (PHG Foundation 2019), available at: https://www.phgfoundation.org/report/algorithms-as-medical-devices.

shown us in her academic and policy work, the freedom to inquire, whether for researchers or indeed any human individual, is not to be taken for granted. Implementing the HRS provides assurance of vigilance, and as I have shown, Professor Knoppers has inspired a generation of scholars to sustain this cause.

Where the regulation of AI- or ML-based medical devices are concerned, we already see that both regulators and regulatory mechanisms are more participatory and responsive, at least to developers and manufacturers at this point. This move towards a more inclusive and dynamic approach to regulation will continue, partly because the goal of enabling our health system to continually improve the quality, safety, and outcomes of healthcare delivery cannot be attained otherwise. Whether PRSS is to be regulated as medical devices or not, the wider regulatory environment must ensure equitable access to safe and effective technologies, and transparently communicate with device users. Moving forward, health institutions and healthcare professionals need to better integrate with PRSS development. This integration ensures that providers can act on knowledge gained from risk profiling. Patients and their caregivers should similarly be involved, even if the nature of participation differs from that of health institutions and healthcare providers. After all, the reliability of risk stratification is likely to depend on effective long-term engagement with patients where risk factors are expected to change over the course of their lives due to lifestyle choices, environmental exposures, and shifts in scientific consensus that results in variant reclassification. Professor Knoppers has shown us that these anticipated changes are not only necessary, but first and foremost the most human-centred course to take.

VIGNETTE

Positivity and Perseverance

Alexander Bernier

First as a research assistant, and later as an academic associate, I was privileged to collaborate with Bartha Knoppers during her tenure as the Director of the Centre of Genomics and Policy. Bartha fostered my passion for applied issues at the intersection bioethics and international data stewardship, which animate my career to this day. Together, we and other colleagues ideated data governance programs for biomedical research repositories such as the Human Cell Atlas, the European-Canadian Cancer Network, and the euCanSHare effort—each of which presented a unique blend of ethical, legal, and scientific conundrums. Working on these initiatives gave me the chance to learn about bioinformatic analysis and personalised medicine tools in rigorous depth, dialogue with the scientists developing them, and ruminate on their societal implications. For me, this sparked wonder.

Bartha and I would meet early most mornings to pore over the minute details of documents with a fine-tooth comb, exchange ideas on policy dilemmas, and transmute general musings into sound academic manuscripts. From the outset, I was strongly encouraged to think outside the box, and to vie for the implementation of idealistic and novel ideas rather than to gravitate toward those which appeared most practicable to implement. Bartha's inimitable blend of utopianism and pragmatism has shaped my own perspective on the scholarly study of law and technology.

Bartha takes unparalleled joy in helping friends and research collaborators cultivate their intellectual potential, and develop new capabilities. She has a preternatural sense for the passions, drives, and interests of those around her. Within the walls of the university, she is always astir. Deftly marking up manuscripts drafts with handwritten notes bearing insightful questions. Printing out publications, news articles, and event posters that relate to the interests of specific colleagues, and carefully laying them out for those colleagues to find. Convening celebrations for the personal and professional milestones of teammates, complete with a life-size outdoor scrabble board and lavishly decorated cakes.

The legacy that Bartha leaves is not only that of carefully shepherding the development of bioethics, health law, and science administration. She has also empowered budding scholars and practitioners to take personal responsibility for the flourishing of science policy and innovation. Profound faith in the honesty, the talents, and the drive of others is a hallmark of Bartha's approach to leadership. Her sustained belief in others motivates them not only to exceed her expectations, but also those that they might have of themselves.

I have always been struck by Bartha's willingness to selflessly champion the ideas and the projects that her collaborators hold dear to their hearts. No less striking is her continued tenacity, resilience, and graciousness when faced with adverse outcomes.

Academic contexts teach us many virtues. Meticulousness and work ethic are amongst them, as are critical thinking, originality, and independence. However—Bartha, by her own example, reminds us that the scientific endeavour requires, in equal measure, a quite different set of qualities. These are selflessness, camaraderie, humility, and courage. And above all else, sustained passion for, and pleasure taken in, the collegial exchange of ideas.

VIGNETTE

Bartha Maria Knoppers: A Game Changer

Alexandra Obadia

I met Bartha Knoppers at the end of 1997. One meeting with her was enough to convince me to leave litigation and private practice to pursue a master's degree in Law, Biotechnology and Society, a new and innovative program she was leading at the Université de Montréal. Her contagious passion and forward-thinking views on the legal and ethical issues raised by emerging biomedical technologies and genetics ignited a new flame within me, one that would change my career path.

Bartha is a force of nature: strong, graceful, charming—yet determined. She's in a category of her own. She trained and inspired generations of professionals, leaving a tremendous heritage.

But beyond her teaching, Bartha is an innovator and a visionary. She was a pioneer in her field by taking an interest and anticipating the impacts of biomedical progress on law and ethics and putting forward corresponding innovative concepts and frameworks. Her international experience and recognition have contributed to build and advance a new field of law and ethics.

She was also the instigator of major initiatives and societal projects, such as CARTaGENE, the Quebec population cohort and biobank. She changed the course of my career once again, when she solicited me for the position of Director of Legal Services of CARTaGENE, and a couple of years later, trusted me with the position of CEO thereof. Together with her acolyte Professor Claude Laberge, Bartha envisioned CARTaGENE for the benefit of the whole Quebec population, to advance and accelerate health research, and enhance Quebec's position in major national and international research collaborations.

Advancement and innovation in science and medicine, not to mention law and policy, are possible thanks to people like Bartha who believe in a vision, are relentless and have a natural capacity to lead and unify people around a common goal.

Bartha is a game changer for our society. It's a privilege and an honour to be part of her legacy. Her success is ultimately our success as a society.

 | DOI:10.1163/9789004688544_050

Index

www.ingramcontent.com/pod-product-compliance
Lightning Source LLC
Chambersburg PA
CBHW071335230926
51849CB00002B/400
9789004688537